EXCELLENCE IN PRACTICE Series
Katharine G. Butler, Editor

COMMUNICATING FOR LEARNING

Classroom Observation and Collaboration

EXCELLENCE IN PRACTICE Series
Katharine G. Butler, Editor

Conversational Management with Language-Impaired Children
Bonnie Brinton and Martin Fujiki

Successful Interactive Skills for Speech-Language
Pathologists and Audiologists
Dorothy Molyneaux and Vera W. Lane

EXCELLENCE IN PRACTICE Series
Katharine G. Butler, Editor

COMMUNICATING FOR LEARNING

Classroom Observation and Collaboration

Elaine R. Silliman, Ph.D.
Professor of Communication Sciences and Disorders
College of Arts and Sciences
University of South Florida
Tampa, Florida

Louise Cherry Wilkinson, Ed.D.
Dean, Graduate School of Education
Professor of Educational Psychology and Psychology
Rutgers, The State University of New Jersey
New Brunswick, New Jersey

AN ASPEN PUBLICATION®
Aspen Publishers, Inc.
Gaithersburg, Maryland
1991

Library of Congress Cataloging-in-Publication Data

Silliman, Elaine R.
Communicating for learning : classroom observation and
collaboration / Elaine R. Silliman, Louise Cherry Wilkinson.
p. cm.
— (Excellence in practice)
Includes bibliographical references and index.
ISBN: 0-8342-0203-4
1. Learning disabled children—Education—Language arts.
2. Oral communication—Study and teaching. 3. Observation
(Educational method) 4. Interaction analysis in education.
I. Wilkinson, Louise Cherry. II. Title. III. Series:
Excellence in practice series.
LC4704.85.S58 1990
371.9—dc20
90-23748
CIP

Editorial Services: Lisa Hajjar

Library of Congress Catalog Card Number: 90-23748
ISBN: 0-8342-0203-4

Printed in the United States of America

1 2 3 4 5

Dedication

To Paul, Dawn, Scott, Sue, Alex, and Jennifer, whose loving support never waivered; and to all those children who were the real teachers of language and learning.

With contributions by

Amy Stone Belkin, Ed.D.
Language Consultant, The Fisher-Landau Program
The Dalton School
New York

Lauren P. Hoffman, M.A.T.
Supervisor, Communication Development Program
South Metropolitan Association
Flossmoor, Illinois

Table of Contents

Series Preface

Seeing the World of the Classroom

A Playlet

Scene: Mrs. Jones' third grade classroom.

Actors: Mrs. Jones; 26 children; and Miss Smith, a student teacher in her first week of attendance.

Time: Monday, mid-morning, on a fine fall day.

Background: Students, working on a science experiment, are gathered in small groups of three or four. Many have completed the experiment and are writing up or rendering a drawing of the results. Conversations, for the most part well-modulated, fill the classroom.

Action: Mrs. Jones is writing on the chalkboard. Without turning to the class, she issues a directive: "Children, it's time to get ready for recess."

     The children begin to gather up their work. The sounds of chairs being pushed back and children moving around the room fill the air.

     Miss Smith notes that the children appear to understand the specific sequence of actions expected of them. She watches the first group of children who are congregating at the door.

Without turning from her task, Mrs. Jones suddenly and in a very firm voice states, "John, join your group . . . and Mark, I'd like to see you at my desk *now*."

Miss Smith is somewhat startled, now aware that there has been a small scuffle in the back of the room. John, 8 and small, and Mark, 9 and large, have faced off near the coat closet. John now stands silently, face red, fists clenched. Mark hastily puts something in his pocket. Miss Smith wonders what she has missed as Mrs. Jones and Mark both move toward the teacher's desk.

As the children exit from the room, Mary whispers to Alice, "See, I tole you, didn't I? That Mizz Jones has eyes in the back of her head."

Seeing the world of the classroom in its entirety and complexity requires great skill. To truly see that world as it exists would require 360 degree vision. Such vision is not given to most of us. Experienced teachers may develop "eyes in the back of their heads," while those who are new to the classroom scene may miss both obvious and subtle interactions between students as well as between teachers and students.

With this book, Elaine Silliman and Louise Wilkinson help us see classroom interactions in new ways, as well as new roles for those educators who would collaborate in the classroom. As they note, there is a synergy between language, learning, and teaching that can be captured through observation. It may be surprising to realize that the teaching–learning setting utilizes communication as its primary medium for instruction. While reading, writing, and arithmetic have been viewed for many decades as the basic "three R's," and the public may view reading as the quintessential skill to be learned in school, *communication* forms the real basis for academic success. Literacy begins with speaking. Communication is the link to literacy and precedes capturing the world in print.

How does one see into and through the world of the classroom? Drs. Silliman and Wilkinson offer a series of lenses by which the classroom, in all its variations, may be viewed. The authors have addressed the needs of both "special" and "regular" educators as they interpret the uses of observation and consultation used to assess and intervene in this setting. Sensitivity to the dynamics of the classroom and the interactions which take place therein can be increased through the communication-centered approach suggested in this book.

Essential collaborative competencies are described in detail, enabling the reader to understand the functioning of co-participation among teachers, speech-language pathologists, and other team members in education settings. Workable models of co-participation are not easy to achieve because they require both individual and institutional change, as the authors make quite clear. However, with this book they provide a road map of sorts with a variety of paths to make the going easier to achieve successful co-participation.

In explicitly describing the dynamics of classroom and clinical discourse, the authors explore the hidden nature of the cultural and social expectations placed upon children in the classroom. These are not new expectations, but we gain a new appreciation of their extent and their impact as we utilize the various mental lenses provided by the authors. We are provided not only with a road map which is most useful, but also with the theoretical and research findings that border this landscape. The book provides not only a perspective on building a communication-centered approach to learning, literacy, and instruction, it also provides a method for gaining those much-valued "eyes in the back of the head." Those eyes come in handy for looking ahead as well as looking behind. Utilizing the observational approaches suggested here makes the world of the classroom transparent and thus provides a clear vision of the future.

Katharine G. Butler, Ph.D.
Director, Center for Research
and
Chair, Department of Communication
Sciences and Disorders
Syracuse University
Syracuse, New York

Preface

Serving as a speech-language pathologist in schools in the 1990s is demanding. Every day, speech-language pathologists deal with the challenges and complexities presented by the communicative needs of students who bring widely different learning styles, motivations, and abilities to participate in classroom activities. Classroom teachers are confronted with similar problems, although on a broader scale, since they must continuously balance individual with group needs.

The explosion of knowledge on oral language proficiency, learning, and literacy has created new opportunities for developing educational and intervention approaches for children and adolescents with language learning problems. Disciplines contributing to current knowledge include cognitive psychology, educational psychology, linguistics, sociology, anthropology, and communication sciences and disorders. The growing recognition of the interrelatedness of language, learning, and literacy has had a catalyzing effect and also has generated certain dilemmas. For example, many speech-language pathologists face complex decisions about how best to (1) modify the traditional "pullout" role of service delivery into a more comprehensive and collaborative role in the classroom; (2) select assessment tools, including observational tools, that display patterns of classroom communication for individual children; and (3) integrate naturalistic intervention strategies and goals with classroom and curricula requirements for literacy learning.

As a speech-language pathologist and an educational psychologist respectively, our primary purpose in writing this book is to assist speech-language clinicians and educators in their joint work with children. As clinicians and educators work together, they can become overwhelmed by the diversity of research on the relationships among language, learning, and literacy. A vast body of literature is also available on the development of these interrelationships, their disruptions, and on approaches to intervention with children and adolescents who cannot become literate without sustained help. One aim of this volume is to synthesize this diverse and varied body of research so that speech-language pathologists can make informed decisions about: (1) methods of service delivery and (2) the programmatic structures for assessment and intervention.

Both the research included in our book and its application were determined by our perspective on communication development and impairment. We take a sociolinguistic perspective. Sociolinguistic research in schools focuses on the communication of children and teachers in a variety of real classroom situations, as well as some more restricted, experimental situations that mimic these real situations. Despite the expected diversity of studies from this approach, some commonalities do exist. Virtually all of these sociolinguistic studies focus on the processes and patterns of language and communication as they spontaneously occur in classrooms. For example, studies focusing on developmental differences among children have emphasized the learning process for socialization, whereas studies on individual differences in language and communication have argued for the importance of social categories such as gender, ethnicity, and class on learning outcomes.

In writing this book, we have attempted to synthesize sociolinguistic perspectives from the communication sciences and disorders with educational/developmental psychology as applied to children's communicative development. We have enjoyed this process, and it has afforded us the opportunity to learn a great deal from each other and expand our understanding of language and communication. We hope that the result of our collaboration may be helpful to you.

Acknowledgments

The ongoing assistance of Dr. Katharine G. Butler, the editor of the Excellence in Practice series, was invaluable to us in our work on this book. Her contributions exceed these immediate efforts, however. Dr. Butler's insights into the cognitive, social, affective, and developmental dimensions of language learning disability have influenced the direction of research and practice throughout the field. Her multiple roles as mentor, model, and scholar inspire all who are concerned with assisting children to realize their communicative potential.

Several other colleagues contributed to our thinking about issues and approaches to communicative development. In particular, we would like to acknowledge Dr. Margaret Lahey, Dr. Sylvia Richardson, Dr. Geraldine Wallach, and Dr. Carol Westby for their thoughts about communicating for learning; we thank them for providing feedback on applications of these concepts within the classroom setting.

Several colleagues have been generous in allowing access to classrooms where communication-centered, collaborative approaches have been implemented for children and adolescents with language learning differences. We would like to express gratitude for the cooperation and participation of Dr. Amy Stone Belkin, Speech-Language Pathologist for the Fisher-Landau Program at The Dalton School in New York City; Susan Etess, Director of the Fisher-Landau Program at The Dalton School; Dr. Stanley Seidman, Director of the First Program at The Dalton School; Dr. Gardner Dunnan, Headmaster of The Dalton School; The Dalton School teachers who participated in the initial workshop on classroom discourse, Diane Aronson, Nancy Chusid, Kathy Dicks, Beth Dougherty, and Linda Halbreich; Betsy Voss Lease, Program Director, South Metropolitan Association (SMA) in Flossmor, Illinois; Lauren P. Hoffman, Supervisor, the SMA Communication Development Program; and the speech-language pathologists, educators, social workers, career educators, parents, and support staff of the Communication Development Program.

The preparation of the manuscript was assisted by the work of several individuals. Special appreciation is extended to Tonya Daniels, Darci Kline, Donna Kulwicki, Erin Laipply, and Judy Reese, graduate assistants in the Department of Communication Sciences and Disorders at the University of South Florida; Shirley Spencer, Academic Program Secretary for the Department of Communication Sciences and Disorders; and Jane Sherwood, Administrative Assistant, Office of the Dean, Graduate School of Education at Rutgers University. The original art work in Appendix C was created by Robert Cavey of the Wisconsin Center for Education Research. Guidance in manuscript preparation was provided by the editors and external reviewers at Aspen Publishers. Dava Waltzman's review of an early draft of the manuscript contributed significantly to its subsequent revision.

Finally, since this book is a collaborative effort, we would like to acknowledge its joint authorship. The ordering of authorship reflects alphabetic listing only.

Chapter 1

Observing Classroom Communication: A New Beginning for Assessment and Intervention

No matter how one may try, one cannot not communicate. Activity or inactivity, words or silence all have message value: they influence others and these others, in turn, cannot not respond to these communications and are thus themselves communicating. It should be clearly understood that the mere absence of talking or of taking notice of each other is no exception to what has just been asserted (Watlawick, Beavin, & Jackson, 1967, p. 49).

The interdisciplinary perspective taken in this book is that communication unites teaching and learning into a cohesive system of interaction among students and teachers. Because the central goals of education are "to understand and be understood" (Cazden, 1988, p. 76) within the conventions of a literate society, boundaries between communication, teaching, and learning do not really exist.

This chapter introduces three themes that underlie our approach to classroom observation: (1) locating assessment and intervention in actual classroom interactions among students and teachers, (2) fostering a literate orientation to students' learning, and (3) facilitating collaboration among educational professionals through coparticipation. This overview is followed by description of a model for observing classroom communication.

AN OVERVIEW OF THEMES

Locating Assessment and Intervention in Classroom Interactions: New Roles for Speech-Language Pathologists

The first theme is related to the shift emerging in school settings from a primary emphasis on pullout models of service-delivery for language intervention, to the development of models that are based in classrooms. These models can be found in either regular or special education settings.

One reason for this shift is the thrust of many school systems toward mainstreaming and providing the least restrictive environment for students who can be supported in the regular classroom or in comparable instructional environments (Simon, 1987a).

There is a more substantive reason motivating this shift. It is the growing awareness by many speech-language pathologists, teachers, and researchers from a variety of disciplines of the influence of oral language and communication on the acquisition of literacy (Corson, 1988; Garton & Pratt, 1989; Goodman, 1986; Kamhi & Catts, 1989a; Michaels & Cazden, 1986; N.W. Nelson, 1988a; Richardson, 1990; Wallach & Miller, 1988).

The Roles of the Speech-Language Pathologist in Literacy Learning

According to one view, literacy consists of knowing how to speak, listen, read, and write competently (Garton & Pratt, 1989). The stress on this broader view of literacy derives from the recognition that the basic ability to read and write by itself does not necessarily produce an individual who can flexibly apply sophisticated strategies for inferencing and generalizing to an infinite variety of activities and purposes in reading, writing, speaking, and listening (N.W. Nelson, 1988a). The purpose of speaking can vary from chatting to maintain social politeness to lecturing for the communication of new knowledge (Biber, 1988; Scott, 1988). Listening also occurs in different ways and for different purposes. For example, attending to the meaning of a classroom lecture requires different strategies than does attending to the chatter of "cocktail" talk. Similarly, how a book is read for meaning will vary depending on whether the reading is being done for pleasure or for the critical analysis of an issue. Writing differs as a function of its purpose. For example, writing thoughts and feelings in a personal diary is unlike the more impersonal writing of a scientific article to be published (Biber, 1988; Scott, 1988).

One essential concept is that literacy, as a new mode of thinking and communicating, should not be approached as a set of isolated, splintered skills (Miller, 1990; Stewart, 1987; van Kleeck, 1990; Wallach, 1990; Westby, 1989). A literate attitude toward learning, as well as literacy itself, is cultivated through the richness of communicative interactions—initially with parents and, later, with teachers, clinicians, and peers. Classroom-based models of language intervention at the elementary, middle school, and secondary levels tend to be characterized by the incorporation of this concept through the integration of spoken and written language activities with curriculum goals and content (Buttrill, Niizawa, Biemer, Takahashi, & Hearn, 1989; Christensen & Luckett, 1990; Comkowycz, Ehren, & Hayes, 1987; Despain & Simon, 1987; Hoffman, 1990; McKinley & Lord-Larson, 1985; N.W. Nelson, 1989; Norris, 1989; Simon, 1987a).

Miller (1989) describes five roles for the speech-language clinician in literacy-based classroom formats: (1) teaching in a self-contained classroom for language learning disabled students (Hoffman, 1990) or, alternatively, in a regularly scheduled class specifically designed for these students (Buttrill et al., 1989; Comkowycz et al., 1987; McKinley & Lord-Larson, 1985); (2) team teaching either in a regular classroom with the classroom teacher (Christensen & Luckett, 1990; Norris, 1989), in the self-contained classroom with another specialist (Hoffman, 1990), or in a combination of resource and regular class modules with other specialists and the regular education teacher (Despain & Simon, 1987; Simon, 1987a); (3) providing one-to-one intervention (N.W. Nelson, 1989); (4) providing collaborative consultation with regular or special education teachers and other staff (Comkowycz et al., 1987; Despain & Simon, 1987); and (5) providing staff, curriculum, or program development (Despain & Simon, 1987; N.W. Nelson, 1989). The first three roles have in common the direct provision of service, while the fourth and fifth roles find the speech-language clinician acting as a resource for classroom teachers, other special education specialists, administrators, or parents.

Also, because of how individual states usually define and fund special education and related services, the majority of students served through classroom formats have been formally classified as speech-language impaired or learning disabled. Exceptions can be found. For example, California expanded its definition of least restrictive environment to include regular education classroom; therefore, "as long as at least one student within the regular education classroom has a valid IEP, the speech-language pathologist may design activities to enrich the entire classroom while still targeting the specific objectives ascribed to the IEP-student" (Christensen & Luckett, 1990, p. 110).

Simon (1987a) invokes the saying "necessity is the mother of invention" (p. 56) to illustrate another exception. In this instance, a collaborative program was implemented for junior high students who had never been formally classified but who were at risk for educational failure. Because these students did not meet traditional criteria for classification, they had never been referred for any secondary special education program, including speech-language services.

New Roles and Decision Making

A major issue concerns how decisions are made by speech-language clinicians and teachers about the status of individual students' communicative competencies in relation to the demands of literacy learning. Traditional criteria and procedures for identifying a language or learning disability have been criticized on a number of grounds. One line of criticism concerns the lack of scientific and professional agreement on the conceptual definitions of disabilities. Additionally, there is the important fact that the "picture" of severity may change over time. Bashir, Kuban, Kleinman, and Scavuzzo (1983) comment that children with language learning disabilities will "look differently" (p. 101) at different points depending on the specific learning context, the nature of curriculum demands, and the assumptions made about the child's competence as a learner.

A second level of criticism is directed to operational definitions of a disability and the serious problem of misclassification. Current procedures and criteria for identification, such as standardized tests of aptitude (tests of general intelligence) and achievement (tests of language performance and basic skills in reading, writing, and math), have convincingly failed over time to separate children who have individual differences in abilities from those with an intrinsic disability (Fletcher et al., 1989; Hammill, 1990; Kavale & Forness, 1985; Stanovich, 1986, 1988, 1989; Tindal, 1985). In practice, academic failure has come to mean reading ability at least one and one-half to two years below grade level (Sleeter, 1987). Identifying reading failure, then, is relatively easy to accomplish, but identifying a specific handicap as the cause of failure is almost impossible given the state of current procedures for formal assessment (Bryan, Bay, & Donahue, 1988; Kavale & Forness, 1985; Senf, 1986; Tindal & Marston, 1986; Wong, 1986).

These criticisms lead Bryan et al. (1988) to ask whether the overall decline in academic achievement during the past 20 years has resulted in proportionately more children being misclassified as learning disabled, and by inference, language learning disabled. A cultural side to the misclassification question is also pertinent. N.W. Nelson (1988a) points out that the expectation that the entire population should be literate is a relatively new standard originating, in part, from the rapid acceleration of the information explosion and its associated technologies. Thus, increased cultural expectations for literacy also influence decision making about classification standards.

In our view, valid decisions about the scope and nature of children's needs and changes in those needs can be achieved only if referral and assessment practices are directed explicitly to the actual interactional requirements of the teaching-learning situation. To understand why certain children are not meeting expectations in academic, social, and communicative domains, the real situations that students routinely encounter in classrooms should serve as the contexts for decision making. This approach emphasizes the observation of children's interactions with each other and with teachers and speech-language specialists as the tool for more precise description of (1) individual variations in the communicative competencies supporting literacy learning, including the situations in which ability, not just "disability," is displayed, and (2) actual sources of communicative breakdowns that, cumulatively, can result in academic failure and the loss of motivation to learn.

A related decision-making issue concerns how the outcomes of classroom-based approaches are evaluated. In a discussion of program evaluation procedures for language intervention services, Schery and Lipsey (1983) distinguish between program outcomes and the effects of specific teaching procedures on learning outcomes. Program outcomes are often measured by changes in students' performance on standardized achievement tests, which, by their very construction, cannot be sensitive to the differential effects of variations in teaching approaches. These variations in the components of teaching, such as teacher communicative styles, teaching strategies, the curriculum structure, and classroom management procedures, may all be factors contributing to different learning outcomes for individual students (Corson, 1988; Kavale & Forness, 1985). We propose that the systematic use of observation offers a powerful method for assessing the effects of teaching variations on learning outcomes while simultaneously allowing the ongoing documentation of changes in individual student performance. Observational documentation can then be linked to the broader program outcomes of classroom-based intervention.

Fostering a Literate Orientation toward Students' Learning: New Intervention Goals

The pathway to literacy can be described as a continuum along which more planful behaviors are nurtured and applied in increasingly flexible ways to the various purposes of listening, speaking, reading, and writing. *Planful* means that the actions constituting listening, speaking, reading, or writing have been organized in more conscious ways prior to their actual execution.

Planful Comprehension and Remembering

To illustrate the nature of more self-directed planning, consider the following plan recommended by a learning disabilities specialist to improve the "listening skills" of Laurie, a fictional student in a regular fifth-grade class. The purpose of the seven-step plan is to assist Laurie in better following the teacher's verbal directions and explanations (Cerussi & Stern-Levine, 1988, p. 17):

1. Keep your feet, hands, and lips very quiet.
2. Look at the person who is talking.
3. Listen to everything that is said.
4. Think about what you are hearing.
5. Paint a picture in your mind that shows you what to do.
6. Raise your hand and ask questions right away if you are confused.
7. Listen carefully until your teacher is finished. Then repeat the directions to yourself or write them down. That way, you will be sure to remember them. Try saying this: "I was listening to you, but I don't remember everything you said."

Understanding and remembering are the two essential purposes cutting across the domains of listening, speaking, reading, and writing (Baker & Brown, 1984), and they are the core elements of this plan as well. However, for Laurie to use effectively the various procedures for implementing the plan, she must (1) understand the specific conditions that either promote or hinder her comprehension and remembering, (2) be aware when a comprehension or memory problem arises, (3) be able to locate the source of the problem intentionally, and (4) then be able to use the recommended procedures in controlled ways as techniques for resolving miscomprehension or misremembering.

This example serves to capture the critical role of *metacognition* in facilitating and monitoring more planful comprehension (Baker & Brown, 1984; Brown & Palinscar, 1987; Palinscar & Brown, 1984). Metacognition refers to the conscious awareness that one is thinking about thinking, including thinking about strategies for using aspects of cognition and communication in purposeful ways. Metacognitive activity is always an intentional or controlled process, and it is engaged in when information must be actively organized and used for a particular reason, as the example above indicates. Being competent in the use of "meta" strategies means being competent to independently, actively, and intentionally self-direct the process of learning for particular goals. Hence, how a learner plans to approach understanding and being understood (Cazden, 1988) is the essence of the active, self-regulated learning that is the hallmark of a literate orientation to learning.

Learning Potential

A specific objective of interventions directed to the fostering of a literate orientation toward learning is to minimize the risk of educational failure by maximizing learning potential irrespective of whether students are placed in regular or special education. Educational risk can be present when a mismatch exists between, on the one hand, the intellectual and social readiness of individual students to meet the communicative demands of literacy learning and, on the other hand, the standards by which these same students are judged to be communicatively and academically competent. These mismatches may be present at all grade levels. For example, Despain and Simon (1987) report that some marginal students may be less able to make the transition from elementary school to junior high school without some "temporary incompetence" (p. 175). Unless the teaching-learning situations contributing to this condition are carefully analyzed, referral to special education might be the formal action taken (Dudley-Marling, 1987; Miller, 1989; Simon, 1987a).

Learning potential can also be minimized or maximized through the ways in which teaching-learning interactions are organized as the tool for learning. Little attention has been paid to the classroom setting—or even the clinical setting—

with respect to how variations in the interactional dynamics of teaching-learning situations help support children's identities of themselves as competent communicators and learners. The shift in roles for the speech-language pathologist to classroom-based assessment and intervention does require that teaching plans, strategies, and materials be reorganized around communicative goals in the formal classroom curriculum; however, these actions by themselves are not sufficient. Rather, promoting a literate orientation to learning requires careful and ongoing observation of the sociolinguistic organization of teaching and learning. It is through the process of skillful observation that we come to understand how classroom and clinical discourse creates and sustains the communicative contexts for learning. Skilled observation also permits insight into the ways that instructional discourse functions as the primary tool for shaping students' attitudes about themselves as either active, competent learners or passive, dependent learners (Corson, 1988; Palinscar, 1989; Silliman, 1987).

Facilitating Collaboration among Educational Professionals through Coparticipation: New Professional Competencies

It seems clear that, in moving to new roles in the classroom, where real teaching-learning situations are the contexts for assessment and where maximizing learning potential is the ongoing goal of intervention, speech-language clinicians must be proficient in the use of observational tools. The same need for proficiency has been identified for classroom teachers (Stiggins, 1990). Two reasons underscore this need. One pertains to the expectation that decisions derived from assessment procedures or from modifications in classroom or intervention dynamics will be data-based (Damico, 1987; Miller, 1989; N.W. Nelson, 1989). The second concerns the development of skill in evaluating the short- and long-term effectiveness of instructional practices on learning outcomes.

Of no small import is the issue of how speech-language clinicians, general and special education teachers, and other specialists can begin to work collaboratively in order to attain proficiency and to integrate observational tools effectively into classroom communication. Here the focus of collaboration would be those classroom roles involving team teaching, one-to-one intervention within the classroom, and consultation. However, the issues of proficiency and integration are equally applicable to self-contained classrooms taught solely by the speech-language clinician.

At the outset, the implementation of a collaborative structure requires are thinking of roles and attitudes on the part of speech-language pathologists, teachers, and administrators (Simon, 1987a). While there are a variety of definitions of collaboration, common themes include shared responsibility for the design, implementation, and evaluation of students' instructional programs; shared ideas and goals; facilitation of change without confrontation; and ongoing self-evaluation (Idol, Paolucci-Whitcomb, & Nevin, 1987; Marvin, 1987; West, Idol, & Cannon, 1989).

West and Cannon (1988) noted the absence of research from either the regular or special education settings on the repertoire of skills needed to be an effective collaborator; however, it appears that fundamental competencies are not necessarily equivalent to traditional didactic skills. In a large-scale study of special educators, West and Cannon (1988) used a Delphi process to achieve consensus on essential collaborative skills. (In this process, skills are generated and then continuously refined into smaller sets according to the rating values and the degree of consensus achieved for each skill; it is noteworthy that speech-language pathologists or supervisors of speech, language, and hearing services in the schools were not included on the rating panels.) Four sets of competencies were rated the most essential. In rank order of agreement, these competencies were (1) the capacity to communicate goals and objectives clearly in both oral and written forms; (2) the ability to show active attention to and interest in the perspectives of others, for example, by acknowledging, paraphrasing, reflecting, clarifying, elaborating, and summarizing; (3) skill in facilitation, that is, eliciting and sharing information, defining and exploring problems, and helping to find alternate solutions to problems; and (4) the ability to solicit and give continuous feedback that is specific, immediate, and objective. A conspicuous parallel can be drawn between these essential collaborative competencies and the active, self-regulated, planful learning characteristic of the literate mode of thinking and communication.

The intent here is to establish these four collaborative competencies as a frame of reference for the notion of coparticipation. Coparticipation is the basic interactional mechanism for achieving collaborative approaches to classroom communication. The heart of coparticipation is a dialogue between speech-language clinicians and teachers that "assumes a parity between participants. The purpose of such a dialogue is not to give information or impose findings: it is to provide participants with ways of looking critically at social circumstances, so that they, themselves, can take action to make change" (Mehan, 1979, p. 205).

The goal of coparticipation is to assist speech-language pathologists, teachers, and others in regular or special education settings to become their own instruments of change. In this context, change can be defined as a "metadialogue" that results in two outcomes. One is the alteration of attitudes about traditional roles; the other concerns the development of the skill repertoire underlying effective collaboration.

Clearly, institutional change is not an easy task. However, meaningful changes can be initiated at the individual level if those who are directly responsible for educational or clinical decision making understand the situations they must deal with on a daily basis (Mehan, 1979; Ripich, 1989). Mehan (1979) notes that people who are oblivious to the nature of particular situations will not readily accept others' telling them how to think and act.

Central to the work of meaningful change is the need for teachers and clinicians to combine efforts through coparticipation to observe students directly in actual classroom interaction. Proficiency in the direct observation of actual classroom interaction can function as a powerful means for understanding teaching and learning as a social-communicative process. The use of systematic observation can also reveal interactional sources of students' abilities in communication and learning, uncover hidden sources of interactional breakdowns that culminate in judgments of failure, and lead to intervention strategies better grounded in students' individual needs and learning styles.

THE OBSERVATIONAL LENS MODEL

Observing in the classroom is more than just looking at events. Rather, classroom observation can be conceptualized as a series of snapshots that depict different views of events. Figure 1-1 illustrates this concept using the observational lens model.

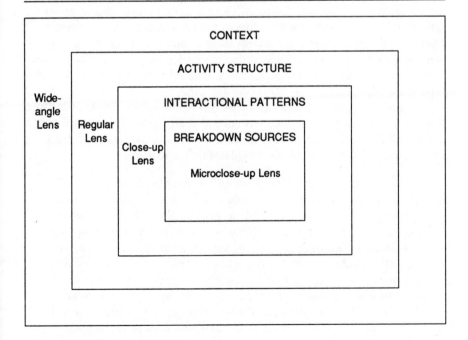

Figure 1-1   The Observational Lens Model

This model is conceptually similar to the zoom lens model of observation employed by van Kleeck and Richardson (1988). Both models address the whole child from the perspective of the broader interactional system that mediates language learning in its earlier and later phases. Both view the function of the speech-language pathologist as similar to the function of a systems analyst (Calfee & Sutter, 1982). The two models are distinguished by their focus. The zoom lens model is oriented toward developmental assessment, while the observational lens model is intended to link developmental goals with instructional goals.

The observational lens model approaches observation as a dynamic tool for making the meaning of classroom events more transparent. Selection of the most appropriate tool for observing is always dependent on the decisions made about the *purposes* of observation, because these purposes determine how events are interpreted and what questions can be pursued (Cherry, 1981; Prutting & Kirchner, 1983; van Kleeck & Richardson, in press). The importance of specifying observational goals cannot be overstated, since "to observe without knowing at least fairly well what and why one is observing is usually to blunder" (Dollaghan & Miller, 1986, p. 108, paraphrasing Kerlinger, 1973).

Like a camera lens with its filtering effect, human observers filter the behaviors comprising events. The lenses through which information is filtered are those cognitive mechanisms that allow us to construct interpretations about the actions of ourselves and others relative to the context and goals of interaction. Moreover, different observational tools filter information in different ways, so that only selected factors can be seen through the lens being used. The outcome is that any snapshot of reality represents a reduced version of an event, not a copy of the total event (Ochs, 1979a; Zukow, 1982).

As a way of relating purposes to lenses, we will use the example of Kelly, a fictional 10-year-old female who has entered fourth grade in an urban public school. While Kelly is a composite of similar children, the classroom teacher's identification of Kelly's problems should be familiar to readers:

> Kelly is a shy girl who is consistently at the bottom of the class in most academic areas. Her oral reading skills are fair; she often cannot get the gist of what she reads and has poor word attack skills. She also has serious problems with spelling, which is further complicated by her illegible handwriting. Her language skills are poor, as well. She cannot remember the differences between nouns, verbs, and adjectives and sometimes has a hard time communicating her ideas. The result is that she loses the interest of her classmates because of the time it takes for her to relate her message. Math concepts are her strongest area. I really feel sorry for her because she tries very hard to do well and is not a troublemaker. She works well to complete her assignments.

There are times, however, when she has a poor attention span and is easily distracted by her classmates. But she seems to work to the best of her ability when paired with high-academic students. I know that Kelly has had academic problems at least since second grade, but she appears to have gotten by. I'm really concerned about her now because she certainly has a poor self-image.

The Wide-Angle Lens

As indicated in Figure 1-1, a wide-angle observational lens is best suited for the purpose of capturing the contextual landscape in which classroom interaction is taking place. The context of interaction consists of the physical setting of talk as well as the participants engaged in talk, their communicative roles, the activities they share, and the topics being talked about. The context also includes the channel in which communication takes place and the particular discourse genre constructed through topics (Scott, 1988). For example, the channel of communication can be spoken, written, or gestural, while different discourse genres, such as narration, argumentation, satire, explanation, or chatting, can very across channels (Biber, 1988). The context, therefore, is not a fixed set of features but a dynamic system that constantly changes according to what teachers, clinicians, and children are doing together—and how they are doing it—in order to make sense of each other (Bloome & Knott, 1985; Erickson & Shultz, 1982; Romaine, 1984).

The teacher's description of Kelly is one kind of observational tool. It offers a wide-angle view of situations, activities, and conversational partners that lead to judgments about personal attributes (e.g., Kelly is shy, tries hard to do well, and is not a troublemaker), sources of failure (e.g., Kelly cannot remember the differences between nouns, verbs, and adjectives), and sources of success (e.g., Kelly seems to work to the best of her ability when paired with high-academic students).

Many checklists and rating scales also yield a wide-angle perspective, because they produce a surface view of communicative behaviors comparable to the view provided by more traditional standardized screening measures (see also van Kleeck & Richardson, in press). For example, a checklist developed by Genishi and Dyson (1984) focuses on observing the general contours of a child's interactional pattern in using oral language; Weiner and Creighton (1987) offer a checklist for teachers to identify language behaviors associated with school readiness; while Gruenewald and Pollak (1990) utilize a student-language-use inventory to judge the occurrence or nonoccurrence of four categories of communicative functions in different classroom situations.

The Regular Lens

A regular observational lens allows the power of magnification to be increased when the purpose is to define how the context is framing a particular classroom activity, including individual children's participation within that activity. The outcome of observing through the regular lens is a description of the interactional system underlying the particular event.

Regarding Kelly, the lens might be focused on language arts (when Kelly's problems become more visible) or during math (when more of her abilities seem to be displayed, according to the teacher's wide-angle synopsis). Elements of the activity structure that should be described include (1) the physical aspects of the language arts instruction (the location, scheduling, and supportive materials, such as books, blackboards, etc.), (2) the cognitive and task components of the language arts instruction (content and appropriateness of curriculum materials, how goals are presented, expected outcomes, when and how feedback is provided), (3) how language is used to form and sustain language arts as a communicative event, and (4) the social organization of the language arts instruction (participants, how grouped, whether learning is teacher or peer directed, nature of conduct management).

Calfee and Sutter (1982) applied these components of the regular lens to the classroom assessment of individual students during small-group discussion activities. Checklists and rating scales can also serve as a regular lens when embedded within the context of learning events. Bedrosian's (1985) checklist focuses the observer's attention on variability in specific discourse skills that a child may produce as a function of different activities. A rating scale developed by Prutting and Kirchner (1987) is intended to be used in different situations. It assesses the appropriateness or inappropriateness of a variety of verbal, nonverbal, and paralinguistic factors related to communicative competence. The outcome is an overall communicative profile for distinguishing patterns of pragmatic problems in different clinical populations, for example, language learning disabilities versus fluent aphasia in adulthood.

The Close-Up Lens

The close-up lens is applied when the observer elects to grasp in finer detail a specific layer of classroom discourse and its effects on a group as a whole or an individual student within the group. One example of a close-up view is the Wilkinson and Calculator (1982) model for request characteristics of the effective speaker. In this model, children's requests to obtain information and action are categorized according to six parameters: (1) degree of directness, (2) designation to a specific listener, (3) sincerity, (4) revision when necessary, (5) the extent to which the request is on-task, and (6) whether the request is responded to appropriately.

Returning to Kelly, let us assume that the regular lens showed a general pattern of Kelly's requesting information more often during math than during language arts. During the middle portion of the math lesson, students were reorganized into small work groups, and Kelly was placed with high-achieving students. The close-up lens of the effective speaker model revealed that Kelly's partners repeatedly encouraged her to use them as resources to clarify information when she did not understand aspects of the task they were collectively expected to accomplish. In a very real sense, Kelly's conversational partners were providing external metacognitive support in assisting her to plan how to "ask the right question" in this small-group activity. As a result, her requests for information, when they occurred, often met the six criteria of the effective requester, possibly because of the social support readily available.

In a comparable peer work group during language arts, Kelly's partners were three "average achieving" children who seemed to prefer working on tasks independently rather than together. In this situation, Kelly initiated requests for assistance less frequently, and when she did make these requests, they tended to be ignored.

In contrast to the regular lens, the close-up lens permits the observer to reach a deeper layer of classroom interaction. This lens also allows the observer to define more precisely the social circumstances that facilitate more effective communication for a child like Kelly and, in the process, can help to modify more general perceptions about a child, such as "She is shy" or "Her language skills are poor."

The Microclose-Up Lens

At the microclose-up level, observations of interactional patterns are sifted into a finer layer for the purpose of examining critical sources of communicative breakdowns. Recall that, in the wide-angle view, Kelly's teacher conveyed the information that Kelly sometimes had a hard time communicating her ideas and, as a result, often lost the attention of her classmates. The information obtained from the close-up level of observation indicated that Kelly's requests for assistance were frequently ignored or not responded to fully in the language arts peer group. The tight focus of the microclose-up lens serves to locate potential sources of communicative breakdown that could account for this pattern.

For example, one breakdown source may have resided in the composition of the work group, whose members valued independent performance rather than cooperative learning. Possibly because of her apparent lack of confidence in being able to manage the language arts tasks by herself, Kelly consistently tended to select less socially appropriate linguistic strategies to solicit the help of her peers. Rather than choosing linguistic forms that communicated a direct, on-task need for information, such as "What's that word?", Kelly approached the communicative goal less planfully; that is, her strategies tended to be more indirect, ambiguous in intent, and off-task. One strategy was the use of indirect forms, for example, "I can't see your paper"; the other tactic consisted of shifting her posture to invade her peers' space in order to "see" what they were doing. As a consequence, Kelly continuously received social feedback from both her peers and the teacher that her actions were intrusive and distracting. Her visible reaction was to withdraw from the group's activities.

Based on the overall pattern of findings, it might be appropriate to ask whether modifying the actual communicative contexts in which our fictional Kelly must function will assist her to (1) use more planful linguistic-communicative strategies for requesting information, (2) use these strategies more frequently and with increasing independence across a variety of classroom activities, and (3) understand explicitly why and in what circumstances using these strategies is important. The ultimate test of any modifications derived from the four observational lenses would be the extent to which Kelly's sense of confidence as an active learner has been enhanced and is expressed in how she actually performs.

CONCLUSION

In this chapter, the three major themes of the book are introduced, and their relationship to systematic observation of the communicative processes of teaching and learning is discussed. Observation can be conceived of as a series of mental lenses that serve to filter classroom communication in different ways. These lenses are capable of yielding increasingly refined pictures of variation in interactional events, from the broad context to the fine details of conversation. Depending on the reasons for observation, each lens can be used by itself or in combination with the others. The purposes of observing determine which of the four lenses should be selected, when they should be selected, and how they should be focused.

LOOKING AHEAD

Chapters 2, 3, and 4 elaborate on the framework and themes presented in this initial chapter.

Chapter 2 is devoted to a discussion of the sociolinguistic approach to communicative competence, considers the mentalistic and interactional perspectives underlying concepts of assessment and intervention, and concludes with a merging of these two perspectives for the interpretation of communicative behaviors.

Chapter 3 addresses the notion of how the interactional requirements of schooling can enable or disable language and literacy learning. Two sources are explored: (1) the hidden nature of cultural and social expectations for classroom competence and (2) individual differences among students regarding their level of classroom competence.

Chapter 4 concentrates on the third interactional source regulating the acquisition of metacognitive and metalinguistic strategies for language and literacy learning: the actual dynamics of classroom and clinical discourse.

Mutual understanding about the classroom as a communicative context is a precursor to collaborative planning by teachers and speech-language clinicians and their selection of observational tools. Chapter 5, coauthored with Amy Belkin and Lauren Hoffman, offers strategies for the fostering of this mutual understanding through the process of coparticipation. Focused on are two collaborative roles of the speech-language clinician in creating a communication-centered classroom. One is the role of teacher in a self-contained or resource classroom, and the other is the role of consultant to regular education teachers.

Chapter 6 begins the presentation of observational methods. Topics discussed include the purposes and goals of direct observation, the general types of observational systems for sampling students' interactions, and the reliability and validity of observational information.

Chapter 7 is devoted to the advantages and disadvantages of various procedures for recording students' interactions, including the use of technological aids.

Chapters 8, 9, and 10 include detailed discussions of the three kinds of observational tools: categorical tools, narrative tools, and descriptive tools.

A decision-making model for the selection and integration of these observational tools is described in Chapter 11.

Chapters 12 and 13 are concerned with communication-centered intervention in the classroom and the documentation of its outcomes over time.The metacognitive and metalinguistic bases of an active, planful orientation to learning are examined first in Chapter 12. Adapting Brown's (1982) model as a framework, planful learning is considered as the product of an interactive process mediated by the learner's background knowledge, the specific learning activity, the content to be learned, and the goals of learning.

Chapter 13 addresses the discourse of effective teaching as a supportive scaffold through which more planful learning strategies can be gradually facilitated within routine classroom activities and flexibly transferred to a broader array of curriculum objectives. Recommendations are also made for selecting among the various kinds of observational tools as the means for monitoring the progress of individual students over the short and long term.

Three additional resources are Appendixes A, B, and C. The first two appendixes, co-written with Amy Belkin, expand on the principles of coparticipation described in Chapter 5 by detailing procedures that can be selected to enhance awareness of classroom communicative contexts. Appendix C complements the discussion in Chapter 7 of technological aids for obtaining samples of students' language use in the classroom. Specific procedures are outlined for obtaining good quality audio and video recordings.

Chapter 2

Teaching and Learning As Communicative Processes

In this chapter we first describe a sociolinguistic approach to communicative competence in the classroom. Second, the relevance of theory for effective instructional practices is addressed. Third, we discuss two complementary perspectives on the origins and development of communicative competence—the mentalistic and the interactional—and their application in describing potential sources of a language learning disability. Finally, a perspective is presented that merges the mentalistic and the interactional orientations.

A SOCIOLINGUISTIC APPROACH

Sociolinguistic studies focus on the communication of school-age children and their teachers in a variety of classroom situations, including some that may attempt to mimic "real" situations in more restricted, experimental ones. Because research considered to be sociolinguistic has been generated within a variety of disciplinary perspectives (education, linguistics, psychology, sociology, anthropology, and communication sciences and disorders) and across disciplines, generalizations about guiding theoretical assumptions and consequent methodological practices are somewhat problematic. For example, psychologists have investigated individual differences in language and communication; linguists have studied the development of communicative functions of some primary school children; sociologists have studied the regulation of social order through communicative processes, such as turn-taking and attentional norms; educators have studied the organization of formal activities, such as the lesson; anthropologists have investigated verbal and nonverbal aspects of communicating within and between cultural groups; and clinical scientists in the field of child language disorders have explored many of these same parameters as they intersect with language, learning, and literacy acquisition in children with language learning disabilities.

Despite the apparent diversity of even the few approaches just cited, some commonalities are apparent throughout the corpus of sociolinguistic research. Virtually all researchers have studied the processes and patterns of language and communication as they occurred spontaneously in the classroom. Differences in communication that are associated with selected social variables, such as gender, ethnicity, and social class, have been examined. Developmental differences have also been investigated, with the emphasis on children's social roles as learners, not on chronological age per se.

In addition to a common focus of research, another similarity found across sociolinguistic studies is their use of *descriptive tools*, which are characterized by five key elements: (1) the use of some technology, such as audio or video taping, as the basis for transcription; (2) units of analysis, which may be predetermined categories for the coding of language or categories that emerge from the data; (3) retrospective analysis of audio and visual recordings in order to allow the observer to note patterns and sequences of talk that may occur very fast in real time and elude even the most perceptive of observers; (4) multiple analysis, for example, the analysis of syntax, pragmatic functions, the lexicon, discourse relations, or paralinguistic cues, among other dimensions; and (5) knowledge of the context within which recordings are made so that interpretation can be as accurate and complete as possible. A full discussion of descriptive tools in comparison to other tools used in observational approaches to assessment and intervention is included in Chapter 10.

IS THEORY PRACTICAL?

A major goal of this book is to bridge the gap between theory and practice, which are sometimes seen as incompatible. This gap is often visible in graduate courses in communication disorders, where it is not uncommon for students to ask their instructor, "Is this going to be a practical course?" Moreover, it is also not uncommon for continuing professional education activities for practicing speech-language pathologists to be guided by the dictum "Make it practical!" Both the question and the guideline have as an underlying assumption that theory is dissociated from principles of practice and, as a result, should be avoided as impractical.

The issue of incompatibility has been addressed in a limited way. For example, Johnston (1983), Lund and Duchan (1988), and others (e.g., Muma, 1986; van Kleeck, 1985) present the argument that the dissimilarity among approaches to assessment and intervention found in both clinical and educational settings derives from the differing theoretical frameworks held by researchers and clinicians. Furthermore, the nature of the clinician's theoretical assumptions affects how assessment is defined, what diagnostic questions are asked, how the clinician sees his or her role as an interventionist, what methods are selected to facilitate changes in competencies, and how progress is evaluated.

However, the relations among assumptions, the definition of roles, and the actual practices do not always correspond (Fey, 1986; van Kleeck & Richardson, 1988). A clinician may adhere to the theory that the facilitation of communicative competence emerges from a diverse set of enriching interactional experiences. The method of intervention, however, may actually consist of practicing specific "splinter" skills in isolation. Examples of this method might include practicing linguistic rules for producing complex sentences that are unconnected to meaningful communicative activities or practicing the sequencing of a pictorial story divorced from the purposes of story telling. As Wiig (1989) observes, children acquiring nonfunctional communicative skills cannot readily use these skills outside of the situations in which they are taught. Isolated practice as a pedagogical approach to learning in the classroom is not immune from criticism either. Applebee and Langer (1983) argue that the emphasis on splinter skills has resulted in "extensive taxonomies of questioning techniques, to legions of workbook and textbook activities providing 'practice' in one or another component skill, and to outlines of ideal lesson sequences" (p. 168).

Because there are competing theories of language learning and of language learning disabilities and gaps between an individual clinician's theoretical assumptions and his or her actual practices, an important qualification should always be kept in mind. The selection of any approach to assessment or intervention, including the use of standardized tests, procedures for obtaining and analyzing samples of language, software packages, and commercial therapy materials, "involves adopting the author's view of language" (Lund & Duchan, 1988, p. 7). As a result, if theory and practice are to be related as complementary sides of the same coin, clinicians need to make their own assumptions explicit about language and communication as a means of self-clarification about roles, processes, and procedures (Muma, 1986; van Kleeck & Richardson, 1988). Two sources of assumptions about linguistic-communicative processes and their developmental disruption are explored in the next section.

BELIEFS ABOUT HUMAN BEHAVIOR

Behavior is action or performance in a particular circumstance. From a practical point of view, all educational and clinical decisions about who may be impaired are interpretations. These interpretations emerge from social judgments, which are sets of expectations about how human beings should act (Mehan, 1983, 1987; Mehan, Hertweck, Combs, & Flynn, 1982; Mehan, Hertweck, & Meihls, 1986). Wong (1986) cautions that "in all classification decisions, value judgments do come into play, whether we (openly) acknowledge them or not" (p. 6).

In a similar way, the set of assumptions (or beliefs) that we hold about scientific inquiry into child development is based on what Gavelek and Palinscar (1988) describe as our "metatheory" (our philosophical orientation toward) about the origins and shaping of human functioning. Two such metatheories are mentalism and interactionalism.

Mentalistic Orientation

In a mentalistic view of communication development and disorders, the focus typically is the internal processes the individual actively employs in becoming a proficient language user. Internal processes are those mental, or intrapersonal, processes through which cognitive, linguistic, and social knowledge are acquired, organized, accessed, and used for specific purposes. An implicit premise is that how an individual acquires internal knowledge about communication subsequently "influences the act of communication itself" (van Kleeck, 1985, p. 3). Hence, children are viewed as active and independent builders of their own learning who abstract the underlying rules of the linguistic-communicative system from their interactions with the linguistic and nonlinguistic world. Their overall direction of development is conceptualized as an evolution from the individually motivated, intrapersonal domain to the collectively motivated, interpersonal (social) domain (Muma, 1986; Silliman, 1984; van Kleeck, 1985).

A variety of different theories and their applications stem from this philosophy of science, for example, stage-based Piagetian and neo-Piagetian theories, information-processing theories, skill-based theories, and linguistic theories (for comprehensive reviews, see Kamhi & Lee, 1988, and Snyder, 1984). In communication disorders, frameworks for understanding the relations and possible sources of disruption among cognition, communication, and learning can vary significantly according to the salience of behaviors. Our intent is not to provide a full account of these frameworks but to select models illustrative of approaches in which intrapersonal processes are described as the primary sources of language learning disabilities. In this context, the term *sources* refers, not to etiology, but to descriptions of behavioral patterns.

Sources of Disability

The Wiig and Semel (1984) framework accounts for relationships between oral language competence and academic achievement. Their model attempts to explain disruptions in language learning within the information-processing mechanisms that are believed to regulate language processing and production. For example, memory deficits in retrieval and recall are believed to influence various perceptual, linguistic, and cognitive aspects of language comprehension and production. These aspects might include recall of phoneme sequences; retrieval of words (semantic units); the retrieval of semantic classes involved in verbal associations, such as antonyms, synonyms, subordinates, or super-ordinates; recall of semantic relations underlying the understanding of "verbal analogies, cause-and-effect relationships, and linguistic concepts that require logical operations" (Wiig & Semel, 1984, p. 30).

Catts' (1989a) model of phonological processing is a more circumscribed way of thinking about information processing as it relates to connections between linguistic functions and sources of disruption in learning to read. Catts defines phonological processing as the linguistic operations utilizing the phonological structure of the language. Five types of related processing activities are identified in the utilization of the phonological code: (1) encoding of phonological information in long-term memory, an operation in which sensory input is transformed into a representational form for relating sound to meaning, for example, on tasks requiring the oral reproduction of a string of newly learned nonsense words; (2) retrieval of phonological code information where phonological representations are accessed from long-term memory, for example, on word recall or rapid naming tasks; (3) recoding of phonological information in short-term memory in order to keep it active on tasks in which a series of digits, letters, words, or sentences is to be repeated as accurately as possible; (4) active manipulation of phonemic segments, a form of phonological awareness that occurs, for example, in explicitly recognizing the syllabic and phonemic constituents represented in a printed word or analyzing how many phonemic segments exist in a word presented orally; and (5) at the level of production, planning and rapid motor execution (articulation) of nonsense words or other complex phonological sequences, such as *seashells, blue brush,* and *she sells shirts* (Catts, 1989b). Planning, retrieval, and execution also are reflected in the demands of oral reading. While reading out loud, children must quickly and accurately retrieve the pronunciations of printed words (Catts & Kamhi, 1987).

Based on research evidence, Catts (1989a) locates two possible sources of breakdowns in phonological processing. One is at the *encoding* level, the level at which phonological information is represented in long-term memory. Depending on the task, speech perception information is not used efficiently to derive the phonological structure of spoken words accurately or automatically, a situation that can have a significant impact on language and learning. For example, less proficiency in the planning and execution of complex phonological sequences may be the result of encoding difficulties, since, if one cannot readily organize the order of phonemes in a word, accuracy in production will be affected. Also, if phonological encoding is disrupted, then rapid retrieval of words may be impaired. Words either are not phonologically represented in the "mental lexicon" or, if encoded at some level, are not fully elaborated in terms of the richness of lexical features (Kail & Leonard, 1986) or well integrated with phonological representations (Catts, 1989a).

The other source of breakdown may occur at the level of *accessing* phonological information. Even if phonological information is encoded sufficiently, there may be difficulties in employing efficient strategies for retrieving that information. Rapid retrieval on naming tasks or on tasks requiring the accurate repetition of sentences or digits demands the use of memory strategies to keep information active in short-term memory. If efficient memory strategies (e.g., mnemonic, rehearsal, categorization, and elaboration strategies [Brown, 1982; Pressley, Borkowski, & O'Sullivan, 1985; Rogoff, 1990]) are less accessible for spontaneously remembering disconnected pieces of information, then more processing resources must be devoted to the act of retrieval itself. As a result, additional processing constraints on comprehension or production are created (Blachman, 1989; Catts, 1989a).

Modes of Processing

Catts (1989a) points out that the strength of these findings and related interpretations regarding possible sources of breakdown is dependent on the confidence placed in the validity of tasks and procedures and the representativeness of subject samples. Given these qualifications, the basic interpretations derived from studies of phonological processing are consistent with a mentalistic model of information processing in problem solving proposed by Sternberg (1987a, 1987b). The model is a variation of schema theory (e.g., Anderson & Pearson, 1984; Brown, 1982; K. Nelson, 1986) and specifies three interrelated information-processing components or mental processes: (1) planning components, which regulate decision making about how problem solving is to be approached and evaluated; (2) performance components whose purpose is to execute strategies developed by the planning components; and (3) knowledge acquisition components. The following discussion focuses on knowledge acquisition processes and learning how to solve problems, which begins with making sense of the situation (Sternberg, 1987b).

According to the model, when novel information is present in natural contexts, such as in the case of the above paragraph, it is always embedded in less relevant information. An initial task for the learner, therefore, is to selectively encode, in order to focus attention on what information is essential for making sense relative to the purpose for doing so. The encoding is selective in that some level of controlled, or conscious, processing is activated. For example, when unfamiliar words are encountered during the reading of the above paragraph, such as *knowledge*, selective encoding will be used in an attempt to decipher those clues in the text that will be most relevant for assigning meaning to these unfamiliar words. Moreover, "a good selective encoder will be able to spot these clues among the vast amount of textual information that is irrelevant for this particular purpose" (Sternberg, 1987b, p. 692). Simply stated, the good selective encoder is one who can readily separate the essential from the trivial.

Next, this newly encoded information about *knowledge acquisition processes* must be fit into a larger whole (an organizational schema or structure) through the process of selective combination. To continue with Sternberg's (1987b) example of an unfamiliar word, it is insufficient to figure out relevant clues from seemingly unconnected pieces of information; rather, these clues need to be combined into a plausible definition of the new words if understanding of their meaning is to take place in relation to the broader theme being conveyed.

Finally, the process of selective comparison must be employed to relate this new meaning to meanings previously stored in long-term memory. For example, a new meaning for *knowledge acquisition processes* is only useful to comprehension when it can be coherently related to and integrated into existing knowledge schemas. Integration allows going beyond prior understanding of knowledge acquisition and application of the meaning of *knowledge acquisition processes* in new ways. Application in new ways is the general meaning of *transfer* or *generalization*.

The three controlled processes of selective encoding, selective combination, and selective comparison are seen as interdependent: "Deciding what information to encode and how to combine it does not occur in a vacuum. Rather, encoding and combination of new knowledge are guided by retrieval of old information" (Sternberg, 1987a, p. 150).

In the transition from the novel to the familiar, performance becomes automatized. The individual no longer has to purposefully direct conscious attention to a task that previously placed a heavy demand on the allocation of cognitive resources (Sternberg, 1987a). You need only think about first learning to drive a car and the amount of controlled processing resources that must be brought to bear in order to become a proficient driver. With experience, however, the process of driving becomes relatively automatic and only becomes more conscious when an unexpected event happens, such as a car swerving into your lane. Then the schema for driving returns to some level of controlled processing so that you (hopefully) can avoid an accident.

When information, including linguistic information, cannot be managed routinely through automatic modes of encoding, combination, and comparison, then more of the existing processing resources need to be consciously allocated to the mastering of a new task (Snyder, 1984). Consequently, rather than being viewed as delayed, many language learning disabled children may be more aptly described as perpetual new learners. Because they do not readily infer connections between the old and the new, they are continuously confronted with having to allocate more of their processing resources in less flexible ways over longer periods of time to thinking consciously about the mechanics of new tasks (Wallach & Miller, 1988). They become bogged down trying to figure out what they are supposed to be doing. Less resources can be devoted to how the tasks should be done.

Wallach and Miller (1988) ask whether the phonics versus reading comprehension controversy could be better approached, in the case of disabled students, by incorporating the distinction between controlled and automatic information processing. Because some children must intentionally devote more time (i.e., processing space) to figuring out the phonemic constituents of printed words (they cannot yet do so automatically), comprehension of what is read becomes sacrificed. Thus, it takes them much longer than their nondisabled peers to master the same task (Sternberg, 1987a). Research on the phonological-processing problems displayed by language learning disabled students (Catts, 1989a; Catts & Kamhi, 1987; Kamhi & Catts, 1986) is one source of evidence for the perpetual new learner description.

Strategy Inefficiency

The metacognitive notion of strategy inefficiency, mentioned in Chapter 1 and referred to as one potential source of disruption in phonological processing, also contributes to understanding the persistent metalinguistic problems associated with language learning disabled children and adolescents (van Kleeck, 1984a; van Kleeck & Schuele, 1987; Wallach & Miller, 1988; Wiig, 1989). Metalinguistic knowledge refers to the awareness that components of the language system itself, its sounds, words, meanings, syntax, and intents, can be logical problem-solving tools for reflecting on that system.

In a real sense, metalinguistic knowledge pervades the understanding and expression of more literate forms of communication in the realms of listening, speaking, reading, writing, and spelling. It is also the kind of knowledge typically accessed by many standardized measures of language performance (Silliman, 1984; van Kleeck, 1984a). Examples of metalinguistic tool use include (1) understanding that words can have multiple meanings depending on contexts of use (e.g., "They are folding chairs," "The movie was cool," etc.); (2) analyzing letter-sound relationships; (3) manipulating the multiple functions of print from reading street signs to writing poems; (4) learning nonsense words; (5) comparing and explaining the grammaticality of utterances and why one linguistic form is more socially appropriate than another; (6) resequencing language elements, as in pig Latin or other miniature languages; (7) rapidly retrieving names from a category; (8) understanding and appreciating figurative uses of language, including verbal humor, idioms, similes, metaphors, and proverbs; (9) acquiring a second language; (10) solving a variety of verbal analogies (e.g., "Which of the following words does not go with the others: aunt, cousin, sister, friend?" "All blocks are green. This is a block. Therefore, _____.") (Nippold, 1988a, p. 160); (11) revising or repairing a message as it is being communicated; and (12) adjusting the style of speaking, listening, reading, and writing to fit the situation (Gillam & Johnston, 1985; Nippold, 1988a, 1988b; Nippold, Martin, & Erskine, 1988; Nippold & Sullivan, 1987; van Kleeck, 1984a; van Kleeck & Schuele, 1987; Wallach & Miller, 1988; Wiig, 1989).

Strategy inefficiency essentially means that problem solving, be it practical or formal, is not approached systematically as a process for planning what is going to be accomplished, monitoring what happens as it develops, evaluating the results, and revising the plan or its manner of execution as necessary (Baker & Brown, 1984; Gavelek & Raphael, 1985; Sternberg, 1987a).

Practical Problem Solving. The following example of practical, "on-line," efficient problem solving in communication is drawn from Wiig (1989): "You are at a professional conference. You see a colleague you have not seen for some time. You want to make contact [the goal or result], but you cannot remember your colleague's name [the problem]. What will you do [strategic planning]?" (p. 4).

Wiig offers several courses of action that she herself might use to achieve the goal of discovering a colleague's right name. To assist her in recalling the person's name, which also involves activating the controlled processing mode, she might first try recalling where they first met, which contextualizes the recall process. Then she might attempt to utilize metalinguistic tactics for accessing the name, monitoring and evaluating the effectiveness of these tactical alternatives relative to the internalized re-creation of the context: "Her name was something like Jane . . . or Joan . . . I think it was Jen—no, Jennifer. She was from Australia. Her last name was a long one. Oh yes, it rhymed with Jennifer. It was Westminister . . . no, but it ended in 'inster,' I think. Was it Minister or Glennister? Glennister. That's it" (Wiig, 1989, p. 4).

Since the success of this approach can be verified only by actually addressing the colleague, another plan is formulated for that purpose, a plan that might be altered according to how interaction develops. The example demonstrates that strategic efficiency in practical problem solving is also characterized by flexibility in managing one's repertoire of resources for information processing. Note also that efficiency, flexibility, and spontaneity are not mutually exclusive properties but define together how human information processing actually functions.

Formal Problem Solving. During the 1980s, the strategy inefficiency of many students designated as learning disabled became well documented (e.g., Deshler, Warner, Schumaker, & Alley, 1983; Leong, 1989; Palincsar & Brown, 1984; Schumaker, Deshler, & Ellis, 1986; Wong, 1985; for a review, see Silliman, 1987, and Chapter 12). Recently, this concept has been extended to the potential understanding of the connections between a language impairment and a learning disability. In addition to the phonological-processing research referred to earlier

(Catts, 1989a; Kamhi & Catts, 1986), four other avenues of research yield tentative evidence that reduced flexibility in efficiently managing the allocation of processing resources may be a distinctive characteristic of disabilities in language *and* learning as these behaviors come to be expressed, at least during the school-age years.

One area of research concerns word retrieval patterns of language disabled children. Findings are available from a variety of lexical-processing tasks probing rapid naming, accurate recall of category names, and accurate recall of specific words mentioned in oral stories (Kail & Leonard, 1986; Leonard, 1988). Lexical planning in discourse has also been explored (German, 1987; German & Simon, in press). In Kail and Leonard's (1986) analysis, evidence fails to substantiate that word-finding problems of language impaired children are products of a specific retrieval deficit. Rather, because disabled children tend to encode words more slowly into long-term memory, their representational network of lexical meanings and semantic relations is not elaborated as richly as their normally learning peers. While a child may "know" a word to the extent that it is sometimes understood and produced, knowing in this sense is not equivalent to understanding that the word has multiple meanings. Less elaborated representations can then result in slower and less flexible access to the very retrieval strategies that support speed and accuracy in lexical selection for performance on rapid naming and word recall tasks.

The higher frequency of word-finding indicators present in the discourse of language disabled children, such as pauses of six seconds or more in the lexical search for a word, is also attributed to less flexible retrieval strategies as assessed by telling stories from pictures (German & Simon, in press). Often, these children may be described as "slow retrievers" (Silliman, 1984; Westby, 1984) or as having a problem "getting going" (Merritt & Liles, 1987); that is, they may "know" the words they want to express but cannot quickly gain access to them (German & Simon, in press).

Less flexible resource allocation is also implicated in other kinds of investigations with language learning impaired children, including: (1) semantic-syntactic processing in the learning of miniature languages (Johnston, Blatchley, & Olness, 1990); (2) verbal analogical reasoning processes on story recall and transfer tasks (Kamhi, Gentry, Mauer, & Gholson, 1990); and (3) at the level of discourse processing, the comprehension and production of oral narratives (Merritt & Liles, 1987, 1989; Roth & Spekman, 1986; Westby, 1984, 1985, 1989; for a review of studies, see Silliman, 1989, and Chapter 8). This last area of research is rooted more in an interactional view of development and learning than in the mentalistic tradition. It is included for comparative purposes.

Learning a miniature language is comparable, on a restricted scale, to learning a second language (Johnston et al., 1990). A miniature language has a different lexicon and may have a different word and morphemic order from English declaratives (verb-subject-object rather than the more familiar subject-verb-object), but it still expresses the same semantic relations, such as the relations between objects (e.g., existence, possession, action, etc.) (Lahey, 1988).

Verbal analogic reasoning is an example of selective comparison (Sternberg, 1987a) and entails the linking of a familiar situation with a novel situation when the two situations may be similar in some respects and dissimilar in others (Kamhi et al., 1990; Nippold, 1988a; Nippold & Sullivan, 1987; Sternberg, 1987a). It is also an essential form of logical reasoning socially valued and cultivated by schooling (Rogoff, 1990). A common type of analogic reasoning task is the syllogism, for example, A is to B as C is to D (Nippold, 1988a). Another is the dilemma. In this type of task, children are presented with a hypothetical problem and asked, after training, to discover possible solutions. For example, they might be asked to figure out how a farmer can get his fox, goose, and some corn across the river to his house without anything being eaten (Kamhi et al., 1990, p. 142). Moreover, because analogic reasoning involves inferencing, it has an important bearing on any student's classroom comprehension and on comprehension in general. Regardless of the educational setting and level, teaching by analogy is a common device for connecting experience presumed to be familiar with the content being taught, as indicated by this passage from Nippold, Erskine, and Freed (1988): "A preschool teacher presenting a nutrition lesson might explain that children need food just as cars need gasoline, and a college professor discussing the origins of language development might compare the process to a growing plant: Nature provides the seed that is nurtured by a stimulating and responsive environment" (p. 440).

The interest in oral narrative comprehension and production has increased for three reasons. The first is that narratives, as a particular kind of discourse, offer a window for viewing individual differences among children in their ability to infer the intentions of others and their scope of creativity in using language to entertain and to report on personal experience. Second, as Stein (1983) observed, the social and cognitive functions of narratives are intertwined because stories represent social human problem–solving situations. Narratives have a purpose and a predictable internal structure, and these properties help to guide comprehension in the oral domain and in reading (Brown, 1982). The third reason for research in this area is a practical one. Narratives are an integral part of classroom events, for example, the activity of sharing time in the primary grades. Almost every child can tell a story, and oral narrative competency appears to be an important precursor for effective participation in a broad spectrum of literacy activities (Cazden, 1988; Michaels & Cazden, 1986; Stein, 1983; Westby, 1989).

Despite the somewhat disparate variations across these three strands of research, there is commonality. All of them require tasks for organizing and attending to multiple dimensions of language and communication in strategic ways in order for new knowledge to be acquired and transferred to different situations. Caution is needed in interpreting the generalizability of patterns from one research strand to the other. However, some stability in patterns can be discerned, which is consistent with findings from investigations on phonological and lexical processing.

Relative to the shifting processing demands inherent in learning a miniature language, solving story analogues, or understanding and producing narratives as a cohesive whole, language learning disabled children manage tasks at a slower rate than their normally developing peers. Moreover, slower task acquisition suggests limitations in the automatic accessing of efficient and flexible strategies for performing the three parallel functions of new knowledge acquisition. One function is to decide what parts of the information flow are most relevant for the task purposes (encoding), the second is deciding how the parts fit together within an organizational structure that guides making sense of that information (combination), and the third is going beyond what is known by inferring how the new information can be applied to novel situations (comparison) (Kamhi et al., 1990; Sternberg, 1987a; Wallach & Miller, 1988).

Breakdowns in one or all three of these parallel functions will disrupt what is learned about linguistic-communicative information, how it is elaborated and organized into a system, and how it can be used strategically for a vast array of purposes in listening, speaking, reading and writing. From a clinical perspective, the weak "encoder" may be the kind of child often described as having a restricted vocabulary (Kail & Leonard, 1986; Leonard, 1988), as having inadequate word recognition (Kamhi & Catts, 1989a, 1989b), or as being a slow retriever (German & Simon, in press; Merritt & Liles, 1987; Silliman, 1984; Westby, 1984). The weak "organizer" may be the kind of child who is described as not being planful as a conversational partner in managing communication (Brinton & Fujiki, 1989; Merritt & Liles, 1987, 1989; Roth & Spekman, 1986; Westby, 1989). Finally, the weak "transferrer" may be the kind of child who appears to be more "context-bound" and to be less flexible in the use of language in new situations (Wallach & Miller, 1988). Clearly, less flexible resource allocation can be a significant factor in constraining advancement in language and learning.

The etiology of these five symptom clusters remains unknown, primarily because of the complexity of the relationship between etiology, patterns of language behavior, and changes in patterns with development. Pennington (1989) advises that, although symptom clusters may be correlated with a language learning disability, it does not necessarily follow that they are part of the cause. The cliche "correlation does not equal causation" is valid in this instance. To complicate matters even further, similarities in the symptom clusters can originate from different causal factors (whether genetic, biochemical, or neurological) or can share a common underlying cause (Bashir et al., 1983; Geschwin, 1985). Two hypotheses for common causal factors are genetic heritability

(Pennington, 1989) and immunological mechanisms that become dysfunctional during early fetal development (Galaburda, 1989).

Two Assumptions

In our view, mentalistic metatheory engenders two apparently incompatible assumptions for explaining the processes and patterns of a language learning disability.

> *Assumption 1:* Behavior (that is, performance) is the product of under-lying internal processes that, in some sense, are relatively independent of particular contexts; therefore, behavior within a particular content domain can be considered as relatively consistent across different contexts of use.

While one needs to be wary of overgeneralizing, an assumption of this kind generally presupposes that, for the purposes of research, assessment, or intervention, adults and children understand situations in similar ways. This presupposition can influence interpretation of students' performance on research tasks conducted in a laboratory setting, standardized tests administered in the clinical setting, or other kinds of controlled tasks regardless of setting.

For example, it may be presumed that strategies used by children on controlled tasks administered in a research or clinical situation to assess the recognition and interpretation of multiple meaning sentences, such as *He took her picture* or *I got new glasses* (Wiig, 1989, p. 242), resemble similar linguistic strategies applied to the interpretation of multiple meanings in a dissimilar situation, such as the ongoing flow of classroom discourse during a sharing time activity. A similar presumption may also guide interpretation of strategy use in the classroom based on the use of an observational tool, such as a checklist. If the premise is that classification strategies regulate the comprehension of mathematical sets, geographic and scientific concepts, and synonyms and antonyms, the results of observation may then be interpreted within a Piagetian system for the developmental level of classification strategies (i.e., perceptual, functional, or superordinate/categorical strategies) displayed across curriculum areas (Gruenewald & Pollak, 1990).

An unresolved issue for the transferability of strategy use to theoretically similar tasks in dissimilar contexts, such as the linguistic and classification strategies just mentioned, concerns whether the identical set of strategies is actually being applied (Gavelek & Raphael, 1985). In other words, are the lexical retrieval strategies solicited by rapid naming tasks (Kail & Leonard, 1986) or the analogical reasoning strategies prompted by a story dilemma task (Kamhi et al., 1990) in the experimental or clinical situation identical to the strategies for lexical retrieval and analogical reasoning employed in actual classroom situations and elsewhere? Or, as Kamhi et al. (1990) speculate, are the strategies not identical but analogous in ways not yet understood? A third possibility is offered by Rogoff (1990). Strategy use may often be tailored to the particular situation of the activity to which it is being applied. For example, Wiig's (1989) practical problem solving showed that retrieval strategies were specifically tailored to meet her need to access a name.

Assumption 2: The levels of language behaviors, their phonology, semantic content, and syntax, should be assessed in the social communicative contexts that the linguistic system continuously serves.

While many mentalistic models presuppose that behavior is relatively consistent across different contexts of use, at the same time they must deal with the fact that variability will occur (within limits) as a function of the context. Moreover, many, but not all, mentalistic approaches adhere to the principle that a child's linguistic-communicative system should be evaluated in multiple conversational contexts and advocate the use of naturalistic and controlled observation and other "informal" procedures, depending on the purposes of the assessment. However, views on what constitutes naturalistic and controlled observation of conversational contexts may differ, leading to a discrepancy between the assumption and its actual implementation. One reason for this discrepancy is the variability in definition of a conversational context. For example, Fey (1986) states only that clinicians should evaluate children's language use in conversational contexts. Lahey (1988), in contrast, provides a detailed description of how variations in physical settings, conversational partners, activities, and the degree of structure imposed affect the amount of information obtained as well as the type of language behavior observed. Others (e.g., Hubbell, 1988) recognize that clinicians and teachers are a major component of the conversational context; therefore, the ways in which individual children "read" that context (interpret its meaning) significantly influence the actual communicative behaviors displayed.

Chapters 3, 4, 6, and 7 address conversational contexts in more detail. However, it is worthwhile to consider K. Nelson's (1990) description of the dilemma of context, a dilemma that is captured in the two contrasting assumptions of the mentalistic orientation and, to some extent, of the interactional orientation. According to K. Nelson (1990), the statement that context is inseparable from all learning is not a controversial matter. What remains to be resolved are the processes by which the child learns to interpret the complexity of interactions in which conversation occurs. K. Nelson (1990) crystallizes the dilemma:

On the one hand every situation needs to be interpreted in terms of its specific contextual features, which requires close and detailed analysis of the contributions of (conversational) partners; and on the other hand, no such analysis can be generalized to other situations . . . . In

short, accepting the fact that context matters implies accepting the fact
that no one child, situation, dyad, or whatever, can stand for children,
situations, or dyads in general. (p. 94)

In approaching this complex predicament, K. Nelson (1986, 1990) proposes
that context is not an objective "thing" that can be physically replicated but is
instead a subjective mental schema, or cognitive structure, for interpreting
events. Wiig's (1989) retrieval of a mental context as a strategy for recalling her
former colleague's name is a striking illustration of this formal definition. While
Nelson's theoretical framework differs in substantive ways from others discussed (e.g., Catts, 1989a, Kamhi et al., 1990; Kail & Leonard, 1986; Sternberg,
1987a, 1987b), the notion of context as a knowledge structure has comparable
implications for the description of language learning disabled children as perpetual novices:

> When a child enters into a situation, whether a familiar routine like
> getting dressed or a strange one such as an experimenter's "game," an
> event representation is called up that guides the child in interpreting
> what is going on, what can be expected to happen next, and what sorts
> of language are appropriate for the situation. In the event that a situa-
> tion is novel, the child may have no appropriate event representation
> to call up, and he or she may then need to concentrate all of her atten-
> tion and cognitive processing on making sense of what is taking place.
> In this situation, then the child may not talk at all, not knowing what is
> expected of her or what language is appropriate to use, and having no
> cognitive processing "space" available for interpreting or expressing
> language." (K. Nelson, 1990, p. 97)

Thus, in terms of the child with language learning differences, it can be
speculated that the more familiar an event is in relation to the child's existing
schemas, the greater the potential that more processing resources can be allocated to the planning and executing of linguistic strategies fitting the child's performance within the event. Conversely, the more novel the event is in relation to
existing schemas, the greater the probability that more cognitive resources will
have to be expended in making sense of what is happening at the expense of linguistic resources. In effect, if a child is observed only in those contexts whose
structures are not well understood by that child, then critical aspects of linguistic-communicative competence may be missed (Lahey, 1988; K. Nelson, 1990).

Interactional Orientation

A central tenet of the interactional orientation to development and disorders is
that children learn from a diversity of interactions with others. The core of in-

quiry, therefore, is the set of social processes through which cognitive and communicative abilities are acquired and have meaning.

Again, variations of this orientation are found in specific theories. These include the work of the Russian psychologist Vygotsky (1962) (for interpretations of this work and its relevance to learning and education, see Wertsch, 1985, and Wertsch and Stone, 1985), sociolinguistic approaches cited earlier (see also Chapters 3, 4, 5, and 10), and pragmatic accounts of language development and disorders (Bates, 1976; Duchan, 1984; Halliday, 1975; Lund & Duchan, 1988; Prutting, 1982; Prutting & Kirchner, 1983, 1987; Snyder & Silverstein, 1988).

Despite the divergent viewpoints of these theories, there is a shared notion that significant individuals in the child's social world mediate the child's interaction with that world and thereby determine which aspects of experience the child will be exposed to (Day, French, & Hall, 1985). An elaboration of this notion is that the ways in which people organize communicative events (i.e., how rules are structured for who can speak, when and where speaking can take place, and for what purposes) reflect a society's enculturation process (Heath, 1983, 1989). The origins and continuous development of human behavior are viewed as the product of interpersonal processes between the adult and child, because, as Bruner (1985) states, "There is no way, none, in which a human being could possibly master that world without the aid and assistance of others for, in fact, that world *is* others" (p. 32). The direction of development is then considered as proceeding from the interpersonal (social) domain to the intrapersonal (cognitive) domain as defined by the progressive internalization of mental processes. In contrast with the mentalistic orientation, which conceives of the child as an independent builder of knowledge, here the child is regarded as initially an active collaborator with significant others in his or her learning and as only later becoming capable of being an independent learner.

Three Assumptions

Several interrelated assumptions are also linked to an interactional metatheory.

Assumption 1: How we interpret the meaning of behavior displayed at any given point in time (e.g., how competently language is used) is inseparable from the social context in which that human activity is taking place.

A discourse exchange from Frankel (1982) illustrates this assumption. A parent has been called to her child's school, which is located in an urban Hispanic neighborhood, to attend an educational placement conference. The parent approaches the school receptionist. Neither the parent nor the receptionist knows one another.

Receptionist: Habla Espanol?
              (silence)
Receptionist: HABLA ESPANOL?
              (silence)
Onlooker: (In a loud whisper) Sarah! That parent isn't Spanish
              speaking. She speaks English!
Receptionist: Oh! Habla Ingles? (p. 33)

This conversation reinforces the point made previously. How two people act (behave) depends on how they interpret the same event. Stated simply, the way we act is inseparable from our joint understanding of how we are expected to act in any situation (Hall & Cole, 1978). What normal communicative behavior means, then, will vary depending on how persons interpret or misinterpret the situation. The school receptionist, despite contradictory evidence, interpreted the parent's competence in a particular way, namely, she assumed the parent spoke Spanish. The end result was a breakdown in communication.

Assumption 2: The meaning of an individual's action can only be interpreted by understanding the dynamics of interaction.

Let's return again to the example of the school receptionist and the non-Spanish-speaking parent. The receptionist initially assumes that the parent is Spanish speaking based on her prior experiences in this situation. This assumption leads the receptionist to provide a request for information in Spanish. The silence of the parent is most likely interpreted by the receptionist in an ambiguous way—she does not know what the silence means. Is the parent hard of hearing, inattentive, or what? The result is that the receptionist cannot interpret the silence. She needs to say something to keep the conversation going but assumes "that physical alignment or hearing is in question but not the language itself" (Frankel, 1982, p. 34). The subsequent silence of the parent communicates continued misunderstanding. Even with the new information given by the onlooker, which makes explicit that the receptionist's assumptions are in error, the repair that she selects is inappropriate. A mismatch in expectations continues to prevent the establishment of a shared understanding. This conversation illustrates the notion that what behavior means at any given moment in time must be approached from what people are doing together to make sense of each other's actions.

Assumption 3: The phonological, lexical, semantic, and syntactic components of language behaviors always have an integrated function, that of communication (Rees, 1979).

Since the function of an utterance is to communicate (Searle, 1975), every act of speech can be considered as multifunctional (Halliday, 1975). More broadly, because speech is the verbalized expression of language, it unites cognitive, social, and affective functions of human behavior (Cazden, 1988). The "Habla Espanol?" conversation clearly shows these three functions. The elliptical interrogative "Habla Espanol?" (what is literally said) conveys propositional, or informational, content, which is a cognitive, or representational, function. At the same time, it also has a social function, that of accomplishing the pragmatic goal of obtaining a response to a request. This same utterance has an affective function as well, that of communicating an attitude or belief about the other major participant in the dialogue. The manner in which we interpret the affective function is a powerful contributor to our social identities and influences how we interact with others as a consequence (Erickson & Shultz, 1982).

MERGING PERSPECTIVES

Our perspective merges intrapersonal and interpersonal views of behavior, as shown in Figure 2-1.

Recall that every utterance has cognitive, social, and affective functions. In Figure 2-1, the interpersonal processes appear as the processes through which at least two persons interact (participate or collaborate) to create and sustain communication (discourse), including their roles in communication. Also represented are those cognitive (intrapersonal) processes that serve to make sense of what is taking place. Cognitive processes, therefore, have an interpretative function. The assumption is that comprehension is always a sense-making activity

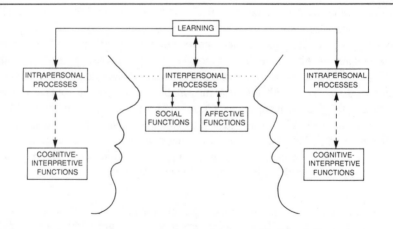

Figure 2-1 Model of Learning As the Outcome of Intrapersonal and Interpersonal Processes

regardless of whether the domain of interpretation is oral or written. Two general premises anchor this merged perspective.

Communication Is a Collaborative Process

In this merged perspective, the analysis of behavior shifts from the individual as the only unit of analysis to the interactive behavior between two individuals (a dyad) or more. The central idea here is that communication, in the strictest sense, is the shared understanding (interpretation) of what is really meant by what is literally said, as the "Habla Espanol?" conversation demonstrates. It follows that communication is always a social process constructed and sustained through collaboration with others.

The Meaning of Behavior Is Inseparable from the Situation in Which It Occurs

The second premise entails that the interpretation of performance should be based on typical classroom activities. If the intent is to develop new collaborative roles for assessment and intervention, then students' behavior has to be considered as inseparable from the context in which learning activities actually take place. In other words, while the results of learning are always measured individually, the process of learning in the classroom always takes place within a social organization of group membership (Dreeben, 1984). What teachers and students, or even clinicians and students, are doing together in their specialized roles defines the meaning of performance.

Bloome and Knott (1985) offer another way of conceptualizing learning as the outcome of a complex interplay between interpersonal and interpretative processes (Michaels & Cazden, 1986, p. 132). The interpretation of students' communicative behaviors is dependent on two interrelated sources of information. One source is the interpersonal context of learning as jointly constructed by teachers and students through the dynamics of classroom discourse. This source is explored in Chapters 3 and 4. The other is the intrapersonal context of learning, which is made visible to others through the individual student's patterns of communicative performance in classroom activities. Consideration of a disability, then, always entails the analysis of an intrapersonal (internal) disorder within interpersonal contexts (Bloome & Knott, 1985).

CONCLUSION

Beliefs about the origins and development of knowledge determine the nature and scope of theoretical descriptions of what is learned and how it is learned.

Theory, in turn, determines the kinds of research questions that are investigated and the kinds of methodologies that are employed to implement the research process. Theory also has an impact on the definition of clinical and educational roles and on the implementation of educational and intervention policies, programs, and procedures. Often, incompatibility may exist between the knowledge base of theory and research and how it is actually applied to everyday situations.

The synthesis of mentalist and interactionalist metatheories (orientations) indicates that each reflects differing perspectives about the conduct of scientific inquiry on the origins and development of knowledge and the sources of its disruption. Each operates with differently focused assumptions. As is typical of the study of complex behaviors, each often has difficulty understanding the other's perspective including the language used to describe each perspective. To some extent, the seeming conflict between these metatheories may be analogous to the apparent conflict in the different ways of perceiving an elephant in the classic parable.

Mentalistic orientations have made significant contributions toward clarifying possible sources of breakdowns in the processing of linguistic information. They have also delineated some of the linkages between these breakdowns and learning to be literate. Studies have shown that the ability to automatize new learning rapidly and to apply it in less effortless ways to novel situations is a distinctive feature of the efficient and flexible language user. Inefficient and less flexible use of processing resources, on the other hand, seems indicative of the so-called perpetual novice, the child who needs to allocate existing resources in consistently effortful ways over longer periods of time to manage the language demands of the classroom or intervention setting. A major issue for mentalistic approaches is reconciling the assumption about the relative consistency of language-processing strategies across their contexts of use with the recognition that strategy use varies as a function of how children interpret the meaning of any specific conversational context.

Interactional orientations, on the other hand, have made equally significant contributions to the understanding of language learning as a collaborative process for socializing children into the conventions of their culture, including the culture of schooling. Because communication is always a collaborative process, the dynamics of communication regulate the interpretation of events as well as the permissible ways in which language can be expressed to achieve cognitive, social, and affective goals. In the merged sociolinguistic perspective presented here, it is proposed that intrapersonal processes regulating individual learning cannot be separated from the actual interpersonal contexts of the classroom.

The Interactional Contexts of Disability: Expectations and Individual Differences

The concepts presented in Chapter 2 serve as the foundation for our approach, which emphasizes that interactional contexts create opportunities for language and literacy learning. Given the complex nature of interaction in the classroom and the range of individual differences among children in their communicative competence, the causes of the less adaptive behaviors that are interpreted as academic failure may not always reside within the child. A disability may be located in the interactional requirements of classrooms. Moreover, if not understood, these requirements can obstruct rather than facilitate the learning of children who do have an inherent disability. Potential difficulty can arise from three sources: (1) the nature of teacher, parental, and child expectations for classroom competence; (2) individual differences in children's classroom communicative competencies; and (3) the ways in which discourse is structured in school, including the intervention setting.

This chapter is devoted to the contributions of expectations and individual differences to judgments of competence. Discussion of classroom and clinical discourse is reserved for Chapter 4.

TEACHER, PARENT, AND CHILD EXPECTATIONS REGARDING CLASSROOM COMPETENCE

Being judged as competent involves knowing how to participate effectively in the many kinds of classroom activities within and across classrooms. Among these kinds are teacher-directed, large-group activities, such as sharing time and lessons; peer-directed learning; and independent activities, for example, completing assignments alone. Much of the recent information on teachers' expectations for successful performance emerges from sociolinguistic studies on literacy learning in kindergarten and the early primary grades among mainstream and cultural minority children. "Good" or "better" students typically know how to do the following:

- They manage one task at a time, completing that task on schedule independently (Erickson & Mohatt, 1982).

- They wait for a speaking turn without interrupting others, since it is understood that the teacher has the right to establish the rules of talk, including the permissible ways in which knowledge can be expressed (Erickson & Mohatt, 1982; Fivush, 1983; Heath, 1983; Wilcox, 1982).

- They fit their style of discourse to the style the teacher uses in directing lessons (DeStefano, Pepinsky, & Sanders, 1982; Heath, 1983; McTear, 1985). Examples of style fitting include (1) giving only minimal responses to teacher requests for factual information (e.g., "What day is today?" or "What color is this crayon?") and (2) being able to repeat key lexical items as a semantic tie for explicitly connecting the response to the teacher's question, a public demonstration that a "complete sentence" can be produced (e.g., "Today is Tuesday," "The crayon is red").

- They separate essential from trivial information in lesson activities, such as activities involving analysis of sound structure (Blachman, 1989; N.W. Nelson, 1984) or the retelling of a story after listening to it (Tattershall & Creaghead, 1985; Westby, 1989); they also integrate any new information into existing knowledge (Ripich, 1989).

- They monitor and attend to the teacher's constantly shifting expectations regarding the form of verbal response (Bloome & Knott, 1985; Bloome & Theodorou, 1988; Mehan, 1979; Spinelli & Ripich, 1985). As an example, within a matter of microseconds, the "good" student can shift from the expectation to give a single word response when called on to the expectation to ask any questions about what is not understood once the teacher is finished giving answers (Green & Weade, 1987).

Each of these strategic or "know-how" skills must be acquired, and the rates at which they are acquired may differ considerably depending on the nature of children's socialization experiences. Research has documented that certain groups of cultural minority children bring to school different social experiences for how these information-processing strategies are to be used. Among the diverse sociocultural groups that have been studied are (1) urban black children (Cazden, 1988; Gee, 1985; Michaels, 1986; Michaels & Cazden, 1986), (2) black and white children from rural working class communities in the same region (Heath, 1982a, 1983), (3) native Hawaiian children speaking Hawaiian Creole (Au & Kawakami, 1984; Au & Mason, 1983; Kawakami & Au, 1986; Tharp, 1982), (4) Native American children (Erickson & Mohatt, 1982; Philips, 1972; Westby & Costlow, in press; Westby & Rouse, 1985), (5) Asian children who are recent immigrants to the United States (Cheng, 1987, 1989), and (6) Chicano children (Wilkinson, Milosky, & Geneshi, 1986).

Two examples, presented in the following sections, will help to illustrate how differences in sociocultural frameworks influence expectations for the meaning of competence.

Teachers' Expectations

One example of conflicts in expectations between students and teachers comes from the work of Michaels (1981, 1986) who investigated black and white children's production of narratives during "sharing time" in their elementary classroom. In this common speech event in the early elementary grades, teachers call on students to share stories with the class. Michaels found that black and white children differed in the style of topical development of their stories and that, as a result, their narratives were differentially evaluated by teachers. White children produced *topic-centered* narratives, which focus on a single object or event. A typical topic-centered narrative is one produced by Burt, who is in the first grade (adapted from Michaels, 1981, p. 428):

Burt:	Well last Saturday/ this . . . last Saturday/ well we played/ against/
Student teacher:	(interrupts) sh sh
Burt:	another soccer team/ and/ well the last team we played against/ we uh lost/ and this team/ this time/ we/ they/ this was the first time/ that they played against another team// and it was/ three nothing/ and we were three//

Black children, in contrast, tended to produce *episodic* narratives, which focus on multiple objects and events. The following personal experience narrative, produced by eight-year-old Carla in response to a topic about fighting with brothers and sisters, is characteristic of this structure (see Appendix B for notations):

Carla:	Um—we be *playing* with them/ When my mother be home/ We be out/ we be home/ we be playing/ You scared/ You colored blind/ And one time he bumped his head/ And we was laughing/ And he was laughing/ And he was getting ready to get us/ And we hide from him come out *boo* go like that/ We had some *fun*/ (narrative continues)

Because an episodic structure conflicted with teachers' expectations for what constitutes a good story, the narratives of the black students were interrupted more often than the narratives of the white children; thus, the stories of the black students were more likely to be negatively evaluated by teachers.

One of the implications of this work is that stylistic differences can be misconstrued by teachers and speech-language clinicians as indicative of a "language deficit," particularly when a child's literacy learning is not commensurate with expectations for achievement. The predominant "oral" style that some black children, like Carla, display in their narrative productions may represent a different way of planning out and clustering units of oral discourse than that found in Burt's more "literate" topic-centered narrative (Gee, 1985).

Cazden (1988) comments that many factors may influence a teacher's decisions about the competence of students' ongoing communicative performance. The amount of time available for activities (e.g., sharing time) and the teacher's goals for the activities are two such factors. Because episodic narratives tend to be longer than topic-centered narratives and to be less explicit in terms of the thematic connections among multiple topics, the outcome may be that episodic narratives are more difficult to assimilate into the teacher's ongoing lesson goals (Cazden, 1988).

An additional factor affecting this assimilation is revealed in Heath's (1983) research. In her work in the Piedmont region of the Carolinas, she observed that, in story telling, how black children defined what was essential information varied markedly from teachers' expectations about what information was important. Thus, sociocultural experiences also influence children's understanding of what is essential to recall or to tell versus what is trivial. Based on the accumulation of research evidence over the past decade, Michaels and Cazden (1986) conclude that "when a child's home-based interactive style differs from the teacher's style and expectations, interaction between teacher and child is often disharmonious and not conducive to effective help by the teacher or learning by the child" (p. 132). When this disharmony occurs, referral to special education is often the teacher's response (Mehan et al., 1986; Pugach, 1987).

Parental and Child Expectations

The second example of how sociocultural experience can cause misunderstandings about competence is taken from Cheng's (1987) analysis of conflict points between Asian parents' expectations about what schooling is and American concepts of education. According to Asian attitudes and beliefs, (1) students are to be quiet and obedient; (2) students should be told what to do; (3) memorization and observation are the methods for learning; (4) factual information is more important than creativity and fantasy; (5) teachers are not to be challenged; (6) reading is the decoding of information and facts; and (7) social and psychological distance is to be maintained between student and teacher as a sign of status and respect, for example, maintaining eye contact with the teacher is not permissible (Cheng, 1987). Cheng notes that, for many new Asian immigrants whose children enter American school systems, incongruencies often arise between the parents' perception of the teacher's role and the teacher's own perception of that role. The result is that conflicting messages are communicated to children about appropriate interactional styles to be used in the classroom, including expectations regarding how to participate with both teachers and peers. Iglesias (1985) correctly cautions that it is currently impossible to predict accurately what the socialization patterns of any individual family might be. The focus of attention should be placed instead on obtaining a better understanding of the values, traditions, and belief systems that children from cultural minority groups bring to school.

Westby and Rouse (1985) conceive of sociocultural systems as being located on a continuum between high-context cultures and low-context cultures. In high-context cultures, being a member of a group (e.g., family, community, or society) is valued over individual and independent effort, such as intentionally standing out from one's peers. Group membership, then, is the basis of social identity, since the individual "perceives the identity of self as part of the identity of the society" (Cheng, 1987, p. 12). Some high-context cultures also tend to have a different conception of time. For example, preset schedules for completing tasks are less valued, planning is therefore more flexible, and the role that "one person talks at a time" is adhered to less. In contrast, low-context cultures value individualistic and autonomous performance (consider, e.g., American institutions of schooling and attitudes about who is the good student). Social identities that embody these virtues are more likely to receive mainstream approval. Low-context cultures also esteem long-term planning, the completion of tasks on schedule, and the preservation of order in verbal turn-taking (Westby & Rouse, 1985). Discord between belief systems can cause children to try to cope with the resulting confusion by acting out or even withdrawing and becoming nonresponsive. So-called behavior problems are a primary reason given by teachers for a referral to special education (Mehan et al., 1986; Pugach, 1987). Thus, while academic failure may be the institutional rationale necessary to use for referral and identification, in actual practice mismatches in expectations regarding how to communicate appropriately can be the implicit reason for referral (Donahue, 1985; Mehan et al., 1986).

From this perspective, then, the educational failure of some may be located in the ways that children and teachers who come from different sociocultural backgrounds interpret each other's communicative patterns. The misunderstandings that result from miscommunication can be further confounded by cultural barriers.

Individual Differences in Classroom Communicative Competence

A point of clarification is in order here. We are not advocating that sociocultural differences in expectations and communicative styles explain the origin of all educational misclassifications of a language learning disability. Rather, the discontinuities in expectations between home and school may be one source of difficulty, particularly for cultural minority children. A second source returns us to the intrapersonal domain of individual variation in the development of classroom communicative competence.

By the time children, at least first-language learners, enter school, they possess the basic knowledge that language "is a code whereby ideas about the world are expressed through a conventional system of arbitrary signals for communication" (Bloom, in Lahey, 1988, p. 2). By "basic knowledge" is meant that children have an implicit command of the linguistic-communicative system for the everyday demands of comprehension and production. As indicated in Chapter 2, not all children necessarily have control over a variety of metacognitive and metalinguistic strategies that permit more conscious analysis of the components of the linguistic-communicative system and the planning of its uses. These forms of explicit knowledge seem to be facilitated by literacy learning, which, in turn, further influences the organization and accessing of metacognitive and metalinguistic tools and their accommodation to the multiple functions of speaking, listening, reading, writing, and spelling (Ehri, 1989; Garton & Pratt, 1989; Silliman, Campbell, & Mitchell, 1989; van Kleeck, 1984a; Williams, 1986).

At school entry, children have the basic knowledge that (1) language expresses ideas about events, beliefs, and desires; (2) the language code is an indirect means for representing what an individual knows; (3) the code is a system because of its predictable set of underlying rules for combining sounds into words, for combining words into utterances, and for combining utterances into discourse; (4) the code is also a convention reflecting what a given society has agreed about the meaning of words and how they can be used; (5) language consists of content, the expression of topics, which, more broadly, represents the specific idea being conveyed in a particular message; (6) the form of language, its phonology, morphology, and syntax, is the way sound and meaning are connected; and (7) the uses of language are intended to achieve different communicative goals by participating in and sustaining discourse (Bloom, in Lahey, 1988).

To be able to participate successfully in all classroom activities, children must now develop a special competence. This special competence involves the production and interpretation of verbal and nonverbal communicative behaviors in the context of changing communicative roles. According to Mehan (1979), in their new role as students, children "must know with whom, when and where they can speak and act, and they must provide the speech and behavior that are appropriate for given classroom situations. Students must also be able to relate behavior, both academic and social, to varying classroom situations by interpreting implicit classroom rules" (p. 133). Since these implicit social rules are never formally taught but must be inferred, they are often referred to as the hidden curriculum. Examples of the hidden curriculum are the five sets of expectations for judging the good student presented in the previous section.

The communicative competence referred to here must be viewed as an end in itself, that is, it is a competence that students must achieve if they are to understand

and participate in what is going on in the classroom. In addition, this competence must also be viewed as a means of attaining other educational objectives. Failing to understand or participate in classroom communication can preclude students from learning the academic content of the communication. Furthermore, within the same classroom, individual differences in this specialized communicative competence are the rule and not the exception. It cannot be assumed that all children in the same classroom have equally acquired all of the new "rules of the game." For example, research by Wilkinson and her colleagues (Wilkinson & Calculator, 1982; Wilkinson, Calculator, & Dollaghan, 1982) shows that children differ in aspects of communicative competence central to classroom learning, such as appropriately responding to questions. Therefore, it is important for both teachers and speech-language pathologists to understand the complex ways in which language functions in the classroom in order to better determine whether a child who might be viewed as having a "disability" actually has not yet mastered components of this specialized competence. At a minimum, children have to know how to adjust communicative roles, initiate and sustain topics, take turns at talk, and "repair" conversations that are floundering or have broken down.

Adjusting Communicative Roles

Communicative roles are the ways speakers in a conversation use language so that they are understood by others in the conversation. Being understood requires cooperation among all speakers, and communicative roles have both social and structural aspects (Erickson & Shultz, 1982).

The *social aspects* of communicative roles involve the rights and obligations that individuals having a particular social identity are assumed to possess and that subsequently regulate, or control, any instance of interaction.

Some social characteristics can change from moment to moment and are therefore described as "emergent attributes" (Erickson & Shultz, 1982). To understand this concept, consider the Habla Espanol? exchange discussed in the preceding chapter. The initial role relation between the school receptionist and the parent is an institutional relation between strangers who are not equal in authority. It then becomes "an essential task of the senior person in the encounter to inquire into, and then officially ratify, *who the junior person is*" (Erickson & Shultz, 1982, p. 4). This process of "ratification" proceeds, in part, on initial inferences made by the receptionist about the parent's attributes as a speaker and a listener. Successful ratification depends on how adequately the receptionist revises her inferences based on subsequent interpretations about the parent's effectiveness and appropriateness as a conversational partner.

Other characteristics of social identity are described by Erickson and Shultz (1982) as "status attributes." These attributes can pertain directly to an individual by virtue of one's ethnicity, gender, skin color, height, or the existence of a handicapping condition. Status attributes can also operate indirectly through cultural association, such as the language one speaks and the style of speaking used, or through such socioeconomic indicators as occupational choices. Status attributes are brought by speakers to conversations and have a powerful effect on the interpretations of conversations. Recall from the discussion on teachers' expectations that inferences about students' communicative competencies are often based on status attributes that can become the focus of attention in specific interactions (Erickson & Shultz, 1982). One need only think about the social identities of many children, adolescents, or adults who stutter to understand how the status attribute of a physical limitation in speaking repeatedly intersects with judgments by others about communicative competence.

The *structural aspects* of communicative roles concern the coordination necessary for the alternating work of speaking and listening during conversation. Alternation involves turn-taking, which will be covered shortly, as well as precisely timing one's entry into conversation in such a way that the entry is not interpreted as either silence or interruption (Beattie, 1983; Ervin-Tripp, 1977; Silliman, 1984). Cooperation in conversation thus requires reciprocity; once someone takes on the role of speaker, some kind of response is obliged from the listener in order to maintain topical continuity. In other words, at the same time that the person in the role of speaker is addressing another in the role of listener, the listener is simultaneously demonstrating active understanding through nonverbal or verbal feedback or a combination of both (Erickson, 1982).

In sum, the social and structural aspects of communicative roles enable cooperation in conversation. The complexity of the fine-tuned adjustments that a child must make in order to be judged as a cooperative conversationalist in the classroom can be appreciated. From a developmental perspective, Dore (1986) speculates that advances in communicative competence are motivated by the shifting effects of group membership, roles, and obligations in the classroom. Entry into school dramatically changes conversational role requirements. In the mainstream parent-child relationship, the child's role is that of a separate conversational partner, while in the teacher-child relationship, the child must function in multiparty exchanges as an educational collaborator with the teacher and the other children. Among the tasks now facing the child is mastering the hidden curriculum in order to "pass" in the role of a normal student (Dore, 1986). It is not difficult to entertain the premise that children will differ in those aspects of communicative competence critical for passing.

Initiating and Sustaining Topics

Topics are what students and teachers talk about in the classroom. They are drawn from the shared information of students and teachers as derived from shared situations and previous communication. Communication in the classroom occurs when speakers introduce topics and make comments about topics, which then become elaborated, expanded, or cut off.

Brinton and Fujiki (1989) introduced the concept of topic manipulation in conversation. Although they did not specifically relate this concept to the classroom, it can be applied to the issues of concern in this book. Their concept refers to what can be done with topics, including topic introduction, discontinuation, shading, and reintroduction. There are certain prerequisites for introducing a topic, including securing another person's attention, speaking clearly, and cohesively identifying the referents and the relations among the referents. Once a topic has been introduced, it may or may not be continued by other speakers. If it is continued, then the topic is maintained, sometimes with some elaboration or small fine-tuning (shading) that effectively changes the topic. Sometimes the topic is discontinued outright. The differences between abrupt discontinuation of a topic and shading or gliding into a new topic are very subtle. The knowledge that underlies all of these aspects of topic manipulation is also very complex. Students in the classroom need to understand these complexities in order to smoothly introduce, maintain, and cut off topics when conversing with other students and the teacher.

Turn-Taking

Another domain of knowledge that students have to master in order to be effective communicators concerns the rules that determine who gets to talk, when, and for how long. Turn-taking in adult conversation is a relatively efficient process. Sacks, Schegloff, and Jefferson (1974) developed a model of turn-taking that they believed could account for turn-taking during adult conversation. Briefly, the model is as follows:

- If the current speaker selects a person to be the next speaker, that person takes the next turn.
- If no speaker is selected by the current speaker, then whoever speaks first takes the next turn.
- If no one self-selects and takes the turn, the current speaker may continue talking.

Other researchers have discovered that there are elaborate ways that speakers signal to other speakers that they wish to take a turn (e.g., a student may catch the gaze of the teacher, raise a hand, or call out in the classroom).

Few researchers have studied whether and to what extent this turn-taking model adequately describes what children do. Research has clearly established that, within a dyadic structure of participation, children at a very early age are able to exchange turns with caregivers, and even infants appear to have the rudimentary knowledge that turns alternate in conversation and that only one person talks at a time.

However, not all aspects of turn-taking implied by the model described above are mastered in early childhood, and "mistakes" in turn-taking may contribute to the *impression* of reduced communicative competence. For example, Craig and Gallagher (1983) found that not all of the preschool children that they studied knew the difference between long and short pause durations in turn-taking. The work of these researchers and others suggest that, although young children have some concept of pause duration and are sensitive to it, this form of knowledge seems to increase with age and language level. By three years of age, children have become relatively adept at taking turns, and they show some awareness of some of the more subtle aspects of the process, such as pause duration and how to deal with interruptions. Communication can still break down in some situations. Among the most vulnerable situations are those in which there are multiple speakers—situations typical of the classroom.

Silliman and Lamanna (1986) provide an account of the complexities of turn-taking in two special education classrooms for preadolescent children. The focus of their study was the dynamics of verbal overlap versus interruptions during sharing time. One of the classrooms was characterized by a high degree of teacher control over turn-taking, which did permit children to formulate personal experience narratives without significant amounts of interruption by other group members. However, the teacher reserved her conversational right to interrupt, typically for the purpose of conduct management, such as telling the children to be quiet. Although this turn-taking structure did increase the potential for each child to "get a turn," there was less attentiveness on the part of the group to individual contributions. Also, the children most likely to be interrupted by the teacher and other students were the ones who needed more time to formulate what to say. Recall the description in Chapter 2 of the "slow retriever," the child who needed more time to engage in lexical access.

The structure of the second special education classroom differed. Here, turn-taking practices allowed group members to serve as resources for each other in narrative construction. Less interruption but more overlapping of turns was common in comparison to the other class (overlapping involves taking a turn when it is inferred that the current speaker has reached a plausible stopping place). When children overlapped a peer's speaking turn, they most often did so in a resource role, for example, to add new information to the topic on the floor. Although group members were attentive to each other's contributions, participation was limited to the more powerful speakers, who could act as resources for each other and who were skillful at holding the group's attention.

This study demonstrates that children must learn different rules for turn-taking with different teachers. These rules, which are part of the hidden curriculum, need to be inferred, will vary across teachers within the same grade level, and can vary within the same classroom across different activities. Once again, we can see that the knowledge underlying classroom communicative competence is very complex, and students in classrooms need to coordinate and compare all of this knowledge in order to smoothly allocate turns to other students and to teachers.

Repairing Conversational Breakdowns

The final area of competence to be discussed concerns how children deal with breakdowns in conversations. Even simple interactions, both inside and outside the classroom, can be filled with misunderstandings. Despite a general fluency that characterizes communication, language interaction is replete with breakdown opportunities, which are signaled by false starts, incomplete constructions, and attempts at revision of a message's form or content. Research with both children and adults reveals that strategies are used to repair conversational breakdowns, and there is some research on how these repair strategies differ between normal and language disabled students. Repairs can be initiated by either the speaker or the listener and include requests for clarification ("What did you say?"), requests for specification ("What did you mean?"), and requests for confirmation ("Is this what you said?"). Brinton and Fujiki (1989) provide an extensive treatment of repairs for school-age children, including both normal and language disabled speakers. Readers are referred to their treatment for details about the knowledge that children must have in order to be able to function effectively as conversational partners inside and outside the classroom.

We return to the premise that individual differences in classroom communicative competence may be erroneously interpreted as a deficit in basic language competence. These differences need to be considered within the context of particular classroom demands for role relationships, topic formulation and continuity, turn-taking, and the verbal tactics used by teachers and students for the repair of misunderstandings that commonly occur in the classroom.

CONCLUSION

An implication of both sociocultural conflicts in expectations and individual differences in classroom competence is that some children may have differential access to the instructional activities that catalyze literacy learning. Learning is not the transfer of knowledge from teacher to student. Learning emerges from the highly complex interactions among teachers and students in a variety of academic and social activities, all of which involve communication. As Shuy (1988a) observes, the ways teachers talk can make all the difference between success and failure for individual children. In both the classroom and intervention settings, all teaching consists of talk, but not all talk is effective teaching (Silliman & Leslie, 1983; Spinelli & Ripich, 1985).

If the goal is to obtain a richer understanding of why certain children fail to achieve, then approaches to identification, assessment, and intervention need to be embedded in the real interactional situations that children typically encounter in the classroom. In the next chapter, we examine the third interactional source of a disability. Classroom discourse and clinical discourse within a typical situation (the lesson) are compared.

Classroom and Clinical Discourse: The Third Interactional Source of Ability and Disability

Teachers' expectations for students and students' individual differences in classroom competence can influence decisions about whether students are classified as disabled. In this chapter, we examine the communicative demands of the classroom and the clinical intervention setting as powerful influences on decisions about students' abilities and disabilities.

COMMUNICATIVE DEMANDS OF CLASSROOM DISCOURSE

In middle-class, mainstream families, a significant degree of overlap exists between the way language is used in preschool, elementary, and secondary classrooms and the way it is used in the home. For example, the purpose of most teacher-student talk in school is to facilitate students' acquisition of academic information. In addition, research has shown that a great deal of parent-child communication is focused on information exchange during the early years (e.g., Snow, 1977). However, one difference between home and school contexts is that, in school, the content of interactions between teachers and students typically takes place during lessons, and the students' responses are evaluated more frequently and in a more formal way.

Teacher-Student Interactions

Examples of the formality of lessons can be found in the work of several researchers. These analyses show that classroom lessons have a distinct structure characterized by communicative units of increasing size. A very significant unit, from an instructional viewpoint, consists of communicative sequences between teachers and students, which in turn, consist of an initiation (I) by the teacher, a response (R) by the student, and a follow-up (F) by the teacher (Cherry, 1978). It is important to note that this IRF sequence is similar to the IRE (initiation-response-evaluation) sequence discussed by Cazden (1988) and Mehan (1979). In the work of Griffin and Shuy (1978) and Cherry (1978), the next level identified is the topical sequence, followed by phases of the lesson and then by the entire lesson.

Cazden (1988) has identified three important aspects in lessons: (1) The question–answer–follow-up discourse structure of the lesson appears to be the "default pattern" (the IRF sequence), since it reflects "doing what comes naturally." (2) Only a small part of the lesson structure is ever verbalized by the teacher. (3) Children must learn to speak within the structure of the lesson. That is, children must match their discourse style to the teacher's style to demonstrate that they know how to give appropriate and accurate responses in accord with teacher expectations regarding how to perform. These expectations often have to be inferred by students.

The following example is taken from a kindergarten lesson on trees. The first excerpt describes the entire lesson, which lasted only four minutes. The basic sequence of the lesson includes determining various attributes of trees, including types of trees. Two verbatim excerpts, each an example of the IRF sequence, follow:

> The class is gathered in a circle in front of the teacher. The teacher writes the word "tree" on the board and asks if someone can read it. The teacher then asks the students to provide the names of things they think of when they think of "tree." The teacher writes appropriate responses on the board. The lesson ends when the teacher reads a story about trees.

Teacher:	Alright, Mary had her hand up. (I)
Mary:	Tree. (R)
Teacher:	Tree we have. (F)
Teacher:	Arthur. (I)
Arthur:	Cherry tree. (R)
Teacher:	Cherry tree, alright. (F) (Cherry, 1978, p. 48)

This example reveals an important fact about classrooms and children's learning: Students must learn to "read" classrooms in order to participate effectively in school. Children have to learn the subtle cues that a teacher gives to signal changes in the lesson or in her attention. One example is when the teacher just says "Arthur" to call on that student. And in the previous IRF sequence, the fact that Mary had her hand up suggests that Mary knows how to respond to the teacher's overall initiation.

Student-Student Interactions

Students interact not only with teachers in school. Indeed, some of the most challenging situations encountered by students in school occur when they have to interact with other students during lessons. The following excerpt ("What's That Word?" Lesson) illustrates the ways that children use language to request help. This example provides a contrast to lessons dominated by teachers. Additionally, this example presents a central communication between three first-grade students, who have been instructed to "help each other" in their reading group while the teacher is working with another group.

The excerpt shows how one student, Amy, demonstrates through her use of language a strategy to enlist the help of Dave, a reluctant but knowledgeable student. Amy has been successful in obtaining help from Dave in doing her assignment in the previous 15 exchanges between the two of them (e.g., Amy: What's the answer here? Dave: Tent). Amy shifts her attention to another student, Joe, and attempts to enlist his help. Joe does not provide assistance, and Amy shifts her attention back to Dave by requesting his help in providing the answer to a particular question. At first, Dave hesitates and resists Amy's initial request, which is interrupted by Joe also requesting the answer. However, Amy persists and Dave eventually gives in to the pressure and provides the answer. Dave and Amy continue to work on the assignment through collaboration, which consists of Amy requesting information and action from Dave, who provides both.

Amy: Ok, what, what's that word?

Joe: Don't ask me.

Amy: I'll ask him. What's that word (to Dave)?

Joe: Dave, do you know what we should write, like here?

Amy: Right here. (Several seconds elapse.)

I want you to look at my paper. (Several seconds elapse.)

Listen to this.

I've got these words.

I keep gettin mixed up, Dave.

Dave, I keep gettin

Dave: R the, the (The words requested by Amy are provided by Dave.) (Wilkinson & Calculator, 1982, p. 97)

DISCONTINUITIES IN LANGUAGE AT SCHOOL

In Chapter 3 and in the preceding discussion, we saw that effectiveness in the use of language at school is crucial to students' success. But what happens to students who do not communicate effectively with teachers and other students?

Communicative Barriers

Some of the consequences of not participating effectively in school activities are made vivid in the work of Heath (1982). From her description of the language used by black children and their white teachers in a Southern rural community where school desegregation had recently occurred, we have a sense of the educational and communication barriers present for many children. In the following excerpt, one teacher articulates her perceptions about the presumed communicative inadequacy of some students in her class:

> They don't seem to be able to answer even the simplest questions. I would almost think some of them have a hearing problem; it is as though they don't hear me ask a question. I get blank stares to my questions. Yet when I am making statements or telling stories which interest them, they always seem to hear me. The simplest questions are the ones they can't answer in the classroom; yet on the playground, they can explain a rule for a ballgame or describe a particular kind of bait with no problem. Therefore, I know they can't be as dumb as they seem in my class. I sometimes feel that when I look at them and ask a question, I'm staring at a wall. (Heath, 1982, pp. 107–8)

Regardless of ethnic or social class differences in communicative styles, the consequences for students of not learning how to read lessons can be far-reaching. They will be less able to take turns at talk and be more unsuccessful in interacting with other students and teachers. In addition, if these students do not understand the situations they encounter and the communicative demands placed upon them, they may be deprived of the opportunity to participate in classroom lessons. Thus, the discontinuities between classroom conversational contexts and other conversational contexts may present special risks for some students. Examples include students with dialect or communicative style differences (Au & Mason, 1983; Cole, 1989; Heath, 1983; Kawakami & Au, 1986), students who have limited proficiency with English (Bernstein, 1989; Cheng, 1989), and students for whom a developmentally based communicative impairment is the primary risk factor. While the magnitude of these discontinuities may vary, their presence can interfere with the further development of communicative competence and significantly influence overall adjustment to school.

The effects of not knowing the "rules of the game" (the standard ways of communicating in the classroom) are not limited to the obvious problems that these students face in their unsuccessful communications with other students and teachers. In addition to such immediate problems, if these children do not understand the classroom and its unique demands, students may learn little from the classroom experiences in which they participate. Furthermore, accurate assessment of their achievement is unlikely, since access to their knowledge is predicated upon optimal communicative performance. It is important to note, however, that a gap often exists between the explicit purpose of a lesson—the exchange of academic information—and its actual implementation. Research by Baker and Zigmond (1990), Bloome (1987), Durkin (1978–1979), Morine-Dershimer (1985), Shuy (1988a), and others shows that a good deal of discourse during lessons in elementary and middle school concerns the social (or conduct) aspects of being in school, such as being quiet, paying attention, taking out materials, and so on. Little time is actually spent on the content of the lesson (e.g., little reading is done).

Discourse Barriers to Planful Learning

Procedural Display

There are two main sources of evidence for the conclusion that in some classrooms active and planful learning by students may be discouraged or may not be taking place in the ways intended. One source of evidence is Bloome's (1987) research in urban, middle school classrooms, where he identified "procedural display." Procedural display involves the learning of a conversational pattern or routine with the implicit goal of completing the lesson for the lesson's sake.

A specific illustration of procedural display is taken from a vocabulary discussion with a class of eighth-grade students who were primarily black and from a working class background. Following the oral reading of a story about a 17-year-old boy and his loss of religion, the students were individually called on by the teacher to read aloud the dictionary definition of important words from the story. In this example, a student (Michael) is called on to read the definition of "torpid" (Bloome, 1987, p. 135):

Teacher: All right, Michael has found the word in the dictionary, Rodney. He will give us the definition it gives, and then he'll find which one fits your sentence, OK?

Michael: Number one,
          tempora temporary loss of,
          Number one
          Number one,
          has lost most of power
          power of
          convention or failure
          in functioning in functioning
          oration.
          Number two
          lacking in energy or vigor
          vigor.

Teacher: OK.

As Bloome (1987) notes, "Even though the dictionary definition is read and the vocabulary words had twice been placed in the context of the surrounding text, students were unable to determine what the words meant, and they did not respond to the teacher's request for a definition" (p. 135).

In this instance, the oral reading of the definition, rather than understanding its meaning in relation to the surrounding story text, seemed to be the implicit goal of the interaction. The use of this strategy for "getting through the lesson" required only that the students master a conversational routine for participating within the structure of the lesson and be able to demonstrate this acquisition publicly, for example, by displaying their knowledge of how to find a word in the dictionary and reading it aloud. One result is the illusion that learning has occurred. What remains unlearned are the appropriate metastrategies for approaching and mastering a variety of kinds of academic content. Other examples of procedural display are reproduced in the discussion on clinical discourse in this chapter.

The Teacher Talk Register

The second source of evidence for the conclusion that learning can be an inactive activity derives from information about the teacher talk register. A register is a way of talking that marks a specific social role, in this case a particular kind of instructional role.

An instructional register can be either supportive or controlling. In a controlling, or power, register, adult control is exerted in five ways (Cazden, 1988; McTear, 1985): (1) rigid access to the conversational floor, (2) tight management of the topic, (3) a focus on conduct behaviors, (4) the use of procedural display questions, and (5) the requirement that the student provide minimal responses within the adult's frame of reference. Control registers are frequently characteristic of teacher discourse in the regular education classroom (Cazden, 1988) and the special education classroom (Pugach, 1987; Silliman & Lamanna, 1986; Sleeter, 1987). Two central issues for clinical discourse pertain to whether procedural display and control registers are also distinctive features.

COMMUNICATIVE DEMANDS OF CLINICAL DISCOURSE

Because of the influence of sociolinguistics in the 1980s, there was a conceptual shift in language intervention approaches from an exclusively psycholingustic, mentalistic orientation to the social interactionist perspective. Duchan (1984) described it as a shift from "viewing children's language as a representation of their thinking, to a view of children's language as a tool they used to achieve their desired goals" (p. 154) by collaborating with significant others to accomplish the work of communicating. Revised frameworks for language intervention increasingly emphasized naturalistic, functional, and integrated learning (e.g., Kaiser & Warren, 1988; Lund & Duchan, 1988; Norris & Hoffman, 1990), and this change paralleled, sometimes without an acknowledgment of the commonalities by reading experts, the "whole language" movement toward teaching literacy in the regular classroom. Similar to communication-centered intervention approaches, whole language practices are based on the functional premise that listening, speaking, reading, and writing are all interrelated by their shared use as tools for communication. In other words, "What I can think about, I can talk about. What I can talk about, I can write. What I can write, I can read. I can read what I write and what other people can write for me to read" (Stahl & Miller, 1989, p. 89).

Shifts in conceptual orientations and changes in intervention procedures consistent with an interactional view of language and literacy learning are indicators of progress. However, the discourse processes governing how communicative goals for language and literacy learning are integrated may not have been altered to the same extent as have theoretical frameworks and clinical methods (Blank, 1988; Bobkoff & Panagos, 1986; Butler, 1984; Letts, 1985; Panagos, Bobkoff, & Scott, 1986; Panagos & Griffiths, 1981; Ripich, Hambrecht, Panagos, & Prelock, 1984; Ripich & Panagos, 1985; Silliman, 1984; Spinelli & Ripich, 1985; Stone & Wertsch, 1984). Clinicians (and teachers) still face the challenge articulated by Snow, Midkiff-Borunda, Small, and Proctor (1984). Since intervention is a specialized form of social interaction, the challenge remains essential to discover explicitly how clinical discourse is used to enable—or, unintentionally, to disable—children's active participation as collaborators in their own learning.

Two Samples of Clinical Discourse

The notion of clinical discourse as enabling or disabling is illustrated by the two samples that follow. Each excerpt represents different assumptions about what are appropriate behaviors for clinicians versus appropriate behaviors for children. Each also communicates different information about the activity of learning.

Disabling Discourse

This segment of clinical interaction is taken from a public school setting and will subsequently be referred to as the "Speech Rules Lesson." The format of intervention is the traditional pullout format. The participants are three children, Damian (nine years old), Jared (nine years old), and Allison (ten years old), and their clinician. Damian and Allison had been previously grouped together for language therapy. Jared was the newcomer in the group. This session is the first of the new school year, and the clinician begins with an accounting of her expectations for acceptable participation. (See Appendix B for a complete list of notations used in the transcriptions.)

| Clinician: | 1 | Jared has never been in speech before so we're gonna go over speech rules which you guys are familiar with because you've been in speech (.) for two years and we're gonna read the rules and talk about them = what happens when you don't follow the rules/ An' after we do that we're gonna take (.) kind of a little test/ But it's a fun test, ok?/ A test where you get to talk about some pictures and get to do some drawings (.) too/ All right/ Now = usually these rules will be up on my board in my speech room = did you see my room - uh - the rules when you came (.) to my room before?/ |

(Jared shakes his head negatively)

Oh/ You didn't notice them up?/ They're right up on my bulletin board/

(A topic digression now occurs for 1 minute, 35 seconds, with clinician then returning to the main topic in turn 23)

| Clinician: | 23 | Ok/ Let's go over the rules so we can get - um - finished here/ My rules are easy to follow = aren't they, Damian and Allison?/ |

(Both nod their heads affirmatively)

I don't have hard rules but they're something - they're rules we have to follow in speech or we don't have a good time/ Ok/

(Holds up poster board on which are written the five rules)

| Jared: | 24 | I can't read that/ |
| Clinician: | 25 | That's ok/ Uh - can anybody read number 1?/ |

As this sample shows, expectations regarding the form of participation can often take precedence over the process and content of learning. Also being signaled is the hidden message that the clinician will retain control of access to learning. In this instance, these expectations subliminally communicate a less than positive attitude to the children about the purposes of intervention and their roles as participants in this type of social interaction.

Enabling Discourse

The second sample, the Gist Lesson, is also taken from a public school setting. In this case, intervention was provided by the clinician in the resource classroom to three students: Danny (9½ years old), Sam (11½ years old), and Myron (10½ years old). Sam and Myron had been grouped together the previous year; Danny was a new participant. This session was the second of the new school year. The clinician's goal was to support the development of a strategy for "getting the gist" of a story by having each of the boys collaborate in the role of "teacher" and, in that role, evaluate the adequacy of the main points offered by the others. The clinician initiates this segment with a request for a review of the process for participation.

Clinician:	1	Does anyone remember how we participate?/ Refresh our memory/
Sam:	2	Ask them -- you're gonna read that - um - whoever is the teacher has to ask them -- one of them the main idea -- what they think is the main idea/ And . . . and - um - . . . and - um - um - if the teacher doesn't like it -- if they like it . . . um - um - they can change (.) their main idea/
Clinician:	3	Super super/ That was a good job/ (The next 31 turns are dedicated to the three boys taking turns in recalling and summarizing the parts of the story covered in the previous session.)
Clinician:	35	Here's the point where we are going to start today/ Now Danny, you're going to be teacher first/ Do you remember what your two jobs are?/ Go ahead and tell us the two jobs/
Danny:	36	(Reading from a 3" x 5" "memory cue" card) Ask - um - an (.) for mmmmain idea/ Give a better main idea if you don't . . . don't want to . . . if you don't want to use theirs/
Clinician:	37	(Orally reads the next two paragraphs of the science fiction story.)
Danny:	38	Um - him (points to Sam)/ Will you - um - tell us the main point of the sentences?/

Here, the participatory requirement being communicated differs significantly from the previous example. Each conversational partner, not just the clinician, is expected to assume an active role in assisting the others to monitor the process of communication relative to the task ("ask them what they think is the main idea"), evaluate its outcome, and revise the result if necessary ("give a better main idea if you don't want to use theirs"). Moreover, because shared responsibility for decision making seems to be valued, a sense of empowerment as an effective communicator is being facilitated. Feelings of empowerment, in turn, can serve as the intrinsic motivation to communicate in more planful and integrated ways (Hoskins, 1990; Norris & Hoffman, 1990; Snow et al., 1984).

We do not suggest that these two examples of clinical discourse are representative of every clinician's use of language to teach "language." Clearly, individual clinicians, as well as individual teachers, vary in their style of discourse depending on intervention frameworks and personal preferences for organizing and managing particular kinds of interaction. We suggest that the educational preparation of speech-language pathologists and teachers has customarily emphasized theory and method (see also Snow et al., 1984). For example, as language specialists, clinicians have not been taught routinely that, regardless of the specific techniques being utilized, their own discourse simultaneously functions as the interactional framework within which literate communicative contexts are created and as the medium for fostering the communicative competencies that support a literate orientation to learning. Thus, how the discourse of teaching is organized directly affects students' (or clients') understanding of the purposes of activities, what is actually learned about the meaning of learning (Stodolsky, 1984), the degree to which learning potential is realized, and how effectively learning can be applied to new situations. Prutting (1982) regards this last point on generalization as a crucial one: "Generalization issues most likely would be less of a problem if the multiple dimensions of communication became as much of a concern to us as the behaviors we select to remediate" (p. 106). In our judgment, one important clinical skill is the ability to make these multiple dimensions of communication transparent as the method for understanding the scope of their effects.

Earlier, we noted that, like the specialized demands of classroom interaction, language intervention is a specialized form of social interaction. Classroom and clinical interactions are typically instructional events comprised by the lesson, as the segments from the Speech Rules Lesson and the Gist Lesson demonstrate. Clinical discourse is contrasted with the lesson focus of classroom discourse along two dimensions: *structure* and *communicative* roles.

Structure

Some have argued that there is a general structural difference between classroom discourse and clinical discourse. *Structure* refers to repeated patterns of regularity that denote an internal organization of some kind. Bloome and Knott

(1985) describe classroom discourse as multiply layered. One layer consists of teacher–whole class discourse; a second layer is teacher interaction with a single student, which, from the teacher's perspective, is always teacher–class discourse; the third layer is discourse between individual classmates or between a student and the whole class. Rules for appropriate participation can differ within each layer and, indeed, can often conflict (e.g., in how and when children are to attend and to communicate).

Intuitively, it may be reassuring to believe that the structure of clinical discourse is layered in less complex ways, but two practical problems stand in the way of confirming or denying that assumption. One problem is the limited number of formal studies on clinical discourse. Furthermore, most of these studies have been conducted outside of the classroom. A second problem is the lack of an empirically verified body of data on the kinds of clinical discourse patterns that enable or interfere with learning over time (Spinelli & Ripich, 1985). Again intuitively, communication-centered discourse would seem to hold the most promise for the design of programs located in the classroom or in any intervention setting.

Review of existing research on clinical discourse does show that, regardless of whether the situation is dyadic or multiparty, teaching is organized and communicated through a lesson structure. Like the classroom lesson (Cazden, 1988; Mehan, 1979: Morine-Dershimer, 1985; Wilkinson & Calculator, 1982), the clinical lesson is organized sequentially into three phases: the setting-up phase, the instructional phase, and a closing phase. Each of these phases has specific functions, is marked in distinctive ways, reflects how adult-child behavior is organized into interactional sequences (Mehan, 1979), and, within sequences, is multiply layered. Because the least data are available on the closing phase, which terminates the clinical lesson, only the first two phases are reviewed.

Setting-Up Phase

In this phase, clinical discourse is characterized by the use of an interactional strategy, variously described as an *orienting*, a *framing*, or a *preformulation* strategy (French & MacClure, 1981; Mehan, 1979; Silliman, 1984). This strategy has multiply embedded functions, which children must learn to "read" if they are to have access to the learning event. One function of this strategy is to focus children's attention on the purpose or content of the lesson activity that will unfold (Morine-Dershimer, 1985); another is to focus attention on behavioral expectations for participation in that activity. Orientations can vary in their length, in the degree to which they explicitly frame the topic of talk, and in the extent to which the topic is related thematically to the larger purpose of the lesson. For example, the Speech Rules Lesson orientation is both lengthy and specific and is unrelated to the actual "language" task that emerged later on. The

Gist Lesson orientation, in contrast, is shorter in duration, although not necessarily less explicit, and coheres to the broader long-range theme of learning how to summarize the main idea.

Function: Minimize Misunderstanding of Purpose or Content. The first purpose of orientation is to draw attention verbally to the shared topic context of the lesson in order to minimize the possibility of children misunderstanding adult intent. The failure to establish agreement on what is going to be talked about results in dialogue that is limited as a vehicle for communicating information (Grimes, 1982). On another level, Ramirez (1988) describes orientations as metastatements about the structure or organization of lessons that also indicate " 'where we are' in relation to that structure at a given point in time" (p. 139). Orientation typically precedes knowledge testing, which marks the beginning of the second phase of the lesson. French and MacClure (1981) have identified three types of orienting strategies used by classroom teachers to serve the general function of shared understanding. Each can also be found in clinical discourse.

Orienting Strategy 1: Introduce New Activity. The first kind of orientation directs children to attend to particular aspects of a new activity about which they will be subsequently questioned. An example from a language therapy session with a six-year-old, where facilitating language comprehension was the goal, demonstrates one variation of this orienting strategy (Silliman, 1984, p. 311):

> I have some pictures here. And we're going to divide them into piles
> (placing a set of object pictures in front of the child), whether you eat
> something for breakfast, lunch, and dinner or snack, and say what it is.
> You can see it. Here choose a picture (child selects potato chips from
> the pile). What are they?

Note that the clinician did not present the reason for the activity of sorting pictures in separate piles. Rather, the focus of attention was on the *products* of the activity, or what the child already knew or may not have known. In addition, the activity appears to be a multiple purpose one involving a form of confrontational naming. The orientation also communicated that the child was to name a series of foods according to when they may be eaten.

Another example of this strategy comes from a combined kindergarten–first grade special education class for five children with language learning disabilities. The teacher is also a speech-language clinician, and the approach used is "language experience." The specific purpose of the lesson was to introduce a subtheme of a larger unit on chefs. The clinician viewed her intent as facilitating the children's explanations of what chefs do based on their prior visit to the school cafeteria. However, how this intent was expressed was at variance with the purpose of the lesson:

> This week we've been talking about the chef and I have a picture of the chef up here/ (Points to the bulletin board, where a picture of a chef is displayed) And I have one of the tools on that a chef uses/ What's one of the tools that a chef uses -- Look at Mrs. Light (sanctioning a child whose eye gaze was not directed to her)/ What do I have on that a chef uses?/ (Clinician is wearing an apron)

Again, the clinician did not state the broader purpose underlying the introduction of tools or cohesively relate this topic to previous verbal experiences of "talking about the chef" or the social experience of visiting the school cafeteria. Similar to the previous example, this orientation appears to serve notice that the activity will focus on products (naming cooking tools) rather than involve explaining what chefs do with tools.

A third example is drawn from a classroom module with language learning disabled children at the middle primary level. The intervention approach is grounded in whole language concepts. The teacher is also a speech-language clinician, and the activity to be introduced as part of a larger reading unit also involves tools used by a chef. An array of cooking tools, including a cookbook, are displayed on the table where the children are seated. Written on the blackboard is the reading plan: (1) Think about a chef. (2) Look at tools. (3) Write our ideas about a chef.

> Today, we're going to be talking about the different tools a chef uses/ What are some of the things your mom uses?/ What are some of your ideas?/

Although this orientation is similar in some ways to the preceding examples (e.g., the lack of a clear rationale and the focus on products), it differs in two important respects. First, the activity itself is embedded, at least, implicitly, within the larger context of different functions of print, such as the written formal plan of action (which is somewhat ambiguous in directing children to "think about a chef" and "look at tools") and the cookbook, which was a focal point of activity later on. Second, in directing children's attention to their background knowledge ("What are some of the things your mom uses?"), the subsequent product being requested ("ideas") is a metalinguistic one.

Orienting Strategy 2: Review Past Activity. A second type of orienting strategy directs children to review a recent past activity known to have been shared by both the clinician and themselves. Again, the orienting information may be a preface to subsequent questioning about the accurate recall of activity details or their sequencing. The review of speech rules that the clinician provided in the Speech Rules Lesson illustrates one form of this strategy. The purpose was to focus attention on prior experience assumed to be shared social knowledge, which then served as the basis for questions about actual rule recognition ("Can anybody read number 1?") and questions about rule violations ("What happens when you don't follow the rules?").

The Gist Lesson also demonstrates how this strategy can invoke metacognitive awareness about the mental state of remembering but may accomplish this in an indirect way. The clinician specifically cued the children's deliberate recall by referring to memory processes ("Does anyone remember how we participate? Refresh our memory."). In this instance, children needed to infer that the clinician's underlying intent was for them to concentrate on remembering the specific procedures for participation as well as the dual purpose of the activity ("Ask what they think is the main idea, and if the 'teacher' doesn't like it, change the main idea.").

An even more indirect use of this orienting strategy occurred in an upper primary classroom for language learning disabled children, all of whom had been working on a life skills unit for several days. The teacher, a speech-language clinician, opened the lesson by asking for a redefinition of the theme and then broadened the topic to the internal process of review itself:

Clinician:	1	What is a life skill?/
Ted:	2	Something you do every day/
Clinician:	3	What is a life skill you use every day?/
Sasha:	4	Telephone book/
Manny:	5	Checkbook/
Teresa:	6	Using money/
Clinician:	7	Why do we need to review things?/ Why is it good to remember?/

Orienting Strategy 3: Relate New Knowledge to Familiar Knowledge. The last orientation strategy is premised on the adult assumption that children do not have new information readily available; thus, before examining new knowledge, the teacher or clinician "must introduce new interpretive recipes and bodies of knowledge to the child" (French & MacClure, 1981, p. 37) by connecting the already known to the new. Analogies are a common device for connecting the old to the new as the following example shows. It is drawn from a grade 6–7 math lesson with four students who have language learning disabilities. The speech-language clinician is also the classroom teacher:

> This morning, we are going to start learning about subtraction and borrowing/ Knowing how to subtract is very important because we really use it every day/ Like when your parents write a check, they have to use subtracting/ Mary, what are some other reasons you can think of for why we would use subtraction and borrowing?/

In using orienting strategies to establish a shared frame of reference, a major issue is whether the discourse tactics selected will enable children to participate fully in the learning activity. This topic is covered in greater depth in Chapter 13. For the time being, we suggest four questions clinicians may choose to consider in formulating the metastatements that shape the way children understand the lesson as an interactional event.

First, how adequately can the participants infer the purpose and kind of information being sought? When these expectations are not stated explicitly or cohesively (e.g., in the sorting pictures and Speech Rules orientations), then the children are confronted with having to make "on-the-spot assessments," which may be more complicated than the actual activity.

Even if children are able to infer the expectations, as they were capable of doing in the Gist orientation, a second question arises: Does each child have the ability to figure out how specific the clinician wants the answer to be? Questions following the prefacing information can vary not only in the complexity of their form and their preceding reference but also in the complexity of the adult intent for a preferred response. Is the preferred response to "Do you remember what we mainly focused on in therapy last week?" simply an acknowledgement (yes or no) or is a more complex elaboration being sought?

The third question is whether it is developmentally appropriate to focus children's attention continuously on the accurate recall of the products of their knowledge (e.g., "What are they?" "What do I have on that a chef uses?" "What is a life skill you use every day?"). Or is a more facilitative course of action to draw attention to the process of reasoning and its relationship to the relevance of the activity (e.g., "What are some of your ideas?" "Why is it important to review things?" "What are some other reasons you can think for why we would use subtraction and borrowing?")?

The final question is whether individual children have the necessary linguistic means available to provide a preferred response, for example, to explain social or logical cause-effect relations (e.g., "What happens when you don't follow the rules?" "Why is it important to review things?").

In orienting children to what they are expected to do, misinterpretation can occur at any of these levels. An individual child may not be able to infer adequately the nature of the task, the kind of information being required, or the expectations for preferred responses. The clinician may presume erroneously that the child has the linguistic means available to provide the preferred response or may unintentionally communicate that the accurate recall of factual bits of information is the expectation for acceptable performance. The end result of a misinterpretation by either the clinician or the children is a breakdown in communication, which then affects how the activity is actually implemented.

Function: Communicate Participation Requirements. A second function of orientation strategies is to establish conduct expectations, that is, to ensure that children behave in an appropriate way. Spinelli and Ripich (1985) suggest that generally securing and maintaining attention in the traditional pullout setting may be easier than in the classroom setting. One reason is the smaller physical size of the therapy room. Because space is more confined, it becomes easier for the clinician to sustain eye contact and to speak and be heard. However, the limited research base available on this topic does point to the finding that, despite the smaller confines of the therapy room, whether located in a school or nonschool setting, clinicians implicitly convey messages whose goal is to manage the form of children's conduct in listening and speaking. To illustrate, many clinicians, like many classroom teachers, seem to use prescriptive and restrictive conduct rules very frequently (Fivush, 1983), a hallmark of social control. Prescriptive rules include "attentionals," such as "Look," "Pay attention," "You must listen carefully," or even use of the child's name (Spinelli & Ripich, 1985). Restrictive rules are intended to inhibit undesirable behavior at the time at which an activity is initiated (Letts, 1985), for example, "Sit still," "You're not listening carefully," or placing a forefinger on one's lips to indicate nonverbally "No talking." The use of conduct rules to prescribe and restrict behavior is consistent with the teacher talk register referred to earlier. These rules are intended to attract children's attention or to make them display active attention (Cazden, 1988).

A segment from the beginning of a language therapy lesson (Listening Lesson) with Sara, 11 years old, demonstrates the negative effects on communication when the form of displaying attention is simultaneously the procedure for assessing acceptable performance and the goal of intervention.

Clinician:	3	What things did we talk about that might affect how well we listen?/ (Clinician is gazing directly at Sara; 9 seconds of silence follow)
Sara:	4	Not paying attention/
Clinician:	5	Uh-huh (acknowledgement also conveys that Sara is to continue her turn)
		(Sara shrugs her shoulders and looks away from clinician, followed by 15 seconds of silence)
		When might you be a better listener?/ If you slept

		eight hours the night before or if you stayed up until three in the morning watching a movie?/
Sara:	6	Slept/
Clinician:	7	Why?
Sara:	8	Because/ You don't get sleepy in the morning/ (Sara is now looking at clinician)
Clinician:	9	Nice eye contact!

"Better listening" through paying attention appears to be the goal of the interaction; conversely, "not paying attention" is incompatible with attaining better listening. However, in practice, the criterion by which Sara's paying attention is defined and measured is her sustaining eye gaze when being talked to or when she has the conversational floor. Sara's capacity to initiate and sustain a topic about the components of good listening and the variables that might affect it (such as not getting enough sleep) is not as positively valued as the form of her participation. Sustaining eye contact is the aspect explicitly rewarded with the verbal evaluation "Nice eye contact." Thus, Sara is learning that the real purpose of language therapy is meeting the clinician's standard for a preferred form of displaying attention. Similarly, in the Speech Rules Lesson, the clinician is communicating that the content of the lesson will consist of verbal demonstrations by the three children of their understanding of prescriptive and, later on, restrictive rules for acceptable participation in language therapy. In both cases, the implicit message conveyed is that, in adult-controlled interaction, the only way children can regulate their involvement in the ensuing flow of activities is through their degree of attentiveness (Bossert, Barnett, & Filby, 1984).

Instructional Phase

The second phase of the lesson is implementation: the *exchange and evaluation of information*. The previous discussion of classroom discourse indicated that this phase is marked distinctly by the use of elicitations, which are typically requests for information or action. It has been argued that these requests are not genuine requests. That is, the teacher asks for information even though he or she already knows the information; the intent is to confirm whether students also know the information. These elicitations were shown to be patterned interactionally through a three-part, topically related structure: the IRE (initiation, response, evaluation) sequence. The I slot is typically the teacher's, the R slot belongs to the child selected to respond, while the E slot is used by the teacher for evaluation or feedback on both the accuracy and the appropriateness of the child's response. If the child's response fails to be accurate or appropriate, then the teacher will extend the sequence with the same child or with other children until the reply being sought is provided and evaluated. Evaluation can explicitly confirm the child's response, extend the child's response, or repeat a portion of what the child offered (Green & Harker, 1982). Extension and restatement as forms of evaluation can either be overt or implied.

The IRE sequence also appears to dominate much clinical discourse, or at least this is indicated by formal studies conducted in the last decade (Becker & Silverstein, 1984; Letts, 1985; Prutting, Bagshaw, Goldstein, Juskowitz, & Umen, 1978; Ripich et al., 1984; Ripich & Panagos, 1985; Silliman, 1984; Spinelli & Ripich, 1985). Moreover, the IRE pattern seems to be as frequent in articulation therapy as in language therapy (Ripich et al., 1984), and it is also overwhelmingly found in the role play of clinician-client dyads in situations where children are receiving articulation therapy (Ripich & Panagos, 1985).

We examine three of the language intervention lessons cited in the setting-up phase by applying the close-up lens of observation to the patterning of their interactional sequences. These samples were selected for several reasons. First, they seem to be representative of clinical discourse patterns reported in the research literature. Second, they are comparable in structure to classroom discourse findings across grade levels in both regular and special education, including the aspect of multiple layers. Third, the clinicians' instructional models were, in theory, child-centered. Finally, like traditional classroom discourse, the restrictive nature of the discourse patterns symbolize instructional language use that, potentially, can interfere with students' development of an active, planful, and literate orientation to learning. These three lessons, in order of their appearance, are the Listening Lesson, the Speech Rules Lesson, and the Chef Lesson.

The Listening Lesson. The participants are Sara, 11 years old, and her clinician.

Clinician:	11	What other things did we talk about that might help you be prepared to be a better listener?/
Sara:	12	Carry a notebook/ Paper/ Pad/ Pencil too/
Clinician:	13	Great!/ Nice/ Good, Sara/ And how can you tell when someone is really listening to you?/
Sara:	14	Ask them questions/
Clinician:	15	Um-hmmm/ What else?
Sara:	16	You want to know more about it/
Clinician:	17	Good/

Two IRE sequences are embedded in these seven turns (11–17). In turn 11, the clinician requests Sara to recall a list of objects (products) associated with being prepared to be a better listener. In turn 12, Sara accurately supplies the information being sought; that is, her response is contingently related in terms of its function, a reply, and the specific lexical content requested. Her response is evaluated as both accurate and appropriate only retrospectively by the clinician's subsequent positive evaluation in turn 13; the evaluation then closes this topically related sequence. In the same turn (13), the clinician initiates a new IRE sequence in which Sara is requested to recall a verbal process for verifying how others might be listening. Sara provides a response in turn 14 that is appropriate but, perhaps, not as accurate as the clinician might have wanted. The accuracy dimension appears to be questionable, because in the clinician's evaluative slot, turn 15, she conveys neutral feedback ("Um-hmmm"), immediately followed by an another initiation that is elliptical ("What else?") and that functions to repair this sequence through extending it. In turn 16, apparently attempting to fill in missing information in the clinician's previous turn, Sara appears to relate back to information sought earlier in turn 13. She then gives new process information ("You want to know more about it"). Despite the ambiguity of her response, it is apparently accepted by the clinician in turn 17. The positive confirmation "Good" closes this sequence.

The Speech Rules Lesson. The conversational participants in the segment are the clinician and two of the three children in this ethnically mixed group: Damian (nine years old) and Jared (nine years old).

Clinician:	33	Number 2/ (an indirect initiation that means "What is rule number 2?" Jared infers that he has been nominated to reply, since, concurrently with her initiation, the clinician orients the poster board with the written rules toward Jared)
Jared:	34	(Reading) (.) Bee/ (1 sec.+ pause) Big/
Clinician:	35	Damian, do you know what it says?/ Number 2/
Damian:	36	(Reading) Bee (.)/
Clinician:	37	Be polite/ Ok/ Be polite/

This excerpt consists of five turns (33–37) composing an extended IRE sequence. It also shows another variation in repairing a sequence in which individual children do not supply accurate responses. Jared is nonverbally selected by the clinician in turn 33 to read the second rule (earlier Jared had publicly admitted that he could not read the rules on the poster board; see turn 24 on p. 57). He tries to comply. Note that his struggle to decode is signaled by pauses. His ultimate product, "Big," is phonetically related to "Be" but is implicitly evaluated in the clinician's next turn (35) as inaccurate. The evaluation ("Damian, do you know what it says?") shows how any single act of communication is multiply layered. First, the evaluation communicates affective information that may unintentionally reinforce Jared's sense of himself as a nonreader. Second, it conveys dual social information in denying Jared further access to the conversational floor while simultaneously allocating a turn to Damian in anticipation of closing this sequence. Third, it communicates the propositional content that "Big" is a misreading of the word. With his selection, Damian, in turn 36, encounters the same decoding difficulty as Jared. As a probable consequence of the two children's failure to read rule 2, the clinician, in turn 37, opts for another kind of repair to bring closure to this sequence. She fills in the reply herself ("Be polite"), and then restates it, which marks the end of that sequence.

The Chef Lesson. This multiparty lesson takes place in a combined kindergarten–first grade classroom. Participants are the clinician, who is also the classroom teacher, and five children of various ethnic backgrounds.

Clinician:	31	Should I wear this apron to go to church? (Looks at apron)
Sol:	32a	[Nooo] ([ ] indicates choral response)
Mary:	32b	[Nooo]
Larry:	32c	[Nooo]
Lori:	32d	[Nooo]
Joey:	32e	[Nooo]
Clinician:	33	Should I wear *this* to go swimming? (Pointing to the apron)
Sol:	34a	[Nooo]
Mary:	34b	[Nooo]
Larry:	34c	[Nooo]
Lori:	34d	[Nooo]
Joey:	34e	[Nooo]
Clinician:	35	Should I wear *this* if I'm gonna cook something?
Sol:	36a	[Yeees]
Mary:	36b	[Yeees]
Larry:	36c	[Yeees]
Lori:	36d	[Yeees]
Joey:	36e	[Yeees]
Clinician:	37	Yes/ That would be the best time to wear *it*/ Ok/ Let's look up here/

This segment demonstrates another variation of the IRE sequence. Here, the function seems to be to prevent the need to repair a breakdown in children's accurate retrieval of the target information. In this variation, cognitive complexity is simplified as a means of minimizing disruption to the IRE sequence. In both turns 31 and 33, the clinician draws on shared social knowledge of when a white apron would be worn and formulates the content of her initiation as a counterfactual yes/no request. Turns are allocated through an open bid in which all five children are given equal responsibility for affirming or denying the counterfactual content. The expectation is that the extended sequence will be closed when, in turn 35, the clinician explicitly provides the factual content for the children's R slot. Her evaluation (turn 37) repeats the right answer, a form of comprehension check (Letts, 1985), and extends the meaning of "Yes" in referring back to the appropriate time (turn 35) when a white apron would be worn ("That would be the best time to wear *it*"). The use of counterfactuals is also similar to the use of incredulous expressions in the E slot of clinical discourse after a discontinuity in the IR segment has occurred (Letts, 1985). For example, if a child is asked in the I slot, "Who is Roger Rabbit?" (assuming shared social knowledge of Roger Rabbit) and replies in the R slot, "He's my brother," an E slot response might be, "Can that possibly be right?" accompanied by the prosodic features that communicate disbelief in the context of an implied negative evaluation.

Some Additional Features of Clinical Discourse

Three other features of clinical discourse should be noted. The first feature concerns a distinction between the appropriateness and the accuracy of students' preferred responses. A response can fulfill the pragmatic function of answering a question but, in satisfying this function, may not have the exact propositional content being sought by the clinician or teacher. To illuminate this point, consider the following exchange from a high school history lesson in a classroom for students with language learning disabilities (the speech-language clinician is also the teacher):

Clinician: What do we mean by "territory"?/
Student: Large mass of land not claimed by anyone/
Clinician: "Territory" is a piece of land that has boundaries/ That's what you should write down/

One conclusion from this example is that the student has made sense of the question but has not gotten it "just right" according to the teacher-clinician's criterion. Research indicates that, as a general rule, language learning disabled children encounter more difficulty in producing *accurate* replies over a longer period of time than do their normally developing peers (Parnell, Amerman, & Harting, 1986; Parnell, Patterson, & Harding, 1984). We might speculate, therefore, that sources of inaccurate replies are probably located in (1) the semantic-syntactic or cognitive complexity of the request (e.g., the cognitive complexity of reading for both Jared and Damian); (2) the linguistic options accessible to a child, including the richness and coordination of lexical knowledge; (3) the degree to which inferencing is required (assuming it is even possible) to determine the specific semantic content expected (as demonstrated by the "Territory" exchange); and (4) the speed with which an accurate reply must be formulated before losing a turn at talking. Speed of reply is valued in the regular elementary classroom (Allington, 1980), in the special education classroom (Silliman, 1984; Silliman & Lamanna, 1986), and in the traditional language intervention setting (Craig & Evans, 1989; Prutting et al., 1978). The failure to supply responses that are not "just right" can become a serious problem for many language learning disabled youngsters unless these sources are carefully considered in planning this phase of intervention.

The two remaining features seem to be more common in clinical discourse than in classroom discourse. One is the use of external *comprehension checks* (Letts, 1985) in the E slot. While these checks can take different forms, their function appears to be the overt reverification by the clinician that he or she has understood the child. One type of comprehension check consists of repeating, either verbatim or in part, the child's reply from the R slot, as in this example from the Speech Rules Lesson:

Clinician:	What happens when you start being mean and rude to each other?/ (Jared raises his hand and is nominated to reply)
Jared:	You might have to go to the office/
Clinician:	You might have to go to the office/

A second kind of comprehension check combines repetition of the key lexical item being sought in the R slot with a syntactic expansion, which then fills in the proposition that the clinician has been prompting (Silliman, 1984, p. 312):

Clinician:	(Pointing to a picture of an orange) You remember from the time before how oranges tasted?
Child:	Yeah.
Clinician:	How?
Child:	(3.5 sec.) Uh-uh (6 sec.) (Looking at picture)
Clinician:	Sour?
Child:	No.
Clinician:	They were _____? (a lexical "fill-in" prompt)

Child: Sweet
Clinician: They were sweet. Right

The second feature of clinical discourse that may be dissimilar to its counterpart in the regular classroom concerns the overall *complexity* of the IRE sequence. Spinelli and Ripich (1985) contend that IRE sequences found in clinical discourse may be more complex. Depending on the goals of intervention, the clinician may demand attention to the correct *form* of pronunciation and then to the *content* of the reply, as in this example (Spinelli & Ripich, 1985, p. 191):

Clinician: What can we walk through to go into a house?
Child: Winow.
Clinician: Window?
Child: Window.

While there are only anecdotal data to support the notion of increased complexity, the concept can be extended beyond the realm of pronunciation. The Listening Lesson also demonstrates the parallel purposes and multiple layering of many language tasks (Shuy, 1988a). Dual goals occur when children must simultaneously attend to the content aspects of listening and speaking and to the form in which listening and speaking are to be displayed. When children encounter this kind of multiplicity, then effective participation in IRE sequences can become very difficult.

A critical issue for clinicians is the use of the "default pattern" (Cazden, 1988) that characterizes the particular types of IRE sequences discussed in this chapter. What kind of learning actually takes place through this restricted pattern of discourse? The observations of a speech-language pathologist who had received therapy as a child in elementary school still remain highly pertinent for addressing this question:

I can recall my classmates asking me after I returned to the classroom from therapy "What did you do," and my answering "I don't know." Going from the classroom to therapy was a little like walking into the twilight zone. The mirrors, tongue depressors, and exercises of therapy had no counterparts outside of therapy . . . My therapist, like many clinicians, equated her procedures with her goals. Therapy became a succession of contrived tasks that had little to do with reality. The behaviors I acquired could be likened to an elaborate set of parlor tricks . . . I learned some behaviors of a highly specific sort that I used only with my therapist in the confines of the therapy room." (Ripich & Panagos, 1985, p. 343).

We can reconceptualize these cogent observations. Clinical discourse, as reflected in the traditional IRE sequence, is an *interpersonal* context where, too often, the unstated goal is to learn a conversational routine in order to complete the lesson for the lesson's sake. Earlier, in the description of classroom discourse, we referred to these conversational routines as *procedural displays* (Bloome, 1987) used by teachers and children to help them "get through" the lesson together. The Listening Lesson, Speech Rules Lesson, and Chef Lesson also include conversational routines. One important aspect of the agendas of all three lessons is that the children demonstrate that they know how to speak within the structure of the particular lesson. Clinicians use comprehension checks, such as repeating the "correct" answer, to document that the routine has been reproduced according to expectations. The work of Ripich and Panagos (1985) provides additional support for this interpretation. In their research on children's playing of clinician-client roles, they found that treatment responses were best characterized as a speech therapy "dialect" to be spoken under the restricted social circumstances of the therapy room.

Communicative Roles

In Chapter 3, we identified the social and structural aspects of communicative roles. Both of these aspects must be coordinated if a smooth and productive interaction is to occur. The preceding discussion about the structure of the clinical lesson indirectly dealt with the structural component of communicative roles. To be evaluated as competent in the intervention setting, children must learn the particular rules regarding how and when to participate in their alternating roles as speakers and listeners. The focus of this final section is the social roles created through clinical discourse.

We have already noted that a teaching register is a way of talking that marks a specific kind of social role, the instructional role. A teaching register should be differentiated, however, from individual differences in the style through which a register is actually expressed (Cazden, 1988). Stylistic variations are the norm in both classroom and clinical discourse. These variations can include (1) ways in which caring, respect, support, and interest are communicated (Cazden, 1988); (2) combinations of grammatical structures selected to move the lesson along (Shuy, 1988a); and (3) manner in which prosodic features are used (e.g., slower versus a faster rate of speaking, the loudness level, etc.) (N.W. Nelson, 1984). A teaching register, on the other hand, functions as a management procedure for communicating attitudes (expectations) about the roles students are to play in the teaching-learning process. It is conceivable that the very power of the teaching register overrides stylistic variations in teaching.

With the exception of the study by Ripich and Panagos (1985), investigations of clinical discourse have not directly explored children's perspectives of their social roles. Thus, the best we can do is to draw inferences from the results of these studies. These results can be examined for the extent to which they furnish evidence that in clinical discourse, as in the classroom lesson, a control (or power) register is more common than not.

Rigid Access to the Floor

The predominance of the restrictive IRE structure in clinical discourse coexists with a high demand for child responses (Prutting et al., 1978). Even when children initiated requests, Prutting and her associates found that the clinician, in planning a structured task, "responded only to questions relevant to that particular task" (Prutting et al., 1978, p. 137). Overall, studies consistently show that clinicians simply talk more than do their child clients, taking up most of the "communicative space" (Becker & Silverstein, 1984; Letts, 1985; Prutting et al., 1978; Ripich et al., 1984; Ripich & Panagos, 1985). The Speech Rules Lesson and the Chef Lesson are both examples of clinicians' dominating talk. While the two clinicians clearly varied in their styles, they shared this power feature of the teacher talk register.

Tight Topic Management

Studies show some variation in the degree to which clinicians permit children to digress on topics outside of the clinicians' immediate agenda. In one pattern, the clinician does not routinely permit the child to initiate new topics unrelated to the tasks at hand (Letts, 1985; Prutting et al., 1978; Ripich & Panagos, 1985; Ripich et al., 1984); rather, the clinician will redirect the child back to the prior topic. The child's role primarily is to stay on the clinician's topic, as shown in the Listening Lesson and the Chef Lesson. Moreover, in view of the tendency to continue talk for talk's sake, Spinelli and Ripich (1985) contend that the real lesson learned by the child is that "the clinician values the amount of talk rather than the content" (p. 192).

Focus on Conduct

If the notion of conduct behavior is broadened to include how children are to act as listeners and speakers, then this feature of the teacher talk register can also be found in clinical discourse. Even requests to "say the whole thing" (Prutting et al., 1978) can be considered as having a conduct aim. In this case, the child is being told to suspend his or her knowledge of the way language is naturally used (i.e., the knowledge that elliptical replies are normal) and to respond to requests in an artificial way. The focus on the form of displaying listening and speaking behaviors, as well as on the content of listening and speaking, may be more frequent in clinical discourse (Spinelli & Ripich, 1985). The Listening Lesson provided an example of this kind of focus, while the Speech Rules Lesson illustrated a more traditional emphasis on conduct rules, such as "Be polite."

Another facet of the control register evident in classroom discourse relates to how teachers prosodically mark new or important information through altering stress and rate of speaking (N.W. Nelson, 1984; Shuy, 1988a). In both the Speech Rules Lesson and the Chef Lesson, the clinicians combined a slower rate of speaking with stressing of key lexical information. These prosodic changes conveyed that the particular information was essential and should be attended to.

Procedural Display

A fourth feature of the controlling teacher talk register is the soliciting of conversational routines in which children "fill in the slot," providing minimal responses within the adult's frame of reference (McTear, 1985). Conversational routines require that the children take the adult's perspective in the initiation and continuation of topics and assume the role of passive responders (Letts, 1985; Silliman, 1984). In analyzing the structure of the traditional clinical discourse lesson, this feature is also prevalent.

MAKING SENSE OF CLASSROOM AND CLINICAL DISCOURSE

Two major points can be concluded from this comparison of classroom discourse and clinical discourse as instructional events. First, research shows that the structure of traditional clinical discourse, like the structure of traditional classroom discourse, too often provides the appearance that learning is taking place (Bloome, 1987; Cazden, 1988) when in fact it may be inhibiting children's motivation for self-initiated learning (Shuy, 1988a).

Interactions in the classroom and intervention settings, such as those characterized by procedural display, serve as contexts for the learning and enforcement of the hidden curriculum. In all probability, it is the ways in which this hidden curriculum is implemented that lead to variations in the socialization experiences of children who may be less ready, because of differences in development, culture, or learning style, to meet the metacognitive and metalinguistic demands of literacy activities. As just one example of these complex demands, it is well documented that individual differences in children's word recognition abilities are related to their phonological sensitivity to the phoneme as a discrete unit of sound (Kamhi & Catts, 1989a, 1989b; Stanovich, 1986, 1989). Also well documented is the finding that the degree of metalinguistic awareness children bring to school differs depending on their prior experience with a broad array of print materials and the extent to which parental interactional styles emphasize more literate uses of language (Goldfield & Snow, 1985; Heath, 1982a, 1989; van Kleeck, 1990; van Kleeck & Schuele, 1987).

Sensitivity to metalinguistic content and experience with literate conventions, functions, and forms converge at school entry. Children are now learning how to function as members of a group, and the requirements of group membership constrain the communicative roles available to each child. Variations in the experiences of schooling, as communicated through the hidden curriculum, subsequently affect what students learn, what they learn about learning and, as a result, what they learn about their social identities and roles in society. These same variations in the organization of teaching and learning may also account for many of the "poor-get-poorer achievement patterns" (Stanovich, 1989, p. 289) that too often can culminate in a referral to special education. A companion view is offered by Butler (personal communication), who suggests that the power of the teaching register itself, combined with the hidden curriculum, can obscure the existence of subtle problems in language learning. Only after years of "getting poorer" in the face of escalating requirements for academic and social participation does classification finally occur (see also Bashir et al., 1983).

The second point that emerges from the survey of classroom and clinical discourse concerns some possible effects of the hidden curriculum. We believe that the hidden curriculum may foster (1) dependency rather than autonomy as a learner and (2) educational failure rather than educational achievement, particularly for youngsters who fall into the "poor get poorer" category and are eventually designated as language or learning disabled. Formal classification is a type of ability grouping, since such classification is both a legal and social statement about internal competencies. If repeated experiences of group membership participation for these children are primarily ones where (1) the teacher or clinician is the sole source of information and evaluation, (2) procedural display is the dominant activity, and (3) adult control of interaction is the norm, then what is being implicitly conveyed over and over through classroom and clinical discourse is that learning is an inactive process. The long-term consequences of this hidden message may be a social identity at whose core is the notion that the student "cannot succeed on his/her own" (Schumaker, Deshler, & Ellis, 1986, p. 354) and a dependent attitude toward learning (Bryan, 1986; Dollaghan, 1987; Simon, 1987a; Sleeter, 1987).

In short, too many children may be learning how not to learn. By increasing our awareness of how a disability can originate in, or be exacerbated by, the communicative demands of classroom discourse and how it may be further reinforced through the dynamics of clinical discourse, we may be better able to explain why generalization continues as such a central issue for the long-term effectiveness of intervention.

In this chapter, we emphasize that teaching and learning are communicative processes and, further, that behaviors we often come to interpret as "language problems" can also be conceived of as problems of teaching and learning (Shuy,

1988a). Since the direct observation of teaching-learning dynamics is premised on collaborative participation, we next address coparticipation as an interactional process for facilitating collaborative approaches to assessment and intervention.

Chapter 5

Facilitating Collaboration through Coparticipation

Elaine R. Silliman, Louise C. Wilkinson, Amy S. Belkin,
and Lauren P. Hoffman

At this point, a practical question can be asked: How can one begin to work with regular or special education teachers to create a collaboration whose aims are to foster a literate orientation to language and literacy learning? Because these roles in the classroom are precursors for effective integration of observational information into classroom communication, this chapter addresses the concept of coparticipation as central to building collaborative programs.

COLLABORATION AS A CONTINUUM

Much of the literature on collaborative models has been concerned with the philosophy and practicalities of collaborative consultation. This concept was adopted initially within the field of learning disabilities because of the need to provide more effective teams to deal with the increasing number of learning disabled students who were being mainstreamed (West & Brown, 1987). West et al. (1989) view collaborative consultation as a problem-solving process for "classroom teachers, special education teachers and other support staff, and school administrators . . . [whose purpose is to] influence effective collaboration among those professionals concerned with *prevention* of serious learning/behavior problems in at-risk students and improved *coordination of instruction* and *remediation* for already identified exceptional students" (p. i).

West and Brown (1987) acknowledge that, with the exception of a few states, the specific roles and responsibilities of classroom consultants have not been codified in job descriptions for special educators at either the state or local agency levels. The same lack of specification most likely applies to the speech-language pathologist and may account for one type of barrier to be overcome in shifting to classroom-based service delivery, which may or may not include consultation.

Moreover, the existing body of information on the attitudes and professional competencies underlying successful collaboration in regular and special education has also focused on the consultant role (Damico, 1987; Dudley-Marling, 1987; Idol et al., 1987; Marvin, 1987; West & Cannon, 1988; West et al., 1989). Even in those states where consultation is formally recognized as an optional model of service delivery, significant variability exists among state guidelines with regard to the formal competencies to be expected of a collaborative consultant (West & Brown, 1987). Variation in the definition of skills can create an additional barrier to change because of the confusion that may arise when there is no consensus about requisite skills.

Major attention has been paid to the role of consultant. However, we suggest that *collaboration is a continuum of joint effort* involving a variety of team members who may perform different roles at different times. Hence, the skills that result in effective consultation are the same as those needed for collaboration.

For example, along the collaborative continuum, the speech-language clinician may join with the learning disabilities specialist to teach in a self-contained or resource classroom using modularized instruction. At some point in the school day, the speech-language clinician may work with one or two children from the class who need more specialized help with particular aspects of communication, fluency, or articulation. At another point, the speech-language clinician may act as a consultant to regular education teachers in order to integrate meaningful communicative contexts into the teaching-learning process or to provide follow-up assistance for students who have been mainstreamed. The permutations along the continuum of collaboration vary depending on several factors, including (1) existing policies at state and local levels, (2) the extent to which individual school units encourage innovativeness in service delivery, and (3) the willingness of individual administrators and staff members to engage in collaborative activities.

COLLABORATION AS A LONG-TERM DEVELOPMENTAL PROCESS

The shift to using collaborative programs in the classroom requires planning. Furthermore, it should be recognized that achieving new roles in the classroom may take many years, and continuous refinement of goals, procedures, role relationships, and personal reactions will be an inherent part of effecting long-term changes. Idol et al. (1987) characterize the process of implementing change as developmental, that is, "These changes involve planning, learning new behaviors, and adapting to new routines. Because change is a personal experience, it involves a wide range of individual differences in rate of implementation, feelings, and reactions" (pp. 6–7). These authors identify seven stages of concern that can be anticipated in the implementation of collaborative approaches. These stages also illustrate the role that metacognition plays in restructuring a mode of thinking. For that reason, our discussion of the seven stages is presented in metacognitive terms.

The first stage is characterized by minimal awareness, or concern, about the need for change. In the second stage, more conscious awareness emerges about change, and some interest in discovering more about details may be manifested. Since the availability of new information may generate intrapersonal conflicts concerning the change, the third stage is marked by reflections on the affective dimensions of change: "The person is uncertain about the demands of change, personal adequacy to meet those demands, and role with respect to the change" (Idol et al., 1987, p. 7). Examination of these personal conflicts and questions leads to the fourth stage. Here, the focus shifts to procedural issues, such as the efficiency, organization, scheduling, and time demands of the change. The hallmark of the fifth stage is increasing objectification of the concept of change and the strategies for implementation. The focus now becomes the benefits of change for students, including such issues as the relevance of new approaches for students' learning, the strategies to be used, and how outcomes are to be evaluated. The sixth stage is actual implementation of new approaches through collaboration with others. The seventh stage, which is never fully completed, involves ongoing monitoring, evaluation, and revision of the strategies of change. Idol et al. (1987) note that, through the processes of monitoring and evaluation, collaborators can now deliberately attend to ways of creating more powerful generalizing benefits from the change, including alternatives or modifications.

A shift to collaborative ways of thinking does require a restructuring of how role relationships and responsibilities are interpreted. This restructuring occurs on both intrapersonal and interpersonal levels. As Idol et al. (1987) point out, because this shift is developmental, it should be expected that each participant, including the speech-language clinician, will react differently and at a different pace during the implementation of collaborative programs and procedures.

COPARTICIPATION AS THE BUILDING BLOCK FOR COLLABORATION

In Chapter 1, we referred to the work of West and Cannon (1988), who found four problem-solving competencies essential for effective collaborative consultation. All of these competencies were communicative in nature. Briefly, they · are (1) capacity to communicate relevant information clearly, both orally and in writing, using language that leads to a shared sense of responsibility and joint "ownership" of ideas; (2) ability to communicate active interest in and understanding of the opinions and perspectives of others; (3) proficiency in obtaining information from others in order to develop joint action plans for individual students; and (4) ability to provide feedback that is explicit, clarifying when necessary, and directed to "areas of strength or effectiveness and areas that need improvement" (Idol et al., 1987, p. 48).

These competencies change constantly as the participants negotiate their work. Negotiation concerns how the participants share an understanding of the purpose, content, and form of collaboration and how the collaboration comes to be interpreted, reinterpreted, and modified through their shifting frames of intrapersonal and interpersonal reference (Green, Weade, & Graham, 1988). Intrapersonal frames of reference are the sets of expectations that participants bring to interactions. They derive from "past experiences, knowledge, perceptions, emotions, values, cultural assumptions, abilities (e.g., cognitive, social, linguistic, physical), and so forth" (Green et al., 1988, p. 15). Interpersonal frames of reference arise from interactions as they actually unfold. An analogy offered by Erickson and Shultz (1982, p. 9) may be helpful in this regard. Although computers can be programmed to talk, they still cannot be built to act as "engaging conversationalists." Only people can act in this way, even when using computers to communicate, because only people are capable of coparticipating to make sense of the meaning of messages, from minute to minute, in real time.

We propose that coparticipation is the keystone for mounting and sustaining long-term collaborative approaches in classrooms. Coparticipation is the process by which speech-language clinicians, teachers, and other specialists can jointly learn to look critically at the structure and dynamics of classroom interaction through developing common frames of reference. Coparticipation is also prerequisite for the implementation of curriculum-based approaches to language assessment and intervention. N.W. Nelson (1989) defines communication-centered curriculum approaches as the incorporation of actual curriculum contexts and content in order to focus "intervention toward functional changes that are relevant to the child's communicative needs in the academic setting" (p. 171).

The goals of coparticipation are twofold. One aim is to assist potential team members, including the speech-language clinician, to become agents of change. Central to the process of change is enhancing mutual awareness of (1) the hidden aspects of communication and social organization, (2) varying language usage, and (3) communicating in classrooms in ways that constitute teaching-learning events (Mehan, 1979).

A second goal of coparticipation is focused on students. The common frames of reference generated through coparticipation can guide participants to view the curriculum, the language of the curriculum, and the discourse of teaching as a dynamic whole. Westby and Costlow (in press) discuss the traditional assumption that students identified as language learning disabled (or learning disabled) need to have their learning simplified; otherwise, they would not be "disabled." Those who subscribe to this "simplification hypothesis" often approach the student's problem in terms of "splinter skills." That is, the components of oral and written language, phonology, semantics, syntax, and pragmatics are separated into discrete elements and are then taught separate from meaningful communicative contexts. Some of the negative consequences of this approach are discussed in Chapter 4. In the contrast, Westby and Costlow have shown that students at risk for academic failure because of language learning gaps or students with a language learning disability have their learning potential maximized only when learning is approached as an integrated experience. The creation of collaborative learning contexts is based upon the view that (1) speaking, listening, reading, and writing all share the same language derivations; (2) all have communication between people as their paramount purpose (i.e., speakers and listeners or writers and readers); and (3) all can only be interpreted within the communicative contexts of their occurrence.

To illustrate the potential richness and diversity of collaboration through coparticipation, two communication-centered, classroom-based approaches are described next. One approach, that of the communication skills component of the Fisher-Landau Program at The Dalton School (New York), is based on having the speech-language clinician function in the dual role of consultant to and coteacher with the regular education teacher. A major focus of this approach is the student in the lower primary grades who may be at educational risk because of language learning differences. The second approach is designed for students from the preprimary (kindergarten) through secondary levels who have severe language learning disabilities. The communication development component of the South Metropolitan Association (Illinois), a large special education program for students with low-incidence handicaps, is predicated on a model in which the speech-language clinician functions in the role of coteacher with other specialists in self-contained classrooms. The coteaching structure is applied across all grade levels, including high school.

Each of these approaches may be only rarely available in schools in the United States. For example, the communication skills component of the Fisher-Landau Program operates in The Dalton School, an independent day school for gifted students, and is not subject to some of the fiscal and policy constraints present in the public special education system that often make change difficult. An important point, however, is that intellectual giftedness and individual differences in communicative competencies can coexist. Further, if this coexistence remains unrecognized, it can imperil the educational success of certain students who are viewed at risk.

The Communication Development Program of the South Metropolitan Association is a public school program, but students are sent to it by school districts who do not have sufficient numbers of speech-language staff or adequate services to meet students' needs. The comprehensiveness of the program and the range of participants may be unique. As an example, school social workers join with speech-language clinicians and teachers of the deaf, who have been selected because of their educational preparation in language and speech development. Also, career educators serve as consultants to primary classrooms. Beginning with junior high, the role of the career educator is to act as a coteacher with the other team members.

Because exceptions are often at the cutting edge, they also illuminate the practical and reciprocal connections between theory and practice. While these programs differ significantly in their funding sources and to some extent in their structure, they share several important features. One such critical feature is that theoretical assumptions about the multiple interrelationships among "cognitive, social, linguistic, and academic functioning" (Hoffman, 1990, p. 85) serve as a framework for intervention. This framework, in turn, can then enrich models of development and guide the evaluation of intervention effectiveness. A second feature shared by both programs is their emphasis on the central role of communication development or communication skills in the services offered. A third shared feature is their continuous evolution over time as collaborative partnerships, an evolution that is consistent with the seventh stage of change described by Idol et al. (1987). Neither of these exceptional programs represents utopian ideals, but they exemplify what can be practically accomplished for students when true collaboration is realized through ongoing coparticipation.

THE SPEECH-LANGUAGE CLINICIAN AS CONSULTANT TO THE REGULAR EDUCATION TEACHER

Consider a classroom through the eyes of its teacher. There is probably nothing more disconcerting to any teacher than to have a student whose interactional and learning styles are incomprehensible. Frequently, such a student may be so confusing that the teacher is even uncertain how to describe that student's learning differences, much less how to devise teaching strategies that will be more effective in helping the student to learn. Moreover, as concern about the student grows, the teacher may feel obligated to communicate his or her general observations with the student's parents. Thus, from several standpoints, the teacher's immediate needs are to understand the student's language learning differences and how to teach to them.

In some ways, Kathy, a third grader, typified the student whose problems place her at risk for academic failure. In casual conversation, Kathy was spontaneously verbal and engaging. However, in class, she presented language and learning differences that seriously affected her ability to participate:

Kathy was often distracted by visual materials in the room. When responding to the teacher, she would frequently look around at these materials and give several answers while facing the bookshelf. Other students were also a constant source of distraction. Additionally, her attention was pulled away by background noises, and she would comment on sounds coming from other classes as well as from her own class.

Kathy appeared to engage in self-distracting behaviors as well. She would rock in her chair, change chairs, stand up at her desk, or play with any incidental object, such as a plastic cup left over from snack. On these occasions, Kathy would ask for repetition of directions that were well within her cognitive and linguistic capabilities.

While she often required teacher repetition of directions and their sequence, Kathy had little difficulty remembering the gist of a story read to her. Although she struggled with the story's temporal order of events, she could recall essential information, including key vocabulary items, and was able to answer detail questions as well as questions that required inferencing. This suggested that when the structure of remembering was preformulated (as it is in a story recall activity), Kathy had fewer problems retaining and retrieving information that promoted her understanding.

In the case of tasks where Kathy had to activate strategies for retrieving and evaluating information in more controlled ways, she often encountered difficulty expressing content succinctly. This was particularly true when task demands were metalinguistic, for example, when comparing or defining word meanings was involved. In these instances, Kathy characteristically favored two coping strategies. In one, she alternated between discussing the pros and cons of the topic as if she were playing a ping-pong game. For example, when asked to contrast a watch and a clock, a metalinguistic task involving the comparison of semantic similarity, Kathy replied, "A watch is worn on your arm. A clock can't be carried. Well, you *can* carry a clock but it's not easy. Unless it's a small clock. Then you can carry it. But it's not as easy as carrying a watch." When asked to define a word, her second strategy was to give tangential information within a rhetorical framework rather than attempt to zero in on the word's specific meaning. For example, when asked to define *invented*, she replied, "*Invented.* It's something . . . . How do you think cars were made? Somebody invented them. How do you think games were made? Somebody invented them."

Kathy appeared to be aware of her problems in retrieving the explicit information being sought. She would frequently conclude her responses with metacomments, such as "But that's not the point" or "There's so many ways of thinking about it."

Kathy's apparent difficulties with language retrieval may have indicated limitations in the speed or efficiency of her lexical search strategies for selecting the appropriate meanings for integration into her discourse. Her comments on the language process itself suggested a search problem on some level (German & Simon, in press). However, from a practical point of view, Kathy's teacher saw a student who was exhausted by the end of the day from her inability to be centered and to self-regulate her resources. To reiterate, the teacher needed to understand Kathy and needed to know how to help her within the context of the regular classroom.

The Communication Skills Component of the Fisher-Landau Program

The communication skills component of the Fisher-Landau Program at The Dalton School was established in 1985. (A description of the Fisher-Landau Program is provided in Appendix A.) The development of this component was based on the practical philosophy that classroom teachers and other specialists needed to (1) become more formally aware of the communicative strengths and differences of the students whom they taught and (2) have available to them methods and materials that utilized the context of the classroom curriculum as the medium for facilitating students' communicative growth. Therefore, the purpose of collaboration with teachers was to offer each student, including the student with language learning difficulties, the best opportunity to develop communicative skills that would enable successful participation in the curriculum. This guiding principle allows both the teacher and the student to be served and, on a broader scale, immerses all students from prekindergarten through grade 3 in language learning activities across all academic content areas throughout the school day.

Organization of Intervention

The communication skills program is organized according to three levels of intervention: (1) individual, (2) small group, and (3) whole class. In keeping with the notion of the least restrictive environment, the premise is that language intervention should approximate the level of classroom participation in which a student is most capable of being successful. Individual sessions are used when a problem is specific to only one student in a class or when learning would proceed most readily in a one-to-one situation. As one example, prior to developing activities for a unit on Aztec civilization, Kathy was seen individually for several orientation sessions. The purpose of these sessions was to assist her in understanding the general relevance of focusing on a specific topic and attending to foreground information.

Semiweekly small-group lessons are designed to generalize skills acquired in individual sessions into a somewhat more complex set of group participation requirements. As Kathy felt more confidence in being able to attend to essential information in situations where the amount of background noise varied, she was transitioned into a small language group within her classroom. Small groups are used the most frequently, because they have the advantage of facilitating language learning strategies common to several children, including the student who is in formal need of assistance. Since teachers from preschool to third grade levels frequently divide their classes into three small groups, each of which runs simultaneously, the result is that all students are engaged in semiweekly language activities relevant to the curriculum. Hence, with few exceptions, all students are engaged in communication skills groups, which are integrated across these grade levels, and the speech-language clinician assumes the role of coteacher.

At various times throughout the academic year, the speech-language pathologist teaches all students in whole-class lessons. In the beginning of the school year, the purpose is diagnostic. The first lessons serve to identify which students may have difficulty managing the language of instruction. During the school year, whole-class lessons serve as a means for evaluating the extent to which particular children have been partially or fully successful in internalizing strategies practiced in the small-group sessions. Finally, at the end of the academic year, whole-class lessons are utilized to assess how adequately the children of interest have now assimilated and transferred new strategies to a fuller range of classroom activities.

Coordination of Planning

The speech-language pathologist consults individually with teachers on a weekly basis in 30-minute planning sessions. In these sessions, observations about students' learning styles might be jointly reviewed, the meaningfulness of teaching strategies might be mutually evaluated in the context of the curriculum and the student's linguistic-communicative goals, or lessons and materials might be designed collaboratively. When requested, selected readings about aspects of communicative development are shared.

Ongoing Parental Communication

In developing and maintaining an individualized program for a student, the parents receive help in understanding the nature of their child's language learning differences. They are apprised of their child's profile of communicative strengths and difficulties, how this profile relates to curriculum aims, and the ways in which the communication skills program serves as a bridge between curriculum modification and the student's current learning level and style. In subsequent parent meetings (to which the teacher is always invited), parental feedback and perspectives are encouraged, communication skills activities are described, the student's progress is discussed, and suggestions are made regarding a home program or other support services during the school year and the summer months.

In addition, a letter is sent to all parents that suggests a variety of language learning activities that can be used during the school year and the summer months. This letter is disseminated by the consultant and the teachers to parents of all students in prekindergarten through third grade. Additional information on specific activities and materials is provided to parents when requested. Moreover, teachers routinely send home letters highlighting current curriculum units and projects. Communication skills activities that support these units are often incorporated into these descriptions.

Benefits of a Classroom-Based Communication Skills Component

There are multiple benefits to embedding this kind of communication skills program within the regular classroom. Such benefits accrue whether the communication skills program is designed for all mainstream classroom children or specifically for children with language learning differences. When all students participate, the communication activities assist the development of students' metacognitive and metalinguistic skills, which, in turn, tend to make students more active listeners of instructional and peer language. Moreover, these activities may catalyze students to be effective, explicit speakers.

When children with language learning differences are the sole participants in small groups within the classroom, the communication skills activities facilitate practice of language skills. Second, if students' attention in the classroom is a problem, then the classroom itself becomes the setting for the students to apply and practice more efficient focusing strategies. Third, it is common for other children in the classroom to explore the small language groups and then ask to join them. The inclusion of other children allows those selected for the language groups to benefit from the modeling of more linguistically competent children. It also provides them with an opportunity to be "in" and gives them a sense of social status not typically found in pullout groupings.

Significant adults in the students' lives also benefit from an in-class communication skills program in three ways. First of all, both small-group and whole-class lessons are held with the teacher present, and the lessons are designed to encourage the teacher to join in or to observe. An important consequence is that the teacher's understanding of how intervention goals and procedures are implemented is enhanced. Second, classroom-based programming demonstrates to the teacher how readily communication skills groups can be incorporated into the ongoing life of the classroom. Finally, parents come to view communication as central to their child's academic and social success.

The Process of Facilitating Collaboration through Coparticipation: Supporting Kathy

At the outset, it is important to note that collaborative efforts need not begin on a large scale. In fact, coparticipation is probably best approached from a support relationship established between a classroom teacher and the speech-language clinician in order to meet the needs of a particular at-risk student, including a student who may be returning to the mainstream setting. Exhibit 5-1 outlines the parallel focus of the consultant model in creating shared observational lenses for Kathy.

Phase 1: Creating an Initial Frame of Reference

In this instance, Kathy's teacher was aware of her own need for assistance. Procedurally, the teacher was further supported at this stage of concern by the school's Student Services Committee, which determines and coordinates services offered to students with problems in academic, language learning, and social-emotional areas. The teacher's need for assistance was further motivated by her practical desire to incorporate strategies and materials that would help Kathy participate more successfully in a forthcoming social studies unit on Aztec civilization. Thus, from a functional perspective, Kathy's teacher was potentially open to exploring possible courses of action with the speech-language clinician.

As shown in Exhibit 5-1, the first step taken by the speech-language clinician was to focus observational lenses on Kathy in a variety of teaching-learning interactions using a systems approach, for example, van Kleeck and Richardson (1988). In this particular model, three communicative contexts of the classroom are selected for observation. One context is teacher-directed lessons. These are chosen, with the agreement of the teacher, according to the different levels of verbal demand and different styles of teaching that may be operating across academic content areas. The selection of lesson variations may also be made easier when content areas are departmentalized (e.g., language arts versus math, reading versus art, or science versus music). A second lesson context observed, also chosen with teacher concurrence, is defined as an optimal one. Here the student's motivation and his or her ability to participate effectively are indicative of best effort. The third context observed involves peer-directed classroom play in which the student of interest is a group member, for example, block-building, painting, or cooking activities. In all of these observational contexts, the student is not made aware of being the focus of observation.

Exhibit 5-1   Parallel Focus Consultant Model, Communication Skills Component of the Fisher-Landau Program

PHASE 1: CREATING AN INITIAL FRAME OF REFERENCE

Student Focus	*Teacher Focus*
Goal: Describe communicative patterns of student potentially at risk for language learning difficulties.	Goal: Facilitate observational skills in recognizing and understanding a student's language learning differences.
1a. Observe student within the interactional system of the classroom, selecting representative communicative contexts (types of observations should range from whole-class and small-group lessons to peer play in the classroom).	1a. Facilitate ability to observe student's actual language use through joint agreement on activities where specific communicative behaviors can be assessed.
1b. Develop a profile of student's communicative strengths and needs for intervention support.	1b. Facilitate awareness of possible sources for student's display of strengths and problems.
	1c. Facilitate ability to analyze discourse choices to determine if teaching strategies are enabling or interfering with successful participation.

PHASE 2: FACILITATING JOINT OWNERSHIP OF INTERVENTION GOALS AND PROCEDURES

Student Focus	*Teacher Focus*
Goal: Maximize opportunities for use of active strategies that will enable successful participation in the curriculum.	Goal: Facilitate ability to integrate language learning strategies within and across curriculum areas.
2a. Determine long- and short-term goals.	2a. Share goals based on agreement with observations and other forms of assessment findings (screenings, standardized instruments, etc.).
2b. Develop strategies and their order of introduction relative to goals.	2b. Communicate possible strategies; agree on feasibility in relation to curriculum goals.
2c. Facilitate linguistic communicative strategies through individual, small-group, and whole-class lessons within the communicative contexts of the curriculum.	2c. Create different types of curriculum activities designed to facilitate a range of communication skills.
	2d. Facilitate integration of appropriate strategies into teaching discourse and curriculum presentations.

A parallel focus of this phase of collaboration is on the teacher. The aim is to develop the teacher's observational skills so that he or she can recognize and better understand the student's language learning differences. Initially, the teacher and the speech-language clinician can choose to design diagnostic lessons that will explore particular communicative behaviors. These lessons can be implemented by the teacher with the speech-language clinician present. Or, in accord with the continuum of collaboration, the roles may be reversed. When the speech-language clinician teaches the lesson, the teacher is afforded the opportunity of observing students like Kathy with concentrated attention. A joint frame of reference is potentially created for follow-up discussion.

One outcome of this initial phase is the development of a profile. Its purpose is to describe the student's communicative strengths and needs in terms of the system components within which the child interacts, including linguistic, social, and academic components. This profile is constructed from the observational information and from supplementary sources of information, such as screening results, any previous evaluations, other teacher and parental reports, and standardized tests. (Profiles are discussed further in Chapter 11.)

This phase of coparticipation also presumes that the teacher's perspective on the student's profile is critical for confirming that findings are consonant with classroom patterns and learning style. A parallel outcome of this phase, therefore, is a broadened awareness on the part of the teacher of possible reasons for Kathy's strengths and weaknesses in language learning and how particular teaching choices may enable or interfere with Kathy's more effective participation. In other words, based on the speech-language clinician's interpretation of Kathy's patterns of behavior, the teacher assesses whether this information makes sense to him or her. The essential question is whether the speech-language clinician and the teacher can now begin to understand Kathy through the same observational lenses.

Phase 2: Facilitating Joint Ownership of Intervention Goals and Procedures

The second phase of the parallel focus model, as outlined in Exhibit 5-1, consists of facilitating mutual responsibility for intervention goals and implementation. The student-focused goal in this phase is to facilitate an active orientation toward language and learning that will enable the student to deal better with curricular demands.

For example, specific goals for Kathy addressed particular aspects of her linguistic-communicative system as that system was actually applied to classroom demands regarding the Aztec theme. The teacher-focused goal was to support the teacher's ability to integrate—and to modify when necessary—teaching-learning strategies within and across curriculum areas. From the teacher's perspective, use of the curriculum as the substance of intervention is effective for two reasons. First, use of the curriculum helps the teacher figure out how to integrate language learning strategies into what is actually taught. Second, the curriculum can act as a bridge between language intervention and the modification of academic content, thus allowing language intervention to be demystified to some extent.

Use of the curriculum as the substance of intervention also has multiple advantages for the speech-language clinician. It permits the clinician to become familiar with the curricular demands that confront the student with language learning differences while simultaneously offering a perspective from which to view a particular school's academic content over the course of several years. Most importantly, it maximizes the opportunity for students to generalize linguistic-communicative strategies in more naturalistic ways.

Using the format of the Aztec theme, Kathy's teacher and the clinician decided to prepare jointly small-group and whole-class lessons. The teacher chose reading and related materials from which the Aztec unit would be developed and then shared them with the clinician. The clinician, in turn, suggested various Aztec activities tied to specific communicative goals for Kathy. Based on these recommendations, the teacher then determined which activities were most feasible given the overall scheme of the Aztec unit as well as the needs of the other students in the class.

Next, the teacher and clinician worked together to develop the actual activities and materials. In this particular situation, the teacher had never created gamelike activities from curricular material and she requested assistance. These activities and materials were then categorized as appropriate for use either at the introduction of segments of the Aztec unit or at points where knowledge about various facets of Aztec life would be required. Exhibits 5-2 and 5-3 show sample activities in which Kathy's communicative goals were integrated into the larger curricular theme.

Both of these activities were implemented after some prior background knowledge had been obtained from class readings and discussions on Aztec life. Since Kathy had difficulty organizing information on her own, both activities also provided her with a preformulated structure in which she could participate most successfully. The sacred ball game activity was supervised by the clinician as a method for linking the topic-focusing objectives of individual sessions with Kathy to the broader communicative context of a small language group. The activity required that, in order to retrieve information derived from the Aztec theme and evaluate it as on target or off target, Kathy simultaneously had to monitor her attentional state and the appropriateness of her social role as a group member. During this activity, the clinician functioned as an external support, helping Kathy to recall from their individual sessions why staying "on target" was important. Self-monitoring of the attentional and social dimensions was

Exhibit 5-2   Communicative Goals, Activities, and Materials for Kathy: Staying on the Aztec
Topic (Small Group)

Goals:	Kathy should be able to identify the main topic, recognize when she is on or off the topic, and recognize appropriate and inappropriate social behaviors.
Activity:	Tlachtli (a sacred ball game). Choose the answer that is most on topic (requires attending to and retaining key information).
Materials:	A board depicting the sacred ball game, with spaces for moving pawns to a predetermined end (a hoop); a series of cards. Each card has an Aztec question on one side (e.g., "How did Aztec parents punish their children?") and three answers on the other. One answer is on topic (e.g., "Children were poked with cactus needles and thrown into a pool of ice-cold water"); another is tangential to the question content (related but not exactly on topic, e.g., "Children were considered disobedient if they did not follow parents' rules"); and the third is off topic (e.g., "The Aztec people got their food from farming").
Instructions:	"Getting the sacred ball through the hoop requires thinking about the answer best fitting the question." A child rolls a die and moves the resulting number of spaces on the board. Another child picks a card and reads the question and the three answers to the first child. The first child then selects the "best fit" answer.
Outcome:	Children cooperatively evaluate why the choice best fits the question. Kathy is specifically encouraged to assess realistically the strategy she used, monitor its effectiveness, and monitor the effectiveness of her participation in the group.

considered essential because previously Kathy had often been a distracting influence in small groups and had provoked other group members into similar off-task behaviors.

The second sample activity, note taking on aspects of Aztec life during a whole-class lesson, was initially implemented by the teacher. This activity was aimed at the larger goal of attending to essential information, this time utilizing a written outline as an organizer for retaining and recalling key details. Again, Kathy was required to monitor her attentional state and evaluate the ways in which the activity was easy or difficult for her. In fact, Kathy found this task to be motivating because of the external structure provided by the outline.

As the teacher developed a greater sense of proficiency in integrating appropriate strategies into her teaching discourse and curriculum modifications, she began to invite the clinician to join her in a coteaching format. At this point, the teacher had reached the fifth stage of change in collaboration. She understood how an integrated approach was beneficial for Kathy's growth in academic, communicative, and social areas as well as for the growth of all of her students. Furthermore, the clinician and teacher gradually began to assume equal responsibility for small-group and whole-class lessons. Based on continuing consulta-

Exhibit 5-3   Communicative Goals, Activities, and Materials for Kathy: Taking Notes on the Aztec Life (Whole Class)

Goals: Kathy should be able to attend to the main topics as a result of being supplied with an anticipatory schema for organizing essential facts; she should be able to sustain attention throughout the lesson by writing down important facts.

Activity: Prior to the actual lesson, the teacher writes on the blackboard unusual vocabulary that is needed in describing Aztec life (e.g., loin cloth) and talks about the meanings. Children are asked to predict what topics might be discussed based on the vocabulary items and their previous knowledge. Students are then given an outline that indicates the main topics to be discussed and highlights the number of facts to be found under each topic.

Materials: The outline is organized as follows:

Work

    The husband's work

        1. _____

        2. _____

        3. _____

    The wife's work

        1. _____

        2. _____

        3. _____

Housing

        1. _____

        2. _____

Clothing

    The men's clothing

        1. _____

        2. _____

    The women's clothing

        1. _____

        2. _____

Instructions: As facts relevant to each topic are heard, fill in each line with one or two words.

Outcome: Students read what they have written and compare the relevance of items written to the specific topic heading. Again, Kathy is asked to evaluate honestly how she performed.

---

tion with the clinician, the teacher also began to be more independent in implementing activities, a mark of the sixth stage of change, and was on her way to the seventh stage, where new skills are transferred to other curriculum areas. For example, the teacher could sequence the presentation of activities so that they were coordinated with her curriculum. Additionally, she could take responsibility for selecting which children in the class would work the best with Kathy in the clinician's semiweekly small groups. Moreover, she could modify her own teaching discourse as a function of children's needs (previously, self-monitoring of discourse as a tool of teaching had not been part of her repertoire). In a real sense, there was mutual ownership of intervention goals and activities. The teacher and clinician had negotiated an interchangeable set of observational lenses through which change for Kathy could be effected, continuously evaluated, and revised.

Increased awareness by teachers of interactional patterns in the classroom, accompanied by an enhanced sense of competence with an integrated approach, may then nurture a further interest in the fine-tuning of teaching discourse. To support this interest, Appendix A contains suggestions for organizing a series of in-service or workshop sessions on the analysis of classroom discourse. Appendix B offers detailed procedures for transcribing, notating, coding, and analyzing videotapes of classroom interaction. The content for both appendixes derives from a synthesis of discourse analysis procedures and their actual application over a several year period in teacher workshops conducted by the communication skills component.

Final Comments on Gaining Access to the Regular Classroom

Even though there may exist a shared frame of reference for understanding the communicative patterns of an at-risk student, the teacher may continue to feel conflicted about how to integrate communicative goals into the curriculum. Consistent with the third and fourth stages of change described earlier, this conflict may persist and be expressed in various ways. For example, resistance to incorporating the clinician's goals into the curriculum may be apparent. Or the teacher may evidence, over a long period of time, total dependence on the clinician to teach lessons to the individual student, a small group, or the whole class. A third pattern can also be manifested. Even after agreeing on goals, objectives, and teaching-learning strategies for a specific student and also on the actual classroom implementation, a teacher may continue to request over an extended period that the speech-language clinician conduct all classroom-based intervention separately from the curriculum. In this instance, the teacher may still be assuming that, because the clinician is the outside expert who can remedy children's problems, the content of intervention, even if irrelevant to the curriculum, will assist students in eventually catching up. As was the actual case with Kathy's teacher, it may take as long as two years for a teacher and clinician to move through the stages where personal doubt, time management, or control issues remain as primary agenda items. Idol et al. (1987) further note that, when certain system-level circumstances are present, such as extremely autocratic or nonsupportive administrators or the existence of a serious fiscal crisis, then mitigation of the difficulties of change may not be possible.

Assuming that circumstances are minimally favorable for increased access to the classroom, it can be anticipated that the two phases of coparticipation will evolve at different rates and may take different directions. As for gaining broadened access, the experiences of those in the communication skills component of the Fisher-Landau Program suggest that two activities need to be supported explicitly. One is the development of model lessons, related readings, and materials shared with the teacher; the other is positive recognition by the clinician of the academic, social, and related contextual richness of the classroom. Offering positive observations, combined with readings and other materials that further the teacher's instructional goals, can become an effective means for communicating that the clinician is an advocate for the child and the teacher. Information can be provided on the underpinnings of various linguistic-communicative behaviors. Lesson outlines for small-group communication skills sessions may be designed to highlight how content is related to curriculum aims, how activities are implemented, and how each child actually performed. Materials can be left in the classroom in order to give the teacher an opportunity to try out language-enhancing activities when he or she chooses to do so.

The parallel focus consultation model demonstrates that collaboration through coparticipation is a continuum along which role relationships can shift dynamically in meeting a child's needs in the regular classroom. At the same time, the model shows that meeting a child's needs is facilitated through the cohesive coordination and implementation of active strategies for the promotion of interrelationships among language, learning, and literacy.

THE SPEECH-LANGUAGE CLINICIAN AS A COTEACHER IN THE SPECIAL EDUCATION SETTING

The South Metropolitan Association

The South Metropolitan Association (SMA) is a cooperative association of 55 public school districts located in two counties in Illinois (South Cook County and North Will County). Its purpose is to provide special education services for children with low-incidence handicaps, including severe disorders of communication, hearing, vision, and behavior; orthopedic and other health impairments; autism; and other multiply handicapping conditions (e.g., mental retardation) often associated with additional physical handicaps.

Among the educational programs offered by the SMA are (1) a parent-infant program for infants and toddlers with special needs; (2) an early childhood program serving young children (ages 3–5) with delays in communication, social, emotional, or cognitive development or with deficiencies in hearing, vision, or motor skills; and (3) a communication development program for children and young adults (ages 5–21) who have severe language and speech problems that interfere with educational progress. A variety of diagnostic services are also available to individual districts and SMA programs. These include multidisciplinary evaluations for diagnostic purposes or for possible educational placement or alternative programming; audiological evaluation to determine the extent and nature of a hearing loss and, when indicated, further evaluation, hearing aid selection, and follow-up; functional vision assessment; and vocational assessment for older students. Medical diagnostic services (pediatric, neurological, psychiatric, and ophthalmic) are available through consultants.

The Communication Development Program

The Communication Development Program, established in 1978, is guided by a literacy-based philosophy of communication intervention and a transdisciplinary model of implementation. The program's design is explicitly intended to integrate reading, writing, speaking, listening, spelling, and handwriting across all instructional experiences within a framework of metacognitive and metalinguistic strategies (Hoffman, 1990). These six aspects of literacy learning take precedence over any particular curriculum content to be mastered, at least at the elementary level. In contrast, in the communication skills component, the curriculum area to be learned influences which aspect of literacy learning will be emphasized.

The Communication Development Program is a mature, cohesive, and multileveled collaborative partnership whose components have been formalized in a program manual (Lease & Hoffman, 1990). Because of program maturity, the seven stages of change for effecting collaborative relations have already been addressed. However, the two phases of coparticipation—creating shared frames of reference and facilitating joint ownership of intervention goals and activities—continue to suffuse every aspect of program functioning. These phases will be related across six programmatic aspects: the program philosophy and intervention principles, the transdisciplinary model, the organization of intervention, the content of intervention, the coordination of planning, and parent communication and coparticipation.

Program Philosophy and Intervention Principles

The program's philosophy originates in research on the powerful role communicative competence plays in classroom success, and it recognizes that a language learning disability is a chronic condition that significantly impacts on all areas of conceptual, linguistic-communicative, and social development. Three principles derive from this philosophy (Hoffman, 1990; Lease & Hoffman, 1990): (1) communication and learning are inseparable processes, (2) the purposes and outcomes of all learning experiences must be directly meaningful to the student if generalization to other contexts is to occur, and (3) parents are coparticipants with the transdisciplinary team members in the creation and maintenance of a literate orientation to learning.

The program's philosophy is further operationalized through six intervention principles, which serve the dual purposes of program goals for students and a common frame of reference for coparticipation (Hoffman, 1990; Lease & Hoffman, 1990):

1. The goal of learning is to enable students to become responsible, active learners. In achieving this goal, students continuously learn how they learn best by incorporating into all instruction metacognitive and metalinguistic strategies consistent with the students' levels of ability.

2. Active learning is facilitated through enhancing students' self-awareness of intrapersonal strengths and weaknesses in a variety of areas. Students engage in weekly self-profiling of progress in reading, mathematics, science, language, art, physical education, and social relationships with peers, family members, and other adults.

3. Active learning is also dependent on how adequately the everyday purposes and applications of what is being learned are understood (e.g., why learning to read and write particular content is important or why completing a specific task, such as filling in a job application, is relevant).

4. Literacy learning unfolds along an oral-to-literate developmental continuum (Westby, 1985); that is, children progress from being primarily oral communicators to being capable of more literate communication in both the oral and written language domains. A major goal of integrated programming, therefore, is to promote a smooth transition from oral to literate uses of communication.

5. The ultimate aim of communication-centered programming is to "assist students in functioning in environments that are the least restrictive given their needs, abilities, and the academic contexts in which they are required to function" (Hoffman, 1990, p. 85). The least restrictive environment ultimately may be the regular classroom of a student's neighborhood school. Approximately one fifth of students return to regular education programs through transitional support services and follow-up consultation. However, for a number of students, the most supportive setting may remain the self-contained classroom.

6. Another essential goal of integrated programming is to help students understand and make realistic decisions about their personal interests and vocational objectives. Facilitating their understanding and decision making begins in the lower primary grades, where they are exposed to units on the world of work. It continues through the secondary level, where they study specific skills for particular jobs, participate in skill awareness activities, and acquire job-seeking and maintenance skills.

The program's philosophy, premises, and intervention principles undergird the observational lenses for assessment and intervention. The expectation is that each speech-language pathologist and the other team members will demonstrate a working knowledge of this framework as evidenced through the compatibility of actual functioning with the overall programmatic framework (Lease & Hoffman, 1990). New clinicians are asked to consider the compatibility of their lenses with the program's constructs by means of a style assessment. They are asked, in essence, to examine potential areas of conflict between their professional belief system and the program's philosophical orientation. For example, in evaluating their style preferences, clinicians reflect on (1) the type of student who is the most difficult to interact with (e.g., an aggressive student, a nonverbal student, an unpredictable student, a hyperactive student, etc.); (2) their dominant view of themselves in various team member roles (e.g., organizer, facilitator, follower, harmonizer, compromiser, etc.); (3) their teaching styles (e.g., democratic, persuasive, or authoritarian); (4) the preferred qualities of persons they will work with on a team; and (5) personal qualities, values, or styles they would be unwilling to compromise, (e.g., a coteacher might insist on applying a behavior management system in the classroom).

Transdisciplinary Model

The Communication Development Program utilizes a transdisciplinary model, and, as in the communication skills approach, assessment and intervention are closely intertwined.

Assessment. Table 5-1 summarizes the program's holistic approach to assessment. Attention is directed to a student's linguistic, cognitive, social, and physical systems and their interactions (Hoffman, 1990). Observation functions as the means for viewing and analyzing system interactions, and standardized instruments are used only as a supplement to observation. This integrated approach then functions as the basis for developing or, in the case of the triannual reevaluations, modifying overall intervention planning for the individual student (Lease & Hoffman, 1990).

The diagnostic team routinely consists of a speech-language pathologist, a teacher of the deaf (referred to as an educator), the school psychologist, a school

Table 5-1   Integrated Diagnostic Assessment (Communication Development Program)

Team Member	Student Focus	Types of Tools and Content
Speech-language pathologist	Communication status	*Observation:* linguistic-discourse skills in classroom and with the examiner (e.g., requesting and clarifying information, responding to questions, commenting about events, topic maintenance, use of referents, semantic-syntactic complexity of formulations, etc.); metacognitive awareness of strengths and weaknesses and of strategies that may be used; writing skill (awareness of word and sentence structure, punctuation, and referents); inferencing skills, including identifying main ideas in oral and written passages and class materials; phonological, voice, and fluency status
		Standardized measures: language comprehension and production; problem solving
Educator (teacher of the deaf)	Educational status	*Observation:* learning style in classroom, including awareness of strategies to assist understanding; comprehension of functional life skills.
		Standardized measures: functional reading and math skills; metalinguistic awareness
Psychologist	Intellectual and perceptual status	*Observation:* dominance, balance, and eye tracking
		Standardized measures: WISC-R and related measures of perceptual-motor and academic functioning
Social worker	Social-emotional status	*Observation:* perceptions about self, interpersonal relations, and school obtained through student and parent interviews; parental understanding of programming needs and impact of communicative difficulties; classroom and home interactions
		Standardized measures: adaptive behavior inventories (administered to parent)
Career educator	Vocational skills status	*Observation:* student interview on interests, vocational aims, and perceptions of strengths, values, and attitudes
		Standardized measures: interest and ability inventories and surveys

social worker, and, depending on the student's age, a career educator. Roles adjust along the continuum of collaboration according to the phase of assessment (described as a "case study"). For the purposes of the actual collecting of information within a system and its interpretation, the speech-language pathologist and each of the other team members is responsible for his or her area of expertise. Following completion of the within-system assessments, roles expand in order to develop an integrated diagnostic summary of the whole student. This summary leads to goals and objectives for future programming and is reflective of the collective responsibility assumed by the transdisciplinary model.

As an illustration of a coordinated set of communicative, academic, and social goals, consider the following recommendations for a 16-year-old male placed in the Communication Development Program. The evaluation was conducted in compliance with the triannual assessment requirement of P.L. 94-142: (1) To improve memory and retention of class-related information (strategies should be encouraged for this purpose, such as rehearsal, requests for clarification, highlighting of critical information, and use of fact sheets). (2) To improve verbal formulation skills (use of a framework might be encouraged, e.g., focusing on the relations among *who* was involved, *what* happened, *how* it happened, *where* it happened, and *why* it happened). (3) To facilitate the identification and explanation of strategies he can use to assist him in academic and daily life. (4) To improve his ability to relate ideas and experiences in all academic areas through reading, writing, listening, and speaking activities. (5) To provide more opportunities for enhancing self-image, increased success in interpersonal relationships, and greater independent functioning; participation in an outside program that would specifically address these areas would be beneficial.

The student's educational program is then coordinated through a case manager who is a member of the classroom educational team for that student. The case manager is often the speech-language clinician. The student's parents or the student's guardian is also a member of the team.

Intervention. Each communication development team, from kindergarten through high school, consists of a speech-language pathologist certified by the American Speech-Language Hearing Association (ASHA), a certified teacher of the deaf (referred to as an "educator"), a certified school social worker, a certified career educator, and an aide. Teams are usually assigned a cluster of approximately 14 students, and team members function as coteachers in the classroom. All team members are expected to use and expand knowledge within their own area of expertise, develop expertise in the related disciplines of the other team members, and exchange partial teaching roles with one another; hence, role expansion and role release are main features of the intervention phase of the collaborative model.

The reciprocity between role expansion and role release then functions as an interactional mechanism for sustaining joint ownership of ideas, goals, and activities. Hoffman (1990) crystallizes this point:

Obviously, the speech-language pathologist must have learned how to organize a classroom, work with groups, and teach academic subjects. This has occurred via in-service training, additional coursework, and observation of colleagues. The speech-language pathologist also assists the other team members in understanding the students' speech and language delays/disorders and describes how they can best meet the students' speech and language needs. The educator learns how to incorporate the students' speech and language goals into lessons and assists the other team members in understanding the students' academic levels and needs. The social worker also learns about the students' speech and language difficulties and focuses on improving their socialization skills and interpersonal relationships during real situations in the classroom, on the playground, and at recess. (p. 87)

In a very real sense, the speech-language pathologist's role can be viewed as the fulcrum for coparticipation, while the student's communicative needs are the core around which this transdisciplinary model of coparticipation revolves.

Organization of Intervention

Classroom events are structured through whole-group and learning station (or small-group) activities. At the elementary and middle school levels, paired students rotate among three learning stations, and each station focuses on an activity related to the specific topic. For example, at the middle school level, since language and literacy activities occur throughout the day, one learning station might focus on topic-related vocabulary, another on spelling and writing, and a third on comprehension and problem solving. An aide may manage one of the learning stations under the supervision of the speech-language clinician and the educator. The whole-group cluster is utilized at the beginning of the lesson for discussion on the specific topic and at the end to compare and contrast new information with previously acquired material on the topic. A comparable structure is used at the high school level.

Students' specific speech and language objectives, including strategies to be applied, are woven into all instructional interactions. These goals are displayed in the classroom so they can be referred to and utilized by the students and the individual team members. As one example, if a communicative goal for a student is to expand the situations in which different wh-questions are understood, then assistance is provided by "all team members in academic subjects, classroom activities, and social work therapy" (Lease & Hoffman, 1990, p. 18). The latter type of therapy is conducted in large and small groups as well as individually. Similarly, if a social goal is to increase opportunities for the student to be a cooperative member of a group, then this goal is also facilitated across all classroom activities (Hoffman, 1990).

Individual therapy is provided by the speech-language pathologist, usually in a separate area of the classroom, to children who have phonological, fluency, or oral-motor problems in addition to their language learning difficulties. These sessions are scheduled, most typically, during the opening or closing activities of the school day.

Content of Intervention

Speaking, listening, reading, writing, spelling, and handwriting are supported across curriculum areas by three superordinate focuses: (1) the development of literacy along the oral-literate continuum, (2) the development of metalinguistic skills, and (3) the development of metacognitive skills. Exhibit 5-4 presents an outline of a language arts topic unit that also bridges science and social studies. Its theme, the arctic regions, was selected and directed by children in the lower primary cluster from options offered to them. These language learning disabled children were six to seven years old. The theme, its content, and the implementation strategies illustrate four major points. First, they demonstrate how oral communication and literate communication are interwoven through the construction of meaningful experiential activities (see Exhibit 5-4, sections IIA, IIIA, and IVA). Second, they are a practical means of facilitating collaboration through coparticipation since students and teachers collaborate on the selection of themes, the planning of tasks, and the evaluation of individual student performance. Third, like the communication skills approach, this integrated activity is the antithesis of the simplified learning and isolated practice commonly used with language learning disabled children (Westby & Costlow, in press). Finally, the activity itself is intended to maximize children's learning potential in challenging and motivating ways.

Following is a discussion of the three superordinate focuses mentioned at the beginning of this section.

Literacy Functions. The focus of the unit on the communicative functions of literacy is implemented within a developmental perspective. Citing Goodman (1986), Hoffman (1990) organizes literacy functions along a continuum that is reflected in the outline in Exhibit 5-4. The continuum proceeds from building awareness of different communicative functions of print to expanding access to books, magazines, and other kinds of print materials (e.g., maps and globes), expanding students' sense of the style and forms of written language, and translating this into meaningful reading and writing. Along this continuum, children are continuously assisted in using reading strategies for learning how to learn, as shown in Exhibit 5-4 (see sections IID, IIID, and IVD).

Metalinguistic Awareness. The superordinate metalinguistic focus also crosses topic areas and tasks (see Exhibit 5-4, sections IIB, IIIB, and IVB) and

Exhibit 5-4 Integrated Language Unit for Lower Primary Students: The Arctic Regions (Communication Development Program)

I. Introduce unit
   A. Discuss students' prior knowledge base
   B. Develop chart indicating their knowledge about the unit
   C. Write plan of activities for the unit
II. Expand knowledge about the arctic regions
   A. Reading and writing activities
      1. Refer to map and globe
      2. Refer to books and stories about these regions
      3. Find articles in newspapers and magazines about these regions
      4. Design library center in room with print information about these regions
      5. Make tundra or arctic circle maps and label the regions
      6. Develop wall mural in classroom and label the regions
      7. Develop chart summarizing new pertinent information
   B. Metalinguistic activities
      1. Identify long and short words from the print information relating to the unit
      2. Complete word search activities (include words from the unit)
      3. Alter the content of a story by manipulating the words
   C. Spelling and phonics activities
      1. Identify spelling words from the content of the unit
      2. Review specific phonics rules
      3. Develop word banks and word charts
   D. Reading strategy activities
      1. Use picture cues when reading information
      2. Use first sound of word to decode
      3. Determine which word makes sense
      4. Discuss whether or not students utilize reading strategies
   E. Metacognitive activities
      1. Discuss what was easy and hard in the unit
      2. Discuss which activities were the most informative
      3. Discuss how students appeared to learn best
III. Expand knowledge about arctic animals
   A. Reading and writing activities
      1. Discuss animals to be studied
      2. Read books about the animals
      3. Write stories about the animals
      4. For each animal, research the following information
         a) size
         b) color
         c) enemies
         d) food
         e) habitat
         f) term for the young
      5. For each animal, complete experiential activity
         a) whale; melt blubber
         b) walrus; measure tusks
         c) polar bear; change colors

Exhibit 5-4 continued

    d) arctic fox; view videotape
    e) arctic hare; develop tundras
    f) lemming; measure with yarn
    g) penguins; demonstrate how they hold eggs
  6. For each animal, develop booklet with pictures and print
  7. Make oral presentations to regular education and special education classes in the school
  B. Metalinguistic activities (similar to IIB)
  C. Spelling and phonics activities (similar to IIC)
  D. Reading strategy activities (similar to IID)
  E. Metacognitive activities (similar to IIE)
IV. Expand knowledge about Indian tribes and Eskimos
  A. Reading and writing activities
    1. Explore Indian tribes
    2. Discuss where Eskimos live
    3. Refer to map and globe
    4. Read books and stories about Eskimos
    5. View videotape about weather conditions and take notes with pictures and/or print
    6. Discuss Eskimos' appearance
    7. Draw pictures of Eskimos and label information
    8. Discuss Eskimos' method of travel
    9. Discuss reasons for their travel
    10. Locate articles in newspapers or magazines about Eskimos
    11. Write and act out story about Eskimos for parents
  B. Metalinguistic activities (similar to IIB and IIIB)
  C. Spelling and phonics activities (similar to IIC and IIIC)
  D. Reading strategy activities (similar to IID and IIID)
  E. Metacognitive activities (similar to IIE and IIIE)

stresses two related developmental aspects. The first is cultivating the integration of the emerging phonological awareness of phoneme-grapheme relationships essential for word recognition (Kamhi & Catts, 1989a) with the development of phonetic spelling skills (Ehri, 1989a) (see Exhibit 5-4, sections IIC, IIIC, and IVC). To support this integration, students engage in activities in which they identify variations in the duration of vowels (i.e., long versus short words) and create and expand their own word banks. As words are recognized (e.g., the names of arctic animals), these new words are written on cards, which are kept in a personal word bank (a recipe box). New words are also written on a wall chart kept visible in the classroom as an external reference. Other integrative activities emphasize variations in print context, such as searching for familiar words from the unit when their directionality is altered through a modified anagram format or finding words related to the names of arctic animals by looking through newspapers and magazines. Students then make charts of these new words to share with one another.

A second metalinguistic aspect moves beyond the recognition level to the manipulation, or more conscious alteration, of word meaning. For example, if a story is read about an arctic fox, and children know the story well, they will place stickers over the name or attributes of the fox whenever these appear in the text and assign a new name and new attributes. The new words must make sense given the context. A book is then created with these variations.

Metacognitive Awareness. Important facets of the metacognitive focus are its embeddedness in a planning mode (see Exhibit 5-4, section I) and the building of metacognitive awareness directed toward self-evaluation (see Exhibit 5-4, sections IIE, IIIE, and IVE). The plan of the lesson and the order of activities remain visible for reference and are reviewed daily. Based on their prior knowledge base, students are first asked to predict what information might be learned. They are then asked to think about possible ways to learn about that information, to choose the best strategies for acquiring information, and to evaluate their performance relative to reading and writing activities and strategies.

The purpose of self-evaluation is to help students progressively develop an enhanced awareness of their strengths and difficulties. This self-awareness is intended to enable them to understand the usefulness of strategies applied to their own performances. Students are asked to assess continuously what activities were easy and hard and which activities and strategies were most helpful to their learning. This form of self-assessment also encourages students to give themselves a "pat on the back" for their strengths. For example, if a communicative goal for a student is to develop more effective strategies for understanding verbal directions, the first step is to assist the student to recognize that following verbal directions is often difficult. The student is then supported in identifying situations in which following directions is easier or harder as well as strategies to use when directions are not understood, such as learning how to request explicit clarification or assistance.

All students, preprimary through high school, rate (using a 1–10 scale) and graph their abilities monthly in ten areas: speech, language, math, reading, writing, gym, art, music, behavior, and friends (see Exhibit 11-8). After these personal profiles are completed, they are used as visual tools to help students keep track from month to month of what they can do and what they find difficult to do. These profiles may also become the basis for discussing changes that can be made.

A relevant issue is how students of different ages, developmental levels, and severity levels understand the purpose of the metacognitive superordinate focus. For example, when students are asked what the graphing process is used for, variations will emerge as a function of their degree of awareness of learning as a purposeful state of understanding. A preprimary child might respond, "So we can learn stuff . . . stuff we're good and bad at." A primary level child might state, "So you can learn . . . see if you're sad or happy about something hard or easy. Gym, reading, counting numbers is easy. Art is hard." An upper primary child might state, "It shows how I'm doing in the work. I'm good at running in gym and drawing designs. It's hard for me to put pictures in order, to glue papers, and to write in cursive." Finally, a high school student might state "It's good for evaluating values and what subjects you are good in."

Coordination of Planning

As in the case of the communication skills model, coordinated planning is an instrumental process in the communication development model. Planning is the instrument by which common frames of reference are focused on students in the application of intervention principles derived from the program's philosophy and objectives. Furthermore, coordinated planning is the instrument by which the speech-language pathologist and other team members sustain joint ownership of ideas, goals, activities, and procedures along the continuum of role maintenance, extension, and release. All team members recognize that the contributions of each directly influence the functioning of all.

Systematic planning time is built into each team's schedule. Members of the team meet twice weekly, once for a general planning session on particular topic units, material development, or the use of specific intervention techniques and once for discussion about individual students. Aides may or may not attend these planning meetings; however, even if they do not attend, their input is actively sought and integrated, when appropriate, in order to maintain a shared understanding of the needs and progress of individual students.

Parent Communication and Coparticipation

The sixth basic component of the Communication Development Program concerns parental communication and coparticipation (Lease & Hoffman, 1990). Ongoing communication is considered vital, because students with communication problems often encounter difficulties in keeping their parents sufficiently aware of current activities. The parents are viewed as full members of the student's educational team, have the right to participate in the team in accord with P.L. 94-142, and are invited to observe the student's program throughout the school year. Home visits are also conducted by the educational team, most typically when a child enters the program in order to ease the transition into the new educational setting. A parent handbook is also disseminated; it contains information on the program's philosophy among other things.

Two additional avenues for coparticipation merit comment: (1) two monthly newsletters intended as vehicles by which parents can develop a more practical frame of reference for understanding the purposes of the classroom activities in which their children are involved and (2) a parent support network managed by the parents themselves under the supervision of the school social worker.

Monthly newsletters. The monthly newsletters are developed by the program's staff. One newsletter is prepared for parents of elementary students and the other for parents of middle and high school students. The articles concentrate on areas of classroom instruction and skill development. Suggestions for home activities to extend classroom learning are also included.

A newsletter for parents of elementary students might present the building of self-awareness as the primary topic. Short examples of actual student responses would be incorporated to help clarify phases of awareness at different cluster levels (preprimary, primary, and upper primary). Recommendations for home follow-up might include activities such as these:

- Ask your child what he or she does in school. Encourage your child to tell you what he or she finds easy versus hard. Let your child know that you understand that some things are more difficult and that what you expect is for him or her to do the best that can be done.

- Share with your child what is difficult for you. Let him or her know the strategies you have developed to help yourself in those areas.

- Give your child specific tasks to do at home. Have your child decide whether the task is easy or hard to complete. If it is difficult, discuss ways to make it easier. Give your child opportunities to excel.

For parents of middle and high school students, the newsletter might describe language-literacy–based programming and the variations in emphasis for middle school versus high school clusters. Specific suggestions for parental interaction at home could include the following:

- Talk together about the unit topic or theme being learned. Share your knowledge of the topic.

- Encourage interest in the topic by pointing out books, magazines, articles, TV shows, movies, and so on, related to the topic being studied.

- Encourage your child's use of language and literacy skills at home, for example, by having him or her write a letter to a friend or relative, write the family's shopping list, read a recipe or directions for a project, or explain the rules of a game being played.

Parent Networking. Another instrument of coparticipation is a parent networking program that enables parents of students with communicative disabilities to interact with each other. The social work staff trains volunteer parents as "coparents" in three areas: introduction/sharing, listening/attending, and the mourning process relative to understanding emotions about a child who has a handicap. A school social worker continues to supervise parent networking through the linking of parents with coparents and, when requested, acts as a resource. A major purpose of the networking is to offer parents opportunities to cope with their own feelings and to move ahead in supporting their children's needs.

CONCLUSION

In this chapter, we emphasize that communication-centered collaboration, regardless of its particular form and educational setting, evolves over time through different stages of development and is supported in its evolution by the dialogic process of coparticipation. Through coparticipation, mutual understanding of the classroom communication system and its continuous interaction with the communicative system of individual students is created and sustained through the use of observational lenses. These lenses allow for integrating a holistic approach to language assessment and intervention into the communicative contexts of the classroom and its curriculum. The lenses have a dual focus. One focus involves the reinterpretation of traditional roles and responsibilities for the clinician, the teacher, and other specialists. This reinterpretation slowly emerges from learning to observe together what students actually do with language in classrooms. The second focus centers on the assumption of joint responsibility for meaningfully integrating students' communicative goals with teaching strategies and activities for facilitating an active orientation to literacy learning.

Two communication-centered models of classroom partnership have been highlighted as examples of how the dual focuses of coparticipation can be accommodated in versatile ways. These models demonstrate that integrated programs can be initiated on a small scale (the communication skills model), expanded to a larger scale (the communication development model), and modified as necessary according to the particular circumstances of implementation. While the two models vary in major aspects of service delivery, including the educational settings in which they operate, the kinds of students being assisted, and the emphasis given to specific curriculum areas, both are based on similar theoretical assumptions about the central role of communication in literacy learning. This framework, in turn, provides continuity and cohesion between the program goals, the program planning, and the assessment and intervention principles and

108 COMMUNICATING FOR LEARNING

practices. Both models provide evidence that collaboration through coparticipation entails more than a static redefinition of roles. Depending on the students' needs and the needs of other collaborators for support, the functions of the speech-language pathologist vary along a dynamic continuum of role maintenance and extension.

Chapter 6

Ways To Record and Store Students' Communication

We are concerned with how children use language in the everyday situations that they encounter in classrooms. Adequate assessment of children's literacy abilities must include an analysis of their use of language in real situations. Assessment can be viewed as a way of collecting information about a child when that information is closely related to the instructional practices in which the child participates, the teaching and learning environments that constitute the child's school experience, and the individual differences among children. *Nonformal* assessment involves the collection of information in a somewhat informal but still systematic manner. It can include a variety of methods and is continuous over the course of the school year. It involves periodic collection of information, for example, tape recording children's oral language so as to be able to note changes in form, content, or use. Use of these methods leads to a more complete picture of each child's strengths, weaknesses, capacities, and abilities in the use of language. Thus, by *nonformal methods*, we mean methods based on direct observation and/or documentation by the school personnel (e.g., coparticipating team members) whom the child encounters daily.

The use of formal assessment instruments (e.g., standardized tests) needs to be supplemented by noticing, hearing, and seeing what children do with and by means of language across varied situations. Formal measurement uses different standards for obtaining information than informal methods. Formal measures have specified guidelines for administration, and the information collected is based on and limited to the content of the test. These measurements are usually taken only once or twice during the school year, and the information is compared with the published normative data that are provided by the publisher of the test. Some argue that formal methods can include procedures that are developmentally and culturally appropriate to particular students. Others, however, do not agree that it is possible to render a standardized test in that way. Nonformal assessment allows tailoring the methods of assessment to the questions asked about children's language; it includes using evaluative procedures that are developmentally and culturally appropriate for the children being assessed.

OVERVIEW

Observation is a method of inquiry. In the context of investigating children's literacy, it can be used to explore the instructional practices in which children participate, the classrooms in which they learn, and the social situations within which teaching and learning occur. Contemporary research has introduced the use of new methods for assessing children's language and literacy abilities. We attempt to bridge the gap between research and practice by suggesting ways that tools derived from research can be incorporated into practices for assessment and the evaluation of progress.

This overview of observational methods includes a focus on the more traditional methods, as well as some of the newer, more nontraditional methods, and ways to combine both types of methods in order to optimize approaches to assessment. The goal is to show how to observe systematically in order to describe children's communicative interactions clearly and comprehensively. As will be illustrated, inferences and conclusions can be drawn that will then allow an understanding of what is really happening in children's communication. The outcomes can guide the design, implementation, and subsequent evaluation of effective intervention.

WHAT IS DIRECT OBSERVATION?

Direct observation is looking at and listening to what individuals do naturally in various natural situations. The purpose of direct observation, as described here, is to help clinicians in their various classroom roles to see clearly what is happening with a child in the classroom.

USING DIRECT OBSERVATION

Direct observation can be used in a variety of ways (Irwin & Bushnell, 1980). First of all, it can be used as a way to obtain new ideas. For example, the clinician who is functioning in a consultant role may be asked by the regular classroom teacher to observe a child who does not verbalize frequently and who therefore does not participate adequately in classroom activities. Or in the role of a team member in the self-contained special education classroom, the clinician can focus attention on the child who has been evaluated as having language and communication problems. Observations in multiple contexts can be used to discover more precisely how that child spontaneously uses verbal and nonverbal communication. During the course of the observations, a pattern may emerge. A child who is usually silent during formal classroom activities may "open up" and interact with other children, using both oral language and nonverbal means, during informal activities, such as play. An examination of the activities when that child talks is needed in order to determine the critical elements associated with this child's language use. For example, what aspects of the different situations seem to be stimulating the "nontalker" to talk? Does the child talk only when the teacher or another adult is not present? Or is the child's talking primarily associated with less formal, more spontaneous opportunities to talk, such as on the playground or in the cafeteria?

A second reason for directly observing children in the classroom is that observation can be used to find out specific answers to specific questions. The child who may appear to be dysfunctional in certain aspects of language use, according to an evaluation, may spontaneously exhibit these aspects in other settings. It is important to become familiar with the variety of communicative contexts that the child routinely encounters in order to locate those in which the child demonstrates the extent of his or her actual communicative competence and versatility.

For example, it is important to discover if the word-retrieval and related fluency problems that formed the basis of the original referral and that were substantiated by formal evaluation are associated only with certain conversational contexts. These contexts might include the following: (1) when the teacher calls on the child in class and, in effect, places a "spotlight" on the child, and (2) when the clinician engages the child in the dialogue of one-to-one intervention regardless of whether this dialogue takes place in the classroom or in a separate therapy room. It may be the case that word retrieval and flow of expression are enhanced in other teaching situations, such as when the child is learning with a friend or a familiar adult. Again, a child whose written language sample or whose performance on a paper and pencil test reveals a very low level of grammatical complexity may actually produce far more complex language when interacting with a friend or when he or she has chosen the topic of conversation.

A third reason for observing children in typical classroom situations is that it can help in understanding the limits of individual children's communicative competence. For example, an observant clinician can gain insight by looking at how students interact with each other and to what extent their skills at turn-taking are limited by their language learning problems. Consider a particular child who is placed in a self-contained classroom for learning disabilities. The teacher observes that the child often avoids participating in formal class lessons (e.g., the child seldom initiates contributions to the topic being talked about). Upon further discussion with the clinician, the teacher may note that the child seems increasingly reticent to talk in general and is not very successful at communicating when he or she does talk. Observation reveals that the child does not talk very spontaneously during class lessons. But this may not be unusual. As reviewed in Chapter 4, recent research has documented that teachers, even special education teachers, do most of the talking during classtime, even as much as two-thirds. The child, however, also has difficulty obtaining and holding the conversational floor in group situations, such as during a reading group with four to six students when the teacher sits with the group only some of the time. In this situation, the expectation is that each child in the group must get and hold the floor in order to take a turn at talking. It would be logical, then, to observe that same child in a slightly different context, where the teacher is present during the entire reading session, is responsible for allocating turns, and makes sure that each child has the opportunity to finish his or her turn at talking without interruptions. In this second conversational context, the child may offer more contributions related to the topic and express them with more varied semantic-syntactic complexity. That child may behave very differently in the two situations, even though both are considered to be "small-group" situations. Perhaps the observation also reveals that, when the child is alone with only one or two other children who are friends outside of school, he or she manages conversation more actively. This example illustrates that some aspects of the communicative context seem to be crucial in creating the perception that a child's "language problems" are more severe than may actually be the case. A comprehensive understanding of a child's language and communicative competencies should include this kind of information.

A fourth reason to observe children is for the purpose of ongoing evaluation. In the case described above, it is critical to look very carefully at the situation where the teacher regulates turn-taking in the group and the informal situation with one other child in order to determine which aspects could account for the extent of nonparticipation demonstrated by the child. In both situations, the pressure on the child to continually compete for a turn at talk is minimized compared with the situation where many children are constant contenders for the floor. Even more specifically, the child's participation decreases (1) when the child has to keep track of what he or she wants to say while simultaneously figuring out how to get and hold the floor and (2) when the child does not have sufficient time to plan ahead what he or she wants to say. Which of these two explanations reflects what is really influencing the quality of this child's performance? What seems to be triggering this kind of minimal participation and impeding the child's access to more optimal communicative interactions? More observation should lead to the answers to these questions. Once the specific interactional contributors to the presenting problem have been identified, intervention strategies can be designed and integrated into classroom communication to assist the child in actively managing these communicative situations (see Chapters 5 and 13; see also Brinton & Fujiki, 1989; Hoffman, 1990; Hoskins, 1990; Wallach & Miller, 1988).

Many insights are possible through the use of observation. For example, inconsistencies in performance across situations and factors within situations that trigger what appears to be impaired performance may be discovered. Looking at multiple levels of language use, in both oral and written domains, is important for gaining a full picture of communicative competence.

SYSTEMATIC METHODS OF DIRECT OBSERVATION

Using direct observation is like taking a series of snapshots of the strengths and weaknesses in children's language use. And like snapshots, observation requires a tool or set of tools. These tools are referred to as observational systems. It is critical to select the system that is most appropriate for the specific purpose of the observation. Consider the example just described, where concern is expressed about the adequacy of a child's communicative participation. It would be important for the clinician to select a tool that would allow the hearing and seeing of the multiple layers of communicative participation in sufficient detail and in particular situations so that the extent of the problem the child is having could be understood. How do the child's strategies for interacting interfere with opportunities to participate and learn across classroom activities involving speaking, listening, reading, and writing?

The first step is to create an observational system or choose an already existing one. Each system consists of a way of recording and storing examples of a child's language use and a way of examining these examples so that inferences and conclusions can be drawn that will be helpful in guiding the development and evaluation of intervention strategies.

There are literally hundreds of observational systems to choose from (perhaps as many as a thousand). Following is a brief overview of the basic issues that each clinician or user must contend with in selecting an observational system. Essentially, there are three basic questions that can be asked about any observational system: (1) What *goals* can be met by using the system? (2) Is the nature of the system *open* or *closed?* (3) How is the child's language use *recorded* and *stored* for later examination (Evertson & Green, 1986).

GOALS

As discussed in Chapter 5, one principle of collaboration through coparticipation is that team members must have a general sense of how language is currently used in the classroom. Thus, one might want to know whether there is a high level of talk by students or whether those in the teacher role do most of the talking. Also, is there a premium on students' listening to what the teacher says, since he or she is not likely to repeat the same content? What is the nature of the teacher's language use? Does the teacher rely heavily on asking questions, eliciting answers, and then providing evaluation?

Some research has shown that students are more likely to talk when they are working in small groups such as are commonly used for teaching reading and math in elementary school and sometimes used in programs at both the elementary and secondary levels for communicatively impaired students (e.g., Hoffman, 1990). It may be important to find out when small groups are used in the classroom, how often they are used, and what kinds of oral language demands are placed on children in these situations. Elizabeth Cohen, a researcher at Stanford University, has found that, unless a small group is monitored and guided to a large extent by the teacher, the group is dominated by a few children (Cohen, 1984). These children are particularly "good talkers" and are adept at getting and holding the floor, and thus the other children appear not to be as involved in the teaching and learning taking place in the group.

On the other hand, one might want to know in detail about several aspects of a child's language use in the classroom. If so, a different approach would be followed. A system would need to be used that allows (1) careful analysis, perhaps in multiple ways, of samples of the child's discourse and (2) a way to describe the instances of discourse in which there is interest. For example, after situations have been identified where children are allowed to talk during classtime, collaborators may choose to make audio or video recordings of the child's discourse. These technological aids should be considered as external supports for live observation, since they are permanent records that can be continuously available for documenting the effectiveness of assessment and intervention decisions for all students. It may be discovered through the use of these aids that a high incidence of self-interruption accompanies attempts by the child to get the conversational floor in small-group lessons (e.g., the child has trouble "getting started," as suggested by a high frequency of false starts and excessive use of "um"). These attempts often do not result in an opportunity for the child to complete what he or she intended to say because his or her turn is either interrupted by peers or the teacher unintentionally interrupts to select another child. If the goal is this kind of detailed analysis, then it would be necessary to use an audio or video record.

OPEN AND CLOSED SYSTEMS

Closed Systems

Observational systems can be open or closed. Closed observational systems are those that contain a specific number and set of categories for observation, for example: (1) teacher's question, (2) teacher's praise, (3) teacher's rebuke. In closed systems, the specific categories are usually derived from a particular theory or way of looking at the world; they usually focus on only one narrowly defined dimension. In the examples given above, the concern is the functions for which teachers and students use language in classrooms. None of the individual categories overlaps any of the others. For example, when a teacher gives praise, the teacher cannot at the same time be rebuking the student. Because of this feature, closed systems are said to have *mutually exclusive categories*. New categories cannot be added to closed observational systems. If behavior is observed that does not fit into the system that is being used, it cannot be included. That behavior is then referred to as *non-codeable*. All categories that compose the system must remain, even if behavior fitting into one of the categories is never observed in a real classroom. As a result, closed systems are said to have *exhaustive categories*.

A well-known and popular example of a closed system is the Flanders System of Interaction Analysis (Flanders, 1970). It consists of only ten categories (Exhibit 6-1). Seven of the categories refer to teachers' language (functions) and three refer to students' language. Flanders was particularly interested in studying the relationship between teachers' talk to children and the nature of classrooms, and he chose to study classrooms when both teachers and children had chances to talk.

This system has actually been used in classrooms by observers. The observers classify each utterance used by teachers and students into one and only one of the categories listed in Exhibit 6-1. The decision about which category to place an utterance in is made immediately after the utterance occurs. This system has also been used extensively in teacher training activities to provide prospective teachers with a way to look at their actual teaching and its effect upon their students in actual classrooms, such as the quality and quantity of students' participation. Flanders found that teachers were less likely to criticize children and be very directive when they were supportive and accepting of what children said. Flanders claimed that when teachers became aware of the effects their talking had on the children in their classes, they were better able to modify their styles to achieve the kind of classroom communication desired.

Open Systems

Open systems may also contain preset categories, but these categories are not necessarily mutually exclusive. Simultaneously categorizing one utterance in two or more ways is characteristic of open systems, since the focus of these systems tends to be broad and centered on more than one dimension at a time. A particular utterance, for example, the question, "The capital of Montana is Hel-

Exhibit 6-1   The Categories of the Flanders System of Interaction Analysis

---

1. **Teacher accepts feeling:** Accepts and clarifies the feeling tone of the students in a non-threatening manner. Feelings may be positive or negative. Predicting or recalling feelings are included.

2. **Teacher praises or encourages:** Praises or encourages student action or behavior. Jokes that release tension, not at the expense of another individual, nodding head or saying, "um hm?" or "go on" are included.

3. **Teacher accepts or uses ideas of student:** Clarifies, builds, or develops ideas suggested by a student. As a teacher brings more of his own ideas into play, shift to category 5.

4. **Teacher asks questions:** Asks a question about content or procedure with the intent that a student answer.

5. **Teacher lectures:** Gives facts or opinions about content or procedure; expresses his/her own ideas, asking rhetorical questions.

6. **Teacher gives directions:** Gives directions, commands, or orders to which a student is expected to comply.

7. **Teacher criticizes or justifies authority:** Makes statements intended to change student behavior from nonacceptable to acceptable pattern; bawling someone out; stating why the teacher is doing what he is doing; extreme self-reference.

8. **Student talk-response:** Student makes a predictable response to teacher. Teacher initiates the contact or solicits student statement and sets limits to what the student says.

9. **Student talk-initiation:** Student initiates talk. Unpredictable statements in response to teacher. (As student introduces own ideas shift from 8 to 9.)

10. **Student silence or confusion:** Pauses, short periods of silence and periods of confusion in which communication cannot be understood by the observer.

Source: From *Analyzing Teaching Behavior,* (p. 34) by N. Flanders, 1970, Menlo Park, CA: Addison-Wesley Publishing Co. Copyright 1970 by Addison-Wesley Publishing Co. Reprinted with permission.

---

ena, isn't it?" can simultaneously be categoried as (1) a request for information (a function of language), (2) a tag question (a syntactic form), and (3) an initiation (a way to open a conversational exchange with another person).

Open systems do not necessarily cover all that will be observed, since they are often derived from observations of real language use, not just from thinking about how language could be used, a characteristic of closed systems. Open systems can be modified, added to, and subtracted from as observations are collected and attempts are made to categorize them. It is obvious that open systems are potentially more complex than closed ones because they have multiple ways of categorizing language and can be modified.

One open system was designed by Merritt (1982b) to examine how elementary school students got their teacher's attention during individual seatwork time. Seatwork is an activity in which the teacher goes from child to child to provide comments, evaluation, or assistance in completing independent work. Merritt made audio and video tape recordings of dozens of actual elementary classrooms, then made transcriptions of what was said and done by teachers and students. She then analyzed these transcriptions to see how language was used throughout the school day.

Merritt discovered some uses of language that she would not have anticipated if a closed system had been employed. For example, she found that, during individual seatwork (when a teacher is involved with one child), it was not appropriate for another child to try to get the teacher's attention. She saw that the normal ways for children to request the teacher's attention in other classroom situations, such as putting up a hand or calling out, simply did not work in this particular situation. The following rule seemed to be operating in the classrooms that Merritt studied: The teacher had to finish working with one child before another could have his or her attention. It was not appropriate for a child to try to "break in" and get the teacher's attention until the teacher was done; furthermore, while waiting, the child must have at least appeared to be busy with school work and not wasting time just waiting for the teacher to become available. Children who did not follow this rule were rebuked by the teacher.

Of course, like all rules, there are exceptions. Upon further observation, Merritt realized that a teacher did, on occasion, momentarily shift attention from the child he or she was working with to attend to another, for example, in the case of an emergency (an injury) or the child's first greeting of the school day. In the following excerpt from Merritt's study, we see Ms. C. is helping Sam, a student, with a task that involves matching color and letters. She has her back to a wall and is facing the door and Sam when a late student comes in the door. Ms. C. momentarily shifts her attention from Sam to the late student (Carter) and greets him, then returns to the task she is helping Sam with. Merritt notes that Ms. C. changes the pitch of her voice when she greets Carter, thereby showing that the greeting is not part of her interaction with Sam.

Teacher:　What color is next to G?

Sam:　White

Teacher:　No, that's G. The letter G is white, but what is the color *Hi Carter (said with higher pitch)* next to it? (Merritt, 1982b, p. 231)

When Merritt began her study of how children get the teacher's attention, she did not know about the "rule" that she would discover; nor was she aware of the exceptions to it. The phrase "Hi Carter" is simultaneously a greeting, a high-pitched utterance, and an utterance not directed to Sam. This careful and detailed study of real language use in classrooms is an example of how an open system can be used.

The examples of open and closed systems presented here have been derived from research on teachers' language use in the regular classroom. However, classroom collaboration presumes that the collaborative team is knowledgeable about the communicative demands of various classroom activities. For that reason, it may be necessary to observe how language is used for teaching as well as by individual children. Appendix B is a resource for that purpose.

METHODS OF RECORDING LANGUAGE

The third major difference among observational systems concerns the method of recording the information. The most obvious method is to record "live," that is, the observer writes down the information as it actually occurs. In using the live method, each instance of a child exhibiting a particular behavior is written down, such as each instance of a response to a question. The kind of response is also noted (e.g., providing factual information or an explanation or clarification). Because of the limitations in our ability to hear and record information live, the observer is generally limited to recording only one dimension of language when relying on this method. Thus, live observation is most commonly used with closed systems, where it is known in advance what behaviors are being looked for and there is only one dimension to keep track of.

Some kinds of behaviors that collaborators are interested in cannot be captured live, particularly if there is more than one aspect of interest, such as the form *and* the function of what a child says. It may not be possible to note both of these as they actually occur. A second possibility is to record events using some kind of technology, such as audio or video recording.

In sum, there are some basic dimensions shared by all observational systems, even though there are many different systems created to meet particular needs. All systems can be described relative to the goals of the observer, the nature of the system (open or closed), and the way in which information is recorded and stored. Each of these dimensions needs to be considered before a system is chosen. If the appropriate system is not available, then one may have to be created. Further, no one system is adequate for all situations. It is more likely that collaborators will have to design a system tailored to the questions being asked about particular students. Chapters 8, 9, and 10 address different observational systems.

RELIABILITY AND VALIDITY

In classroom collaboration, critical decisions about students' functioning may be based on conclusions and inferences derived, at least in part, from observations of children using language in actual classroom settings. It is incumbent upon collaborators to draw their conclusions based on observations that accurately reflect children's actual abilities. There are two main issues concerning the use of observations: validity and reliability. *Validity* refers to the representativeness of what the child actually does as observed and recorded; *reliability* refers to the consistency, stability, and dependability of recorded observations. In this section, these two key concepts are introduced and applied to classroom observations. The purpose of this review is to help speech-language clinicians and their collaborative partners find practical ways to build reliability and validity into their observational methods. This topic is developed further in Chapter 11.

Reliability

Typically, when we talk about consistency, we are interested in having at least two individuals observe the same child and agree that they see essentially the same behavior. When scientists refer to reliability, they often are in fact referring to an agreement that at least two observers reach when looking at the same thing. This is called *interrater agreement*. Often, the terms *interrater agreement* and *reliability* are used interchangeably, because they both refer to consistency. However, they do not mean exactly the same thing, as is shown later in this chapter.

Consistency in observation is important for at least two reasons. First, it is more likely to result in objectivity. If several observers report seeing or hearing roughly the same behaviors, they are being consistent with each other. In that case, we are likely to believe that what was reported did in fact occur. Second, consistent observation guarantees that other individuals, using the same observational procedures, will see the same behaviors. This is an important consideration, because classroom collaboration implies that observation will be done at other times and perhaps with other people. Initially, to begin enhancing the consistency of observation, it is important for team members to agree with findings; this ensures that the findings are not just some "fluke" resulting from the way the observation has been conducted.

Interrater Agreement

Interrater agreement is not exactly the same as reliability. In its strictest sense, *reliability* has a very narrow definition: It refers to the "true" measure of the phenomenon under observation, plus some error. Scientists do not believe that anyone can really ever observe the absolutely true nature of something, such as a child's language ability, without some kind of error clouding the picture. Observation always includes some error due to the observer not really hearing or seeing the object of study perfectly. For example, the clinician may not be able to hear *all* of what the child is saying in the classroom, just some part of what is said. Therefore, what is heard, the observation of the child's language use, gives an imperfect and incomplete picture. Chapter 8 includes a discussion of errors made in observation and ways to minimize them when using rating scales.

Clinicians may be familiar with interrater agreement as a measure of consistency in observation. How is interrater agreement calculated? An example will be helpful to illustrate both the method and the meaning of this measure.

Suppose you are interested in seeing how a particular child uses verbal and nonverbal communication to attract the teacher's attention. You have done some reading and thinking about the various ways children of this age typically manage to get the teacher's attention, and you believe that there are three methods: (1) the student goes up and touches or tugs the teacher (nonverbal, physical), (2) the student calls to the teacher or asks a question (verbal, speech), or (3) the student goes and stands beside the teacher (nonverbal, proximity). You and another observer, who is familiar with the categories of attention seeking, would observe the child in the classroom. Each of you would write down each time the child tries to get the teacher's attention and note the particular method used. Following the observation, both of you, using your notes, calculate the interrater agreement of your observations. You (Observer A) noted that the child tried to get the teacher's attention 26 times; Observer B noted that the child tried only 24 times.

The first step in the calculation of interrater agreement is to *count the number of instances of attention seeking noted by each observer* (see Exhibit 6-2). The second step is to *add the two numbers together*. In this example, the total is 50. The third step is to *calculate the total number of instances in which both observers agreed there was attention seeking*. In this case, the number of instances in which both of you agreed that the child was seeking the teacher's attention is 20. The fourth step is to *divide the total number of agreements by the total number of observations*. In this case, 20 should be divided by 50, which equals .40. The fifth step is to *multiply the ratio by 2*. The resulting ratio, in this case .80, is the interrater agreement. The reason for multiplying the original ratio of .40 by 2 is that there were two observers. Even if there had been perfect agreement, the ratio would have been only .50, since there were only half as many agreements as observations. Multiplying by the number of observers corrects for this.

In educational and clinical research, there are more complicated ways of calculating reliability, since interrater agreement is not a perfect measure of consistency (see the classic text *Essentials of Psychological Testing*, Cronbach, 1970, for more details).

Consistency

Classroom collaborators, as observers, are interested in having their individual observations be accurate and consistent with those of other team mem-

Exhibit 6-2   Steps in Calculating Interrater Agreement

		Observer A	Observer B
1. Count the number of instances student seeks attention as noted by each observer.	Physical	10	9
	Verbal	11	8
	Proximity	5	7
	Total	26	24
2. Add together the number of instances noted by each observer.	Total	50	
3. Count the number of instances both observers agreed a certain kind of attention seeking occurred and calculate the total number of agreements	Physical	7	
	Verbal	8	
	Proximity	5	
	Total	20	
4. Divide the number of agreements by the total number of observations.		$20 \div 50 = .40$	
5. Multiply the result by 2 (since there were two observers). This final number is the interrater agreement.		$.40 \times 2 = .80$	

Source: Adapted by permission of the publisher from Boehm, Ann E., and Weinberg, Richard A., *The Classroom Observer: A Guide for Developing Observation Skills* (New York: Teachers College Press, © 1977 by Teachers College, Columbia University. All rights reserved.), p. 35.

bers so that the most complete picture of what is really going on can be attained. One way that the consistency of observations can be increased is to develop specific definitions of the kinds of verbal or nonverbal behaviors to be observed. These definitions are sometimes referred to as *recognition rules*. When recognition rules are effective, they allow unambiguous notation of the verbal or nonverbal behaviors of interest and reduce the possibility of incorrectly noting similar behaviors. Duncan and Fiske (1977) have distinguished between explicit recognition rules, which are based on formal and abstract definitions, and implicit recognition rules, which are based on a collection of examples of the behavior.

An explicit recognition rule might consist of a list of characteristics of the behavior. For example, a tag question, according to one formal definition, is a sentence "consisting of an auxiliary verb plus pronoun, attached to the end of a statement in order to convey a negative or positive orientation" (Crystal, 1985, p. 303). An implicit recognition rule, in contrast, consists of many examples of the behavior without any abstract definition linking all examples. Consider the phenomenon of tone of voice. We are able to convey a variety of emotions through alterations in tone of voice. You and another observer may listen to many tape recordings and eventually agree on when you hear an angry tone of voice, a happy tone of voice, and a neutral tone of voice. You are then able to note these different tones when listening to people speak. In this case, you have developed a set of implicit recognition rules for tone of voice, and you probably have a high interrater agreement with that one observer. Problems can develop, however, when you try to teach another person the rules, since you cannot describe the behaviors using formal definitions that apply to all real instances.

Duncan and Fiske (1977) have argued that reliability of observation is maximized when the recognition rules are explicitly stated *and* clearly defined during the training period. They also note that it is important to have the categories clearly different from each other. In the example above, it would be important that the happy tone of voice really does differ from the neutral tone of voice.

Duncan and Fiske also suggest that reliability can be increased when the limitations of our ability to encode and organize information are not exceeded, that is, when human information-processing constraints are taken into account. Observers should be asked to make only one judgment of a particular kind of behavior (e.g., tone of voice) at a given time to ensure that they can direct their complete attention to listening or seeing carefully and to noticing whether, in fact, the behavior in which they are interested has indeed occurred unambiguously. This approach would argue against simultaneously trying to figure out the tone of voice and the syntactic structure of a stretch of speech. If this dual task is attempted, unreliable and therefore inaccurate observations will in all likelihood result.

Duncan and Fiske further recommend that observers be asked to identify behaviors at one given point in time and that they not be asked to think about whether a particular behavior has in fact occurred sometime after the fact of its occurrence. For example, the kind of information that Merritt (1982b) used for her analysis would be very difficult, if not impossible, to obtain if observations were solely based on the on-line talk of teacher and students in the classroom. The nuances that Merritt noticed and that had such importance simply happened too quickly—in a matter of seconds in some cases. The teacher seemed to be doing two things at once: teaching a child mathematics and greeting and directing another child. Merritt always worked from audio- and videotapes as she unravelled the complexities of classroom language. If team members are interested in minute and/or complex behaviors, it is best to work from recordings. Recordings permit the development of a sense of what went on and the freedom to delve deeper once the recordings have been reviewed. The use of technology in observation is discussed in Chapter 7.

Two final ways of increasing reliability are (1) to practice observing through reviewing recordings and transcripts of interactions in order to ensure that all observers have carefully defined the behaviors prior to the actual observation and (2) to increase the size of the sample of behaviors. It would be important to calculate interrater agreement before doing the real observation and attain acceptable levels of agreement.

The question of what is an acceptable level of interrater agreement does arise. The percentage of agreement that is acceptable is subjective—and is decided by you. Shriberg and Kent (1982) have argued that the level of reliability will differ depending on the purpose of the observations collected. For example, if there was to be an important clinical decision based on a relatively small difference in the child's use of language (whether form, content, or function), it would be sensible to obtain a high level of interrater agreement. Only then can one be confident of the conclusions based on the instances of behavior. However, if the purpose is to make preliminary observations of a child's language capability—to get a general sense of what the child typically produces in the classroom—perhaps a somewhat lower level of interrater agreement would be acceptable. In both research and practice, it is a good idea to base important decisions on data that are as accurate and complete as possible.

In sum, determining the reliability of observations is a critical step in developing a systematic way of observing in classroom collaboration. Observations can be valuable to all clinicians, giving them a true sense of how children use language in the real situations that they encounter. But it is important that the conclusions drawn are derived from data that are accurate and that the behaviors are consistently seen by more than one person on one occasion. In later chapters, we will discuss the kind of samples to take, the way to design observational systems, and the way to incorporate multiple perspectives into observational findings. The major point of this section on reliability is to draw attention to the fact that readiness to observe does not mean preparation to observe. The calculation of interrater agreement is a tool that allows classroom collaborators to prepare themselves adequately for observing children carefully and completely.

Validity

We now turn our attention to the issue of validity. A valid observation is one that truly reflects what the child can do with language. The goal in observing is to be as objective as possible and to not let subjective feelings and/or biases prevent one from seeing "what is really going on." This can be difficult for the speech-language clinician, not to mention other professionals. Obviously, when a child has been referred for evaluation because there is a problem, others have already characterized, or attempted to characterize, the nature of the problem. A complete independent investigation of the child's communicative skills is necessary.

Reliability and validity are not the same thing. It is possible to have very consistent agreement among observers at the same time that what they agree upon is simply not a good indication of what they want to know. For example, it is possible for two team members to agree that a student exhibits a high rate of nonresponding when called on in class; that same student may also be a low achiever in that class. Someone might suggest that the incidence of nonresponding indicates the child is unable to concentrate on class work, which indicates in turn that the child is a slow thinker. This conclusion would probably not be warranted, since research, for example, on sociocultural differences (reviewed in Chapter 3) has shown that nonresponding does not necessarily reflect cognitive deficits. An individual who was not aware of this research would arrive at an invalid conclusion.

Ideally, there should be a match between the area of interest, the focus of inquiry, the questions asked, and the information gathered and analyzed. Consider the following example: Suppose that, as a member of a diagnostic team, the school psychologist refers a child to you for further evaluation. The regular class teacher reports that the child is disruptive when working in small-group activities in class with other children. Furthermore, the child, unlike the other children, does not seem able to get his work done when the teacher is not present, and he seems confused, denying that there is a problem. After some preliminary observation of the child in these small-group settings, you observe that the child is notably unsuccessful in getting other children to provide feedback to him and to respond at all to his requests for clarification. The next step is to formulate a question: Is the child able to request clarification and receive it from other classmates? The following step is to record instances of his attempts to request clarification. The final step is to carefully examine these attempts and determine the effectiveness of this child's use of verbal means to get help. Thus, in designing an observational approach, a set of questions—including who, what, when, where, and how to observe—must be asked. These questions need to be carefully thought through and addressed *before* any observation is initiated.

Genishi (1983), a researcher in child language and early childhood education, studied normal language and communicative development in young children. In Figure 6-1, there is an outline of the steps that she took in her attempt to answer research questions such as these: What are children accomplishing through verbal interaction? What kinds of arguments do children have? How do children take conversational turns during dramatic play? What intonation patterns are associated with student engagement during science lessons?

What Genishi looks at in the classroom is determined by the questions she is asking, and these will affect the kind of information collected, stored, and analyzed. Because Genishi, like Merritt (1982b), sometimes examines very minute details of talk, she must make audiovisual recordings of classroom language. She cannot simultaneously keep track of all levels, nor can she hear, in real time,

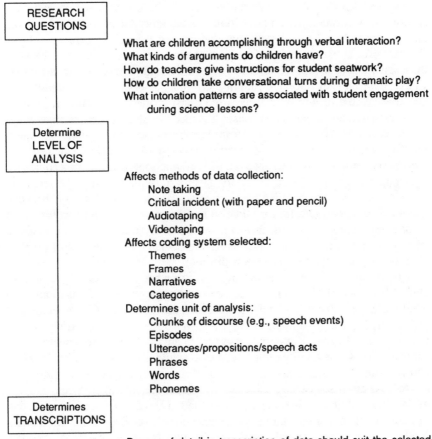

Figure 6-1 Studying Classroom Verbal Interaction. *Source:* Reprinted with permission of Macmillan Publishing Company, a Division of Macmillan, Inc., from "Observation as Inquiry and Method" by C. Evertson and J. Green. In *Handbook of Research on Teaching*, 3rd ed., by M. Wittrock (Ed.). Copyright © 1986 American Educational Research Association.

all intonation patterns of potential interest to her. Genishi's work illustrates that the match between the focus of inquiry, the questions, the potential for using audiovisual recording, among other issues, need to be considered before conducting the clinical observations. Genishi's approach could be adapted for collaborative observations of one or more children for either clinical or educational purposes.

It is very important that interpretations and conclusions be based on actual observations. In addition, it can be helpful to have other kinds of information not directly derived from the observations that support the resulting interpretations. For example, in the case of a referral, are the observations consistent with what the teacher and school psychologist have reported in their referral? Do the observations confirm some problem pattern noted in an assessment of the child's language use based on formal measures (e.g., test scores) or criterion-referenced measures (e.g., elicitation techniques)? It is also possible, if there is an audio or visual record, to replay it for other team members without providing your interpretation and ask them to provide their perspective of the child's language patterns based on this record (Chapter 11 will provide some specific procedures for obtaining this goal). Be sure to ask for specific information from the record to support their conclusions. Finally, prior to any formal procedures for decision making, it is a good idea for the clinician to present analyses and conclusions to other team members and ask them for reactions. If there are discrepancies, it may be illuminating to explore their bases, particularly when the child's presenting problem may represent a complex disorder.

A final validity issue is the extent to which what is seen and what is concluded from actual observation holds true in a wide variety of situations with other participants. How generally true are the patterns that have been observed? How likely is it that communicative breakdowns observed in one setting will occur in others? This is an important question to answer if the assessment is to be complete. Thus, the validity of the claim that a child has a language learning disability or that this disability is "visible" all of the time needs to be carefully considered. As discussed earlier, one child's apparent inability to communicate, exhibited in small groups, was mostly manifested in situations where the child had to fight to obtain and maintain the conversational floor. Even if the child had a disability, the same principle would apply, that is, an intrapersonal disorder would have to be considered within interpersonal contexts (Bloome & Knott, 1985). In such cases, the key to intervention is to carefully construct a series of classroom situations where the child can learn the necessary strategies to develop the confidence to talk in groups when competition for talking occurs.

CONCLUSION

In this chapter, the relevance of observational methods for classroom collaboration has been introduced. Observational methods were presented in the framework of the nonformal assessment of children and the language and literacy skills they use in school. The use of formal assessment instruments (e.g., standardized tests) needs to be supplemented by noticing, hearing, and seeing what students do with and by the means of language across varied communicative contexts.

Adequate assessment of children's communicative ability must include an analysis of their use of language in real situations. Assessment can be viewed as a way of collecting information about a child that is closely related to the instructional practices in which the child engages. Assessment is done by means of a variety of methods and is continuous over the course of the school year. It involves the periodic collection of information (e.g., tape recording children's oral language interactions to note changes in the comprehension and uses of language, including how the components of language interact to create discourse and regulate its understanding). Use of nonformal assessment methods leads to a more complete picture of each child's strengths, weaknesses, capacities, and abilities regarding the use of language.

Chapter 7

Obtaining Samples of Students' Communication

INTRODUCTION

This chapter examines the sampling of a student's language for analysis. It is important to obtain a representative sample. Gallagher (1983) has noted that, in order for a sample to be representative, it must be comprehensive, typical, and optimal. By *comprehensive*, we take Gallagher to mean that the sample should capture in a reliable way the wide range of language comprehension and production of which the student is capable. The sample should also include comprehension and production of language that is *typical* of the student's everyday interactions in the classroom. Finally, the sample should include at least one instance of *optimal* understanding and production of language. Optimal behavior may or may not be accessible at a given point in time; therefore, we recommend substituting at least one instance of the student's most effective language behavior. According to the parallel focus concept presented in Chapter 5, what behavior is most effective is decided jointly by the clinician and other team members. Note that *typical* and *most effective* do not necessarily mean the same. A typical sample can capture what the child is least competent with, while a most effective sample is informative only about situations in which competence is displayed. In any case, what is typical and what is most effective should be agreed on collaboratively. Further, the samples collected for each student should include a wide range of language functions, forms, and content in order to accurately reflect a student's repertoire.

MULTIPLE CONTEXTS

Wilkinson (1982) has suggested that an accurate assessment of students' knowledge of language usage in the classroom should be examined in relevant *multiple contexts.* We cannot assume that language comprehension or production considered appropriate in one context entails that the student will produce appropriate language or understand it in another context. Contexts must be carefully scrutinized so that appropriate ones will be selected in order to provide students with opportunities to demonstrate their most effective performances.

Gallagher (1983) developed a preassessment questionnaire to discover those contexts in which children were most likely to produce language that is typical, optimal, and reflective of all that they know about language. Her questionnaire was developed for a nonschool setting, it was intended to be administered to caregivers (teachers and parents), and it was designed to provide information about children's communication problems as manifested in particular contexts. It may be adaptable for the school setting, however. Using information gathered by means of the questionnaire, Gallagher identified contexts in which to obtain three samples of children's language. Two samples were to be collected in conversational contexts associated with children's high production of language, and the third sample was to be elicited in a clinician-child dyad designed to maximize language production. The important point is that deriving samples of language from more than one context can yield important information about children's language abilities (Gallagher, 1983).

SAMPLING

Once collaborators decide which aspects of students' language are to be explored, the next step is to plan how to take samples so that the production of these aspects of language can be observed in the contexts in which they occur. How can classroom collaborators develop procedures to take samples? The kind of sampling procedure employed needs to be decided on ahead of time. Two sampling procedures, time sampling and event sampling, are discussed below. Each procedure, when correctly used, will help to capture representative samples of students' language that can then be analyzed in order to determine the presence, extent, or nature of a communication problem or changes in how a communication problem "looks" as a function of intervention.

Time Sampling

Time sampling is used when we are interested in the occurrence or nonoccurrence of a particular action or behavior within a specified time period. Wright (1960), a pioneer in this field, has this to say: "The length, spacing, and number of intervals are intended to secure representative samples of the target phenomenon. As a rule, descriptive categories are coded in advance for quick and precise judgments in the field and later efficient scoring" (p. 93). Thus, the time sampling procedure is used most often for frequently occurring actions that can be observed and noted in real time as opposed to time slowed down or repeated, such as through the playback of a tape recording.

An example of time sampling follows. Suppose that you are interested in a second grader's ability to make requests during reading lessons at school. First, listen in on what that student says during the first ten seconds of every five-minute period throughout a given reading lesson to see if that student produced any requests at all. It is necessary to have already decided how to identify requests (e.g., yes/no questions, want/need statements, wh-questions), so that you only have to note whether any occurred. You can record the occurrences of requests on a form such as the one displayed in Exhibit 7-1. At the end of the lesson, you would only have to count up the number of ten-second periods during which a request occurred. If that total is then divided by the total number of ten-second periods during which the student was observed, the result is the percentage of time during which the child made requests.

Alternatively, a record can be kept of different kinds of requests (see Exhibit 7-2). During the observation period, whether or not each particular kind of request occurred must be noted. The sampling does not yield information on the

Exhibit 7-1   Time Sampling Form A: Requests during Reading Lessons

---

Student's Name:

Reading Lesson Periods

9:00   9:05   9:10   9:15   9:20   9:25   9:30

Note: Place a check mark in each lesson time period when the student produces at least one request.

Exhibit 7-2   Time Sampling Form B: Kinds of Requests during Reading Lessons

---

Student's Name:

Reading Lesson Periods

9:00   9:05   9:10   9:15   9:20   9:25   9:30

Note: In each lesson time period, place a Y if a yes/no question is produced by the student, place a W if a wh-question is produced, and place an N if a want/need statement is produced.

---

total number of requests made. After tallying up the kinds of requests over all time periods, you would have an idea as to whether the student has a tendency to produce only certain kinds of requests.

Decisions about taking samples will influence the kind of data collected and the kinds of questions that can ultimately be answered. For example, if there is only information about whether a request has occurred and not about the kind of request, it is not possible to answer questions later about the variety or complexity of requests the student produces.

There are several issues concerning the way time is used in a time sampling procedure. These include determining the length of the observation for that day, the sequence of the observation, and the distribution of the observation. For example, if there is interest in how a student uses language to communicate with the teacher, it is necessary to select academic activities over a longer interval, such as a week, so that the student has sufficient opportunity to talk with the teacher.

One kind of time sampling method, *short-interval sampling*, permits examining the duration of time in which a specific kind of language production occurred. This method makes it possible to discover that, for example, 70 percent of all requests were yes/no questions and only 20 percent were wh-questions. To use this method, the following need to be specified: the length of time overall (e.g., 45 minutes), the beginning point (e.g., the beginning of the reading lesson), and the interval during which the specific language production will be recorded (e.g., every 5 minutes). In this type of sampling, it is important to try to determine how many intervals have to be sampled in order for the sample to be truly representative and how long the observation period must be in order to obtain an accurate ratio of the different kinds of behavior. This method allows us to answer questions such as this: Of all the contacts between the teacher and a student during a given period, what percentage included the use of requests? Short-interval sampling does not permit finding out the actual number of instances of each kind of request.

The second kind of time sampling method is the *small-segment method*, in which small segments of time are taken from the general observational period by using checklists and rating scales. This method, unlike the other, allows notation of each occurrence of the target action (e.g., asking a wh-question). This makes it possible to find out if 50 percent of all the requests produced by a student were wh-questions. It is not possible, however, to answer questions about duration or what preceded or followed a particular action. The language event itself, such as the request, is taken out of the natural stream of speech.

Advantages

Time sampling can be a very efficient method for observing a particular student, but three elements must be decided in advance: (1) the definitions of the actions or behaviors of interest, (2) the intervals of observation, and (3) the coding system and recording format. Time sampling is best used when it is not possible to write everything down but classroom collaborators are interested in obtaining a representative sample that will provide clues about the nature of a student's language problem or changes in how a student is using the language system.

The advantages of using time sampling are many. It can allow focusing on one aspect of a student's problem, thereby enabling one to determine if the problem occurs in some classroom activities but not others. Second, it can provide a way to determine how often the problem occurs and which contexts and activities offer the best opportunity for intervention. Third, it is efficient and cost-effective; it allows the collection of a relatively large number of samples in a relatively short period of time in comparison with other methods. Fourth, it permits collection of information about a student's language production without having to establish rapport with the student, and this can be a great help in some situations. Finally, it readily provides information that can be used for both quantitative and qualitative summaries and analyses.

Disadvantages

The disadvantages of time sampling are significant. First, since time sampling by definition breaks up the natural stream of behavior, the samples are taken out of context and out of sequence. Interpretation of the meaning of these verbal actions can be difficult, since so little is known about what these actions mean in context. Second, time sampling should be used only with actions or behaviors that occur frequently. Third, since time sampling requires the use of predetermined categories, there could be a bias toward finding certain actions or behaviors, even when they may not be there, instead of accurately describing what really occurred. Validity can be a problem with time sampling. Finally, the information collected seldom reveals any cause-effect relationships; it can be noted that a noneffective request has been produced, but the reason why remains unknown.

Event Sampling

Event sampling allows the recording of a particular behavior or the behaviors within a given category each time they spontaneously occur. It is possible to note when the events of interest occur and what behaviors occur before the events. The main advantage of event sampling is that it allows one to observe events as they naturally occur in real contexts. It is important to develop a form and to carefully plan out how to record each target event, noting aspects of context, such as what came before and after the event. The focus of observation must be decided upon, and then possible contexts in which observation would occur can be determined. Only then can events be sampled in a representative way.

In contrast to time sampling, event sampling specifies a focus of observation, such as reading groups, activities involving the whole class, or individual activities, but it does not specify the length of observation. The length of observation is determined by the event itself. For example, if there is interest in a child's narrative production, then recording would start at the moment or just before the narrative starts and would continue until the narrative is completed.

The Flanders System can be used, for example, in an event sample taken in a reading lesson (Exhibit 7-3). Using this system, the following questions could be answered: How much do the students talk in comparison to the teacher? How likely are students to respond to questions?

Advantages

The primary advantage of using event sampling is that it allows the sampling of events in natural units. The events of interest, such as narratives produced during sharing time, are not broken up artificially by the imposition of an arbitrary unit of time. A child's narrative is recorded until it ceases. Event sampling preserves the sense of time and context and includes the events that lead up to

Exhibit 7-3   Event Sampling Form

Student's Name:
Flanders Language in the Classroom

Category	Category Description
1	Accepts students' feelings
2	Praises/encourages students
3	Accepts students' ideas
4	Asks questions
5	Lectures
6	Gives directions
7	Criticizes/justifies authority
8	Student talk—narrow
9	Student talk—broad
10	Silence

Note: Place a checkmark after each category when the teacher or student produces language in that category.

Source: From *Analyzing Teaching Behavior*, (p. 34) by N. Flanders, 1970, Menlo Park, CA: Addison-Wesley Publishing Co. Copyright 1970 by Addison-Wesley Publishing Co. Reprinted with permission.

and follow the event of interest. A second advantage is that this method can also provide information on factors affecting, for example, the narrative skill and can indicate appropriate intervention strategies. Third, event sampling requires relatively little time. With a well-thought-out plan and an understanding of where and when events are most likely to occur, the observation can be directed to just those opportunities. A fourth advantage of event sampling is that it is versatile and not limited, as is time sampling, to those behaviors that frequently and regularly occur.

Disadvantages

Information collected from event sampling may not be as easy to quantify as information collected from time sampling. More time may need to be spent analyzing what has been recorded in order to answer the questions posed. Finally, event sampling still chops up the naturally occurring stream of behavior, even though it takes a larger slice of context. It is possible that team members may not be able to fully answer some questions because of the limitations on context imposed by this method of taking a sample. It is, however, significantly better in preserving context than is time sampling, which fails to respect contextual aspects of the event.

THE USE OF TECHNOLOGICAL AIDS

As noted in Chapter 6, the ability to hear and see language as it is typically produced by students in the classroom is severely limited due to our own information-processing limitations. For example, we can only attend to one thing at a time. Technological aids (e.g., audiotape, videotape, videodisc records, film recordings, timers to switch machines on and off while sampling, voice-activated microphones, and dictating tape recorders) can be of great help. An observer focuses the camera and microphone on a child or children from a particular viewpoint, but there are not preset category systems through which communication is filtered prior to recording and analysis. Segments of the tape can be reviewed or even transcribed subsequent to recording, and multiple analytical systems can be applied to answer diagnostic or intervention questions.

Advantages of Technology

Most clinicians are probably aware of how technology can aid observation by extending our ability to see and hear. Most are also familiar with another advantage of technological aids. Through the use of these aids, it becomes possible to analyze multiple levels of a child's communication system and, in the case of video recordings, to examine the contextual effects of interaction on that system.

For example, by using video recording, hidden aspects of communication are made visible, such as the role of nonverbal signals in facilitating comprehension or how the reactions of other conversational partners may affect a child's ability to revise easily what he or she has just said.

In many school situations, these technological aids are not used routinely for three reasons: (1) the analysis of recorded observations may be too time-consuming given the range of service responsibilities; (2) confidentiality procedures for recording an entire class may not be worked out; or (3) certain pieces of equipment may not be available. Because classroom collaboration requires a shared frame of reference about classroom communicative contexts and individual students' ability to function within those contexts, technological aids become a necessity for the development of skill in observation. As discussed in Chapter 11, not every sample of interaction requires the level of detailed analysis permitted by a transcription. However, becoming a more accurate observer cannot readily be facilitated without the assistance of technology.

Accuracy is undoubtedly increased using technological records, because the observer can analyze the sample again and again. Other individuals can also review the record and a percentage agreement can then be calculated. The final advantage is that the observer can develop a sense of both the child's typical and most effective patterns of language comprehension and production by using analyses of technological records. It may be the case that rarely does the child produce particular sets of forms or functions, and when he or she does, they may be difficult to detect and examine. A record of all that is produced provides more complete information from which the clinician and other classroom collaborators can glean a sense of the child's true communicative repertoire, including the strategies available to comprehend and use language across different learning activities.

Disadvantages of Technology

Using technology to assist the analysis of language does have some disadvantages as well. An obvious one is that making a technological record and subsequently analyzing it involves a large investment of time. The observer would not be able to have the analysis completed in as short a period of time as on-line analyses, such as rating scales and checklists.

A second disadvantage is that using technology can be expensive. While the price of both audio and video recording equipment has decreased considerably during the two decades since they were introduced into language research (e.g., Bloom, 1970), nevertheless, an investment is needed for both the purchase and maintenance of equipment. Some training in the actual use of equipment is recommended. An introduction to the appropriate use of equipment in classrooms for recording students' use of language is included in Appendix C.

A third drawback of using technological records is that the introduction of equipment into a classroom can be considered intrusive by students and some members of the collaborative team and could distort the activities going on. Dollaghan and Miller (1986) have introduced the concept of "observer intrusiveness" to refer to a variety of influences, "including such disparate factors as the physical presence of a camera, microphone, or observer within view of the participants and the comments provided to these subjects" (p. 113).

There are some corrective steps that observers can take to reduce the potential disruptive effects of observer intrusiveness. Masling and Stern (1969) found that students eventually adjust to the presence of an observer providing that both the equipment and the observer had been present in the classroom for some period of time prior to the actual recording of data. One clue to the potential disruptive effect of observer intrusiveness is the presence of comments by those being observed about the equipment or the observers. Once these comments become infrequent, the collaborative team can be reasonably sure that classroom business has returned to normal.

The final drawback of using technological records is that they are not spontaneous. It is necessary to plan to make audio and video recordings. If something occurs on the spot, the only choice may be to write it down or try to remember it, unless the equipment happens to be set up for recording.

GUIDELINES FOR USING TECHNOLOGICAL AIDS

There are five easy guidelines to follow in determining when to use technological aids for observation. First, they should be used when the communication is unfolding so quickly that it simply cannot be reliably heard and written down in real time. Examples include situations involving an individual child who is hard to understand or several children who frequently overlap their speaking turns. Aspects of speech and language occur so quickly and unfold so rapidly that hearing all features is impossible.

Second, technological aids should be used when the language and communicative behaviors of interest are so complex that all aspects of language and communication cannot be focused on simultaneously. For example, a child may compensate for communicative failures by using gestures, which can be misunderstood or missed by observers.

Third, technological aids should be used when action changes subtly so that delineation between the stages is not possible without slowing down the record. One example of this is the integration of gaze behavior and speech, which is the focus of research done by Merritt (1982a). Gaze may shift more rapidly and subtly than speech, and a record available for fine-grained analysis could be helpful to the clinician and other team members in this regard.

Fourth, technology is helpful when sequential changes are so complex that it is virtually impossible to record and analyze speech in real time. There may be a sequence of behaviors associated with communication breakdown, and the changes may be taking place at several levels (verbal, nonverbal, gestural, and paralinguistic) and may unfold very rapidly and in sequence. A technological record provides the opportunity for the observer to look over very carefully what actually took place and to segment the elements associated with disrupted or successful communication. Analysis of communicative successes could be contrasted with breakdowns to disentangle the elements associated with failure. Opportunities for effective intervention could be identified with this type of analysis.

Finally, technological aids can be used to measure a specific parameter of complex language-communicative patterns. For example, you may want to look at the frequency and patterning of false starts, which may be one potential element contributing to communication breakdown. This parameter may be embedded in a complex pattern. Without the verbatim record to examine in detail, false starts tend to be edited from what is seen and heard (Ochs, 1979a).

CONCLUSION

In sum, technology provides a variety of instruments that can be used to make permanent records for analysis at a later time. Technological aids have become more available in most clinical facilities and, increasingly, in schools because of their relatively low cost and ease of use.

In accord with the observation lens model described in Chapter 1, technological aids offer the observer a choice of wide, medium, and narrow focuses that can be directed at particular language and communicative patterns of interest. The making of technological records prior to initiating intervention can provide an accurate basis for comparing before and after. Records can be shared, and different types of analyses can be applied. Technological aids also reduce the observers' dependence on typical instances of language and communication that can be seen in real time. Records preserve the typical as well as the most effective instances, which may occur less frequently.

Chapter 8

Examining Students' Communication: Categorical Tools

In this and the next two chapters, we introduce three kinds of tools that can be used to systematically examine students' language use in school. All of the tools to be discussed have the same basic aim: to capture students' actual language use so that it can be studied and inferences and conclusions can be drawn. Applying the components of the observational lens model, we can consider each kind of observational tool as a different lens with which to examine students' language. Learning to focus all of these tools requires some knowledge of how to use these lenses and practical experience in applying them.

Our first goal is to discuss three kinds of observational tools that can be used for studying children's communicative interactions. We also provide some examples of the kind of information that can be collected. It should be noted that our aim is not to describe which tool should be selected for particular purposes. In the following chapters, we provide more information about how to use the tools correctly and efficiently so that questions about students can be answered as completely as possible.

KINDS OF TOOLS

One important distinction to keep in mind in selecting tools is the distinction between qualitative and quantitative methods. Quantitative methods are characterized by the use of neutral scientific language that is free from context-bound, everyday language. Quantitative researchers seek to report facts unaffected by their values, and their goal is to describe, explain, and predict relationships among a succession of objects and events that occur within classrooms.

In contrast, qualitative methods are characterized by the use of everyday language and focus on what is unique and true at a given time and place. Values are reflected in the reporting, and there can be no facts without particular values reflected in them. Qualitative researchers also seek an understanding of what goes on in classrooms. They believe that understanding is obtained by knowing and experiencing what happens to others within that unique and particular context.

Evertson and Green (1986) have classified observational tools into the following categories: (1) narrative, (2) categorical, and (3) descriptive. *Narrative tools* are open systems that do not have preset categories, and they allow the recording of broad segments of events and behaviors in either oral and/or written form (e.g., a diary). In contrast, *categorical tools* are closed systems that have definite preset categories into which all events and behaviors are coded during the observation; the coded categories are then added up in some manner, so that the observation can be described in a quantitative way (e.g., the Flanders System). *Descriptive tools* are open systems. Streams of behavior, both verbal and nonverbal, are recorded in everyday language, or some other symbol system is used, such as phonetic transcription of speech forms. Central to descriptive systems is the use of transcriptions of the stream of behavior for the purposes of both quantitative and qualitative analyses (e.g., the excerpts in Chapter 4 of classroom and clinical discourse).

All observational tools have these common elements:

1. *A focus of observation.* Whom do you look at or listen to (teacher, child, or both)? What activities, materials, or environmental factors do you record?

2. *A content focus.* What do you want to learn about? Is the focus motor development, social-emotional development, cognitive development, the physical environment, or learning activities?

3. *A coding unit.* What units should be to be chosen to describe the behavior (e.g., requests versus attentionals, tag questions versus wh-questions, story grammar versus propositions, etc.)? How long do you observe before recording and over how long a period do you observe?

4. *A means to record data.* How do you record data? On audiotape, videotape, or with paper and pencil?

5. *A setting.* Where do you record? In the classroom, playroom, or playground?

6. *A purpose.* Why are you observing? Is it to evaluate a child's strengths and weaknesses, evaluate a program, train other people, or conduct a research project?

In selecting the kind of tool that is to be used, each of these elements will need to be carefully considered. Only then can the most appropriate tools be selected to meet your needs.

General Guidelines for Observation

Irwin and Bushnell (1980) provide some basic guidelines for observation that apply no matter which particular tool is chosen. The first rule is to make a clear distinction between what has been seen or heard actually and the conclusions drawn from it. People have a tendency to embellish or see things from their own perspective and to fill in details that may not be there. Second, Irwin and Bushnell suggest that the observer try to observe from the viewpoint of the person being studied. The third rule is not to draw any conclusions that are not backed up by observed facts.

CATEGORICAL TOOLS

Categorical tools are used by researchers when they want to examine communicative interactions across a wide variety of settings and to obtain information about the typical occurrences in which children comprehend or use communication in those settings. From a research perspective, this information may be useful in predicting the future patterns of language production. Because categorical tools focus less attention on individual children and particular patterns of speech, these tools may be of limited use to clinicians and other members of the collaborative team who are interested solely in individual variation. Nevertheless, categorical tools may be useful in providing collaborators with ways to understand certain communicative patterns and problems.

The purpose of any assessment is to provide information that can aid in the decision process relative to particular children. Categorical tools are often used to provide information about many children; however, in their use, it may become obvious that there are some children about whom more information is needed.

Categorical tools are used to record selective behaviors. These behaviors are noted on worksheets or formats and, at a later point, may be counted up and summarized in a numerical representation, such as an overall rating, a summary score, a ranking, a frequency count, or a percentage.

As you will recall, in Chapter 6 the Flanders System of Interaction Analysis (Flanders, 1970) was introduced. The Flanders System is a good example of a categorical tool. First, the units have been derived deductively and prior to the actual observation of children and teachers. Flanders had a conception of what was important in teacher-led discussions; therefore, the teacher is the primary focus of the observation, and Flanders dedicated seven of the ten categories to describing the teacher's speech and action. Second, units in the Flanders System reflect a behavioral approach; each unit represents a variety of particular forms. For example, the verbal aspects of teaching are reflected in seven of the Flanders categories; within each one, many kinds of utterances and actions are included. Finally, units are either discrete (i.e., each behavior can be placed in only one category, as in the case of the Flanders System) or they are continuous (e.g., observed behavior falls between two points on a continuum, as in the case of moderate talkativeness, which falls between talkativeness and taciturnity).

Categorical tools can be very helpful in the collaborative process. For example, the clinician, using the wide-angle lens of observation, may be able to discover a general pattern of language use among a group of children and contrast that with the language use of one child in a variety of settings. An application is provided by Genishi and Dyson (1984), who devised a checklist for describing children's oral language (Exhibit 8-1). Other applications are presented in this chapter.

Exhibit 8-1 Checklist for Observing Children's Use of Oral Language

	Situations	
In each of the following situations:	*Informal Interactions*	*Formal Interactions*
Does the child willingly participate orally?		
Does the child listen attentively to others?		
Are the child's contributions • relevant to the topic? • responsive to others?		
Does the child speak fluently with apparent ease?		
Does the child speak audibly? Too loudly?		
Does the child use nonstandard forms?		
Does the child demonstrate an ability to change language style (word choice, pronunciation), particularly in role-playing activities?		

Source: From *Language Assessment in the Early Years* (p. 204) by C. Genishi and A. Dyson, 1984, Norwood, NJ: Ablex Publishing Corporation. Copyright 1984 by Ablex Publishing Corporation. Reprinted by permission.

TYPES OF CATEGORICAL TOOLS

The types of categorical tools discussed below include category systems, checklist systems, and rating systems. The choice of which tool will depend on several factors, including the availability of information, the amount of time and other resources that need to be expended on observation, and the goals of observation.

Category Systems

Category systems are used by observers to record naturally occurring talk in specific settings. All category systems contain preset categories into which all behaviors are classified. Thus, category systems are essentially classification systems and are used as the events under observation unfold. They can be used during live observation or while reviewing audio or video recordings. These systems seem to work best when a low degree of inference is required in classifying behavior into categories. In other words, they work best when the observer sees a close relationship between behavior as it actually occurs and the coding system. Preparation and training prior to observation are required for adequate use of category systems. Observers need to develop and test each tool before using it for observation.

Requests and Revisions

An example of a category system is the system developed by Wilkinson and Calculator (1982) in studies of effective speakers in grades 1–3.

Wilkinson and Calculator developed the concept of the *effective speaker*, someone who uses knowledge of language forms, functions, and contexts to achieve communicative goals (Wilkinson & Calculator, 1982; Wilkinson & Spinelli, 1982). For example, in the case of requests for action, effective speakers are successful in obtaining from listeners appropriate responses to their requests. Wilkinson and Calculator proposed the model of the effective speaker in order to analyze the use of requests and responses by young children. The model identifies the following characteristics of requests that predict obtaining appropriate responses from listeners (Exhibit 8-2). First, speakers may express acts clearly and directly in an attempt to minimize ambiguity and multiple interpretations of the same speech. For example, speakers may use *direct* forms and specifically *designate* them to one particular listener when making a request. Second, in the classroom, requests that are *on task*, that is, those that refer to shared activities in the teaching-learning situation, are the most likely to be understood by listeners, and thus these types of requests are the most likely to be successful in obtaining compliance from listeners. Third, requests that are understood by

Exhibit 8-2   Request Characteristics of the Effective Speaker

---

1. Direct: Use of linguistic forms that directly signal the speaker's needs. For requests for action, the imperative or I want/I need statements; for requests for information, the wh-, yes-no, or tag question.

2. Designated to a listener: Unambiguously indicates the intended listener through verbal or nonverbal means.

3. Sincere: A request is sincere if (a) the action, purpose, and need for the request are clear; for example, in a request for information, the listener believes that the speaker really wants the information and does not already know the information; (b) there is both an ability and an obligation of the listener to respond to the request; and (c) the speaker has a right to make the request.

4. Revised if unsuccessful: A restatement of a request previously made by the same speaker to the same listener who had not responded appropriately.

5. On task: Related to the academic content or procedures and materials of the assignment.

6. Responded to appropriately: The requested action or information was given or else a reason was given why the action and/or information could not be given.

Source: From *Communicating in the Classroom*, (p. 92) by L.C. Wilkinson (Ed.), 1982, New York: Academic Press. Copyright 1982 by Academic Press. Reprinted by permission.

---

listeners as *sincere* are most likely to result in compliance. Finally, effective speakers are flexible in producing their requests; for example, speakers should *revise* their initial request when compliance from listeners is not obtained.

For each subject in Wilkinson and Calculator's studies, the proportion of requests having each characteristic was calculated. For the purpose of illustrating the amount of variability among subjects and the range of scores for each characteristic, the symbols in Figure 8-1 summarize these distributions as follows: The black circles indicate the lowest and highest proportions obtained among the subjects for a given characteristic; the dashed bar indicates the proportional values corresponding to the 10th and the 90th percentiles of the sample (e.g., 10 percent of the children used direct forms 46 percent of the time or less; 10 percent used them 92 percent of the time or more); and the box indicates the interquartile range, with the median represented by the solid bar in the middle (e.g., half of the sample used direct forms between 55 percent and 72 percent of the time, with a median value of 61 percent).

Some interesting patterns in this figure can be noted. Scores for sincerity and on-task relevance were generally high and of limited variability. Thus, there seems to be a common competence among normally developing children regarding these request characteristics. The remaining four characteristics show much greater variability in scores and a generally lower average performance. The

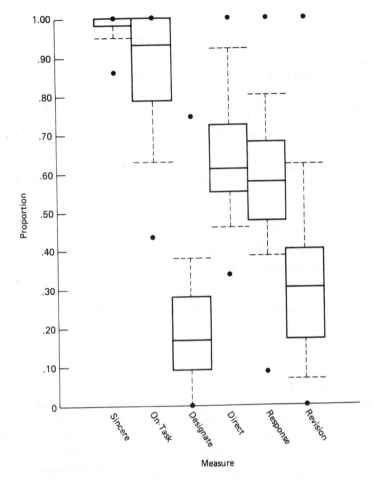

Figure 8-1 Profile of Characteristics of Effective Speakers: Entire Classroom. *Source:* Reprinted from *Topics in Language Disorders*, Vol. 6, No. 2, p. 63, Aspen Publishers, Inc., © 1986.

variability suggests genuine individual differences in the degree to which requests are direct, designated, revised, and obtain appropriate responses.

Figure 8-2 displays the profiles of two children, Juanita and Enrique, regarding the request characteristics. Juanita is an effective speaker, as defined by the Wilkinson model; that is, she usually obtains appropriate responses to her requests (78 percent of the time). She designates many more requests to specific listeners than do other students in this class, and she uses direct forms frequently; her requests are generally on task and sincere. Juanita assumes the role of the leader of the group and its taskmaster, pacing the other students and allotting tasks for each to do. She is in the top half of her class in reading achieve-

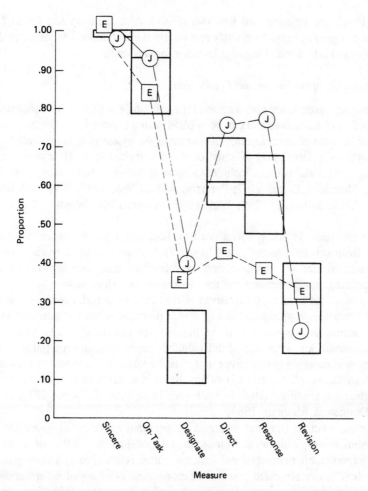

Figure 8-2 Profiles of Juanita (J) and Enrique (E): Individual Differences in Characteristics of Effective Speakers. *Source:* Reprinted from *Topics in Language Disorders*, Vol. 6, No. 2, p. 66, Aspen Publishers, Inc., © 1986.

ment, and she is in the 90th percentile on vocabulary as measured by the Peabody Picture Vocabulary Test.

Enrique's profile suggests a markedly different quality in interaction with other students. He is an ineffective speaker, since he obtains appropriate responses to his requests only 40 percent of the time, and the profile shows that he does not designate his requests to particular listeners.

Other category systems for assessing the pragmatic functioning of language learning impaired children in the nonschool setting can be found in the work of

Fey (1986) and Prutting and Kirchner (1987). Also, Brinton and Fujiki (1989) utilize category systems to classify and interpret clarification requests and the revisions of children with language learning impairments.

Narrative Comprehension and Production

Category systems are also a means for analyzing students' comprehension and production of narratives and can be applied with a narrow focus for this purpose. A brief account of the relevance of narratives for assessment is presented below, followed by a description of some of the categorical tools. (For more detailed reading, additional sources include: Gordon & Braun, 1985; Lahey, 1988; Liles, 1987; Merritt & Liles, 1987; Peterson & McCabe, 1983; Roth & Spekman, 1986, 1989; Silliman, 1989; Wallach & Miller, 1988; Westby, 1984, 1985, 1989.)

The rationale for using narratives as a research, educational, or clinical tool arises from several sources (see Chapter 2). Narratives can be readily solicited, are a natural kind of discourse, and are related to classroom activities, particularly reading comprehension and the composing of written stories.

The practical aspect of narratives is reflected in two dimensions. First, because narratives represent a kind of social problem solving (Stein, 1983), they can function as a window into the planning of discourse. To be planful as a speaker means knowing that (1) individuals' communications are purposeful; (2) others have multiple perspectives that must be taken into account in formulating communicative plans; and (3) others have internal states, such as motives, thoughts, and emotions (Roth & Spekman, 1986; Stein & Glenn, 1979; Westby, Van Dongen, & Maggart, 1989).

Stories, whether fictional or based on personal experiences, share the same communicative planfulness. Stories are temporal-causal chains of events that have a predictable organizational structure, often referred to as a *story grammar*. An "ideal" story structure consists of categories, or types of information, that specify the important elements of a story, relate their interconnections, and cue the retrieval of information in the context of the story structure (Gordon & Braun, 1985). For example, a story consists of information on the setting (time, place, characters, etc.) and the episodes (which develop and link the thematic relationships). An episode can contain a number of elements (Gordon & Braun, 1985; Roth & Spekman, 1986): (1) an *initiating event* or beginning event that causes a response on the part of the character(s); (2) an *internal response*, which represents how a character feels as a result of the initiating event; (3) an *action*, or an attempt to reach a goal or subgoal; (4) a *consequence*, an outcome of the action, whether intended or not; (5) a *reaction*, a feeling, thought, or action in response to the outcome, attempt, or initiating event; and (6) a *resolution*, which expresses the final result and may be inferred rather than explicitly stated. According to Gordon and Braun (1985), not all six subcategories are found in every episode. Moreover, they do not always occur in the order outlined above. For an episode to be complete, however, it must contain at a minimum an initiating event, an action, and a consequence, whether specifically stated or implied.

Mature narratives show certain key elements. Causal events are linked sequentially (temporally) through (1) the purposes or intentions of the characters, (2) the actions that the characters take to reach their goals, and (3) how the results (outcomes) of their actions affect their purposes (Gordon & Braun, 1985; Stein & Glenn, 1979). In both oral and printed narratives, the interaction between story purpose (function), story content (theme or topic), and story structure (story grammar) is the framework for guiding the understanding of information (Gordon & Braun, 1985; Stein, 1982, 1983). Narratives function, therefore, as a real-life demonstration of the interactive nature of discourse comprehension (Stein, 1982; Stein & Glenn, 1979).

A second reason for the practical interest in narratives stems from the opportunity they afford to observe the dynamics of the oral-literate continuum mentioned in Chapters 1 and 2 (Biber, 1988; Scott, 1988a; Westby, 1984, 1985). Language learning disabled children tend to produce "oral" style narratives (Merritt & Liles, 1987; Westby, 1984) that differ in principle from the oral style narratives of many cultural minority children (Cazden, Michaels, & Tabors, 1985; Gee, 1985; Michaels, 1981, 1986; Michaels & Cazden, 1986). Compared with the more "literate," topic-centered narratives of mainstream children, the narratives of some cultural minority children seemed to be characterized by topic association (see Chapter 3). In this kind of narrative, temporal events are not directly linked in causal ways to the narrative theme. Instead, the narrative tends to be a "concrete narrative . . . [whose] meandering away from the 'point' takes the listener on episodic journeys" (Cazden et al., 1985, p. 58, citing Smitherman, 1977). Because causal connections often have to be inferred, comprehension difficulties can be created for teachers or clinicians who may not share the same interpretative schema.

The oral style narratives of language learning disabled students, on the other hand, appear to be based on different grounds, as illustrated from an excerpt of a personal experience narrative by George, a 15-year-old male. His communicative problems had not been previously diagnosed in spite of years of academic failure and a history of language delay. The narrative is a recounting of a horror movie he had seen recently (notations are explained in Appendix B):

> It was all a joke = you know it was/ Um - it was like these people from
> college right=and they were . . . and they were going to this house
> right (.) to live and do their work = ya know/ And then one of them
> started playing around ya know playing jokes on each other = it was a
> whole big joke at the end/ Um - it was (.) really about like (.) ya know/
> It was (.) scarey ya know/ Cause (.) you know/ Cause (.) ya know I
> thought it was all silly and then it started to get serious/ (EPISODE 1)

First of all they were on the boat right onna ferry right/ And this guy
started playing with a knife right -- a switch blade = so the guy threw
it at him right/ And then (.) ... and then they got stabbed um - and
didn't right/ And then the guy falls in the water cleaning it off right (.)
and you could see the blood coming down and everything/ People
dove in there right (.) thinking they were serious/ They came back out
ya know thinking it was all a joke right/ (EPISODE 2)

Then after that = right the guy was swimming around in the water
right (.) and b -- they were getting ready to dock the um - ferry/ And
um - you know like (.) and um - the guy like (.) -- the ferry was coming up to the guy right/ It was all a big joke right/ You know/ It happened to um - you know/ It happened that -- everyone started pulling
jokes on each other but at the end the joke was on two people right (.)
ya know (.) um - (.) ya know/ (EPISODE 3) (Narrative continues
through nine more episodes.)

The style of this kind of narrative has been attributed to three sources of difficulty (Liles, 1987; Merritt & Liles, 1987; Montague, Maddux, & Dereshiwsky,
1990; Roth & Spekman, 1986; Silliman, 1989; Wallach & Miller, 1988; Westby,
1989; Westby et al., 1989; also see Chapter 12). One source is the problem with
role, or perspective-taking. False assumptions are made about what the listener
needs to know because of difficulty in explicitly inferring the listener's state of
comprehension. Another source originates in the problems encountered in organizing the elements of discourse, in making the parts fit together in a cohesive
way. As the discussion in Chapter 2 suggested, these organizational issues may
be related to the less flexible retrieval of narrative schemas that match the situation and combine the temporal-causal relations that linguistically anchor a narrative to its theme. A third source, shown in the segment from George's narrative,
involves planning. In this instance, planning refers to how adequately George
monitors his own comprehension of where he is in the narrative in order to anticipate where he should be going to make the point of the story.

Category Systems in Narrative Analysis

Narratives are solicited typically by two types of activities: *story recall*, often
referred to as "gist" recall, and *story production*. Story recall is used as a means
for assessing the recognition and comprehension of story structure, particularly
the understanding of fictional stories. Story production in theory is more difficult, because, unlike story recall, narrative structure and content must be self-
generated and organized (Westby, 1989). Whether narrative recall and narrative
production yield comparable information for clinical purposes has not been sat-
isfactorily resolved (Merritt & Liles, 1989; Silliman, 1989). Resolution depends,
to some extent, on how narratives are analyzed.

Narrative structure has been the focal point of analysis in research and its clinical applications, most typically through the analysis of episode organization and the cohesion of its propositions and clauses within and across episode boundaries. Less emphasis has been given to the two other essential areas of narrative development. One concerns the instrumental role played by a story's purpose in guiding the nature of comprehension strategies (Stein, 1983). The other is the prerequisite knowledge needed to understand cause-effect relations in the physical realm (e.g., "The hot sun can cause sunstroke") as well as in the psychological domain (e.g., "Tickling the baby makes her unhappy") (Gordon & Braun, 1985; Westby, 1989).

Episode Organization. Using a close-up lens, narratives can be classified in terms of story grammar categories to examine their internal organization in finer detail. For example, the frequency of use of the various story categories can be analyzed. Frequency of category recall is one indicator of the richness of a child's story schema (Merritt & Liles, 1989). Research findings indicate that, while language learning disabled children encounter more difficulty in obtaining the gist on story recall tasks, the frequency of recall of various story categories does not consistently distinguish them as a group from the performance of nondisabled samples. Both use initiating events and consequences equally frequently and internal responses the least frequently (Merritt & Liles, 1987; Montague et al., 1990; Ripich & Griffith, 1988). The suggestion is that difficulties with inclusion of internal responses persist for language learning disabled children and may account for the problems they encounter in understanding and explaining how actions result from different motivational states (Montague et al., 1990; Ripich & Griffith, 1988; Westby, 1985, 1989).

A consistent finding in studies of narrative production is that language learning disabled children, in comparison with normal children, produce more episodes that are less complete. Consistent with story recall findings, incompleteness tends to be related to the omission of internal responses and actions, both of which contain planning information (Roth & Spekman, 1986). George's narrative illustrates this pattern. He produced a 12-episode story, the first 3 episodes of which have been reproduced. Of the 12 episodes, only 3, including episode 2 above, met the criteria for completeness (i.e., the episode included at least an initiating event, an action, and an outcome). In the case of the 9 incomplete episodes, George most often omitted the action, which would have signaled his awareness that the characters had a plan in mind to reach a goal. As a general rule, he also omitted internal responses.

However, a problem with the use of story grammar as a categorical tool for the analysis of personal experience narratives occurs when the story produced is not well formed structurally. This situation is common to the narratives of many language learning disabled children, including George's. Peterson and McCabe (1983) would classify George's narrative as a series of reactive sequences in which a set of changes appear to cause other changes automatically without any planning involved. In other words, events just happen without any causal connection between them. Others (e.g., Cazden et al., 1985) argue that retelling about movies or television shows, regardless of ethnic and social class differences, typically results in a more oral style of narration. Moreover, ethnicity and social class are confounded with each other and with experience in using literate narrative styles. Still others, such as Gordon and Braun (1985), view a story grammar approach as appropriate only for fictional stories like fairy tales, adventure stories, and myths, because these narrative forms most closely approximate the organization of a story grammar. The better fit of fictional tales with a story grammar may partially explain why language learning disabled children have been found to produce more complete episodes in recalling well-formed fictional stories than in generating their own made-up stories (Merritt & Liles, 1989).

A final caution is given by Roth and Spekman (1989). In applying findings on narrative performance to individual children, the statistical significance of patterns in research studies needs to be distinguished from clinical or educational significance. Statistical significance means only that a difference is present in the performance of language learning disabled versus nondisabled samples. Whether this statistical difference is *diagnostically* significant or merely reflective of normal variation is unknown.

Cohesion. Story categories and episode completeness are concerned with the organizational aspects of story knowledge—its macrostructure. Cohesion refers to the microstructure, the topical continuity, or sequential relatedness, of spoken and written discourse constructed through the semantic devices that explicitly glue meaning together within and across utterance boundaries (Halliday & Hasan, 1976). Cohesion indicates what aspects of the topic are the focus of discussion (Sidner, 1983). Consider this narrative from a second-grade basal reader rewritten by Brennan, Bridge, and Winograd (1986) to make it more cohesive and, hence, more understandable for reading comprehension.

Setting:	Mr. Fig was a happy little man. He liked to play in the grass.
Initiating event:	One afternoon Mr. Fig was in the grass by the house. He saw a big bee fly up and over the house.
Internal response:	Mr. Fig wanted to play with the bee but he could not see the bee. Mr. Fig looked and looked for the bee. The bee was down in the grass.
Attempt:	Mr. Fig saw the bee. He ran over to play with the bee.

Consequence: The bee stung Mr. Fig on the nose.
Reaction: That did not make Mr. Fig very happy. He went in the house and the bee flew away. (p. 104)

In this example, the meaning of what is said can be recovered from the linguistic context of the story. We also know that Mr. Fig and the bee should be the focus of our attention throughout the story. Cohesive ties, such as the pronoun *he* and the lexical reiteration of *bee*, among others, serve as explicit search instructions for deciding what elements of meaning must be kept active as the story unfolds.

Section 4 of Appendix B presents a discussion of three types of cohesion found in this story: *pronominal reference, ellipsis,* and *lexical similarity.* Two other types of cohesion present in the story are *parallel structures,* structures in which either the verb phrase or the lexical content or both are reiterated (e.g., "First John blew a gigantic bubble, and then Mary blew one" [Bennett-Kastor, 1986, p. 354; also see Lahey, 1988]), and *connectives.* Unlike the other types mentioned, connectives do not function as search instructions to recover missing information; rather connectives specify how one set of surface structures, such as adjacent clauses within a narrative (Lahey, 1988), are linked to previous surface structures (Halliday & Hasan, 1976). Their developmental order of acquisition in narrative discourse is similar to the order of acquisition for the coding of meaning relations of complex clauses outside of narratives (Lahey, 1988, p. 280): (1) additive relations—*and* (events occur without any internal relationship); (2) temporal relations—(successive) *then, and then, next, just then, after that;* (simultaneous) *when, while;* (3) causal relations—*so, because, therefore, so that;* (conditional) *if* (or *then*); (4) adversative relations—*but, although, only, however;* and (5) comparative relations—*like, as, similarly.* Lahey notes that the frequency of coding different connective relations within a narrative can vary as a function of the task and topic.

In noncohesive dialogue, the meaning of what is said can only be recovered from sources external to the actual language used, for example, in the background knowledge assumed to be shared by conversational participants. This exchange between a clinician and a language delayed child is an example of noncohesive dialogue:

Clinician: What are you doing, Joey?/ What are you doing?/
Joey: I gonna do it/
Clinician: Ok/ What are you doing though?/

In this instance, Joey was stirring a bowl of whipped cream with a large spoon; hence, meaning is located in the physical actions of the child in a particular situation rather than in what is said. A second example of noncohesive dialogue is George's narrative about the movie he had seen.

The analysis of cohesive bonds in narrative use involves an application of the microclose-up lens. This narrow focus allows exploration of how individual children utilize two interrelated language systems for particular discourse purposes, "the system of meaning expressed as 'culture,' and the symbolic system of language" (Eller, 1989, p. 342). Research on the spoken and written discourse of children from culturally diverse backgrounds, including children from distinct, sociocultural areas, such as rural Appalachia, has emphasized sociolinguistic variations in the expression of meaning relations (e.g., DeStefano & Kantor, 1988; Eller, 1989). In comparison, studies with language learning disabled children have concentrated on the symbolic aspect of cohesive relations. The persisting oral style of narrative organization is also reflected in the less frequent and less adequate use of referential devices and causal connectives to tie episodes together in a logical way within and across episode boundaries (Liles, 1985, 1987; Ripich & Griffith, 1988; Roth & Spekman, 1986).

George's narrative shows the difficulty he is encountering in making his topic hang together. In a number of respects, he unintentionally appears to violate the rules of relevance. For example, over 50 percent of his episodes lacked clear-cut boundaries that would signal a transition from one episode to another. The most frequent semantic marker of transition was the use of *and then*, which denoted events occurring successively in time but not causally related. Problems in clearly interpreting episode boundaries can occur when essential components of episodes are omitted. Furthermore, causal linking across multiple episode boundaries is developmentally complex, because more planning is required to execute the appropriate causal connectives in multiple episode stories (Liles, 1987; Roth & Spekman, 1986). Refinement most likely continues into early adolescence.

George's insufficient use of explicit reference created further comprehension difficulties for the listener (or reader). To illustrate, in his second utterance in episode 1, George uses *people* to refer to the focus of discussion, then several words later he refers to this focus again using the personal pronoun *they*. This cohesive tie clearly points back to *people* and indicates that the two lexical items are intended to have the same referent (DeStefano & Kantor, 1988). Similarly, in the same utterance, the possessive pronoun *their* ties back to *people*. From this point on, however, George rarely uses these "rementioning rules" of reference (Sidner, 1983). Recovering the meaning of what he is communicating becomes nearly impossible, because his source of reference is external to what he is saying; that is, his source of reference is his personal experience with the movie events.

Finally, in the absence of referential cohesion, George displays a tendency toward redundancy, or global parallelism (Bennett-Kastor, 1986), where the syntactic structure and lexical content of entire clauses are repeated. For example, the sentence "It was a whole big joke at the end" that occurs in episode 1 is repeated with some variation at the end of episodes 2 and 3 and throughout other episodes. In addition, 4 of his 12 episodes partially repeat the content of preceding episodes, suggesting that, in this situation, he is less able to apply his linguistic repertoire strategically to express new information in elaborated ways.

The limits of use for cohesion as a categorical tool are given by the current state of knowledge about the discourse-processing relations between narrative organization, cohesive adequacy and inferencing. Liles (1987) points out that inadequate story schemas may be predictive of inadequate cohesion, but more sufficient episode structures do not necessarily predict cohesive adequacy in individual children with language learning disabilities. Some children can infer the temporal-causal relationships that integrate episodes, and they will use more adequate cohesive devices across episode boundaries—but at the expense of episode completeness. Others, such as George, may be less able to infer episode integration but will produce more adequate episodes, which, nevertheless, may still be lacking in richness of detail. In other words, given resource allocation limitations, it may not be possible to attend simultaneously to the plan or purpose of the narrative, its organization, and its cohesive integration.

Facilitating this simultaneous monitoring of spoken discourse may be best approached by incorporating written language tools into intervention (Scott, 1989a, 1989b; Wallach & Miller, 1988). One type of tool is the dialogue journal, which is discussed in the next chapter.

Checklists

A checklist is a second type of categorical tool. This tool is used to obtain a relatively large amount of information in numerical form that will be able to address a general question of interest (e.g., "How often do children ask and answer questions during class?" "Is a particular child more likely to ask or answer questions?"). Checklists are typically used on the spot to record what is going on, but they can be used after the fact by reviewing an audio- or videotape.

Prior to the observation, the observer develops a worksheet or form that includes the checklist and other critical features, such as the name of the child or children to be observed and contextual features (activity, time, placement, rules) that may be important for interpreting the information at a later time. Typically, observers are *not* participants in the activity under observation; in addition, as with category systems, they must be well trained prior to the observation. There is no time for learning on the spot, since decisions about what to check off on the worksheet need to be made with split-second timing during the observation.

Checklists are used when there are preset categories of behavior to be observed, and the observer notes the occurrence or nonoccurrence of the behavior on a worksheet. Irwin and Bushnell (1980) give four guidelines that are useful in developing checklists. First, the checklist needs to be developed and tested in conjunction with other observers, such as members of the collaborative team, who presumably are equally well trained prior to the observation. Second, the specific behaviors of interest should be listed separately on the checklist rather than combined into categories. Combining can always be done later, but data cannot be separated after the actual observation. Third, the checklist should be logically organized so that it is easy to use. Frequent behaviors should be listed near the top of the page, while infrequent behaviors should be listed near the bottom. Finally, the organization of the checklist should be consistent with the stated purposes of the observation. If the interest is a particular child, then there should be a separate worksheet for that child. One cannot assume that because there are 20 children in a class, an accurate description of what a particular child does in the classroom can be arrived at by dividing the total behavior noted on the checklist by 20.

Checklists are often a practical means of documenting children's understanding of particular kinds of communicative interactions as well as their participation in these interactions. They are easy to use, and interpretation takes relatively little time, which is a distinct advantage. However, checklists by themselves do not yield details or insight into a child's communicative repertoire.

Genishi and Dyson's (1984) checklist for oral language has already been discussed in this chapter. Another good example of a checklist that applies to normal and disordered language patterns can be found in the work of Bedrosian (1985). She was interested in developing procedures to assess children's knowledge of discourse skills through conversational analysis that could also be utilized across a wide variety of communicative settings. Her checklist focuses on an individual's communicative performance. Bedrosian suggests that her checklist be used on audio or video recordings of a child in at least two of the following kinds of interactions: child-peer, child-teacher or child-primary caregiver, child-clinician-peer, and child-clinician. Bedrosian also comments that it is important to note the kind of setting in which the interaction occurs, and she expresses a preference for a detailed discourse analysis of the child when the purpose of observation is an initial assessment. However, she also believes that a more global analysis can be helpful. Her "molar" analysis can be used by clinicians when time and resource limitations are primary considerations. Exhibit 8-3 portrays her checklist, Discourse Skills Checklist: A Molar Analysis.

Rating Systems

Using a rating system is a third method of recording observations. With this method, preselected behaviors are identified and judgments are made about the quality of the behavior, such as its dynamic versus static nature or quality. Rating systems are typically used at the end of an observation period to summarize

Exhibit 8-3 Discourse Skills Checklist: A Molar Analysis

Name of client: _____

Date of interaction:_____

Type of participant interaction: _____

Type of setting: _____

Length of interaction: _____

Instructions: Check the appropriate skill descriptors.

	Yes	No	Sometimes	Not Applicable

I. Topic Initiations
  A. Frequency of client's topic initiations in comparison to other participant(s) (check one):
    1. None
    2. Less than
    3. Approximately equal to
    4. More than
  B. Subject matter of topic initiations
    1. Able to get attention of listener
    2. Repeats old topics on a daily basis
    3. Initiates new topics on a daily basis
    4. Able to greet others
    5. Able to express departures when leaving
    6. Able to make introductions
    7. Able to initiate needs
    8. Able to initiate questions
      a. Requests for information
      b. Requests for repetition or clarification
      c. Requests for action
      d. Requests for permission
    9. Talks mostly about self
    10. Talks about the other, as well as self
    11. Talks about referents in the past
    12. Talks about referents in the future
    13. Talks about referents in the present
    14. Talks about fantasy-related referents
    15. Calls people names
    16. Uses noises or sound-word play in appropriate situations
II. Maintaining Topics
  A. Able to keep a topic going
    1. Responds to questions
    2. Acknowledges topic (e.g., "Uh-huh")
    3. Offers new information that is related
    4. Requests more information about a topic

156 Communicating for Learning

Exhibit 8-3 continued

	Yes	No	Sometimes	Not Applicable

    5. Able to ask for repetition or clarification if message is not clear
    6. Able to repeat or answer questions about what another has talked about
    7. Agrees with others
    8. Disagrees with others
  B. Not able to keep a topic going
    1. Intentionally evades or ignores a topic
    2. Initiates a topic immediately following a topic intitiation by a prior speaker
    3. Engages in monologues when in a group
III. Use of Eye Contact
  A. Able to use eye contact to designate a listener in a group when initiating a topic
  B. Uses eye contact while listening
IV. Turn-taking
  A. Is easily interrupted
  B. Interrupts others
  C. Answers questions for others
  D. Has long speaking turns
  E. Designates turns for others in a group
  F. Sensitive to listener cues (e.g., can tell if listener is interested or bored)
  G. Excuses self when interrupting
V. Politeness
  A. Able to make indirect requests
  B. Uses commands
  C. Uses politeness markers "Please," "Thank you," "Excuse me"
VI. Observation of Nonverbal Behaviors
  A. Stands or sits too close to people when talking
  B. Stands or sits too far away from people when talking
  C. Stands or sits at appropriate social distances when talking
  D. Uses nonverbal head nods to acknowledge
  E. Uses nonverbal means of getting attention to initiate a topic (e.g., taps on shoulder, points)

Source: From J. Bedrosian, "An Approach to Developing Conversation Competence" in *School Discourse Problems* (p. 238), by D. Ripich and F. Spinelli, 1985, San Diego, CA: College-Hill Press. Copyright 1985 by College-Hill Press. Reprinted by permission.

the cumulative effect of direct observations. In contrast, category and checklist systems can be coded one by one on the spot. Rating systems are most often used to assess global constructs, such as overall question asking, talkativeness, or literacy awareness.

Not all rating scales are alike. Numerical, graphic, and forced choice scales are three common types. In *numerical* scales, a sequence of defined numbers is assigned to particular categories, and then the observer selects the most appropriate numerical representation for the behavior at the time of the observation or later. A three-point scale could be developed for the frequency of question asking: 1 = a high degree of question asking, 2 = a moderate degree of question asking, and 3 = a low degree of question asking.

A second type of rating scale is the *graphic* scale, in which a straight line display is provided with cues along the line corresponding to different degrees of the behavior observed. Observers indicate by placing a mark on the scale whether the degree was high, moderate, or low. One example of a numerical scale is the Rating Scale for Literacy Development (Exhibit 8-4), modified from Heald-Taylor (1987) and used for tracking progress in the components and contexts of literacy development in the collaborative program for severely language learning disabled students presented in Chapter 5 (see also Hoffman, 1990).

Finally, there is the *forced choice* scale, in which the observer is given a set of descriptors and forced to choose the one that best describes the behavior observed. For example, Cheng (1987) listed 34 aspects of language use, and for each she asks the observer to indicate whether the aspect is frequent or infrequent (Exhibit 8-5).

ADVANTAGES AND DISADVANTAGES OF CATEGORICAL TOOLS

The most obvious advantage of many categorical tools is that they are relatively easy and inexpensive to use. However, these tools do take some effort to develop or modify. Because the decisions about which behaviors to focus on must be made prior to observation, the tools have to be carefully developed and the individuals who are going to use them have to be trained to do so correctly and effectively. A second advantage of categorical tools is that a comparatively wide range of behaviors and a large number of individuals can be observed. A third advantage is that the tools can be used on line or with prerecorded data.

One disadvantage is that it is somewhat difficult to specify duration with these tools. Some degree of quality of behaviors can be gleaned from categorical tools other than checklists or rating scales, which is one of their primary disadvantages. Another disadvantage of categorical tools in general is that without adequate training and preparation prior to observation, use of these tools is not reliable. For example, if the intent is to classify narrative categories, then, obviously, observers must be familiar with story grammar approaches. Rating

Exhibit 8-4   Rating Scale for Literacy Development

Student: _____

Rating Scale
1 = not observed
2 = observed occasionally with teacher cues
3 = observed frequently with teacher cues
4 = observed occasionally without teacher cues in structured situations
5 = observed frequently without teacher cues in structured situations
6 = master across subject areas
N/A = not applicable

PRINT AWARENESS	Date	Date	Date
Attends to reading			
Shares reading with others			
Begins to look at print independently (books, calendars, labels, tags)			
Attends to pictures			
Enjoys having stories/information read to him/her			
Handles printed materials appropriately			
Turns pages from right to left			
Recognizes where print begins			
Recognizes where print ends			
Tracks print appropriately			
Comments on characteristics of print (e.g., long words, short words)			

READING STRATEGIES	Date	Date	Date
Pretends to read using pictures as a cue			
Pretends to read using text as a memory cue			
Focuses on print while retelling a story/information			
Reads familiar sight words			
Uses sound cues			
Uses picture cues			
Uses grammar cues			
Uses sentence meaning cues			
Uses word structure cues (e.g., word length, configuration, suffixes, prefixes, root words)			
Uses knowledge of topic and content			
Monitors reading rate			
Monitors understanding of content			

Exhibit 8-4 continued

	Date	Date	Date
Asks questions about content			
Rereads for clarification			
Uses a variety of strategies together			
Explains own use of reading strategies			
Reads smoothly from left to right without pausing between words			

CONTEXTS FOR APPLICATION OF READING STRATEGIES	Date	Date	Date
Material which he/she has dictated			
Familiar material written by others			
Unfamiliar material written by others			
Material with a predictable pattern			
Material without a predictable pattern			
Material important for daily living			

WRITING	Date	Date	Date
Uses random letters to express ideas (A R X for "I went to school")			
Uses first consonant letter sound ("I wx t sk." for "I went to school.")			
Uses increased consonant sounds/letters ("I wit tu skul." for "I went to school.")			
Uses mostly correct spelling			
Writes for a variety of purposes			
Uses mechanics of writing			

Source: From "Predictable Literature Selections and Activities for Language Arts Instruction" by G. Heald-Taylor, 1987, *The Reading Teacher*, 41(1), pp. 6–12. Copyright 1987 by International Reading Association. Adapted by permission.

scales are the most prone to error. Table 8-1 summarizes the kinds of errors that are most likely to occur.

CONCLUSION

Categorical tools are closed systems that have preset categories; they allow for observation and recording of a wide range of behaviors over time and can focus on a large number of individual cases in real situations. By and large, they

Exhibit 8-5 Language Rating Scale

Name: _____

Date of Birth: _____ Today's Date: _____

Observer: _____

Informant: _____

Relationship: _____ Home Language: _____

	Yes	No	F*	I†
1. Imitates	—	—	—	—
2. Asks questions	—	—	—	—
3. Answers questions	—	—	—	—
4. Requests	—	—	—	—
5. Agrees	—	—	—	—
6. Commands or directs	—	—	—	—
7. Pleads	—	—	—	—
8. Says greetings	—	—	—	—
9. Makes suggestions	—	—	—	—
10. Disagrees, argues	—	—	—	—
11. Describes objects or events	—	—	—	—
12. Describes own actions or acts	—	—	—	—
13. Describes a past experience	—	—	—	—
14. Describes future plan	—	—	—	—
15. Describes a picture book, photos, etc.	—	—	—	—
16. Makes commentary	—	—	—	—
17. Protests	—	—	—	—
18. Makes promises	—	—	—	—
19. Expresses humor	—	—	—	—
20. Shows subtle hints	—	—	—	—
21. Initiates topics	—	—	—	—
22. Initiates topic shift	—	—	—	—
23. Uses compensatory strategies	—	—	—	—
24. Uses contingent query	—	—	—	—
25. Gives off-topic responses	—	—	—	—
26. Elaborates on topics already established	—	—	—	—
27. Changes speech, depending on speakers	—	—	—	—
28. Maintains topic	—	—	—	—
29. Role-plays	—	—	—	—
30. Instructs or demonstrates	—	—	—	—
31. Plans forward	—	—	—	—
32. Asks for collaborative action	—	—	—	—
33. Asks for clarification	—	—	—	—
34. Comments on language	—	—	—	—
35. Other	—	—	—	—

* Frequent
† Infrequent

Source: Reprinted from *Assessing Asian Language Performance: Guidelines for Evaluating Limited-English-Proficient Students* by L.L. Cheng, pp. 195–196, Gaithersburg, Md.: Aspen Publishers, Inc., © 1987.

Table 8-1 Common Errors in the Use of Rating Scales

Error	Definition
Error of leniency	Raters tend to rate people they know higher than they deserve to be rated, or, to compensate for possible error, they rate them lower than they deserve to be rated.
Error of central tendency	Raters tend to avoid extremes of high or low in their judgments and rate toward the middle.
"The halo effect"	Originally identified by Edward L. Thorndike in 1920. Tendency to let other information influence the rating. Often raters have a tendency to contaminate their judgments with irrelevancies—a human failing with which all judges and juries are familiar.
Error of logic	Raters are apt to give similar ratings for two items that seem logically related. A child who is rated high on "shows initiative" may be rated high on "works well independently" because the rater assumes that the two are logically related and should be treated in the same manner.
Error of contrast	This error is two-pronged in that we either tend to rate people in the opposite direction from ourselves or rate them as similar to ourselves, depending on how we perceive them and how we view or value the trait being rated.
Proximity error	This was discovered when researchers did intercorrelations of items on a rating scale and found that items that were next to each other or close together in time or space were rated more similarly than items further apart.

Source: From *Observational Strategies for Child Study* (pp. 213–214) by D. Irwin and D. Bushnell, 1980, New York: Holt, Rinehart, & Winston; and from *Psychometric Methods*, 2nd ed., by J. Guilford, 1954, New York: McGraw-Hill, Inc. Copyright 1980, 1954 by McGraw-Hill, Inc. Adapted by permission.

are comparatively easy and efficient to use. Categorical tools are essentially classification systems that are used as events unfold or at the end of an observation period (in the case of rating systems). Category systems and checklists are more commonly found in the assessing or tracking of progress than are rating systems. Summarizing information is not difficult. Interpreting information may be more difficult, because of the absence of detailed contextual information and specific information about the quality of the behavior.

Categorical tools are best used to get an overall sense of communicative patterns with an entire class or, when initial assessment is the issue, with one child. They are not adequate for precise descriptions of communicative skills or problem areas in communication or for evaluating the success of intervention for a particular child. However, specialized category systems, such as those designed to examine request effectiveness and narrative organization or cohesion, can provide a tight focus for initial assessment and for the ongoing assessment of intervention outcomes.

Chapter 9

Examining Students' Communication: Narrative Tools

Narrative tools are used by observers when they want to record everything that happens in a setting, such as the classroom. These tools consist of systematic and detailed written descriptions of what individuals do and say. The best way to convey the essence of narrative tools is to consider a typical example. The following one was taken from an observation of two children in a preschool classroom during three different activities. In this example, Allie uses language to provide information, to accompany action, and to imagine that she is the mother of her doll:

> Three-year-old (3 years, 8 months) Allie is in the 3-year-olds room of a preschool and chooses different activities during "center time." Her first activity is to make a construction paper collage. After she pastes the last piece of paper on her sheet, she matter-of-factly eats some paste and says, "I'm finished!" She then spends about 2 minutes trying to use a plastic socket wrench on a toy car. While she does this, she chants, "dub, dub, dub, dub, dub." She next turns away from the car and picks up a small plastic doll, lying on the floor near the car. She talks to the doll, "I told you to shut up, son! No way, this is no way!" (Genishi & Dyson, 1984, p. 94)

Because narrative tools provide detailed descriptions, clinicians often use them for a variety of purposes. For example, the clinician may be able to extract a critical incident that will illustrate a particular problem with a child and may also be able to provide specific information about the results of an intervention. Clinicians can test hunches by collecting information through narrative descriptions. For example, if it is suspected that a particular child is less verbal only in specific situations involving evaluation by the teacher or students, a narrative technique can be used to gather information from several situations for careful scrutiny and illustrative purposes. In narrative descriptions, the period of obser-

162

vation can vary; it can last only as long as a single incident, such as in the example given above, or it can be a period of several hours, a day, or even longer. Observers typically record events and behaviors as they unfold, and the natural order of events is preserved in the written record.

TYPES OF NARRATIVE TOOLS

There are several types of narrative tools. The choice will depend on the same factors operating for selection of categorical tools: the availability of information, the amount of time and other resources that have to be expended on the observation, and the goals of the observation. In the next section, four types of narrative descriptions are discussed: journals, critical incidents, running records, and ethnographic notes.

JOURNALS

In the broadest sense of the term, a journal consists of retrospective records written about one's own experiences or the experiences of others. There are two types of journals, each of which has different functions. One is the traditional journal in which adult observers record their views of new events and behaviors. The other type, often described as a *dialogue journal*, is utilized in some communication-centered classrooms as a tool for helping students to bridge the gap between the oral style of face-to-face communication and the more literate style characteristic of reading and writing (Staton, Shuy, Peyton, & Reed, 1988).

The Traditional Journal

The journal record is typically longitudinal and requires reported observations of the student or students over an extended period of time. There is no specific training for writing journals, but it is important to be clear in advance about the focus of the questions to be addressed in the written record.

Cazden (1988) cites the following example from Merle Chalon, who as a child had immigrated to England from the West Indies, where she had attended school. In this excerpt, which illustrates the traditional type of journal, Chalon recollects how her London classroom was organized. In that classroom, "a group of children . . . could talk and help each other," which was in sharp contrast to her school experiences in the West Indies:

> We worked in groups a lot. The room was set out in tables. . . . We sat
> on all girls table in one corner. There was my-self and another West

Indian girl and one Asian girl, and whatever the work was we had to read or write about, we could actually help each other, we could talk about it. . . . [This] was new and quite exciting to us. We did quite a lot of work where a group of us would go away with a tape recorder and talk about a particular topic or particular book and then later on report it to the rest of the class. . . . One of the books which we talked about was George Orwell's *Animal Farm* because our teacher found that the children were taking the book at different levels. For some of the children it was merely a book about animals, whereas for people like Fred, who was a boy in the class, he actually understood the political idea of it. . . . People who could understand at that level going away and talking about it, and then coming back and us listening to the tape, really helped in the class. And because the class was often working at different levels, . . . this [working in groups] would enable our teacher to have more time for those children who needed more specific help. (National Association of Teachers of English, n.d. p. 26)

Chalon provides a personal perspective of what it was like to be in a classroom where students interacted and communicated with each other about schoolwork. We can see how the organization of instruction in the London classroom differed markedly from the West Indies classroom. One consequence of this organization was that language use differed to a great degree between the two classrooms. The journal gives the flavor of what it was like to be there in that London classroom and experience classroom instruction organized in this way.

The Dialogue Journal

Dialogue journals have been used with language learning disabled students of ages five to nine as a means for developing their metacognitive and metalinguistic awareness of writing as a dialogue between two speakers (Westby & Costlow, in press). Dialogue journals are intended to assist language learning disabled children to understand that oral language can be written and that print can have different functions (Gillam & Johnston, 1985; van Kleeck, 1990). According to Westby and Costlow (in press), dialogue journals also encourage a more literate style of language use, help in monitoring comprehension, and support the understanding of information that must be inferred. The expectation is that children will collaborate with their teacher, speech-language clinician, and parents in communicating messages through writing.

Westby and Costlow describe three general phases of the discourse continuum (Scott, 1988) that also can be found in journal writing. In the first phase, written dialogue is initiated by the teacher and directed personally to the child in order to convey that written messages have a purpose and meaning. The child may only draw a line or figure or copy parts of words, indicating some awareness that writing has a distinctive look. With repeated experience, children become capable of producing more extended responses on their own. Invented spellings may be a feature of early self-generated responses (see also Ehri, 1989a; 1989b, for a discussion on the developmental aspects of invented spelling). Later on, children are able to evaluate the teacher's written messages, as shown in the following exchange (Westby & Costlow, in press, p. 18):

> Dear Elaine
> Did you have fun playing yesterday? I did.
> I like to play.
>> Love,
>> Lucy

> Dear Lucy
> We Dot
> not ple y
> Yesterday
>> Love Ernestine

Westby and Costlow note that, although Ernestine did not comment on Lucy's getting her name wrong, she did evaluate the truth value of the statement about playing with Lucy.

Once a child can comment on and evaluate the messages of others, the second phase of journal writing begins. Here, written dialogue is initiated by the child and directed to others who are writing in the child's journal (e.g., Ernestine would leave notes for the teacher).

In the final phase, journal writing becomes less oral and personal and more literate and impersonal. The child constructs monologues that are not directed to a specific audience. To illustrate, the child may begin with a short narrative that centers on a single event (Westby & Costlow, in press, p. 21):

> My
> Dad
> wun
> Some
> Mune
> He wun
> looo Dalrs

Some children eventually became capable of producing longer personal experience narratives, such as a description of a trip to the airport or to a restaurant. These more complex narratives often lack complete accuracy in spelling and punctuation; however, they functionally resemble the observations and evaluations of personal experiences found in traditional journal writing, such as the excerpt from Chalon.

Dialogue journals allow the speech-language clinician and other collaborative partners to observe systematic changes in children's metacognitive and metalinguistic awareness as reflected in their journal entries (Westby & Costlow, in press). Moreover, dialogue journals also allow ethnographic applications. Through these journals, it becomes possible to gain more objective information on successful modifications in children's perspectives of themselves as competent communicators.

CRITICAL INCIDENT REPORT

The critical incident report is a second type of narrative tool. This type of tool is used to obtain a relatively small amount of detailed information in a narrative form in order to address a specific question. Critical incidents can be recorded as they occur, or they can be reconstructed after the fact by the team observers (in such cases, it is essential that all the relevant behavior is included in the report). Typically, the observer is not a participant in the situation being observed. Once again, the observer needs to be clear about the question and the focus prior to the observation. Most important is that the team observers recognize when a critical incident occurs, when it begins, and when it ends.

In the following example, Almy and Genishi (1979) report a four-year-old's spontaneous language play. Language play is usually repetitious and rhythmic play. In this example, we see how Robert uses language spontaneously to produce rhyming words:

"Can you read my shirt? It says, 'Thick or thin at Pizza Inn,' inn, min, pin, pin, kin, kee, kee, bee, bee," and then he giggled. The teacher said, "Those words rhymed with *inn*." Robert was silent a moment, then said, "Oh, yeah, they sound like it, right? Yum, yum, tum, tummy!" and he chuckled a little at his understanding of it and patted his stomach. (p. 132)

The observer correctly noted both the beginning and end of the incident. This critical incident report is useful because it provides specific information about

Robert's ability to produce language through rhyming, an early metalinguistic precursor (van Kleeck & Schuele, 1987), which is not uncommon for children of this age. Note, however, that the sequence "kee, kee, bee, bee" does not reflect anything but a sound similarity to the preceding "pin." Although "kin" does rhyme with "inn" and "pin," the teacher mistakenly suggested the last syllables rhymed with "inn." Apparently, only some of the syllables that Robert used were salient for this teacher, which indicates once again the constraints in hearing imposed by the rapid temporal flow of speech. However, this incident exhibits a skill that Robert is developing, even though it represents only a small fraction of Robert's day and interaction at school.

RUNNING RECORD

Running records are used to record *in sequence* everything of significance that is going on with a child or group. The observer does not select what he or she thinks is important but rather writes down all that is possible to record during the observational period. While running records are more complete in some ways, they are not longitudinal and do not preserve the sense of recurring behaviors and events over time that is evident in diaries and journals. On the other hand, running records tend to be more detailed and cover a longer period of observation than do critical incident records. Running records are written in everyday language as the events actually occur, and they are relatively intensive and systematic recordings of the events, capturing as near as possible the complete stream of behavior as it unfolds. Running records form the backbone of case studies, because extensive training in the techniques of recording is not required for proper use of this tool.

An example of a running record is taken from anthropologist Steven Boggs's (1972) study of a Hawaiian classroom. It illustrates the use of this tool to capture the organization and processes of a classroom:

At the end of the count of ten when the whole class is supposed to be sitting on the floor, D is not there. Instead he goes out the door of the class. One of the children calls the teacher's attention to this and she says "D is being stubborn." She then engages the class in a conversation about being stubborn, asking them if they know what it means to be stubborn. Someone suggests that it means to be sad. Someone else says it means bad. The teacher says that you are stubborn if someone asks you to do something and you say (demonstrating) "No, I won't do it!" At this point one of the children says, "Yes. They ask you and you no like." (p. 304)

The following example of a running record is taken from a case study of a Laotian child, aged two years, seven months, who was referred for an initial speech and language evaluation because he formed no intelligible words. The excerpt from Cheng (1987) is a record of the observation that was done at a speech and hearing clinic:

> In the testing room, the child was quiet. Although several toys had been arranged around the room, he showed no interest in them. The child went to the desk, picked up a cup of water that had been placed on the desk, and took it to his seat. He found another cup in a kitchen toy and started to pour the water from one cup to the other; he continued to pour the water back and forth, seeming to enjoy the activity. When asked to look at some pictures, the child did not respond. When asked to play with a doll, the child simply turned away . . . . When the child noticed a jar of tongue depressors in the corner of the room, he went to the jar, opened it, and took out a tongue depressor. Giving the tongue depressor to the clinician, he quickly opened his mouth. The clinician was able to do a thorough oral peripheral examination. (pp. 107–8)

Another example is taken from a 50-minute classroom observation of a 14-year-old language learning disabled student during math. Here, the running record was produced as one part of a comprehensive reassessment to determine the appropriateness of this student's educational placement in a learning disabilities program.

> The teacher had previously reported that Mary had serious difficulty following verbal and written directions, did not attempt tasks independently, and seemed to be shy and withdrawn. Mary was failing in all of her classes. The class consisted of 9 students, 1 teacher, and 2 teacher's aides. Classroom instruction involved participation in various group activities that were centered around stock market investing. Computational skills involved figuring percentage rates on stock dividends. Mary relied on a calculator for computation; however, she had significant difficulty converting fractions to decimals as well as multiplying decimals. She required one-on-one assistance to complete computational tasks. She appeared to have difficulty understanding the teacher's verbal explanations; she did not request repetition or clarification of information but tended to wait for teacher assistance.

The running record is often the tool by which clinical observation is implemented. It is not, however, always defined in this way.

ETHNOGRAPHIC PERSPECTIVES

Ethnographic notes are used to record information obtained during participant observation. Participant observation is a technique used by anthropologists to study cultures and social groups. It consists of a written account of what the observer sees, hears, experiences, and thinks in the course of the observation as well as the observer's thoughts after reflecting on the observed events. Ethnographic notes have an anecdotal quality to them. Within the past two decades, some anthropologists and researchers in language learning disabilities (Ripich, 1989; Ripich & Spinelli, 1985; Westby, 1989; Westby & Costlow, in press) have adapted ethnographic tools to study aspects of education, such as literacy or classroom communication. Ethnographic notes record key events in everyday language. In using this tool, the observer can look back on all that he or she has observed, even if it was not written down, to provide background and a context for the interpretation of behavior. Using this tool effectively does require fairly comprehensive training.

The following example is taken from the anthropologist John Gumperz's (1970) observations of two group of students in a racially integrated first grade in California:

> We observed a reading session with a slow group of three children, and seven fast readers .... With the slow readers she [the teacher] concentrated on the alphabet, on the spelling of individual words .... She addressed the children in what white listeners would identify as pedagogical style. Her enunciation was deliberate and slow. Each word was clearly articulated with even stress and pitch .... Pronunciation errors were corrected whenever they occurred, even if the reading task had to be interrupted. The children seemed distracted and inattentive .... With the advanced group on the other hand reading became much more of a group activity and the atmosphere was more relaxed. Words were treated in context, as part of a story .... There was no correction of pronunciation, although some deviant forms were also heard. The children actually enjoyed competing with each other in reading and the teacher responded by dropping her pedagogical monotone in favor of more animated natural speech. (p. 85)

Using ethnographic notes can also be helpful to the speech-language clinician by providing the participants' perspective on the use of language. Multiple perspective observations can provide clinicians with a clue as to the source of communication problems (e.g., whether there is a mismatch between a teacher's expectation for competent performance and a child's expectation for what is appropriate behavior). Chapter 11 further elaborates on the role of multiple perspectives in validating assessment findings and the tracking of progress.

ADVANTAGES AND DISADVANTAGES OF USING NARRATIVE TOOLS

The different narrative tools discussed thus far have individual, as well as collective, advantages. Most of them allow the clinician and other collaborators to record events in everyday language. Observers can recount what they see as it occurs in a particular environment, and these written records can be reviewed again and again, which then aids the observer in problem solving and planning. The focus of a narrative can be an individual child, a group, or an event, such as the organizing of reading in the classroom. The excerpts themselves are permanent and are made with a minimum use of technological equipment, which keeps their production simple and inexpensive. Furthermore, team members can produce a narrative whenever it is needed and there is time to do so.

These advantages of simplicity are offset, to some extent, by certain disadvantages. First, because of the filtering effect, new observers may find it difficult to decide what to write down. If they are producing a narrative over a long period, the quality and quantity may decline as the time wears on and fatigue sets in. Second, it is sometimes difficult to analyze completely what has been written down, because it may take a long time to read through a narrative and focus on what is germane. This more often becomes a problem with traditional journals, ethnographic notes, and running records, because they are longer than critical incident reports. Recently, ethnographic notes have been criticized for being anecdotal, which supposedly decreases their fitness for scientific use (e.g., they do not make explicit the criteria for categorizing behavior as "good" or "bad"). Further, ethnographic notes summarize information and tend to exclude details. A dialogue journal, on the other hand, can be a systematic ethnographic tool, because it is a longitudinal record of the child's experience in different communicative activities.

CONCLUSION

Narrative tools record a slice of life. They can be used to record, in varying degrees of detail, events, behaviors, and so on, as they unfold. Narratives can be used in real time (on line) or can be written retrospectively based on memories and recollections of events that have just been observed. They can be used to capture one moment in time or to give a longitudinal perspective over time. For example, many language assessments and progress reports reflect the application of a narrative tool.

Because narratives are written in everyday language, it is easy to share them with nonprofessionals and with professionals from other disciplines, such as school psychologists or physicians. Narrative tools can be used individually or together to select and record incidents; they can be combined with categorical and/or descriptive tools, as is seen in Chapter 11. Narrative tools are perhaps the easiest and simplest tools to use, yet their obvious drawbacks can limit the completeness and accuracy of the answers they provide to specific questions.

Chapter 10

Examining Students' Communication: Descriptive Tools

Descriptive tools are used by clinicians to obtain a verbatim account of actual language use and to describe in detail the context within which the language use occurs. Observers typically are concerned with identifying a developing process and/or a pattern of behavior that occurs across situations. The examination of communication breakdowns illustrates how descriptive tools can function as an extra close-up lens. For example, scrutiny may reveal that the source of a breakdown is located in the child's failure to use sufficient cohesive devices to tie meaning together in oral and written narratives.

The hallmark of descriptive tools as they are applied to language is that the stream of talk and accompanying action are recorded in everyday language. Records are sometimes supplemented by notations (see Chapter 4 and Appendix B) that indicate features of the discourse beyond the language used. Although there are many kinds of descriptive tools, a key element of all of them is the use of transcriptions from audio or video recordings of actual talking. Analysis of these transcriptions occurs retrospectively, not live or on line. What's That Word? (Chapter 6), the Chef Lesson, and the Speech Rules Lesson (Chapter 4) are examples of the use of description systems.

Descriptive tools are used effectively to provide detailed records of what was said and done in a given event at a given moment. The analyses of the transcriptions can provide insights that may not be available merely by listening to an exchange among students, as can be seen in the work of Michaels (1986). Recall from Chapter 3 that Michaels investigated elementary school children's spontaneous production of personal experience narratives in school during sharing time (in this activity, the teacher calls on children to share an event or story from the past with the class). In the following example, Michaels gives a verbatim transcription of (1) the narrative produced by a student (Martin), (2) the exchanges with the teacher, and (3) an interpretation of the essential elements of the narrative. Although this example does not involve a communicative breakdown, it

172

does reflect a child's developing competence in organizing personal experience narratives.

Martin:	Yesterday . . . Burt . . . and I was at Burt's house and um . . . this dog was running across the street . . . and uh
Teacher:	What did
Burt:	This dog
Martin:	was running across the street, and a car runned him over and, and he, and he fell . . . down and he was screeching then he died, and his mom, put him on a board and then the bus came, and he and he got
Burt:	called for help
Martin:	called for help
Teacher:	I'm sorry. Life isn't all fun and pleasantry, is it?
Martin:	It was a lost dog.
Teacher:	That's a very sad
Burt:	It was a lost dog.
Martin:	So the guy who owned him, doesn't know he was dead.
Teacher:	Really? Right, that's very sad. That makes me feel very bad. But life's like that. We can't pretend it isn't can we?
Class:	No.
Teacher:	'Cause things like that do happen. Sorry.
Martin:	Yesterday . . . Burt . . . and I was at Burt's house and um . . . this dog was running across the street . . . and uh

Martin's discourse, produced collaboratively with Mrs. Jones and Burt, shows a great deal of rhythmic synchronization. The discourse can be analyzed as containing an *orientation* section (lines 1 and 2), *complication action* (lines 3–11), a *resolution* (lines 12–16), and a *coda* (lines 18, 20, 21), which also serve as Martin's *evaluation* of the discourse. Mrs. Jones provides her own evaluative comments (lines 17, 19, 22–24, 26), which differ in form from Martin's. Martin's comment "It was a lost dog" (line 18) adds additional information about the dog, which ties lexically back to line 3, where Martin originally mentions "this dog." His comment, then, serves several purposes. It adds new and important information about the dog, brings the narrative to a close (also indicated by pronounced falling intonation), and evaluates the discourse implicitly, as if to say, "It's especially sad because it was a lost dog." Mrs. Jones does not overtly respond to this comment, perhaps because she interprets it merely as additional detail rather than as Martin's evaluation and point in telling the story. The comment is then repeated, more loudly and with emphasis by Burt, and then further elaborated on by Martin (line 21) who again evaluates by means of providing additional information. Mrs. Jones then makes explicit the "point" of Martin's story (lines 22–24). She accomplishes this by referring to the event as a whole, standing outside the actual account, whereas Martin's and Burt's evaluative comments are an integral part of the account, and hence remain indirect.*

This example demonstrates again how a categorical system can be applied in order to produce qualitative descriptions.

ELEMENTS

Descriptive tools are characterized by several key elements. First, they depend on the use of some technology, such as audio- or videotaping, as the basis for the production of a transcription.

Second, the initial step in using any descriptive tool is to make a good quality recording for transcription. The next step is to transcribe the audio and video recordings into everyday language, which may be supplemented by other notation as needed. For example, one might choose to note accompanying nonverbal actions or the occurrence of verbal overlaps, interruptions, or prosodic features if these or other behaviors are found to be important for interpreting the interaction.

Third, some descriptive tools specify predetermined categories. One example is the kinds of requests that were focused on in Wilkinson and Calculator's research (1982) on the effective speaker (see Chapter 8). Other descriptive tools allow the categories to emerge from the data, as exemplified by Merritt's (1982b) discovery of the ways in which teachers shift attention or by Michaels' (1986) analysis of Martin and Burt's narrative. These kinds of analyses allow team members to note patterns and sequences of talk that may occur very fast in real time and may elude even the most perceptive clinician. Once again,

---

*Source: From S. Michaels, "Narrative Presentations: An Oral Preparation for Literacy with First Graders" in *The Social Construction of Literacy* (p. 98) by J. Cook-Gumperz (Ed.), 1986, New York: Cambridge University Press. Copyright 1986 by Cambridge University Press. Reprinted by permission.

Merritt's discovery would probably not have been noticed were it not for her painstaking analyses of transcriptions and recording. Her work is similar to Michaels in its notation of detail. Recordings and transcriptions allow for the infinite retrievability of the actual talk as it occurs in real time. In addition, multiple analyses are possible. Observers can analyze the syntactic constructions, the pragmatic functions, the lexicon used, the paralinguistic cues, and the discourse devices, among other dimensions, when using transcription and recordings, as exemplified by Michael's analysis.

Finally, descriptive tools incorporate descriptions of the contexts within which the recordings were made so that interpretation can be as accurate and complete as possible. There are many systems used to describe contexts within which language is used and recorded, such as mappings of the classroom and sociolinguistic analyses. Extensive examples of the use of descriptive tools have already been given in Chapter 4. The discussion of this kind of tool is limited to elaborating its potential uses, advantages, and disadvantages and providing some additional examples.

MAPPING THE CLASSROOM

One kind of descriptive system useful in the study of students' classroom language is illustrated in the work of Wong-Fillmore, Ammon, et al. (1983), who developed a comprehensive way of describing both the instructional and social contexts within which language and learning occur. Their original system specified the key elements to be noted prior to recording language and nonverbal behavior. An extension and adaptation of this system has been used by the authors in their research (Exhibit 10-1).

The system is helpful in achieving a practical understanding of the "ground rules" for language use in classrooms. Having described the classroom by means of the system, the clinician and other team participants will then want to observe the actual discourse used against this backdrop.

SOCIOLINGUISTIC APPROACHES

Sociolinguistic analysis is a kind of descriptive system that provides a powerful way to understand how the discourse of instruction is organized for teaching and learning. As an example, Mehan (1979) used sociolinguistic analysis to discover that classroom lessons have a formal organization characterized by interactional units of increasing size (see Chapter 4). Also, this kind of descriptive analysis was used in discussing the lessons in Chapter 4 and in discussing George's narrative in Chapter 8 (see also Appendix A).

Exhibit 10-1   Activity Description

Name of Activity: _____

Date: _____

Physical Aspects

1. Draw a *map* of the classroom.
2. *Location* (indicate activity on map):

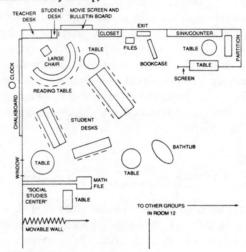

3. *Daily schedule* (indicate activity and time).
4. *Materials* (pencils, books, blackboard, etc.).

Cognitive and Task Aspects

1. Describe the *content* of the material to be learned during this activity. Is it appropriate for this age/grade level?

2. Describe the curriculum *materials* involved in this activity (give specific description). Do all the materials seem to be appropriate for the age/grade level?

3. Are the *goals* for the activity clearly stated? How?

4. What *written products* are to result from this activity? How will they be evaluated? What feedback on these will be given to the students and when? If possible, attach copies of the curriculum materials.

Language Aspects

1. Describe the *language* used during this activity; indicate whether oral or written.

2. How are language *directions* given for the activity? Are there any restrictions on the use of language (e.g., only speak in English)?

3. Could this activity be conducted with *less use of language*? If so, how?

4. If there are students who speak more than one language in this activity, describe their usage.

Social Aspects

1. *Participants* (provide names and indicate where they are located during the activity). Describe the students (age, L1/L2, grade, gender, etc.).

Exhibit 10-1   continued

2. *Activity structure* (large group, small group, individual, pairs). If *groups* or *pairs* are used, describe (a) how the students were assigned (e.g., ability/achievement, friendship, age, grade, language, homogeneous or heterogeneous); (b) stability of assignment; (c) whether the group/pair is directed by the teacher or by a student; and (d) if directed by a student, how the student was selected (by teacher, by students, on what basis).

3. *Management of the activity*. Does the teacher provide discipline? How does the teacher deal with interruptions and discipline during the activity?

The following example is taken from Mehan's (1979) analysis of the lessons that the sociolinguist Courtney Cazden taught in a combined class of first-, second-, and third-grade children in San Diego nearly 15 years ago. One lesson, Birthplaces, was part of a social studies unit that had two objectives: (1) understanding maps, and (2) lessening the psychological distance between Cazden, who resided in Cambridge, Massachusetts, and the children in her multiethnic class. Cazden (1988) used an orientation as an introduction in the following example:

Some people did some good homework last night in finding out where they were, were born or where your family, your parents came from. And Miguel has a little box of colored paper here, and what we're going to do is—if you know where you were born, we are going to put your names up with orange paper. If you know where your parents came from, we're going to put their names up with green paper and pin them right on the map (demonstrating). Now some people were already telling me as soon as they came into school this morning that they had some, they knew some things to put on the map. (p. 31)

According to Mehan (1979), the basic sequence of this lesson includes determining, for each student, the student's or parents' birthplaces, locating the birthplaces on the map, and placing the markers on the map. The following exchange is an example of an IRE sequence:

Teacher: Uh, Prenda, ah, let's see if we can find, here's your name. Where were you born, Prenda?

Prenda: San Diego.

Teacher: You were born in San Diego, right.

In the first turn, the teacher nominates Prenda to take a turn at responding to the question; Prenda does so, and the teacher positively evaluates her response in the third turn, which also functions as a comprehension check.

This excerpt is an example of the kind of analysis that is possible using descriptive tools. Mehan has compared his discovery of the order of lessons to the order of a grammar that students must learn in order to read classroom events, participate effectively in school, and learn the lesson content taught. Children have to learn the subtle cues that teachers give to signal changes in the lesson or her attention.

APPLICATIONS

Returning to our camera analogy, descriptive tools provide the clinician and other collaborators with both narrow and wide-angle lenses that can be aimed at a child with a communication problem or potential communication problem. Dollaghan and Miller (1986) comment that sometimes a clinician will report that a child responds inappropriately to questions or directives. When asked to elaborate, the clinician may not be able to provide more information, such as specific instances, but may reply merely that the child provides inaccurate answers to questions and does not follow directions. These broad, wide-angle conclusions do not pinpoint the specific interactional sources of the communication problem or elucidate the nature of the difficulties a child is having with requests, which makes it difficult to design effective intervention strategies. Dollaghan and Miller and others (Lahey, 1988; Lund & Duchan, 1988; van Kleeck & Richardson, in press) suggest that time could be well spent recording and transcribing the specific interaction exactly as it occurs and then conducting a fine-grained analysis of that interaction to define the problem clearly and in detail. According to Dollaghan and Miller (1986),

> one might construct a taxonomy that at least distinguished between answers to "wh" questions, yes-no questions, tag questions, and choice questions, or the clinician might conduct an exploratory observation of the subject's question answering skills by recording and examining the number of events preceding and following successful and unsuccessful responses to questions. This exploratory phase might lead the clinician to realize that the subject's question answering skill actually varies depending on the degree to which the question refers to some aspect of the "here-and-now" or the degree to which the answer can be produced through use of a comprehension strategy. The clinician could then proceed to construct a taxonomy distinguishing among these events and to write recognition rules for its categories; subsequent observations would yield a much better picture of the specific kinds of questions to which treatment should be addressed. (pp. 120–121)

ADVANTAGES AND DISADVANTAGES OF DESCRIPTIVE TOOLS

In using descriptive tools, observers focus on and record exactly what is said as it unfolds in a particular situation. These original records, on audio- or videotape, are permanent, can be reviewed indefinitely, and are transcribed into everyday language. The transcriptions in turn can be used for illustrative and investigative purposes. The primary advantage of descriptive tools is that they provide a completely accurate record of what language was actually produced in a particular interactional event. Careful analysis can reveal the interactional sources of any communicative difficulty, a more precise picture of the communicative problem, and the aspects of the context associated with communicative breakdowns.

The advantages of the completeness of information and the infinite retrievability of information are offset, to some degree, by certain disadvantages. First, new observers need training to gain proficiency in using descriptive tools. Also, knowing where to point the camera and how to link audio and video recordings to obtain a clear record is not always an easy matter. Second, it is sometimes difficult to analyze an audio or video recording and turn it into a transcription because of noise and other flaws. Third, it is time-consuming and expensive to make audio or video records, transcribe data, and code them, a major disadvantage in school settings, where clinicians' caseloads, even in collaborative models, are often large. Appendix C provides guidelines for use of videotaping in the school setting.

CONCLUSION

Descriptive tools are open systems that (1) may or may not have preset categories; (2) allow for the thorough observation of dialogue in real situations; (3) can be combined to construct systematic descriptions of ongoing behavior; and (4) allow the precise recording of ongoing behavior, verbal and nonverbal, in everyday language, supplemented by other forms of notation as necessary. They cannot be used on line, since they involve a retrospective analysis of transcriptions of records made from audio or video recordings of what actually transpired. Observers can focus the lens at a wide angle, capturing the context within which action and talk occur. However, a tight focus on specific behavior is also possible. Instances of specific communication breakdown can be pinpointed and identified for further analysis. The conditions that preserve, exacerbate, or are simply associated with certain discourse events can be interpreted more clearly by using descriptive tools. Thus, a program of intervention can be developed and assessed over time in a way that most categorical and narrative tools cannot allow.

Chapter 11

Integrating Observational Tools: Steps and Procedures

DEVELOPMENTAL AND INSTRUCTIONAL ASSESSMENT

In this chapter, we offer a method for applying observational tools to the assessment of children's communication skills in classrooms. In many developmental approaches to assessment of children's language and communication abilities, observation is used to link naturally obtained data to intervention goals. These approaches often incorporate sampling the discourse or language of the children under study (Bernstein & Tiegerman, 1989; Brinton & Fujiki, 1989; Fey, 1986; Lahey, 1988; Lund & Duchan, 1988; Muma, 1986; Prutting & Kirchner, 1983; van Kleeck & Richardson, in press). Another common element of developmental approaches is that the continuous evaluation and modification of an intervention plan take place through ongoing assessment.

Instructional (curriculum-based) assessment contrasts with developmental assessment in terms of both goals and setting. Developmental assessment is concerned with comparing a child's development with normal communicative development in order to define specific intervention goals and procedures. This kind of assessment most often takes place outside of the classroom. In contrast, the goal of instructional assessment is to align evaluative and instructional techniques so that curriculum objectives can be achieved in the classroom (Howell & Morehead, 1987; Idol et al., 1987; Weaver, 1988). To meet this aim, assessment becomes an ongoing process within classrooms.

It is not surprising that findings from developmental and instructional assessments may not be consistent. Information from a developmental assessment, by itself, does not always lead to practical strategies that can be used by clinicians and others to improve children's learning. Some attempts have been made to bridge this gap, such as N.W. Nelson's (1989) work on curriculum-based language assessment and intervention, Wallach and Miller's (1988) work on integrating language intervention into the varying cognitive and social demands of the classroom, and Scott's (1989b) approach to integrating writing and reading.

The common thread linking instructional and developmental assessments is their mutual reliance on the use of observational tools. Kagan (1989), a proponent of instructional assessment as an alternative to standardized achievement testing, summarizes four benefits of using observational tools in the classroom: (1) the natural learning setting becomes the focus of observation; (2) individual differences in children's development can be captured more reliably; (3) variations in individual children's progress can be documented across time; and (4) teaching and assessment can be integrated, since teachers and clinicians can tailor instruction and intervention to each child's needs, learning styles, and interests.

As discussed in Chapter 5, new classroom roles for clinicians along the continuum of collaboration mean that clinicians and teachers become resources for each other in implementing and evaluating communication-centered instruction and intervention. The specific model chosen for collaboration may be consultation, team teaching, or a variation of either one, depending on the circumstances of a particular educational setting. The model may incorporate collaboration with regular education teachers, as in the communication skills model, or it may primarily involve collaboration with special educators, as in the communication development model. Regardless of the collaborative model, a central issue is *how* observational lenses and tools can be integrated systematically while maintaining reasonable standards of manageability, accuracy, and validity. A plan for integration is outlined in this chapter. The focus is upon initial assessment; however the general steps and procedures can be readily modified for the multiple purposes of ongoing assessment.

SELECTING AND INTEGRATING OBSERVATIONAL TOOLS

We propose three steps in the selection and integration aspects of assessment: (1) identify whether a problem exists; (2) observe real-time interaction; and (3) integrate and validate multiple perspectives. There are alternate substeps within each of these major steps.

Step 1: Identify Whether a Problem Exists

Identification is the first phase of assessment. This phase is often essentially a matter of screening. Standardized screening measures are traditionally used for identification, and in many states they may be required to determine eligibility for referral. However, in some states, such as Florida, prereferral documentation is necessary on the part of teachers prior to a formal referral, and in California, standardized testing is not recommended for children who are kindergarten age or younger (Kagan, 1989). Thus, observational tools are often very significant in guiding joint decision making by teachers and clinicians on the question of whether or not a problem exists. Even with students who have been placed in special education or mainstreamed into regular education, new problem areas may be reported that then require further description.

Purpose of Identification

When referral from the regular classroom is likely to occur, identification can be thought of as a prereferral activity. The purpose of identification is to ascertain whether educational risk is present for students whose communicative competencies may not be notable until associated with literacy learning (Lahey, 1988). Idol et al. (1987) comment that the identification step in the collaborative process is a vital one: "If the collaborators move too quickly to problem remediation without first drawing the most accurate picture of the problem, consultation is likely to result in ineffective service" (p. 57).

The need for full incorporation of teachers' perspectives has been shown by Mehan et al. (1986) in their work on decision making in special education. Some unintended consequences were found to affect the referral system and subsequently influence who was selected for special education. For example, although uniform referral procedures were intended to decrease variations in teachers' referral criteria, in practice they lead teachers to discover in their students previously undetected symptoms of "disability." Furthermore, how students actually acted in classrooms was not the basis for referral. When teachers viewed videotapes of children they had referred and compared them with children not referred, it became apparent that decisions to refer were only *partially* linked to the students' actual behavior (Mehan et al., 1982). The same behavior in different students might result in one student being referred and the other not. This pattern was interpreted as indicating the role of expectations in the decision to refer. These expectations then mediated how students actually behaved with teachers in the classroom, both as group members and individually. Mehan et al. (1986) propose that it is through this mediating process that the behaviors of certain students come to be "counted" as an index of a disability, which, more often than not, is then confirmed by the psychological assessment.

Because systematic confirmation of a disability seems to be built into traditional, noncollaborative referral procedures, the process of collaboration through coparticipation should reduce unwarranted referrals. In having a shared frame of reference for viewing patterns of interaction, clinicians can better assist teachers in transforming vague perceptions of a problem (e.g., "Kelly has poor language skills and can't work independently") into more precise initial descriptions.

Outcomes of Identification

The selection of observational tools should be linked to the purpose of identification. Several points should be kept in mind. First, the tools chosen should lead to more explicit understanding of the teacher's and parents' views of the child's communicative competencies and readiness for various aspects of language and literacy learning. Second, the tools selected should provide ideas about patterns and sources of communicative breakdowns that signal a "problem." These potential sources can then be explored in greater depth during the next phases of assessment. Based on these two outcomes, a preliminary summary of the problem can be developed that integrates at this point the perspectives of the teacher, parent, and clinician (Ripich & Spinelli, 1985). Because multiple perspectives are taken into account, this tentative summation is a clinical application of ethnographic field notes to the identification process (see the discussion of ethnographic notes in Chapter 9).

Tool Selection in Identification (Wide-Angle Lens)

Recall the Chapter 5 description of the parallel focus model of observation: Before deciding on how observation is to be done, the clinician and teacher must jointly decide on what will be observed. Decision-making elements include the short-term purpose, the focus, the content, the means for recording information (videotape, audiotape, or paper and pencil), the unit of analysis, and the setting.

Since the purpose of identification is to obtain a wide-angle snapshot of potential trouble spots, categorical tools, such as checklists or rating scales, can provide appropriate information by themselves or in conjunction with a narrative tool. A follow-up interview should begin to clarify the problem further, regardless of whether categorical or narrative tools are used.

Checklists or *rating scales* can be preselected if they meet the particular need. Alternately, these tools may be designed in conjunction with teachers in a way that more adequately interfaces with reading and writing activities and strategies (e.g., the rating scale for literacy development created by Heald-Taylor, 1987).

Four general criteria for selecting or developing checklists and rating scales were given in Chapter 8 (Irwin & Bushnell, 1980): (1) there must be a sufficient level of training prior to observation; (2) the behaviors to be observed must be listed; (3) there must be a logical organization of items, as well as ease of use; and (4) the organizational format must be matched to the purposes of observation. Two additional criteria are included here for choosing or constructing a checklist or rating scale: (5) there must be a focus on what children can do (the social contexts of ability) rather than on what children fail to do (the social contexts of disability), and (6) the item content must be presented with sufficient clarity so that the same information can be obtained from a child's parent or teacher.

Checklists and rating scales with a prereferral function are now available for speech-language clinicians to use themselves or to have teachers use. Boyce and Larson (1983, pp. 20–21) offer an informal 20-item rating scale for teacher observation of communicative behaviors in secondary classrooms. Howell and Morehead (1987, p. 229) utilize a 13-item checklist for observing students' application of communication strategies in the upper primary through secondary levels. Ripich and Spinelli (1985, p. 209) have also devised a brief rating scale for elementary-level teachers to use in judging seven general areas of children's discourse behaviors. A language use inventory (checklist) developed by Gruenewald and Pollak (1990, p. 70) also has prereferral applicability for primary- and secondary-level students.

The most comprehensive and formal rating scale is one standardized by Fressola and Hoerchler (1989) on 4,500 students from 27 states and 82 school districts. This scale is intended to be used by classroom teachers for the rating of 68 behaviors related to articulation, voice, fluency and language form, content, and use. Ratings can be transformed into standard scores and percentile ranks for the age span from 4½ to 18 years. Although this scale meets the Irwin and Bushnell (1980) criteria better than the informal checklists and rating scales just cited, three design limitations need to be considered. One type of limitation emerges from the biasing effects created by statements that direct attention to only what a child cannot do (criterion 5). For example, the 42 statements pertaining to language form, content, and use are typically prefaced with *has difficulty, lacks, demonstrates difficulty,* or *exhibits difficulty.* A second design problem concerns the omission in the choice of items, of a clear logical relationship between the oral aspects of communicative competence and their role as precursors for literacy learning (criterion 3). Finally, without extensive modification to the often complex and ambiguous wording of items, this scale, as well as the others cited, would be difficult to use with parents (criterion 6).

A variety of resources can be drawn on from the developmental and clinical literature for constructing a prereferral categorical tool that adequately meets the five design standards (criteria 2–6). Since many choices are available for the selection of content, clinicians should be guided by the degree of compatibility between their conceptual frameworks about language, learning, and literacy and the content to be included in categorical tools. Information is available on precursors of metalinguistic awareness (van Kleeck & Schuele, 1987), including emerging phonological awareness and its application to sound-letter correspondences (Ball & Blachman, 1988; Blachman, 1989); developmental expectations for children's understanding of the forms, functions, and content of print literacy (van Kleeck, 1990); and metacognitive and metalinguistic strategies regulating various aspects of discourse processing and production (Brinton & Fujiki, 1989; Wallach & Miller, 1988; Westby, 1989; Wiig, 1989) (see also Chapter 12). In addition, Cochrane, Cochrane, Scalena, and Buchanan (cited in Weaver, 1988, pp. 206–207) offer a schema for considering the development of print literacy on a continuum from preindependent literacy to independent literacy, while Genishi and Dyson (1984), Ehri (1989b), and Scott (1989a) provide frameworks for observing the communicative purposes and processes of children's writing and phases of spelling.

Narratives can be used as a supplement to a checklist or rating scale. The purpose of a narrative is to make the teacher's perception of the problem explicit. An interview is also a type of narrative tool, at least when its purpose is to define more precisely whether a problem exists, what its dimensions may be, and how the child's strengths are viewed.

The teacher's written narrative in Exhibit 11-1 describes Billy, a child at risk for academic failure. She has interpreted his problems as a set of negative behaviors inherent in him. These behaviors then become symptomatic of probable failure. There is also the concern that a language-processing problem might be the source of his symptoms, despite the lack of any developmental history that points to this diagnosis. The perspective of Billy's mother differed from the teacher's, as noted by the clinician's written summary (Exhibit 11-2).

In Billy's case, narrative information pinpointed a conflict in perspectives about potential sources of difficulty. The teacher attributed the general problem to Billy, while the mother located the source of difficulty in the interactional structure of the classroom and, possibly, the home. Furthermore, communication between the teacher and parent apparently had broken down. What remained to be defined was Billy's overall readiness to meet classroom demands.

Exhibit 11-1 Teacher's Narrative

Billy, a 6-year-11-month-old white male, was completing first grade. His teacher, Ms. Richards, was preparing to recommend that Billy be retained because of his lack of progress in mastering the curriculum. She defined the problem in the following way.

Billy is frustrated by reading. He does not enjoy it, as it is a chore for him. He is reading on level 3 (the first part) and needs to stay with this level until he masters the skills and vocabulary. For example, he has a weak sight word vocabulary and is also somewhat below grade level in English, math, social studies, and science as a result. His spelling is far below grade level. I feel that Billy has a processing problem. He appears to function well orally, although I am not certain about this. His biggest difficulties occur when he has to read or write. He then becomes easily frustrated. He also seems immature for his age, can't pay attention for long, fidgets, often has difficulty following directions, often talks out of turn, and sometimes talks too much.

Exhibit 11-2   Mother's Oral Narrative (from the Clinician's Written Summary)

Billy's mother was upset by the suggestion of retention, believing instead that the open classroom structure of his first grade was not meeting his needs for more individualized attention. While agreeing that reading, writing, and math were difficult for Billy, she was most concerned that he no longer wanted to go to school. She indicated that he did not enjoy reading and had never been a child who sought being read to as a preferred activity. In her perspective, Billy tended to perform less well "on demand" and would seek to avoid situations where his self-esteem was threatened. She also reported a normal developmental history and a lack of any familial history to account for the learning difficulties that Billy was having. The mother further noted that Billy's style of communication was less verbal, similar to his father's style, while her style was a verbal one; thus, Billy may have been receiving conflicting messages about how and when to communicate appropriately.

Collaborative models presume that team members have developed effective interview skills as a means for developing a frame of reference and information base that can be shared with each other and with parents and students. Interview skills are generally defined as skills needed to conduct purposeful verbal interactions, including taking responsibility for conversational development if necessary (Idol et al., 1987). Interviewing is considered as a process of eliciting and sharing information, expressing and discovering feelings in an open manner, exploring problems, and planning for future action to assist students (Idol et al., 1987; West et al., 1989). Critical interview behaviors include (1) being an empathic and active listener, (2) directing the conversation so that its content meets the interview's objectives, (3) wording questions to bridge the respondent's understanding and the interviewer's objectives, (4) asking one thing at a time, (5) making the purpose of question asking clear, (6) using questioning techniques that promote ample opportunity for the respondent to generate contributions and that allow ambiguous or incomplete responses to be clarified, and (7) not "putting ideas into the respondent's mind" (West et al., 1989, p. 125).

Summary of Preliminary Findings

Through the use of categorical and narrative tools, a summary can be prepared that describes the child's general competences and initially interprets the existing problem (Spinelli & Ripich, 1985). To return to the example of Billy, a categorical tool constructed in combination with the narrative reports should accomplish four goals. First, there should be more evidence about the convergence or divergence of teacher and maternal perspectives on Billy's understanding of the forms and communicative functions of speaking, listening, reading, writing, and spelling. Second, more precise documentation should emerge to confirm or disconfirm the teacher's impresson that Billy is "out of phase" with her expectations, as well as curriculum expectations, for literacy learning. Third, the categorical tool should provide quantifiable evidence that educational risk is present. Finally, based on these narrative and categorical tools, particular domains should logically follow for further assessment, if warranted, in order to pursue sources of breakdown in interactional and academic competencies.

The wide-angle view afforded by the preliminary summary shows where assessment lenses should then be focused to obtain an accurate and valid picture. Most importantly, the initial problem summary functions as a collaborative procedure for the next step in decision making: observation of relevant classroom or intervention situations.

Step 2: Observe Real-Time Interaction

In moving to the second phase of assessment, clinicians and teachers need to select the most appropriate observational tool or combination of tools to accomplish four goals: (1) systematic comparison of classroom observational data with the initial summary; (2) revision of the initial interpretation of the problem, if indicated; (3) reconciliation of different perspectives on competencies, breakdowns in competencies, and sources of breakdowns; and (4) developing a plan in which the teaching choices maximize opportunities for effective learning in the classroom in either the regular or special education setting. Anticipated outcomes include enhanced reliability and validity in decision making initially and over time.

This phase is also characterized by an integration of observational tools. The depth of integration will depend on how narrow a focus is required to define patterns of communicative competencies and the sources of breakdowns. Four courses of integration are outlined. Of these four, two are obligatory and two are optional.

Describe the Activity Structure (Regular Lens, Obligatory)

Regardless of the depth of observation, description of the activity structure is obligatory. Procedures for describing the activity structure, including mapping the classroom, were discussed in Chapter 10 (see Exhibit 10-1). Understanding the activity structure is the mechanism by which the clinician and other team members, applying a regular lens, can analyze the physical, temporal, and social organization of the particular activity, including its communicative requirements.

The clinician and teacher need to agree on which activities will be observed, when observation will take place, and the length of observation (e.g., one session versus different sessions over several weeks). For example, in developing an assessment of Billy, representative contexts should be selected from whole- and small-group lessons to peer play in order to define his most typical and most effective communicative participation. Recall that his most typical might occur in situations where Billy seems to be less communicatively competent, while his most effective will occur in situations in which he shows ability.

Obtain a Running Record (Regular Lens, Obligatory)

A running record of the activity is a narrative tool generated from live or taped observation. Its use is obligatory. Through the running record, the clinician is able to record and to recount in writing all that is significant about the activity and individual children's participation in the activity as events occur in sequence. Remember from the discussion in Chapter 9 on narrative tools that, in selecting a running record, the clinician does not predetermine what he or she thinks is important. Rather, the focus of observation is the communicative context through which the activity is constructed and sustained.

Constructing a Running Record. Two variations of a running record (Exhibits 11-3 and 11-4) are taken from the Speech Rules Lesson discussed in Chapter 4. This example of discourse is not one to emulate; rather, the example serves to illuminate how communicative contexts can be unintentionally disruptive for students' learning.

Some background information is in order. The 24-minute language therapy session included the clinician and three children, all of whom were in the regular third grade and came from lower socioeconomic backgrounds. Two of the children, Damian and Allison, were black, and the third child, Jared, was white.

Damian, age 8 years, 11 months, was known to the clinician since his entrance into a Headstart program. This program was located in a public school served by the clinician at that time. At 4 years old, Damian was described as having delayed language development and was also considered to be slow. By Grade 2, he was displaying persistent academic and attentional difficulties. His second- and third-grade teachers reported that Damian only "got along" because of his good survival skills, such as the use of sophisticated cheating strategies. A special education referral was in progress, since Damian's third-grade teacher had recommended retention. He was currently receiving language intervention in a pullout program for 30 minutes twice weekly.

Allison, age 10, was the oldest of the three children and had repeated Grade 1. She was classified as learning disabled, with a language learning disability as the secondary condition. Allison was mainstreamed, however. In kindergarten, Allison used only two or three word utterances, and the concern existed that her mother, a single parent, did not verbally interact with her sufficiently. Since Grade 1, Allison had been placed in a learning disability resource program where an Orton-Gillingham approach to decoding was used. In addition, she also received remedial reading through computerized instruction. The addition

Exhibit 11-3   Running Record A: Topic Construction Focus

Topic 1: An extended opening sequence in which the focus of talk was the new function of the speech room as a TV studio. Damian and Allison were apparently confused between the room's new use as a TV studio for school purposes and its use as a "speech room."

Topic 2: The clinician sequentially announced and expanded on the five conduct rules for appropriate participation in "speech."

1. Walk quietly to and from speech.
2. Be polite.
3. Keep hands, feet, objects to yourselves.
4. Pay attention.
5. Do your best.

The clinician apparently assumed that these five rules were familiar to Damian and Allison but not to Jared, who was a new group member. The rules were made visible through being written on a poster board held by the clinician. Following introduction of each rule, which the children were expected to read but often had difficulty doing, the clinician queried them about the rule's meaning.

Topic 3: The clinician sequentially announced and expanded on three consequences of violating the rules.

1. One misbehavior—name written on the blackboard, just like in the classroom.
2. Two misbehaviors—a note written to the teacher.
3. Repeated misbehavior—student not allowed to return to the speech and language class.

These three rules were also written on the poster board. The same query procedures used in Topic 2 were also followed.

Topic 4: A barrier task was implemented in which each child was to take turns describing the contents of a picture the others could not see. The picture was then to be drawn by the two other children. In practice, each child used a labeling strategy to direct their peers' drawing, such as saying "sun," "house," etc., reflecting their apparent interpretation of the activity.

---

of remedial reading, combined with resource room services, limited Allison to one hour weekly of language intervention.

Jared, age 9 years, 1 month, was new to the school system. He had moved from another county, where he had been placed in a learning disability program. Because Jared had failed the norm-referenced language screening in his new school system, he was placed in a learning disability resource program, with language intervention as an additional resource service for one hour per week.

Exhibit 11-4   Running Record B: Lesson Organization Focus

The purpose of the activity appeared to be to remind Damian and Allison about the rules of conduct for how to behave in "speech" and to introduce these rules to Jared.

The activity was organized into three general segments. The first segment was an extended setting-up phase in which the clinician explained the purpose of the conduct rules and also announced that a "fun test" would take place after the rules were talked about. Embedded in this setting-up phase was a long subsequence introduced by the clinician and cooperatively elaborated on by all three children on the new use of the "speech room" as a TV studio.

The clinician reintroduced the primary topic of the conduct rules, which marked the second segment of the implementing phase. Three distinct events made up this segment:

1. The clinician sequentially announced and elaborated on five conduct rules for acceptable participation in "speech," including the requirement that the children explain the underlying reason why each rule was important. During this event, Damian was sanctioned for his negative attitude, which resulted in his temporarily withdrawing from overt participation. The end of this event was marked by the clinician's review of the reward system for following all of the rules. For example, the earning of 10 stars would result in a prize.

2. The clinician sequentially introduced and expanded on three consequences of violating the conduct rules. Again, the children were expected to explain why these consequences were important.

3. A barrier task was introduced in which children were instructed to take individual turns in describing the contents of a picture not visible to the others and to draw what was described. None of the three children described the picture's content; rather, they only itemized objects from the picture. During Jared's turn, Damian violated the "no peek" rule by visually intruding on Jared's picture. The clinician immediately sanctioned Damian by giving him a token for misconduct.

The final segment was a brief closing phase. This consisted of the children gathering up the barrier task materials, returning them to the clinician, and leaving the session.

Damian and Allison had been grouped together previously in language therapy. They also lived in the same neighborhood. Jared was the "outsider." He was new to the school and relatively new to the language intervention group. The group met in a room in the school from which morning announcements were also televised daily to each classroom.

Although both running records filter observations in a similar way, the direction varies. The focus of the running record in Exhibit 11-3 is directed towards how the activity is put together through topic construction. This type of focus may be sufficient if the intent was to obtain data, for example, on how the three children demonstrated understanding, or misunderstanding, of prescriptive and restrictive conduct rules (Topics 2 and 3); the ways in which they could collaboratively manipulate a familiar topic of interest (Topic 1); or how each managed an imposed topic that required describing a pictured event not visible to the others (Topic 4).

In the running record in Exhibit 11-4, the emphasis is on lesson organization as constructed through topic centering. More child-centered information is also recounted in this running record. Hence, we learn of two instances in which Damian, who was being referred for a possible attentional deficit disorder, was explicitly sanctioned for not following the rules. In one of these instances, he temporarily withdrew from participation. An important question concerns the conditions that promoted less cooperation and less directed attention on Damian's part. If the purpose is to address this question, then the observational lens needs to be narrowed further to the microlevel.

Obtain Several Critical Incidents (Close-Up Lens, Optional)

The critical incident, a narrative tool, is also based on event sampling and videotaping, derives from a running record, and crystallizes a key learning encounter affecting a child's access to participation (Michaels & Cazden, 1986). One qualification in using this tool is that observers must recognize and agree on the beginning and terminating boundaries of the critical incident. As discussed in Chapter 9, a critical incident report allows a small amount of information to be studied in more detail in order to examine a specific question.

Critical Incident A: Does Damian "Tune Out"? At least three interactional patterns could be explored in greater depth from the running record of the Speech Rules Lesson:

- What kinds of linguistic and discourse strategies did Allison use to help Jared and Damian explain the rules?
- As the newest group member and unfamiliar with expectations for participation in "speech," what coping strategies did Jared use to deal with the cognitive and social complexities of tasks that were genuinely difficult for him, such as being called on to read the rules written on the poster board?
- What could be some possible sources of Damian's reduction in on-task attending? (This question is addressed in critical incident A, Exhibit 11-5.)

As noted earlier, a second critical incident involving Damian being sanctioned for rule breaking was identified during the barrier task (Topic 4). His behavior, which led to a reprimand, was similar to his behavior in the first critical incident. The pattern emerging from these critical incidents suggested that the sources of the communicative breakdowns resided less in a lack of ability to focus his attention and more in his need to preserve his feelings of competence and self-esteem. In fact, the analysis of critical incident A indicated that Damian was ca-

Exhibit 11-5   Critical Incident A: Damian's Variability in Sustaining On-Task Attention

---

Damian is attentive throughout the subsequence of Topic 1 and the first portion of Topic 2. He participates appropriately and actively by contributing new information, initiating several requests for information and, in one instance, correcting Jared's inaccurate use of a pronoun. Neither his spontaneous contributions nor his inquiries are always fully acknowledged by the clinician, however.

The critical incident begins near the end of an extended sequence on the meaning of Rule 2 ("Be polite"). Apparently having figured out, or recalling from memory, Rule 3 ("Keep hands, feet, objects to yourselves") and anticipating its occurrence next, Damian solicits permission of the clinician: "I can read next?" His request is ignored, possibly because its timing is not interpreted as appropriate relative to the current topic on the floor. While the IRE sequences continue on the various meanings of Rule 2, Damian is simultaneously, and quietly, negotiating with Allison about which one of them will take a turn to read Rule 3. At the same time, he is also monitoring the clinician's speaking turn, made evident by the direction of his eye gaze, and, then, at a probable stopping point of the clinician's turn, Damian again asks permission to read Rule 3. The clinician responds with the multiple function assertion "I'm going to read rule number three." An immediate change is observable in Damian's posture and body orientation. He slumps into his chair and withdraws from the center of interaction, an action that communicates feelings of disappointment or rejection.

The clinician seems to interpret immediately the meaning of Damian's action. She attempts to repair the situation by directing the children to more cooperative participation with a directive and follow-up confirmation "Let's all read it together. How's that sound?" Still slumping in his chair, Damian passively joins in a choral response. The clinician, still seeking to repair, then nominates Damian to explain the meaning of the rule. He refuses to comply, signaled by negatively shaking his head. As a result, Jared and then Allison take Damian's turn slot and offer explanations.

During this transaction, Damian stares at the clinician. His facial configuration conveys continued anger or hurt. Attempting for a third time to solicit his active participation, the clinician requests Damian to recall how Rule 3 was applied from the previous school year. Damian again refuses to respond. The clinician then explicitly reprimands him with "Damian, you've been begging me to come to speech. Now you're here and let's act nice, OK?" This sanction is immediately followed by a fourth attempt at reconciliation with the choice request, "Do you want to read [Rule] Number 4?" (which, in reality, may have been an indirect directive). Damian again shakes his head to indicate no and is seen to place his hand over his mouth, where it remains for the next 20 seconds.

The terminating boundary of this critical incident occurs with the introduction of Rule 5 ("Do your best"). Damian begins to participate more visibly. His tentative reentry was marked in two distinct ways: (1) his verbal actions in being a resource for Allison (i.e., giving her a "right" answer for Rule 5) and his choral reading of the rule; and (2) his nonverbal action of leaning forward towards the table, which indicated rejoining.

---

pable of attending to and tracking multiple layers of the communicative context. He could simultaneously attend to the specific aspects of the topic being talked about, detect and correct an error in pronoun use by another child, look ahead to what was coming next, and figure out its meaning. Moreover, even when Damian appeared to tune out through his withdrawal from participation, he did not close down his information-monitoring systems. Rather, his actions elicited reactions from the clinician that subsequently influenced his further actions. He continued to monitor carefully the events going on, waiting for the appropriate time to reenter the discourse in a face-saving way.

When Damian dealt with familiar events in a non-knowledge-testing situation, such as Topic 1, his contributions were relevant but not always acknowledged. When Damian determined that tasks were more difficult and that independent performance, such as reading the first two rules (Topic 2), was the primary way by which knowledge was assessed, he attempted to reorganize complexity by seeking cooperative assistance from others. For example, he requested from the clinician that Jared be the first to read the rules. When he had information, such as the content of Rule 3, readily accessible, he tended to misread the ongoing interaction for when to enter conversation or when to shift topics, thus violating timing rules for cooperative turn-taking. When he had to infer answers in the absence of less visible social supports for deriving an accurate response (the Topic 4 barrier task), then he tended to use inappropriate behavior to obtain missing information. This had also been observed by Damian's second- and third-grade teachers, who characterized his coping actions in terms of cheating.

Sufficient information may now be available from the close-up level to engage in the joint planning of intervention, contingent on the existence of comparable running records and critical incidents obtained in the classroom setting. For example, what had previously been described as an attentional deficit can be reconsidered from an alternate perspective. The less desirable social behavior that Damian often manifested may be the outcome of repeated experiences in which significant adults in his life unintentionally failed to interpret his communicative efforts as signals of the need to have his competence recognized.

Critical Incident B: The Deception of Appearances. The second critical incident is taken from the Chef Lesson, which was also presented in Chapter 4. The ethnically mixed kindergarten class for language-impaired children consisted of three boys and two girls who ranged in age from five years, three months to six years, one month. Three of the children, including both females, were white; one male was black, while the third male, Larry, came to the United States from Vietnam when he was 24 months old and lived with his English-speaking grandmother, who only spoke English to him in the home. This particular core of children had been together for one and a half years. They were being taught by a teacher who was also a speech-language clinician.

The content of the 45-minute lesson derived from a visit the children had made earlier that morning to the school kitchen. Children were seated in a semicircle on chairs facing the teacher, the cooking materials, and a bulletin board with a picture of a chef and a recipe card pinned to it. The curriculum goals of the lesson were structured around a community helper unit. Specific objectives included alphabetic recognition using the chef concept and related cooking materials and expansion of oral communication skills, including the learning of appropriate rules for turn-taking.

The running record of the lesson indicated two major components. In the first phase, a 15-minute multiply embedded orientation and implementation phase, previous letter-sound associations were reviewed ("Mr. M for munching"), a new association was introduced as the correspondent for the cooking activity ("Mr. T for tasty roll-ups"), the functions and tools of the chef were presented, and, finally, the ingredients and measuring devices for making the tasty roll-ups were announced and physically handled on an individual basis by each child. IRE sequences dominated as children were queried about each topical aspect. The teacher's turn allocation rules were primarily open bid or filling the R slot chorally. The children seemed to have an implicit understanding of these two rules.

The second phase, which lasted 25 minutes, was introduced with "Now, we're gonna pretend we're chefs," followed by IRE sequences on identifying the actual cooking tools and ingredients. These ingredients included bologna, cream cheese, Worcestershire sauce, onion, and chopped pineapple. Implementation began when children were individually selected to take turns in either grating the onion or mixing the various ingredients. The question addressed from the running record concerned Larry's tendency to volunteer information less often than the other group members (Exhibit 11-6). The teacher-clinician defined volunteering as children self-selecting to contribute information.

This critical incident revealed for the teacher-clinician that appearances were deceiving. That is, her organization of discourse conflicted with her assumptions about classroom management and curriculum goals and procedures. One area of conflict involved the turn allocation procedures that were employed. She used an open bid style instead of nominating individual children in the belief that nomination provided children with less accountability in knowing when to take a turn. This form of speaker self-selection did avoid placing individual children in the spotlight to respond and reduced the frequency of nonresponding. However, through analyzing critical incidents, the teacher-clinician came to understand that, in supporting the children's ability to select themselves as speakers with a minimum of interruption, she unintentionally created a situation in which passive responding to her framing of topics was the *rule*. Additionally, although the chef activity was conceived as collaborative, it was implemented in a way that allowed children access to the cooking phase only by the teacher-clinician's individual selection.

A second area of conflict related to the teacher-clinician's perspectives about Larry. His tendency to not volunteer frequently as a speaker was initially attributed to a developmental language delay. The suggestion was that his level of linguistic development was comparable to his peers in the group. Larry's cultural

Exhibit 11-6   Critical Incident B: Larry's Volunteering of Information

---

During the first phase of the lesson, Larry responds appropriately to open bids, although he does not do so frequently; however, on several occasions, he adds new information to the teacher's request content. During the second phase, Larry is the last to be called to take a turn at grating the onion. The teacher asks him, "What are you doing?" and he responds, "I'm grating," which is followed with an E slot neutral evaluation and comprehension check, "Ok, you're grating." Larry then returns to his seat. The mixing activity starts next.

The critical incident begins when Sol completes his turn at stirring the ingredients and Mary is nominated for a turn. Sol walks back to the semicircle and sits in Mary's seat. Larry turns to Sol and sanctions him for violating possession with "No/ It's not your chair." The teacher-clinician then momentarily redirects her attention to Larry and tells him that Sol's action is acceptable. The camera view then shows Larry observing Mary during her stirring turn and his directing his eye gaze to her as she returns to Sol's former chair. During this same segment, the teacher-clinician is simultaneously commenting on the completion of the stirring phase. In the middle of her speaking turn, Larry, who has not been called on to participate in the stirring, walks to the ingredient bowl, picks up the spoon, and begins to stir. His unexpected action interrupts the teacher-clinician in midutterance and surprise is visible on her face. She asks him whether he had been called to come up. In response to an apparent rebuke, Larry noticeably steps back from the table and shakes his head to indicate no.

The end of the critical incident is marked by Larry's immediate return to his chair. During the remainder of the activity, he neither independently responds to requests for information nor expands on others' contributions.

---

and bilingual background were considered less germane to explaining this delay. The videotaped running record and the resulting critical incident focused attention on the degree to which Larry was dependent on observing the actions of his peers in order to feel more secure about how he should perform. Furthermore, Larry's reaction to Sol taking the wrong chair indicated that earlier he had misinferred the degree of stringency about the chair possession rule or that he was having difficulty sorting out, or simultaneously attending to, which rules held at which times.

The second possibility was supported by the critical incident analysis. Larry was one of two children selected to grate the onion. Two other children, Sol and Mary, were selected separately to stir the tasty roll-up mixture. Larry seemed to anticipate being selected after Mary based on his observing her return to the chair and his previous schema for turn-taking in an activity of this kind. He was not attuned to the clinician's nonverbal cues (e.g., her change from facing the group to facing the mixing bowl) or even to what she was saying as a conclusion to the stirring. The result was a mistiming of a turn. His embarrassment was visibly obvious when the teacher-clinician sanctioned him with "Larry/ Were you called up here?"

The issues arising from this and other incidents involving Larry make more salient the question of cultural or bilingual discontinuities that may be operating to produce a picture of Larry as developmentally delayed. More precise information on his level of linguistic-communicative development is needed and can be obtained through the use of descriptive tools. More detail about Larry's developmental history, including the style of discourse into which he has been socialized, is also needed.

Obtain Transcribed Samples of Selected Dynamics of Interaction (Microclose-Up Lens, Optional)

A verbatim transcription is a descriptive tool whose content should be derived from a videotaped record as opposed to an audiotape record alone. This tool is selected when the purpose is to acquire more detailed information about a significant developing process or pattern of behavior that occurs across contexts. In short, a transcription is the means for making the familiar obvious at the microscopic level of analysis. The anticipated outcome of choosing this tool is an accurate and comprehensive picture of the multiple dimensions of communicative interactions and disruptions.

Some Issues Related to Transcription. As stated in Chapter 10, a transcription is a retrospective account of a stream of talk that defines an event as a critical incident. This in-depth method of analysis will be selected when the purposes of observation have not been sufficiently satisfied through running records or critical incidents analyses. Again, as with running records and critical incidents analyses, multiple samples should be obtained. Procedures for transcription have been outlined in Appendixes A and B.

The distinction between language sampling and discourse sampling warrants clarification, since the two terms are often used interchangeably. Language sampling focuses on how the child uses aspects of language in a particular context of use. Discourse sampling, in contrast, is concerned with how a specific kind of discourse event, such as a question-answer sequence, a narration, a lesson, or peer teaching, is negotiated by its participants. Both procedures often produce similar kinds of information. For example, discourse sampling can yield information on a child's use of semantic-syntactic relationships or the kinds of phonological processes employed. However, since language sampling is concerned with what the child does, it cannot provide as rich information on the discourse devices jointly utilized by the child and his or her conversational partners to initiate, sustain, repair, and terminate turn-taking or topic sharing.

A second issue pertains to the relationship between the length of a discourse sample and its representativeness (Gallagher, 1983; see also Chapter 7). Lahey (1988) recommends obtaining a minimum of 30 minutes of continuous event sampling from different situations or over several different days for a sufficient sample of child utterances. Obviously, the longer and more diverse the samples, the more confidence one can have in the reliability and validity of the outcomes. However, transcription of even 30 minutes of dialogue can be extremely time-consuming for clinical purposes in both the school and nonschool settings.

An alternate approach is offered by Lund and Duchan (1988), who emphasize obtaining and transcribing a variety of discourse events, for example, story telling, participation in classroom lessons, and peer play. Their approach is essentially the one incorporated into the observational plan being discussed here— with an important modification. Time management in transcription is enhanced when agreement exists that a particular segment of events merits closer examination. Since the clinician and other team collaborators, including the parent or caregiver, must agree that certain running records and critical incidents are representative events, the standard of external validity has been established for a particular transcript. Furthermore, if the purpose of a microclose-up analysis is to *describe* the dynamics and layers of interaction and their influence as sources of communicative breakdowns, then the previously identified critical incidents should direct the focus of transcription. Two examples of this tight focus follow.

Transcriptional Analysis A: Communicative Breakdowns Located in the Hidden Curriculum. The critical incident from the Chef Lesson indicated some unintended breakdown effects of the teacher-clinician's turn allocation rules. These unintentional outcomes reflect the hidden curriculum at work. Their dynamics differentially affected the group as a whole and individual children within the group, such as Larry.

Transcription of this critical incident, as well as other comparable ones, resulted in the teacher-clinician's interpretation that the primary issue impacting on children's learning had little to do with knowing how to take a turn. Rather, despite the operation of a less rigid turn management style, the social structure of learning was organized in a way that promoted children's using language with minimal variability in form or function. Child language use consisted of either elliptical single word responses to lower-level *who* and *what* or *yes/no* requests or elliptical responses elicited from the nonverbal context of their here-and-now actions, as in "What are you doing?" (referring to physical actions, such as stirring, grating, or tasting). Across the events of the classroom, language was seldom encouraged as a means of predicting what might happen next, organizing the cooperative actions of others, summarizing what had occurred, inferring motives or emotions, and clarifying the intentions of others. Because the teacher-clinician wanted to prevent "failure," she unintentionally created conversational routines as the substance of learning (see Chapter 4 for a transcription and discussion). The reality of implementation bore little relationship to facilitating children's oral communication skills or to linking more literate uses ("metauses") of language to communicatively appropriate reading readiness activities.

Transcriptional Analysis B: Communicative Breakdowns Specific to an Individual Child. Transcription can also be focused on the individual child. The following example illustrates a purpose of a microclose-up analysis that is concerned with examining sources of communicative breakdowns specific to an individual child (Exhibit 11-7). The transcription was derived from critical incidents involving the discourse event of sharing time in a special education classroom for children with language learning disabilities (Silliman & Paris, 1984). The focus was Cary, 11 years old, who often had difficulty in formulating his topics smoothly in order to keep his peers' attention. In this segment, Cary literally jumped into the conversation when he inferred that an opening had occurred for contributing a "scary" personal experience.

The following kinds of analyses can be applied to this excerpt: (1) narrative cohesion, (2) level of utterance complexity, and (3) patterns of repair attempts. The false starts and self-repairs indicate Cary's attempts to formulate simultaneously *what* to say and *how* to say it. False starts are failures to correct an utterance successfully. However, depending on the discourse sequence, false starts may really be a type of metalinguistic repair called *bracketing*, which is "the insertion of material, as if in brackets or parentheses, in the middle of an otherwise intact sentence" (Cazden et al., 1985, p. 53). With self-repairs, the speaker corrects a source of difficulty so that the dialogue can proceed smoothly (Schegloff, Jefferson, & Sacks, 1977). The beginning of each repair attempt is underlined in the transcript.

Exhibit 11-7   Cary's Narrative of a Scary Personal Experience

---

(*C* refers to Cary and *T* to teacher; for the meaning of notations, refer to Appendix B).

C   254   Once (.) - we were in the house right/ One day we were going for a match (.) car
          -- *Matchbox* car/ It - it wasn't raining that day/ We -- and we left -- we tri -- we
          looked for all a them = picked 'em up/
T   255   mmhm/
C   256   And we didn't find that one/ One day -- the next day it was raining w -- me and
          my brother had my shorts on/
T   257   mmhm/
C   258a Or bathing suit on/ Right/ (.) um - and then when we did it w -- I saw the car out
          there = saw it a couple of days but I forgot to pick it up/ An then (.) when there
          was lightning and thunder I went right out there to get the car/ And you shoulda
          -- I got so scared/ I pick up the car and it felt like the lightning went right
          through me/
          And {I got scared}
T   258b   {It might have}
C   258c because the li -- all the light - all the light went right (.) by me/ I ran right back
          inside = I was scared/

In this example, there are eight self-repairs. Six are lexical (turns 254, 256, and 258c), the remaining two are syntactic (turn 258a). In the first lexical repair (turn 254), Cary detects a violation in the word form and corrects it by retrieving the explicit name. The three lexical repairs that occur within the last utterance of turn 254 suggest attempts to use a recurring, or parallel, grammatical structure as the repair procedure for linking successive clauses (Bennett-Kastor, 1986; Lahey, 1988). The two lexical repairs occurring in turn 256 are located across different utterance boundaries and have different functions and outcomes. The first is a successful correction through specification of content (e.g., "one day" to "*the* next day"). The second fails to connect the first clause ("*the* next day it was raining w --") to the proposition that constitutes the repair sequence ("*me* and my brother had my shorts on or bathing suit on") (turns 256 and 258a) and may represent an abandonment of a difficult clausal construction in favor of an easier construction (Brinton & Fujiki, 1989). The attempt to repair does serve to recover the identity of the ambiguous "we" mentioned earlier.

The three remaining repairs could be analyzed in a similar manner. For example, the syntactic repair in turn 258a ("*I* saw the car out there = saw it a couple of days but I forgot to pick it up") is comparable to bracketing, the inclusion of material within the host sentence, which suggests a more complex use of syntactic resources (Cazden et al., 1985).

The use of a descriptive tool, like a transcript, provides some evidence of planning and production processes at work in naturally occurring situations, such as a child's sharing time narrative. The segment from Cary's transcript shows how the overlapping cycles of verbal planning and production (Beattie, 1983; Catts, 1989b) are always influenced by the conceptual and social requirements of conversation. In terms of conceptual demands, the argument can be made that Cary in his communicative role as a narrator is engaging in an easier form of discourse production, since narratives have a more predictable structure than other kinds of discourse (Ochs, 1979b). The existence of self-repair attempts indicates that, at some level of metalinguistic awareness, Cary detects when he is encountering trouble with either the speed or efficiency of retrieving the appropriate referential relations for coding his intent. Moreover, detection may be enhanced by the syntactic role surrounding the trouble source (Brinton & Fujiki, 1989). Despite the evidence that he is aware of trouble points, their resolution does not always occur on an automatic level. Rather, Cary's attention seems to be directed towards the demand of working on these referential trouble sources out loud. As a consequence of having to allocate his attentional resources in this manner (e.g., to planning out connections between syntactic roles and meaning relations), there is a production breakdown in the cohesiveness of his story and a compromising of his status as an effective narrator.

One can also consider the social dimensions of Cary's dialogue on planning and production. Recall that Cary had been described as jumping into a turn.

Ochs (1979b) suggests that, when social and conceptual requirements are equally demanding, an overall effect is the production of less well-planned discourse:

> In some cases, a communicator cannot plan the form of his communication because the situation in which he is participating requires more or less continuous monitoring. For example, in spontaneous conversation, who will assume the floor, when the floor will be assumed, and what will be communicated are negotiated on a turn-by-turn basis. The participant in such a situation must attend closely to each turn in order to deal with each of these questions . . . . Where turn-taking is locally managed in this sense, it may take priority over the expression of well-formed propositions for the communicator. (p. 75)

The analysis presented here corroborates the initial description of Cary's problem but goes far beyond wide-angle statements such as "Cary doesn't know how to take a turn." The analysis also illustrates a major contribution of the microclose-up lens to "slowing down" the interaction and allowing important clues to emerge about what is happening.

Step 3: Integrate and Validate Multiple Perspectives

The final phase of assessment is critical, because it entails "confirming the accuracy of observations" (Ripich & Spinelli, 1985, p. 205). Since the generalizability of conclusions cannot be separated from the validity of findings, identifying and resolving differences in interpretations of the data are essential. The viewpoints of the teacher, the clinician, the primary caregivers, and the student need to be obtained, integrated, and validated for the observational tools selected. Any discrepancies must be reconciled so that an accurate and complete summary of findings can be obtained (Ripich & Spinelli, 1985; Ripich, 1989). Some validation procedures are discussed in the next section.

Validating the Teacher's Perspective

Videotape Records Available. One validation procedure that has clinical utility derives from ethnographic research in special education (Mehan et al., 1986). Its implementation is predicated on the availability of videotaped records. The first step is to ask the teacher and/or other team members to review the written description of the activity structure and the running record. Discrepancies in the viewpoints of the teacher and clinician about the accuracy of these written records should be discussed prior to the viewing of the videotape. If the teacher has prepared a separate description of the activity structure or a running record, then the two sets of written records should be compared for consistency.

In the second phase, the teacher and clinician view the videotape together. The teacher's role is to stop the tape when of any the following events occur (Mehan et al., 1986):

- The child of interest is engaged in something about which the teacher would like to comment.
- Either the teacher or children other than the target child are doing something that warrants comment.
- A contrast is observed between the target child's "behaviors" and abilities and those of other children in the activity.
- Behaviors occur that are related either to the reason for a potential referral or to the initial problem summary.

Once this review is completed, a modified set of these procedures can be followed for viewing critical incidents or reviewing transcriptions (depending on the observation and the specific questions of interest). One important issue is whether the teacher's interpretation of an incident as critical is similar to the clinician's. If perspectives differ, then it becomes important to know what sequences of events captured on the videotape are defined as key events by the teacher. The task then becomes one of merging viewpoints as the means for drawing an accurate portrait of the child relative to the academic and interactional requirements of the classroom.

Videotaped Records Unavailable. If a videotaped record is not available, then team members need to compare their written accounts before preparing a final summary. For example, in the transdisciplinary team assessment of the Communication Development Program (see Exhibit 5-4), the five team members, including the speech-language clinician, meet to discuss their observations and other assessment findings. The actual report of the assessment and accompanying recommendations are then team generated. This document represents a joint integration of perspectives on a student's communication status, learning style and strategies, intellectual potential, self-esteem, and vocational interests, values, and attitudes.

Validating the Perspective of the Parent or Caregiver

The second component of validation consists of validating the perspective of the parent or primary caregiver. Interview techniques, categorical tools, and multiple informants are commonly used for identification, the first phase of assessment. However, these same methods are not necessarily as useful when the purpose is to document the validity of an observational assessment. The viewing sessions are designed to obtain the collaborative perspective of team members and can be adapted for use with a parent or caregiver. For example, the videotape can be stopped when the child is doing something that the parent or caregiver considers significant. Critical incidents can be jointly reviewed to determine if the parent or caregiver interprets the pattern of behaviors in a manner similar to the teacher and the clinician.

Several problems arise regarding the modification of the viewing session technique in educational settings. One is the issue of confidentiality, since the videotape contains a record of other children in addition to the target child. In the nonschool clinical setting, this issue is minimized, because assessment typically is focused on dyadic interactions, such as between the clinician, parent, or caregiver and the child. The second problem is the sensitivity that parents and caregivers sometimes have to viewing videotapes of children under their care. One solution to this problem is to use extracts of the written transcripts that concern only the target child. The parent or caregiver is then asked to review these excerpts and to decide whether they accurately depict the child's competencies and problem areas. Multiple samples of a child's narrative from sharing time, and the child's use of requests in different classroom activities are just two examples.

If the observation does not include a microclose-up lens, an alternative is for the clinician to provide a detailed verbal summary on the different kinds of observation that were conducted and the patterns that emerged. The parent or caregiver should be asked whether this summary is consistent with his or her perspective of the child and to elaborate where appropriate. If inconsistency emerges, then areas of disagreement need to be resolved.

Validating the Student's Perspective

The final component in validation is understanding the student's perspective. Not much research is available on this topic, however.

Ripich and Panagos (1985) studied how elementary-age children with articulation problems role played clinician-child "speech therapy." Ripich (1989), using an interview format with 16 children enrolled in school intervention for articulation disorders, elicited behavioral descriptions of roles associated with the speech-language clinician versus the classroom teacher. Neither of these studies specifically addressed the ways in which a communication problem influenced children's views of themselves or even how children with a speech or language disorder defined their world (Ripich, 1989).

Re-Create Familiar Communicative Contexts. One recommendation is to re-create familiar communicative contexts in order to probe how a given child views the world of talk. The following ethnographic interview format, developed by Morine-Dershimer (1985) for students in Grades 2 to 4, was designed to obtain information on their perspectives about the rules and processes of classroom discourse:

- How are children expected to talk in your classroom? When do they talk and what kinds of things do they say? What else can you tell me about how children are expected to talk in your room?
- How can you expect the teacher to talk in your classroom? When does she talk, and what kinds of things does she say? What else can you tell me about when the teacher talks, or what kinds of things she says?
- Suppose there was a new boy (or girl) in your classroom, and you wanted to help him get to know about the class. What would you tell him about how children talk in your classroom? What else would you tell a new boy about how children talk in your class? What would you tell a new boy about how the teacher talks in your classroom? When does she talk, and what kinds of things does she say? (pp. 211–12).

In addition, a series of sentence stems can be used in a modified cloze procedure to identify a child's perspectives on the rules of discourse holding with (1) different conversational partners, such as a teacher versus a parent or friend (e.g., When my teacher wants me to be quiet, she _____; When my mother wants me to be quiet, she _____; When my friend wants me to be quiet, he or she_____), and (2) different types of communicative situations (e.g., I don't talk when _____; I ask a question when_____; When I need help, I _____) (Morine-Dershimer, 1985, pp. 44–45). The sentence stems for the teacher are reproduced below (Morine-Dershimer, 1985, pp. 212–13):

1. When the teacher wants us to get quiet, she . . .
2. When I want to ask the teacher something, I . . .
3. If I know the answer to a question, I . . .
4. If I don't know the answer to a question, I . . .
5. If I need help, I . . .
6. I talk quietly when . . .
7. When the teacher talks, I . . .
8. I don't talk when . . .
9. The teacher doesn't talk when . . .

10. At recess I talk to . . .
11. When I finish my work, I . . .
12. During a lesson, I talk to . . .
13. I ask a question when . . .
14. The teacher asks a question when . . .
15. Before we begin to work . . .
16. After we finish our work, the teacher says . . .
17. The teacher says "good" when . . .

These types of ethnographic formats can be used in conjunction with other specialized probes, such as the following, designed to obtain knowledge about strategy use in reading:

- What do you do when you read and you know that there will be a test on the story later? (Older/better readers tend to be aware of the need to use a strategy, such as rehearsal.)
- Can you do anything as you read that would make what you read easier to remember? (Older/better readers tend to cite such strategies as note-taking, remembering the main points, and self-testing as helpful aids to remembering.)
- What would you do to find the name of a place in the story? (Older/ better readers suggest strategies as a "skim" strategy, while younger/poorer readers are more likely to reply "just read".)
- What would you do so that you can remember a story to tell it to your friend? (Older/better readers mention attempts to remember the important parts of the story; younger/poorer readers tend to say that writing down the story is the best way to remember.) (Pressley, Forrest-Pressley, Elliot-Faust, & Miller, 1985, pp. 28–29)

Self-Profiles. McKinley and Lord-Larson (1985) argue that adolescents with a suspected language learning disability should be told why they are being assessed, what behaviors will be assessed, how their performances are evaluated, and the implications of the findings for their academic, social, and vocational goals. If intervention is warranted, students should be active partners in identifying goals and objectives and in determining priorities for their communication. It is rightly claimed that adolescents must take responsibility for effecting change in their communicative competencies. Indeed, if a youngster remains unmotivated to act as his or her own agent for improvement, the recommendation is that "the adolescent not be forced into intervention services" (McKinley & Lord-Larson, 1985, p. 7).

One tool for helping language learning disabled students as young as kindergarten age to see themselves as their own agents of change is the self-profile (Hoffman, 1990; Miller, 1990). In Chapter 5, the student profile used by the Communication Development Program was discussed (Exhibit 11-8). This profile is a means for students to assess easy versus hard activities, their strengths and weaknesses in these activities, and changes in perspective over time as the result of strategies learned to facilitate their learning. This self-assessment, which is completed monthly beginning in kindergarten, becomes a mechanism for establishing initial baselines on the perception of abilities. It then serves as a self-tracking tool for the mutual evaluation of change by the student and teachers, including the speech-language clinician. The continuous use of profiles also allows the creation of a permanent portfolio.

Miller (1990) utilizes profiling by the child to design an individualized intervention program. Among the dimensions of the profile is the child's assessment (done in conjunction with the teacher) of his or her learning status in various linguistic-communicative areas. For example, in the areas of understanding humor, understanding narratives, and decoding print, the child's ratings are keyed to five categories: prebeginner, beginner/emerging, intermediate/transitional, stronger, and strongest. Clearly, this method permits the child, as well as clinicians, teachers, and parents, to understand the importance of building on competencies in designing intervention. The resulting profile may indicate that the child sees him- or herself as strongest in understanding narratives, as strong in understanding humor, and as a prebeginner in decoding print. Miller (1990) notes that, in using this method, the child "was not compared to his peers; rather, he was encouraged to develop a sense of himself as a competent learner who could develop abilities in those academic areas in which he had previously encountered difficulties in school" (pp. 21–22). For definitions of each learning category and the general process of profiling, the reader is referred to Miller (1990).

CONCLUSION

In this chapter, a plan has been proposed for applying the tools of observation to the linking of developmental and instructional assessment in collaborative learning situations. Components of the plan include identifying whether a problem exists, observing real-time interaction, and integrating and validating multiple perspectives. The integration of four tools for observation of language used by students in real classrooms has been discussed. Use of two of these tools, the activity structure description and the running record, is obligatory; since together they allow an overall understanding of the communicative context. Depending on the continued purposes of observation, two additional tools can also be applied: the critical incident and the transcription. Prior to observation, it is

Exhibit 11-8   Student Profile, Communication Development Program

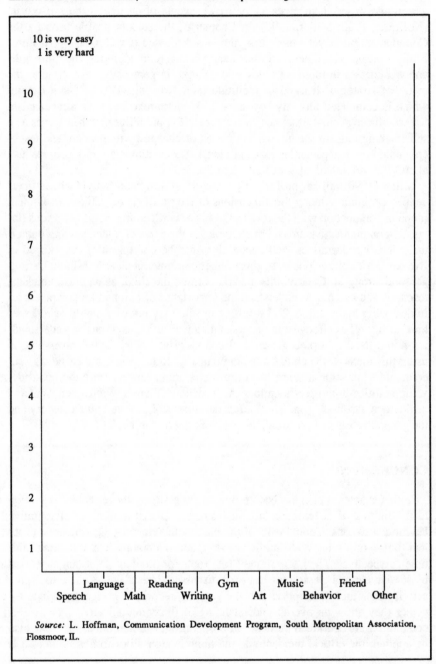

Source: L. Hoffman, Communication Development Program, South Metropolitan Association, Flossmoor, IL.

imperative to define clearly the level and kind of observational data needed to understand the problem. Selection of the appropriate tools will allow a better understanding of competencies and sources of difficulty as they occur and will provide a clear direction for planning collaborative intervention. Finally, it is essential to integrate the views of others (e.g., the student, the parent or caregiver, the teacher, and other team members) in order to make the assessment complete. Another major advantage of integrating multiple perspectives is that it provides a way for all of those involved, including the student, to take an active role in intervention.

Chapter 12

School Learning and Learning Potential: Planning for a Communication-Centered Approach

Obtaining systematic observations of children's communication can lead to the development of appropriate intervention goals and procedures, which, in conjunction with communication-centered learning, can maximize the potential of individual students. As we argue, the preference for communication-centered versus whole-language approaches is predicated on the assumption that language always works in holistic ways. *Communication-centered* means that learning, in order to be literate, must be an active, functional, and interactional process. This is because it is accomplished through discourse between people across curriculum domains and the specific channels of communication, whether oral or written. Communication is simultaneously the focus of literacy learning and the tool for facilitating more effective participation in literacy-learning activities in school.

Several key factors influence whether a particular approach will be successful for a child. Lahey (1988) summarizes some of the factors to be considered in planning intervention goals: (1) social experiences that may be constraining language learning potential, for instance, the quality and frequency of parental interaction patterns (e.g., Conti-Ramsden, 1990; Porter & Conti-Ramsden, 1987) or the quality and purposes of teacher-child or clinician-child interaction (see Chapters 3 and 4); (2) the nature of collaboration in facilitating language learning, including collaboration among parents, peers, and others who are important participants in the child's daily life; (3) the relevance of the settings for intervention (e.g., the classroom, playground, clinic room, and home) and the number and cycling of goals for language learning within and across settings; and (4) based on the observational tools previously applied, the language and communicative behaviors to be facilitated, as well as the means for facilitation. In the next chapter, we address the topic of effective teaching discourse as a tool for promoting literate uses of language and communication. In this chapter, we discuss two areas that are central to the collaborative planning of communication-centered intervention for maximizing children's learning potential.

One area, which is related to self-esteem, involves the adequacy of teaching-learning situations and strategies for nurturing students' awareness of themselves as capable communicators. The second area concerns the interactive nature of learning, including the metacognitive and metalinguistic bases of an active orientation to learning. An understanding of these interactive relationships is a prerequisite for designing teaching-learning situations and strategies that will enable learning to proceed more planfully across the multiple communicative functions of literate language use.

SELF-ESTEEM AND LEARNING POTENTIAL: THE PROBLEM OF TRYING HARDER TO DO BETTER

One theme of this book is that the perpetuation of a passive orientation to learning can be a result of the traditional social organization of teaching and learning. In the traditional structure, literacy activities are isolated into separate skills, and "getting through" the lesson becomes a substitute for real involvement in learning (Bloome, 1987; Bloome & Theodorou, 1988).

A dependent attitude towards learning can have serious cognitive, social, and affective consequences for any learner but especially for students with language and learning difficulties, whether placed in special or regular education settings. Often these students invest much effort in trying harder to succeed. Kronick's (1988) description of the planning problems encountered by many learning disabled students dramatizes some cognitive consequences of "try harder" strategies:

> Learning disabled persons . . . may have poor imagery of immediate or extended time and so misjudge the amount that they can accomplish in a period of time, thus over- and underplanning their use of time. If, in addition, they utilize concrete thinking and have a poor ability to establish priorities, they may not resort to problem solving to reorganize their time and ensure that critical tasks are completed and less critical ones deferred or abbreviated. Eventually they are faced with a backlog of incomplete tasks, and the amount of anticipated work overwhelms and hence further disorganizes and overwhelms them. Similarly, LD students who are inefficient at preorganizing a task and in determining the precise focus and the amount of effort expected by teacher or parent may put so much effort into tasks that each task looms as overwhelming. Some concretely believe that every essay must reflect all

that is known in the world about a given subject and that every test written should include a synthesis of the body of human knowledge on the subject in question. Others include so much detail that time runs out before their assignments can be completed . . . . (p. 48)

In addition to cognitive influences, social and affective variables equally affect the tenuous relationship between self-esteem and learning potential in many language learning disabled students. Bashir (1989) highlights the influence of these variables:

As children with language disorders advance in school, these children become increasingly aware of their difficulties and worry about themselves. The awareness takes many forms, but often is associated with a loss of motivation, depression, anger, and a reluctance to participate in learning, including remedial activities. Children become anxious and often verbalize their concerns for themselves. Some children create inaccurate "theories" about themselves, theories that need to be addressed and changed if the children are to gain an optimal perspective of themselves and alter their motivation and desire to learn. (p. 186)

The coexistence of negative self-esteem and an increasingly "reluctant" and anxious attitude towards learning can also lead professionals to believe erroneously that the child is not trying hard enough to learn (N.W. Nelson, 1989; Sleeter, 1987). One consequence is that the professionals unwittingly apply another version of the "try harder" approach (e.g., "If only Damian would try harder to listen," "If only Kathy would try harder to pay attention and not be so easily distracted by her classmates," or "If only Billy would try harder not to get so frustrated when he sounds out words"). The implication is that the amount of effort expended is causally related to how well a student will do, and thus the student comes to attribute success to effort alone (Schunk, 1989). But the problem does not disappear. Too often, no matter how much effort is invested, the result is the same. A cycle of failure is activated when the student is confronted with many classroom and intervention activities, possibly because the appropriate knowledge base or strategies are not readily available or accessible. The outcomes may then be (1) less persistence in completing activities, (2) less consistency in selective attention, (3) a reaction to obstacles encountered as if they were impossible to overcome, (4) a tendency to blame oneself when the verbal messages of others are communicated inadequately, and (5) a resulting reduction in confidence in onself as a competent communicator and learner (Bryan, 1986; Donahue, 1985; Kronick, 1988; Meline & Brackin, 1987; Palinscar, 1989; Pearl, Donahue, & Bryan, 1986). These outcomes may then function causally in perpetuating further academic failure (Torgesen, 1989), creating a self-fulfilling prophecy of learned helplessness and of being an outsider (Donahue, 1985).

To illustrate how these negative effects may partially originate in teaching-learning activities, we return to the "try harder" intervention plan formulated for a fictional fifth-grade student, Laurie, who is a "poor listener" (see Chapter 1). This seven-step plan was intended to help Laurie in understanding and remembering her teacher's verbal directions and explanations in a more systematic way. Briefly, the steps were (1) keeping feet, hands, and lips quiet; (2) looking at the person who was talking; (3) listening to everything that was being said; (4) thinking about the information being heard; (5) painting a mental picture of what to do; (6) asking questions immediately if confused; and (7) repeating the directions to herself or writing them down in order to remember them (Cerussi & Stern-Levine, 1988, p. 17). The prediction is that Laurie will try hard to use these components but that she will not become a more effective comprehender, a result that may further reinforce her inaccurate beliefs about her learning potential and overall competence (Bashir, 1989).

THE MEANING OF EFFORT: INTEGRATING THE META CONNECTIONS WITH COMMUNICATION AND LEARNING POTENTIAL

A Word on the "Metas"

During the first half of the 1980s, van Kleeck (1984b) asked the question whether meta matters for practically helping children and adolescents to become more proficient language learners. Van Kleeck's question concerned the development of metalinguistic knowledge. Others (e.g., Wallach & Miller, 1988; Westby, 1989; Wiig, 1989) have answered this question with a resounding yes by offering clinical frameworks that explicitly incorporate metalinguistic and metacognitive principles into goals for language and literacy learning.

Research with learning disabled populations (e.g., Brown & Palinscar, 1987; Schumaker et al., 1986; Wong, 1985) addressed this same question with respect to classroom-based instructional approaches for facilitating an active learning-how-to-learn orientation to reading comprehension. This work revealed the central role of metacognition in students' understanding of the interactive nature of learning (Brown, 1982).

Metacognition

Although not a well-defined concept, metacognition is generally considered to encompass other forms of meta-awareness, such as metalinguistic knowledge, metacommunicative knowledge, and metacomprehension (Gavelek & Raphael, 1985; van Kleeck, 1984a). Chapter 1 included a discussion of metacognition as the conscious awareness of thinking about thinking and as a process for directing how one goes about learning in purposeful ways and transferring this learning flexibly. This self-directive process is constituted by four related expressions of internal guidance (Brown & DeLoache, 1983):

1. *prediction* of the anticipated goals one wants to achieve in learning (the *why* question)
2. selection of the most appropriate *strategies* to reach these goals (the *how* question)
3. continuous *monitoring* of one's level of understanding as the means for troubleshooting (the *what's happening* question)
4. ongoing *evaluation* of outcomes, both the goals and subgoals, in order to revise the effectiveness or efficiency of learning strategies when necessary (the *what happened* question)

Silliman et al. (1989) reviewed some of the unresolved issues involved in defining metacognition and its relationship to metalinguistic awareness. These issues include (1) variability in definition, (2) the sources and rates of development of metalinguistic awareness, (3) differences in the organization or functions of automatic versus controlled processing, (4) the exact boundaries between cognition and metacognition and how to assess the point of awareness, and (5) whether conscious awareness is always necessary for metacognitive activity. All of these issues remain unresolved in one form or another despite over a decade of research.

Metalinguistic Knowledge

The same issues of definition that plague metacognition also are problems for the definition of metalinguistic knowledge. However, there is consensus that metalinguistic knowledge appears to be a specialized application of metacognitive knowledge (Bialystok & Ryan, 1985; Silliman et al., 1989; van Kleeck, 1984a). In this specialized use, linguistic elements, such as sounds, words, meanings, and sentences, are selectively attended to as independent objects of analysis separate from the purposes of communication.

Metalinguistic knowledge, like metacognition, is characterized by choice and control (Garton & Pratt, 1989) and appears to consist of a diverse range of abilities rather than being a homogeneous ability (Bialystok, 1986; Birdsong, 1989). Much of literate language use, including reading and writing, are associated with metalinguistic forms of knowledge, because the elements of choice and control are central to the access and use of these forms (for further discussion, see Garton & Pratt, 1989; van Kleeck, 1984a, 1984b; van Kleeck and Schuele, 1987; Wallach & Miller, 1988; Wiig, 1989). Access can be thought of as a pathway for guiding the routing of information in order to make it more salient for cognition.

Metacommunicative Knowledge

Metacommunicative knowledge is sometimes, but not always, distinguished from metalinguistic knowledge by virtue of its attention to

communication that "goes along with" language. As a speaker talks, much more than words are exchanged—messages accompanying language communicate such things as how the speaker feels about what he or she is saying, how he or she feels about the listener (along power and affect dimensions), how the message is to be interpreted (e.g., as a joke, seriously, ironically), whether the speaker would like to continue talking some more before the listener takes a turn, etc. All of these messages can be said in the actual words but none of them has to be communicated in the actual talk (van Kleeck, 1984a, pp. 130–31).

The kinds of metacommunicative awareness associated with language can vary considerably. One example is communicative sensitivity to message adequacy, for example, deciding how a message is incomplete or ambiguous (Wilkinson, Wilkinson, Spinelli, & Chiang, 1984), or whose fault it is (Meline & Brackin, 1987). Another is metacommenting, which can be used to admit an error in comprehension monitoring (e.g., "I thought I was the only one forgetting to write 'Mar' instead of 'February' " [Shuy, 1988b, p. 86]) or to evade responsibility for retrieval failure when specific information is being requested (e.g., "There are so many ways of thinking about it").

Metacomprehension

Metacomprehension is concerned with how cognitive activity is modified in order to promote and monitor one's state of comprehension (Gavelek & Raphael, 1985; Palinscar & Brown, 1984). Question asking, whether provoked by external sources, such as teachers, clinicians, parents, or reading material, or generated by oneself, is viewed as an important procedure for facilitating and clarifying the comprehension of spoken and written discourse. Adult question asking forms the core of traditional IRE sequences, discussed in Chapter 4. The high frequency of questions in classroom and clinical discourse attests to the power of belief in their role as a major tool for enhancing understanding (Blank, 1988; Brinton & Fujiki, 1989).

Research on these forms of metaknowledge has not established, as yet, boundaries between each, differences between them, and their specific connections to literate language uses. For example, while it seems intuitively plausible that metacognition and metacomprehension are processes with some kind of "executive" function, it is less clear that metalinguistic and metacommunicative awareness have a similar executive function. Rather, they seem to consist of specialized content about how parts of language and communication work. With these cautions in mind, some possible connections are examined in the following sections and applied to the meaning of effort.

A META THEME

Recall from Chapter 1 that understanding, being understood, and remembering are described as the essential purposes of learning (Baker & Brown, 1984; Cazden, 1988). These purposes are the implicit motivations shared in common by the communicative processes of listening, speaking, reading, and writing. We listen and read to understand and remember the communications of others. We speak and write so that our communications are understood and remembered by others and as an aid to our own understanding and remembering.

Since these purposes form the core of a communication-centered approach to learning, the problem now facing the speech-language clinician is organizing the purposes into an actual program. Chapter 5 describes in detail two communication-centered approaches. The primary goal of both approaches involve the facilitation of listening, speaking, reading, and writing either within curriculum areas (the communication skills approach) or across curriculum areas (the communication development approach). Both incorporate in different ways three superordinate foci: the development of metacognitive skill, the development of metalinguistic skill, and the development of literacy along the oral-literate continuum. These foci are now dissected further, since their articulation is critical at the level of the individual child and at the programmatic level.

By way of illustration, consider outlining an idea for a unit and then using this unit to demonstrate some of the planning issues involved at the individual child level for integrating the meta connections with communication and learning potential. The unit that is discussed here has been taken from a secondary-level English curriculum developed for learning disabled students (Florida Department of Education, 1987); it has been modified for discussion here.

Learning activities are to be structured around the theme of the development of the English language, a theme that seems quite appropriate for a discussion of communication, learning potential, and their meta connections. This theme is a rich one, encompassing cultural topics (the contributions of different cultures to our language), geography (the different origins of our language), and language arts (theories about the formation of language, mechanisms of language change, histories of words, and derivations of surnames and first names). To keep the discussion manageable, the particular learning activity highlighted concerns the origins of surnames and first names, specifically, rules that explain the endings of last names and the origins of meanings for first names. Examples of these rules include the following (Florida Department of Education, 1987, pp. 329–30):

- If your last name ends in -sohn or a common ending like -stein, -berg, -burg, -mann, -er, your last name comes from the German language. This includes Yiddish.
- If your last name ends in -ski, your last name comes from the Polish language.
- If your last name ends in -quist, -rup, -holm, -strom, -dahl, -gren, -by, -tjen, your last name comes from Scandinavia. This includes the Swedish, Norwegian, Danish, and Icelandic languages.
- Girl names

  Brenda: a firebrand or sword (German)

  Donna: little princess (Spanish)

  Karen: the pure (Greek)
- Boy names

  Jimmy: the supplanter (Hebrew)

  Jorge: earth worker (Greek)

  Tony: a twin (Aramaic)

The theme, as well as the particular learning activity, can be characterized as a special case of word consciousness. This form of metalinguistic knowledge refers to the awareness that word meanings are separate from what they represent in the real world and that words can have different underlying meanings as agreed upon by the members of a linguistic community (Bloom, in Lahey, 1988; van Kleeck, 1984a).

THE META CONNECTIONS AND THE INTERACTIVE NATURE OF LEARNING

Literacy learning is a complex and interactive process (Brown, 1982). The extent to which planning activities on the unit will be effective for an individual student is dependent on how adequately four interactive factors are taken into account (Brown, 1982): (1) the learner's prior experience, (2) the specific learning activities, (3) the content to be learned, and (4) the task purpose. Each of these factors is discussed in turn.

The Learner's Prior Experience

The first factor is the student's prior knowledge regarding the learning activities, in this case, the student's knowledge of names. This knowledge consists of knowledge about the world (e.g., all human beings have surnames), knowledge about language form and content (e.g., names can be linguistic entities), and attitudinal knowledge about ourselves and others (e.g., names communicate social and cultural identities). It also includes strategy knowledge about how to act in order to get things done, including communicative strategies (e.g., if we want to get another's attention, we can use his or her name). From a practical perspective, a strategy can be considered generally as a "technique, principle, or rule which enables a person to function independently and solve problems in ways that will result in positive consequences for the person and others around him/her" (Schumaker et al., 1986, p. 333).

Prior knowledge originates from and is continuously expanded and enriched by the social and cultural experiences that adults and children collaborate in. According to Rogoff (1990), these experiences include (1) the circumstances of participation whether the home, a day-care center, or a playground; (2) the activities, materials, and roles for engaging children that come to have significance for them, for example, book reading, television watching, visiting relatives, taking trips, playing with toys, taking care of a sibling, playing a musical instrument, helping to cook dinner, and being a student; and (3) the appropriateness of activities, materials, and roles, for example, selecting books or puzzles that are adjusted to a child's skill and interest levels and upping the difficulty as skill levels and interests change.

Children develop knowledge of ways of talking about familiar events, their purposes, and causal relationships from the social arrangements and engagements (in all their richness, scope, and variation) (see Chapter 2; K. Nelson, 1986). The richness of the knowledge that is acquired and the extent to which it has been coordinated into a flexible network for specialized information-processing purposes, such as those involved in metacognitive and metalinguistic activities, have been identified as the most important determinants of oral language and reading comprehension (Brown, Campione & Day, 1984; Catts, 1989a, 1989b; Gavelek & Raphael, 1985; Kail & Leonard, 1986; Kamhi & Catts, 1986, 1989a; Meline & Brackin, 1987; Menyuk, 1983; Pearson, 1984; Pearson & Gallagher, 1983; Pressley et al., 1985; Wong, 1985). The representational richness of the information-processing network allows one to make sense of the problem initially by (1) recognizing and selectively encoding information relevant for sense making; (2) selectively combining, or integrating, this new information with known information into a plausible understanding; and (3) then selectively comparing what is now known with what still needs to be known and assessing how it needs to be known in the particular context (Kronick, 1988; Pearson, 1984; Rogoff, 1990; Sternberg, 1987a). Through this inferential process, one can not only "read between the lines" (Wallach & Miller, 1988) but also "read beyond the lines" (Wilson, in Weaver, 1988) in order to evaluate how novel problems in different contexts are related to familiar experience.

An important issue concerns how basic knowledge about language and communication comes to be more specialized and elaborated for the purposes of literate communication, including the multiple functions of classroom discourse. Wallach and Miller (1988) note that

> students must use and process classroom discourse, which . . . is complex and somewhat decontextualized. Teachers and clinicians ask students to analyze and correct various aspects of their language every day. Additionally, students are asked to discuss the differences between narrative and expository text. They are asked to edit their manuscripts, to write better sentences, and to analyze their conversations. They are asked to analyze words and deal with sound-letter correspondences. (pp. 146–47)

The learning activity on the recognition of the origin of surnames and first names obviously requires this kind of specialized knowledge.

Analyzed Knowledge

Bialystok and Ryan (1985) provide some insight into the issue of specialized knowledge. Although their framework does not explain the exact mechanisms by which language knowledge is transformed into metalinguistic knowledge, it introduces the concept of analyzed knowledge as a prerequisite for solving metalinguistic problems, such as identifying and explaining the cultural or geographic origins of written surnames. In this instance, successful performance is contingent on the richness of prior experience with names as indicators of social or cultural identity combined with the accessibility of underlying knowledge of phoneme-grapheme relations, the spelling system, and word meaning (Ehri, 1989b). All are required for problem solving. In other words, "success" can be translated to mean how adequately the student can make explicit linguistic representations about (1) phonological rules, (2) the symbolization of phonemes by graphemes, (3) spelling rules, and (4) the meaning of human names (Bialystok, 1986; Ehri, 1989b). Previously, these representations may have been only implicit.

According to Bialystok and Ryan (1985), if an aspect of language or communication is nonanalyzed, it remains at an automatic level of processing. As a result, it cannot be readily applied to new communicative contexts in intentional ways, remaining limited to highly familiar contexts. Think of being in a country whose language you do not understand. In spite of the fact that you are a proficient comprehender and producer of English and a literate person in terms of your metalinguistic knowledge of English, the foreign language is simply inaccessible because its structure, meanings, and intents are unfamiliar. Your use of that language may be restricted to contexts in which words (e.g., *thank you* or *goodbye*) can be applied in nonanalyzable ways in social routines.

Once new information is sufficiently analyzed, it returns to the automatic mode until the need occurs for deliberate retrieval. Aspects of linguistic knowledge can be analyzed—and therefore accessible to explicit awareness—once they become encoded and integrated into a network of linguistic categories and relations. For example, in addition to familial bonds, human names can be related by categories of cultural kinship, geographic kinship, or even etymology. This network can then be utilized to draw inferences about these categories and their relations. "A natural consequence of such analysis of language knowledge is an increase in one's consciousness of that knowledge and hence one's ability to express it" (Ryan & Ledger, 1984, p. 166).

We can add to this statement that another natural consequence is the ability to manage comprehension as an active inferential process, as this formal example aptly demonstrates: "Emma observed each passenger who came aboard. Every one of them was welcomed by her cheerful greeting. Looking into both mirrors, Emma drove the yellow vehicle back onto the country road" (Wallach & Miller, 1988, p. 115). Based on our prior experience, we probably inferred initially that Emma was a flight attendant. With more information, some kind of inconsistency became detected (i.e., "It no longer makes sense that Emma is a flight attendant"). This inconsistency may then trigger explicit analysis of the semantic-syntactic relations among sentences in order to modify the initial premise and evaluate the consistency of the revised inference. Analyzed knowledge is integrated with our real-world knowledge of what people do when they drive a yellow vehicle in which many passengers are carried. Our prior experience leads us to the plausible inference that Emma is most likely, but not necessarily, a school bus driver.

The distinction between nonanalyzed and analyzed knowledge is not viewed as an either-or distinction. As Table 12-1 shows, analyzed knowledge is approached as a continuum of metalinguistic demand from little or no demand for a particular aspect to a high degree of demand. Where the student's performance in the learning activity will fall is a function of the specific problem-solving requirements and the student's current level of development. The second dimension, metacognitive control, is described below. However, it is pertinent to note that Bialystok (1986) defines metalinguistic ability as "that portion of language development for which high levels of both skill components are required [and a] metalinguistic task [as] a problem whose solution places relatively high demands on these skill components" (p. 499).

The summary of metalinguistic tasks in Table 12-1 is not intended to be exhaustive or even indicative of different developmental levels. In fact, the examples listed probably capture many kinds of analyzed knowledge demands typically found on standardized tests of language development and reading achievement in which skills are assessed in isolation from meaningful communi-

Table 12-1 Metalinguistic Tasks Classified According to Demands for Analyzed Knowledge and Metacognitive Control

Demand	Type of Tasks*
Low Analyzed Knowledge—Low Control	Repetition of "normal" sentences ("The cat chased the dog"; "The dog was chased by the cat")
	Synonymity judgments, including paraphrases (different surface structures have the same or similar meanings, e.g., "The cat chased the dog" vs. "The dog was chased by the cat")
	Correcting sentence violations involving morpheme deletions ("Yesterday John bump his head")
	Reading a text for the purpose of obtaining specific facts
Moderate Analyzed Knowledge—Low Control	Grammatical acceptability judgments for sentences whose literal meaning can "make sense" ("We cannot go home"; "The large rock walked down the hill"; "The happy pencil rolled off the desk" [Tunmer & Grieve, 1984, pp. 96–97])
	Maze procedures in which the contextually appropriate word is selected from a set of distractors (e.g., "They felt a soft wind _____ (walk) (little) (pass) them by" [Howell & Morehead, 1987, p. 178])
High Analyzed Knowledge—Low Control	Explaining (defining) the meaning of parts of speech, sentences, words, etc.
	Explaining the source of linguistic ambiguity
	Formulating sentences based on contextual constraints of controlled words (e.g., given "scared" and "your," make up a sentence [Wiig, 1989, p. 246])
	Identifying sentence subject and predicate
	Explaining a linguistic rule for why one verb is used rather than another (e.g., "ask" vs. "tell")
	Diagramming sentences
	Correcting (proofreading) an unfamiliar text for spelling and typing errors
	Formulating cohesive discourse when topic is unfamiliar and/or conversational partners are unfamiliar with each other (requires establishing shared frames of reference through linguistic means alone)
High Analyzed Knowledge—Moderate Control	Segmenting words into phonemes using phonemes as the salient information
	Identifying word boundaries in sentences printed without spaces
	Monitoring the communicative adequacy of complete, incomplete, or ambiguous messages

continues

Table 12-1 continued

Demand	Type of Tasks*
High Analyzed Knowledge— High Control	Reordering sets of words or paragraphs from scrambled orders to form a meaningful whole
	Correcting or editing (proofreading) one's own text for both form errors and meaningfulness
	Formulating a classroom lecture
	Engaging in formal debate (logical argumentation)
Moderate Analyzed Knowledge— Moderate Control	Cloze or fill-in procedures in which words in a passage are systematically blanked out and the contextually appropriate words are to be produced (e.g., "_____ was fascinated with the _____ aspect of war" [Howell & Morehead, 1987, p. 175])
	Repetition of deviant sentences, which requires overcoming tendency to "normalize" (e.g., "Teeth your brush" [Tunmer & Grieve, 1984, p. 92])
	Repetition of nonsense strings
	Correcting sentences with word order violations (e.g., "Teacher the read a story" [Garton & Pratt, 1989, p. 144])
Low Analyzed Knowledge— High Control	Judging linguistic ambiguity (the same surface structures can have different meanings, e.g., "He took her picture" [Wiig, 1989, p. 242] or "The man picked up the pipe" [Tunmer & Grieve, 1984, p. 88])
	Anomalous word substitutions (substituting a word for a target word and thereby violating semantic-syntactic rules, e.g., "spaghetti" for "they" in the sentence "They are good children" or "smart" for "long" in "The cat has long legs" [Bialystok & Ryan, 1985, pp. 236–37])
	Fluent self-repair of one's own discourse

*Compiled from Bialystok and Ryan (1985), Birdsong (1989), Garton and Pratt (1989), Meline and Brackin (1987), and Ryan and Ledger (1984).

cative contexts (e.g., sentence repetition, judgments of grammatical acceptability, corrections of semantic and syntactic violations, sentence formulation, scrambled sentences and passages, cloze procedures, and repetition of nonsense strings).

Degrees of proposed difficulty are also included in this table. For example, there is a difference between proficiency in using tag questions in the everyday discourse of social routines—such as saying "It's a nice day, isn't it?" which does not ordinarily demand deliberate analysis but which could demand it in some circumstances—and proficiency in writing a formal recognition rule for identifying children's tag questions in the observation of classroom discourse. The ability to explain a linguistic rule, much less a system of interrelated linguistic rules, demands a relatively sophisticated level of metalinguistic analysis. The degree to which factual knowledge about tag questions has become more elaborated through a formal network of hierarchically arranged categories of questions probably determines the degree to which that knowledge is easily and spontaneously accessible in a specific learning context (Bialystok & Ryan, 1985). Similarly, linguistic demands for analyzed knowledge are increased when topics are less familiar or when conversational partners do not share the same frames of reference and the inferring of meaning is dependent on the explicit use of cohesive ties (see, e.g., the discussion on George's narrative in Chapter 8).

Thus, in planning learning activities, such as those designed to facilitate metalinguistic development, a number of considerations need to be entertained for each student. These include (1) the overall richness of the student's prior experience, including language experience; (2) the degree to which he or she has accessible analyzed knowledge of various aspects of language, such as knowledge of phoneme-grapheme relations or of the multiple meanings words can have; and (3) the adequacy with which this knowledge has been organized into a workable structure for fostering comprehension through the activity.

The enrichment of both unanalyzed and analyzed knowledge is a challenging, if not formidable, task for any clinician. One suggestion for approaching this task is to use semantic maps as a procedure for introducing a theme, such as the English language theme under discussion (Wilson, in Weaver, 1988). Students can brainstorm with the clinician or teacher about the kinds of information that might be needed in developing the theme, which serves as the "organizer." The map can be developed to reflect the kinds of questions students might ask about the theme. Major questions and subquestions are then arranged around the topic. For example, the questions might include these: "How are words formed?" "Where do names come from?" "How do people's names relate to places?" "What do the spellings of names tell us about who people are?" Brainstorming can also be directed towards such issues as (1) the kinds of information resources students will need to address their questions, including print and nonprint resources (nonprint resources would include other people); (2) how information should be gathered (interviewing parents and school staff and using newspapers, magazines, and books); and (3) how information will be reported to others (e.g., writing a story, giving a simulated "newscast," developing a word bank of names, drawing a poster to depict relationships among names).

Wilson (in Weaver, 1988) notes that the process of semantic mapping is planful, stresses information gathering as a holistic communicative activity, derives from self-generated questions of personal interest rather than imposing an adult agenda, and encourages students' transactions with texts "they read and those they write and share with other class members" (p. 318). In emphasizing the tools of communication as the means for obtaining new experiences, the student's potential for learning how to learn is being cultivated.

Specific Learning Activities

The semantic mapping description illustrates that the specific learning activities the student engages in are inseparable from the strategies chosen for learning to occur.

In a planful approach, selection of the most appropriate strategy for managing a learning activity occurs only after assessment of what the problem or task is, including how important it is for accomplishing a particular purpose (Brown, 1982; Gavelek & Raphael, 1985; Kronick, 1988). The fact that the student can generate questions about *what* might need to be known about the origin of people's surnames and first names, consider *why* it may be important to know, think about *how* those questions might be answered, and suggest *ways* for that information to be communicated supports this conclusion.

We now examine some issues related to the student's spontaneous selection of strategies. Let us assume that the student is now going to have to study for a multiple choice test on the origins of names (the learning activity). The student probably will need to apply metacognitive tools for intentional remembering, since lists of facts about name derivations must be retained. The two overlapping dimensions of analyzed knowledge and control in Table 12-1 suggest that reading information resources for factual retention, such as a text, generally require less expenditure of linguistic and cognitive resources (low analyzed knowledge—low control). Presuming that the student can process the particular text for the most important facts, she or he may employ mnemonic or verbal rehearsal devices because these strategies are often the most efficient for this kind of remembering (Brown et al., 1984; Pressley et al., 1985). Also, the format of multiple choice tests might make less of a demand on resources. As Table 12-1 shows, multiple choice formats are a type of maze procedure (Howell & Morehead, 1987) in which there is a moderate demand for analyzed knowledge. Choosing from a set of foils involves inferring the most appropriate semantic "fit" based on the saliency of cues from the sentence structure. Moreover, if the fit can be recalled, it need only be reproduced.

On the other hand, when the student is processing a verbal report by other students on the findings of research on name derivations, the student must deliberately listen in order to get the "gist." The use of either a mnemonic or verbal rehearsal strategy would not be as effective for imposing an organizational structure on the material and making it more comprehensible and thus retainable (Brown et al., 1984). Suggesting to the student to write down what he or she thinks is important to remember implies some form of summarization via note taking or outlining. Bialystok and Ryan (1985) point out that, without the analyzed knowledge of what information is essential to write down, applying a strategy that presumes controlled use "can have only minimal impact" (p. 230). The implementation of appropriate strategies, as opposed to their indiscriminate use, is always dependent on the ability to encode and analyze what information is important (Gavelek & Raphael, 1985).

However, even if the student now has an adequate base of analyzed knowledge for tackling the multiple choice examination or the verbal report, including tools for remembering and summarizing, this may be insufficient for successful performance if the information is not easily retrievable (Bialystok & Ryan, 1985; Brown, 1982; Gavelek & Raphael, 1985). We all are familiar with situations in which we know what we are supposed to do (i.e., the analyzed knowledge exists) but cannot readily think how to do it. We have problems making connections between our analyzed knowledge and the appropriate strategic knowledge to be accessed in a given circumstance.

Why don't we always use the strategies we have available when the situation calls for their use (Brown, 1982; Pressley et al., 1985)? While the answer to this question remains conjectural, two possibilities emerge from research on this topic that might explain why the student is not spontaneously applying appropriate comprehension strategies in certain types of learning activities (Bialystok & Ryan, 1985; Dollaghan, 1987; Meline & Brackin, 1987; Pearl et al., 1986; Pressley et al., 1985):

1. The strategy is available but not accessible because (a) all of its components are not fully networked; (b) the components are elaborated but a temporary breakdown occurs in retrieval as a function of task demands; or (c) the inaccurate inference is drawn that its use would not be helpful in the particular circumstance or would demand more effort than the student wants to expend on the specific learning activity.

2. The comprehension strategy is being used but the student cannot efficiently monitor from moment to moment when the strategy is working well and when it is not.

Both of these explanations evoke the cognitive control component outlined in Table 12-1.

Cognitive Control

In the Bialystok and Ryan (1985) model, the cognitive control dimension is defined as those metacognitive operations that function to retrieve (select) and coordinate the relevant information appropriate for task solution (Ryan & Ledger, 1984).

> If the relevant information is not obvious, then selection [retrieval] becomes difficult; if a variety of sources must be consulted, then coordination becomes difficult; if a number of processes are independently involved, then speed or fluency becomes difficult.... Similarly, the control to coordinate information becomes more important where monitoring procedures are required to oversee several facets of a problem, such as form and meaning, or meaning and context, and so on. (Bialystok & Ryan, 1985, pp. 213–14)

Low Analyzed Knowledge—High Control. In effect, control procedures support appropriate strategy use. These procedures regulate access to analyzed knowledge. As one example from Table 12-1, high control demands in solving metalinguistic problems are found in activities where linguistic ambiguity must be recognized and then resolved (but note that explaining the source of ambiguity shifts the direction of demand to high analyzed knowledge—low control). If the ambiguity is detected at first, its resolution presumes availability of the analyzed knowledge that similar surface structures can express many different meanings. Then multiple sources of alternate information must be deliberately attended to, coordinated, and compared within the context of occurrence.

The ease or difficulty of solution resides in the frame of reference that must be re-created. Wiig's (1989) illustration of these frames of reference is instructive: "Assume that you knew your friend had been to an optometrist and she said to you, 'I got new glasses.' You would interpret her statement to refer to eyeglasses because of your prior knowledge. When you read a novel, it might require more effort to interpret ambiguous sentences because you must recreate the context and remember and integrate prior topics, information, and intents" (p. 242). The key word here is "effort." Effort and degrees of control coincide. Degrees of control can be refined into the resources that must be devoted to searching and retrieving the appropriate information sources, integrating these sources, and then monitoring and comparing the outcomes relative to some criterion of adequacy, such as the facilitation of comprehension (Gavelek & Raphael, 1985).

High Analyzed Knowledge—High Control. Demands for monitoring increase when the pull on analyzed knowledge and control processes are equally strong, for example, when multiple sources of information must be retrieved and coordinated. An example of high demand on both components is the scrambled story, a tool sometimes used to assess the effects of instruction on narrative comprehension. Fourth-grade children, both good and below average readers, were asked to read the following scrambled version of a second-grade level story, and "their task was to try to remember everything they could and put the pieces back in order" (Fitzgerald & Spiegel, 1983, p. 5):

The Wolf and the Bird with the Long Neck

He soon felt terrible pain in his throat. He wanted to stop the pain. Suddenly, a small bone in the meat stuck in his throat. He could not swallow it. The Bird told the Wolf to lie down on his side. He had him open his mouth as wide as he could. Then the bird put its long neck down the Wolf's throat. With his beak, the Bird pulled on the bone. At last the Bird got the bone out. At last a Bird with a long neck said he could try. "Will you please give me the reward you said I could have?" said the Bird with a long neck. The Wolf grinned. He showed his teeth and said: "Be happy. You have put your head inside a Wolf's mouth and taken it out again safely. That is all the reward you will get." A Wolf was eating an animal he had killed. He tried to get everyone he met to take the bone out for him. "I would give anything," he said, "If you would take it out." (Fitzgerald & Spiegel, 1983, p. 6)

Even the most skillful of readers will find that the reordering of the story demands increased mental "effort" and is a highly directed strategic activity of choice and control (Garton & Pratt, 1989). Monitoring of how the elements fit together to make sense occurs continuously because multiple sources of information must be coordinated (e.g., story grammar categories, categories of cohesive devices and sentential relations, purposes of stories, real-life knowledge of wolves and birds, etc.) and interrelated with the various kinds of analyzed knowledge retrieved (e.g., specific types of story grammar categories, specific kinds of meaning links within and across sentence boundaries, inferring connections among structure, content, and purpose).

The strategies each reader uses to accomplish the goals of remembering and understanding may be similar in many respects and different in others. Some may search out the story grammar categories as the key clues for ordering story elements; others may first search for the theme using the title as a main clue; still others may focus on the "purpose" or moral of the story, which has both entertainment and teaching functions (e.g., "Beware of the gift giver" or even "Every person alone is sincere; hypocrisy starts when a second person enters"). Kronick (1988), K. Nelson (1990), and Rogoff (1990) remind us that, in real-life learning situations, no two contexts are identical; hence the same strategies may not be selected each time a similar task is encountered. An effective strategy in one situation for dealing with scrambled information, like carefully examining each sentence in order to find temporal connections, may not be effective in a situation where the scrambled information has a high frequency of unfamiliar words that serve as a barrier to discovering the temporal connections. In this situation, alternative routes to the same goal may have to be adopted. We could look up the unfamiliar words in the dictionary or use others as external resources for helping us figure out the solution (Wilson, in Weaver, 1988).

Higher degrees of demand for controlled processing are also influenced by the social structure of tasks (Heap, 1988) for which efficiency and speed are expectations for success or are *interpreted* by students as expectations. For instance, when the student is allocated a turn by the teacher or clinician for the purpose of explaining the derivation of a name, the real or imagined expectation to respond quickly in order to keep a turn can increase the load on the control component (Bialystok & Ryan, 1985). The result for some students may be a breakdown in strategy execution. Similar variability in strategy execution can also occur when timed tests are given or when testlike situations are created to assess the speed and fluency of skill in word retrieval during picture description (German, 1987; German & Simon, in press).

Thus, the more automatically any student can skillfully (fluently) execute selection, integration, and comparison (e.g., in understanding what is read or heard), the more the demands for control and analyzed knowledge can be reduced (Bialystok & Ryan, 1985). Enhanced automaticity also allows for flexibility in problem solving (Brown & Ferrara, 1985; Premack, 1989). The less evidence of automaticity (e.g., lack of fluency in analyzing the functions and features of print and their relationships to units of oral language), the more likely the student will remain a perpetual novice in using communicative tools for literacy aims. With automaticity in control processes, one can rapidly shift strategies for different purposes, such as retaining factual information, clarifying an unfamiliar word, summarizing essential information, reconciling inconsistencies in meaning, or reordering illogically presented information (Bialystok & Ryan, 1985; Brown, 1982; Brown & Ferrara, 1985; Sternberg, 1987a). In a very real sense, strategies are flexible applications of controlled choices.

Some Practical Implications

The Bialystok and Ryan (1985) framework for planning a communication-centered approach has many important implications, which are discussed below.

Instructional Implications. The first implication concerns instructional decision making. The selection and sequencing of learning activities needs to be balanced by careful scrutiny of their level of demand for analyzed knowledge versus controlled processing. Each of these components overlaps the other, and each illustrates how existing knowledge will be used strategically for particular problem-solving purposes. What is easy for one child will be difficult for another. The trick is to select meaningful learning activities that are neither too easy nor too hard. Also requiring thoughtful analysis are the conditions under which a student is asked to deal with a task, such as the expectation for the speed of performance.

The task-analytic model in curriculum-based evaluation presumes that "a student must learn the subcomponents, or prerequisites, of a task in order to learn the task" (Howell & Morehead, 1987, p. 27). The analyzed knowledge–cognitive control perspective complements the task analysis model, because it allows for the recognition that most school learning consists of metalinguistic and metacognitive demands. These demands must be examined in the selection of meaningful communicative activities and in the teaching of strategies that permit students to manage their own learning more efficiently. The departure from the task analysis approach occurs at two points. One point of divergence occurs when "skilling and drilling" (Wilson, in Weaver, 1988) become the aims and methods of learning; the other concerns the notion of teaching prerequisite (subcomponent) skills. Because analyzed knowledge and control processes seem to develop in tandem and support each other, it is questionable whether there are clear-cut developmental sequences that can be directly taught (Westby & Costlow, in press).

Developmental Implications. The account by Bialystok and Ryan (1985) is a parsimonious one for understanding sources of development in metalinguistic awareness. In their view, metalinguistic skills and literacy skills are not causally related but are promoted through the underlying and intersecting components of cognitive control and analyzed knowledge, both of which share a cognitive basis. As suggested above, advances in each of these components, either through natural development or through immersion in communication-centered learning, affect the enhancement of both.

This account is consistent with the position that metalinguistic awareness and basic language acquisition are interwined from the beginning. Evidence comes from the spontaneous attempts of preschoolers as young as two or three years old to play with, comment on, and correct aspects of the sound and meaning systems. (For a fuller discussion of these behaviors, see van Kleeck & Schuele, 1987.) Garton and Pratt (1989) elaborate on this position. They believe that metalinguistic abilities develop gradually from spontaneous reflection on parts of language into deliberate attention based on the mastery of the different forms involved in language use. Spontaneous reflection can often arise from trouble sources in communication or from other rare events (K.E. Nelson, 1989), such as "the existence of speech repairs in one's own speech, the existence of errors such as mispronunciations in the speech of others, words that are difficult to pronounce, words that rhyme with each other, and characteristics of the written word which, given its more visible and permanent form, will be more salient than the spoken word" (Garton & Pratt, 1989, p. 135).

Thus, in Bialystok's (1986) interpretation, both aspects of processing—analyzed knowledge and cognitive control—appear to support language development from its earliest to more advanced phases. Which component predominates at any point in time may depend on the aspect of language or communication that has reached some level of conscious awareness (Garton & Pratt, 1989).

Awareness can be momentary initially, such as when a child recognizes a mispronunciation in his or her own speech, including oral reading errors (see Wilson, in Weaver, 1988, on reading miscues) but is unable to correct it. The most advanced level of awareness is found in the ability to *explain* how and why units of language work, such as what a word means or why the same sentence can have different meanings. Similarly, momentary awareness may be reflected in a child's recognition that a conversational partner's message is incomplete or ambiguous. But doing something to correct the communicative breakdown, such as requesting clarification, probably requires more control. Explanation of the source of the breakdown or justifying why a breakdown occurred most likely demands analyzed knowledge of metacommunication, since evaluation of communicative intents is involved (Meline & Brackin, 1987).

Wilson (in Weaver, 1988) suggests that aspects of the reading process can be brought to a more formal state of metacomprehension for individual students by using integrated procedures. A student can be guided to talk about places in the text where "trouble" occurred through discussion of what was learned from the text and how it was learned. For example, the student can be invited to reflect on his or her reading and to talk first about how well she or he did. Problems, such as a reading error, can then be focused on jointly, and the student can be encouraged to analyze the reasons for the problems and to comment on or ask about the story or about the manner in which the story was read (see also Chapters 5 and 11 on supporting students' perspectives on task ease or difficulty). A further suggestion from Wilson is to invite children to use each other as resources for the strategies to apply when encountering an unfamiliar word. Self-monitoring of reading efficiency can be supported by having the student make a check in the margin of the reading material at the point where a trouble spot occurs or underline the exact place. The trouble spots can then be reviewed and discussed further in order to help the student develop more productive strategies. If particular problems did not occur or were independently resolved as they occurred, then the student can be asked to note how the reading went (easy, not so easy, etc.) and to turn in that information on a bookmark. Alternatively, a simple rating form can be utilized for self-assessment, which can also be subsequently discussed.

Implications for Individual Differences. The third value of the Bialystok and Ryan model is its capacity to accommodate individual differences (Birdsong, 1989). It is relatively well documented, for example, that variations in metalinguistic knowledge are a product of how preschool socialization experiences directly encourage spontaneous attention to the properties of spoken language and to the forms and functions of a vast array of print (Goldfield & Snow, 1985; Heath, 1989; van Kleeck, 1990). Essentially, this type of documentation has been concerned with unanalyzed knowledge, since it emphasizes the precursory knowledge children acquire. The nature of the specific learning activity and the extent to which control is required have not been considered as rigorously in explaining differences in a child's performance over time or differences between children (Garton & Pratt, 1989). Depending on the task demand, including the implied or explicitly stated expectation for speed of performance, individual children will naturally show variation according to the level of analyzed knowledge and cognitive control being required. Differences reside less in the child than in what that child is being asked to do.

Implications for the Oral-Literate Continuum. A final contribution of the framework is its augmentation of the oral-literate continuum. This can be illustrated by the dialogue journal, discussed in Chapter 9, a technique that supports the transition from oral to literate styles of communication. The initial purpose of dialogue journal writing is a developmental one—to apply "what is known about how to use oral language in a written form . . . in real-life, natural, appropriate, and motivating tasks" (Shuy, 1988b, p. 87).

Westby and Costlow (in press) identified three phases along the oral-literate continuum found in dialogue journals: (1) the adult addresses written messages to the child and the child responds with whatever writing resources he or she has available (e.g., scribbles, copies words, invents spellings, etc.); (2) the child initiates written dialogue addressed to others, such as notes; and (3) the child generates more literate message forms, such as brief narratives directed not to a specific person but to a more general "listenership." Invented spellings appear to be prevalent across all three phases.

These three phases of dialogue journal writing are also interlocked with phases of analyzed knowledge and control for the phonological, lexical, and spelling systems. Ehri (1989b) defines the spelling system as the visible symbols for thinking in terms of sounds as separate units and for consciously manipulating them. In this perspective, all three forms of analyzed knowledge—phonological, lexical, and alphabetic—interact to facilitate development of each system. By analyzing children's spelling errors, conclusions can be drawn about analyzed knowledge of the spelling system.

The earliest stage in the development of the spelling system is the *precommunicative* stage. The spellings resemble print (e.g., the child may scribble, write numbers, or write *ML* for *dog*), but the child's attention is on the meaning and functions of the message, not its forms, which remain unanalyzed. Note that, while the form may be precommunicative in the sense of not being conventional, the child's message is always communicative.

In the *semiphonetic* stage, the names or sounds of letters are used to spell, but the choices are logical nonetheless (e.g., *PL* stands for *pickle* [Ehri, 1989b,

p. 358]). Westby and Costlow's description of Ernestine as she progressed through the first phase of dialogue journal writing suggests that her spellings contained many semiphonetic elements (see Chapter 9). Ehri (1989b) would interpret Ernestine's pattern as follows. If a lexical search does not result in the retrieval of the specific word, then a plausible spelling will be generated by using existing knowledge of the spelling system to make a best guess (a prediction). Hence, children at the semiphonetic stage probably have some momentary or shifting ability to focus their attention on *connections* among word meaning, word pronunciation, and the visual form of these connections symbolized in spelling.

The third stage is the *phonetic* stage. Here spellings are generated that contain all the letters for all of the sounds in the word, a growth in ability related to knowing how to spell vowels. Analyzed knowledge of the spelling system creates a specialized schema that allows learners "to make phonetic sense of individual spellings and hence remember them" (Ehri, 1989b, p. 358). Ehri's research findings suggest that when the spelling system is learned, it permeates phonological knowledge and fundamentally influences how learners approach the sounds they believe are in words. Ehri gives the example of children who know how the nonsense words *tadge* and *taj* are spelled, which then gives rise to a letter strategy in phonological segmentation (i.e., *tadge* is segmented as four sounds, with /d/ and /g/ separated, while *taj* is appropriately segmented as three sounds).

In supporting transitions along the oral-literate continuum, dialogue journals create natural contexts for students with language-learning differences to attend to the connections among sound, meaning, and spelling (see also Scott, 1989b, on using natural contexts for expository writing). Ehri (1989b) advocates that students be taught how to invent semiphonetic spellings by using their partially analyzed knowledge of letter-name or letter-sound relations before phonics instruction is introduced. Play with these precursory connections within dialogue journals also permits phonological awareness and phonics activities to be integrated naturally (see, e.g., Blachman, 1989). In addition, prediction of possible connections and their anticipated outcomes is naturally built into dialogue journals and capitalizes on children's normal tendencies to make best guesses based on the context of the messages being communicated. Furthermore, in embedding sound-meaning-spelling connections within this kind of learning activity, three conditions for the development of any language skill, including specialized abilities, are satisfied (K.E. Nelson, 1989; Shuy, 1988b): (1) if one is going to learn to write, read, and spell utilizing metaknowledges and metaprocesses, then many multipurpose opportunities have to be provided for doing so; (2) every learning activity must be meaningful and motivating; and (3) the demand for analyzed knowledge versus control in the particular learning activity must also occur meaningfully so that the student can monitor it and progressively learn how to resolve trouble sources in strategically flexible ways.

Nature of Content To Be Learned

The preceding discussion shows that the learner's prior experience and the nature of the specific learning activity cannot be dissociated readily from each other. The factors operate not in isolation but interactively. The same is true for the third factor affecting learning how to learn: the content to be learned. Content that is more readily comprehensible is also learned more easily regardless of whether the medium for comprehension is oral, pictorial, or printed. Stated another way, the closer the content fits what the student can potentially understand and is interested in, the greater will be the compatibility between the content to be mastered and the existing knowledge base (Brown, 1982; K. Nelson, 1990). The issue is not familiarity per se but compatibility.

Factors affecting compatibility should be well known by now. They include (1) predictability of the content; (2) its demands for analyzed knowledge and control; (3) the organization of information, that is, the format and order in which information is presented; and (4) the level of inferencing required (Blank, 1988; Brown, 1982; Howell & Morehead, 1987; Wallach & Miller, 1988). As a general rule, children are less adept than adults at inferring overall thematic content when materials are inadequately structured, illogical, or linguistically ambiguous (Pressley, 1983). For example, a scrambled story task would increase the likelihood of incompatibility, because it violates the predictable order of story categories. The format of information also exerts a strong influence on compatibility, as illustrated by the following two variations in testing formats (Howell & Morehead, 1987, p. 93):

Test A

2	8	7
+2	+6	+2

8	7	5
–6	–3	–2

Test B

$2 + 2 =$ 7   6

               –3   +8

$8 - 6 =$

$5 - 2 =$

$7 + 2 =$

Both tests have the same content, in the sense that the numerical problems and operations are the same; however, they differ in physical alignment and the groupings of problems. In Test A, the task is simplified inasmuch as the format is vertical and each example is grouped by the type of operation. Test B, in comparison, appears harder, because the content is presented in both vertical and horizontal formats and the operations of addition and subtraction are mixed. The strategies used to solve the Test A problems may not be easily transferred to Test B, since, with the latter, one first has to recombine and then compare the problem elements in order to understand that the same problem sets are being represented. Even though familiarity exists about addition and subtraction, most likely at an automatic level of processing for older children and adolescents, Test B requires the activation of more controlled processing before familiar operations can be applied. Howell and Morehead (1987) speculate that students who perform well on tests like Test B will have fewer problems in the everyday use of addition and subtraction than those who score high only on tests with the Test A format. Further, if students' learning experiences with math problems are primarily ones in which a Test A format predominates, then they will be less able to transfer the same analyzed knowledge to somewhat dissimilar situations.

Task Purposes

A major tendency of children with language learning disabilities is to rely on rote strategies. At best, these strategies for verbatim remembering may be helpful only in tasks having a highly predictable structure or sequence (Kronick, 1988), as is the case when facts need to be retained (e.g., telephone numbers, state capitols, historical dates, etc.). How any student understands the purpose of the learning activity—what is being required as the outcome of comprehension—is the fourth factor and the one most closely linked to motivation. Brown (1982) underscores the importance of understanding what is being required, since the nature of the comprehension goal also determines the kind of strategies that will be employed.

Returning to the learning activity on the origins of names, the ways in which the student approaches that activity are contingent on the motivation for learning about how language works and what this information will be used for. Will it be used for learning about the derivation of names without any experiential relevance to the student? Or is the starting point designed to help the student generate his or her own questions about why this activity might be personally interesting and beneficial? Will it lead to the awareness that the process of learning can be its own reward? Knowing what the problem is and why it is important are critical for focusing attention on how learning is going to happen.

Recall from Chapter 4 that the completeness and explicitness of task themes and orientations are crucial for the ways in which learners execute activities. Most importantly, students need to be guided in ways that will enable them "to take stock of what they already know" (Wilson, in Weaver, 1988, p. 287) in order to set their own purposes for using the tools of communication.

CONCLUSION

To recapitulate, all learning can be considered to be the result of how prior experience, the specific learning activity, the content to be learned, and the understanding of task purpose function together to "enable or disable the learner" (Gavelek & Palinscar, 1988, p. 279). Because these components constitute the why, how, what, and when of individual learning, they are central to the planning of a communication-centered approach.

Good comprehenders in both the spoken and written domains readily employ these critical thinking skills to facilitate and monitor their comprehension at any given point in time (Bialystok & Ryan, 1985; Brown & Palinscar, 1987; Dollaghan, 1987; Gavelek & Raphael, 1985; Weaver, 1988; Westby, 1989; Wong, 1985). These learning-how-to-learn skills allow them to do the following (Brown & Palinscar, 1987; Palinscar, 1989; Wong, 1985):

- understand the purpose of a task, whether that purpose is explicitly stated or must be inferred
- clarify task demands when necessary
- activate the appropriate background knowledge, both experiential and specialized, in order to bring meaning to what is being said, read, written, and spelled
- allocate attentional resources so that concentration is focused on relevant content at the expense of more trivial information
- deploy appropriate "debugging" or monitoring strategies to repair comprehension breakdowns, such as requesting clarification from others or, in the case of reading, decreasing the speed of reading, rereading ambiguous material in order to find clues, or engaging in self-questioning
- evaluate the outcomes of comprehension relative to the purposes of the task and the compatibility of understanding with prior knowledge and common sense

While "trying harder" is necessary, it is an insufficient method for any learner, especially for a child whose communicative competence puts him or her at serious risk for academic and social failure. What is often described ambiguously as poor comprehension or poor listening skills may actually represent difficulties with the underpinnings of a planful approach to learning. These difficulties often entail reduced awareness of the purposes of tasks, what is known, what needs to be understood, strategies for dealing with the task and its theme, how to monitor current and anticipated comprehension needs, and how to evaluate progress and outcomes in understanding (Westby, 1989).

Chapter 13

Scaffolding Classroom Discourse into Communication-Centered Intervention

The final chapter is devoted to a discussion of the discourse scaffolding within the context of the communication-centered classroom. Some recommendations are given for ways that observational tools can be used to evaluate individual needs for discourse scaffolding and to document progress over time.

Applebee and Langer (1983) specified some principles for discourse scaffolding in the classroom. Communicative competence with spoken or written language originates from two interrelated sources: (1) the communicative events that children routinely participate in and (2) the kind and degree of social support received from knowledgeable adults and peers. These competencies are not taught directly; rather, the route from acquisition to eventual mastery of any skill is mediated through the scaffolding nested in teaching discourse (Palinscar & Brown, 1987). Scaffolding refers to the guidance an adult or peer provides through dialogue as the way of doing for the child what the child cannot yet do alone without assistance (Cazden, 1988).

BRINGING TOGETHER LEARNING TO COMMUNICATE AND COMMUNICATING TO LEARN

Goals and Methods in the Discourse of Intervention

All integrated perspectives share the same basic view that children's oral language is the bridge to literacy (Stahl & Miller, 1989). This philosophy can be seen in several intervention programs that have been described in the literature. However, data on the long-term effectiveness of these programs are currently not available.

For example, Despain and Simon (1987) outline a plan for integrating language development and curriculum objectives for low-achieving sixth graders at

234

academic risk for an unsuccessful transition to middle school. Buttrill et al. (1989) describe the direct teaching of learning strategies developed by Schumaker et al. (1986) to foster problem-solving and conversational skills in language learning disabled youngsters at the secondary level through the alternate language classroom (see also McKinley & Lord-Larson, 1985). Norris (1989) describes another strategy-based approach with mainstreamed language learning disabled children at the elementary level. Actual curriculum materials are used in small reading groups as the medium for enhancing proficiency with oral communication strategies for predicting, clarifying, and informing. Applying a Piagetian framework, Gruenewald and Pollak (1990) focus on how the classroom teacher can match curriculum, instructional, and language needs in students with learning difficulties. Others (e.g., Blank, 1988; Hoskins, 1990; N.W. Nelson, 1988b; Scott, 1989a, 1989b; Wallach & Miller, 1988; Westby, 1989, 1990; Wiig, 1989) provide a rich base of information for incorporation into an integrated perspective.

The most comprehensive of the integrated approaches that emphasize collaboration are the communication skills and communication development programs described in Chapter 5 (see also Hoffman, 1990). Lease and Hoffman (1990) also describe three modes of providing lessons that are related to purpose setting, monitoring, and students' self-evaluation of their own performances. Each team member is expected to implement the following three components across all learning activities: (1) *introduction*, or orientation, whose function is to motivate interest and participation (the relevance of lesson purposes and steps are stated and interrelated with the students' experiential knowledge); (2) *pacing* of information in order to monitor continually each student's comprehension of and attention to lesson organization and goals; and (3) *closure*, in which the main points of the lesson are summarized through the students' paraphrasing of the activities that occurred. Throughout the lesson, consistent and immediate feedback is given as a procedure for supporting the development of self-evaluation.

However, despite the positive (and welcomed) trend towards integrated communication in the classroom, the dynamics by which communicative goals are to be achieved have not been clearly stated. For example, the strategies intervention model (Schumaker et al., 1986), which is designed for learning disabled students and extensively field tested within the classroom (Florida Department of Education, 1989), does not specify how dialogue should be structured in the classroom so that particular strategies will be acquired flexibly for a variety of purposes in and out of school. This omission is a significant one, since, as Kronick (1988) points out, "learning strategies to achieve in school is not the same skill as producing focused thought and behavior" (p. 15). Similarly, the whole language approach (Goodman, 1986) advocates that learning for all students is best facilitated when language functions are integrated in communicatively relevant ways across the curriculum. However, this approach does not address the discourse basis by which learning can be integrated. (An extensive review of whole language approaches in the regular classroom is provided by Stahl & Miller, 1989; see also, King & Goodman [1990], and Norris & Damico [1990] for specific applications to language intervention.)

In terms of language intervention strategies, many clinicians are most likely to rely on an eclectic combination of procedures as the primary techniques for supporting new language learning and its transfer to different situations. These techniques may be cast in the form of modeling and be direct and indirect. Embedded within modeling may be instances of commenting on the child's actions (Constable, 1986; Lahey, 1988), expansion, and recasting, among other techniques. Expansion and recasting are somewhat similar, because in both techniques portions of the child's preceding utterances are restated and new semantic or syntactic information is added (Fey, 1986). K. E. Nelson (1989) states that recasts are critical opportunities for the child to analyze and compare new forms within the framework of discourse sequences. When the child produces an utterance, for example, "That a doggie," a recasted reply is made immediately, such as "That's a doggie and he likes you." The adult simultaneously retains the child's essential meaning and extends it through a new structure (for further discussion, see Conti-Ramsden, 1990).

The intent here is not to examine these language-teaching strategies, since others have already done so (Fey, 1986; Lahey, 1988; K. E. Nelson, 1989); rather, it is to place them within a larger context of modeling and induction. Significant variability exists in the language intervention literature regarding the meaning of modeling and rule induction, variability that is partially accounted for by differences in theoretical frameworks (e.g., Cole & Dale, 1986; Connell, 1987; Fey, 1986; Kaiser & Warren, 1988; Kamhi, 1989; Lahey, 1988; Leonard, 1981; Naremore & Hopper, 1990; Norris & Hoffman, 1990; Nye, Foster, & Seaman, 1987).

Modeling

The goal of modeling is to provide verbal examples that the child will internalize. In its most dynamic meaning, a model is a blueprint for drawing the child's attention to similar instances (Cazden, 1988). The elements within the blueprint selected for attention will vary according to the constantly shifting purposes and requirements of interaction. Modeling, on the other hand, can be the strategy selected to make blueprint elements salient at a particular point in the flow of interaction.

Modeling strategies can be directive and nondynamic, directive and dynamic, and reciprocal and dynamic. The terms *directive* and *reciprocal* refer to the amount and kind of adult responsibility assumed for initial learning and subsequent transfer. A directive strategy is not the same as a direct method (Lahey,

1988). Indirect methods are sometimes described as forms of incidental teaching. Directive and reciprocal modeling can function either as a direct or indirect method for facilitation depending on its actual implementation.

Directive and nondynamic modeling is most visible when eliciting an imitation from a child is the desired goal, for example, when the clinician's intent is to solicit an exact or modified repetition of a form that has been produced by the child incorrectly. It is also the most direct form of modeling. Lund and Duchan (1988) cite the example of a child who says /t/ for /s/, followed by the clinician saying "Say this after me: sss, sss, sss" (p. 38). If the sound can now be reproduced, we consider that child to be "stimulable" for the /s/ (or any other form being solicited, including the whole word). The nondynamic nature of this model is reflected by the fact that the clinician is providing an example to learn, not a sample to learn from (Cazden, 1988). Fey's (1986) account of the role of modeling strategies in teaching specific linguistic constructions to language impaired children contains many similar examples of directive, nondynamic choices.

Modeling strategies can also be directive and dynamic. The following conversational sequence shows how the clinician's modeling choice can serve to focus the child's attention on specific elements of the child's message in need of clarification:

Child:	This big bear was chasing Donald down the road.
Clinician:	What?
Child:	This big bear was chasing Donald.
Clinician:	What?
Child:	(no response)
Clinician:	The big bear was doing what?
Child:	Chasing Donald along this road.
Clinician:	Oh, now I get it, the bear was chasing Donald down the road.
Child:	Yeah. (Brinton & Fujiki, 1989, p. 179)

The choice of "The big bear was doing what?" was a modeled clarification strategy, more indirect in intent, but timed to direct the child to attend to the specific elements in his own message that the listener (the clinician) wanted to have clarified. The child must subsequently infer (recover) those elements.

Strategies for modeling can be reciprocal and dynamic, as well, and these probably approximate everyday interaction more closely, because the focus is on communication as an event. Wilson (in Weaver, 1988) describes invited demonstration, an indirect procedure in which children are invited to bring their favorite books and magazines to school. The teacher also brings his or her favorite book and participates in the activity along with the children, discussing, drawing, writing, or responding to questions from the children. This type of invitational modeling conveys to children that reading is a communicative event having value for both the teacher and the students. Another version of this same strategy is found in shared reading. The teacher prepares highly predictable material for children to read (or write about) in a group (rhyme, story, song, etc.); then together, they "master" it, for example, through repeating it. Next they read it together as a group, and then individual children are invited to locate and read certain lines and, later on, to locate certain sounds, words, and word endings. This kind of modeling strategy has several purposes. It "invites" children to focus more deliberately on units of language (forms) and cultivates opportunities to recognize and analyze metalinguistic connections among sound, meaning, and spelling (see Chapter 12). The next section elaborates on reciprocal and dynamic modeling.

Naremore and Hopper (1990) correctly point out that, while modeling may be important for learning to communicate and communicating to learn, the processes by which children originally learn from a blueprint and its modeling strategies and then transfer this learning to new situations remain unknown (see also Fey, 1986). Another issue is a technical one. When modeling is applied to the classroom for intervention purposes (see, e.g., Cole & Dale, 1986; Norris, 1989), the distinction between strategies that are reciprocal and dynamic versus directive and nondynamic should be explicitly described. Otherwise, clinicians will encounter difficulty in replicating them.

Rule Induction

Rule generalization presupposes the induction of a cross-situational rule from repeated experience with individual samples (models) (Lahey, 1988). In other words, the child discovers an analogy between one situation and another similar one. Fey's (1986) concept of focused stimulation is an illustration of how directive and dynamic modeling procedures can be centered on the induction of the auxiliary, *can't*. Focused stimulation is intended to structure the conversational context in such a way that the child will be indirectly led to produce the form. The clinician or parent uses multiple examples of the target form, typically in a contrived activity designed for this purpose:

Clinician:	I have a dog that can fly. False Assertion
Child:	Doggie not fly.
Mother:	Doggies can't fly. Expansion
Clinician:	Can't doggies fly? Recast
Child:	No.

Clinician:	I think they can.
Child:	Nope. Bird fly.
Mother:	Doggie can't fly. Birds can fly. Expansion
Clinician:	Oh, that's right. Doggies can't fly. They don't have wings. (Fey, 1986, p. 210)

Lahey (1988) comments that the effectiveness of focused stimulation will be dependent on the child's level of developmental sensitivity for the target form.

Again, the features of the social context that support and sustain the flexible use of rule induction need to be made clear (these features include the learning activities that originate strategies, the content for strategy application and its compatibility with prior experience, and the purposes of learning). Otherwise, directive modeling for rule induction remains susceptible to the criticism that it is no more than "barebones instruction" (Pressley, Johnson, & Symons, 1987, p. 85).

The Directive Scaffold

Directive modeling and rule induction, whether dynamic or nondynamic, all represent different models of discourse scaffolding. Each version offers assistance to children who cannot learn to communicate and communicate to learn on their own; however, each version also teaches children something different about what it means to communicate and what communication is used for. Although intervention may be aimed at bridging the gap between oral styles of language use and literate styles of language, the actual discourse strategies employed may not always achieve this goal.

Figure 13-1 indicates some of the assumptions of the directive scaffold. The teacher or clinician retains responsibility for what the child should be learning (K.E. Nelson, 1989) based on assessment of current (base line) performance. Dynamic and nondynamic modeling strategies are chosen as methods for the teaching of content. The child's performance is assessed through summative evaluations, which provide information on what happened after it happened (Howell & Morehead, 1987). Evaluations usually are done at the end of a lesson or unit. With repeated exposure to the teaching procedures and content, the expectation is that the child will induce connections among examples (generalize) and be capable of independently monitoring similar learning outcomes across comparable contexts.

The assumptions of directive scaffolds, particularly assumptions that are nondynamic, may be recognized in the conversational routines examined in Chapter 4. At the same time, directive scaffolds can perpetuate an erroneous un-

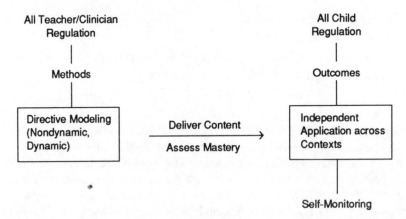

All Teacher/Clinician Regulation

All Child Regulation

Methods

Outcomes

Directive Modeling (Nondynamic, Dynamic)

Deliver Content → Assess Mastery

Independent Application across Contexts

Self-Monitoring

Figure 13-1 The Directive Scaffold. *Source:* From "The Instruction of Reading Comprehension" by P.D. Pearson and M.C. Gallagher, 1983, *Contemporary Educational Psychology, 8*, pp. 317–344. Copyright 1983 by Academic Press. Adapted by permission.

derstanding on the child's part that therapy is something "done" to him or her (Hoskins, 1987). Finally, directive scaffolds, while valuing problem solving through active participation on the child's part, tend to provide indirect guidance where exposure to a model or rule is too often equated with sufficient support for the child to perform independently. Failure to make the leap to independent performance may then lead to the inaccurate conclusion that the child is "context-bound" or less flexible in strategy application.

SUPPORTIVE SCAFFOLDING OF COMMUNICATION-CENTERED LEARNING

Supportive scaffolding is a blueprint for learning and has the potential to align the procedures of communication-centered learning with its goals. Moreover, a supportive scaffold incorporates modeling and rule induction into a more cohesive system for structuring the discourse of intervention.

What Is a Supportive Scaffold?

The principles of a supportive scaffold can be found in Vygotsky's (1962, 1983) theory of the origins of higher order cognitive functions. The development of these metafunctions for organizing one's own learning activities is conceived of as a process of gradual internalization that proceeds from the social (interpersonal) plane to the individual (intrapersonal) plane. Campione and Brown (1987) describe how this internalization is accomplished within and across cognitive and communicative domains through the process of supportive scaffolding:

> At the outset, the child and adult work together, with the adult doing most of the work and serving as an expert model. As the child acquires some degree of skill, the adult cedes the child responsibility for part of the job and does less of the work. Gradually, the child takes more of the initiative, and the adult serves primarily to provide support and help when the child experiences problems. Eventually, the child internalizes the initially joint activities and becomes capable of carrying them out independently. At the outset, the adult is the model, critic, and interrogator, leading the child toward expertise; at the end, the child adopts these self-regulation and self-interrogation roles. (p. 83)

This view of the supportive scaffold as a dynamic process is captured in Figure 13-2.

Scaffolding can be considered from both a developmental and intervention perspective as a process through which control is gradually transferred from the adult to the child for planning, monitoring, and evaluating goals, courses of actions, and outcomes. All three guidance functions—planning, monitoring, and

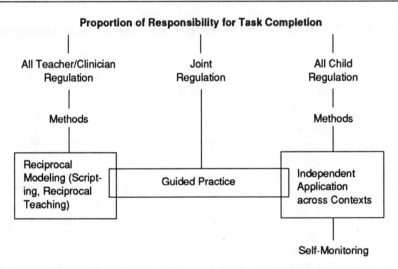

Figure 13-2 The Supportive Scaffold. *Source:* From "The Instruction of Reading Comprehension" by P.D. Pearson and M.C. Gallagher, 1983, *Contemporary Educational Psychology, 8*, pp. 317–344. Copyright 1983 by Academic Press. Adapted by permission.

evaluating—constitute the essence of self-regulation or proficiency in the independent application of skills for problem solving (Brown & Palinscar, 1987; Palinscar & Brown, 1984). Specific teaching strategies found in the support scaffold are described below.

Rogoff (1990) extends the Vygotskian framework in characterizing this internalization process as the pathway each child takes from being an apprentice thinker and talker to becoming an expert. Apprenticeship provides the beginner with access from the known to the new through the connections made within the context of communication between what a child already knows and what he or she must learn in order to take on gradual responsibility for new situations. Learning why, how, when, and what to communicate can be viewed, then, as a special kind of scaffolding process that, in Cazden's (1988) phrasing, naturally "self-destructs . . . as the need lessens and the child's competence grows" (p. 104).

Two essential teaching components of the supportive scaffold are discussed next: collaboration through discourse support and the transfer of responsibility.

Collaboration through Discourse Support

Parent-Child Scaffolding

A classic example of the gradual evolution from external regulation to self-regulation is the natural development of skill in being a collaborator in question-and-answer sequences (Heath, 1982). Initially, the parent interacting with a young infant will assign intent to the infant's facial expressions and other physical movements:

> *Mother:* (addressing her 2-month-old infant). You don't know what to make of all those lights, do you?
>
> Pause (3 seconds)
>
> *Mother:* That's right, I know you don't like them. Let's move over here (picks up infant and moves away from lights). (Heath, 1982, p. 110)

In this illustration, the parent engages in a "pseudoconversation" (Heath, 1982) in taking on the communicative roles of requester and responder. Note also that a turn-taking pause occurs between the requester and responder slots. At this point, the parent is externally guiding the infant's role as a conversational partner, a form of explicit regulation that is most likely automatic (Rogoff, 1990). The parent, by responding to the infant in a way that signifies the existence of shared understanding, and does for the infant what he or she cannot yet accomplish alone without help.

Gradually, the infant's capacity to engage in a broader array of reciprocal interactions evolves. For example, at ten months old, in looking at a picture book with the parent, the infant may point to a colorful picture while coordinating pointing with vocalizations. The parent interprets the infant's intent as a request for information and may expand on it with, "Yes, that's a doggie, a big doggie." With repeated experience in a variety of question-and-answer situations, combined with further development of the communicative repertoire, the middle-class child is eventually able to participate in abbreviated request-response routines, as this segment from Heath (1982) demonstrates:

Mother: (looking at a family photograph album with Missy, age 2;3) Who's that, Missy? (The mother has pointed to the family dog in one of the pictures.)

Missy: That's Toby.

Mother: What does Toby say?

Missy: Woof, woof, (child imitates a whine), grrrrrr, yip.

Mother: Where does Toby live?

Missy: My house. (pp. 110-11)

As the process of internalization evolves further and is influenced by a range of experiences with literacy forms and functions, questioning now assumes wide application as a comprehension facilitating strategy (Brown & Palinscar, 1987). For instance, self-questioning is a form of internalized dialogue whose self-regulating purpose is to elaborate understanding in oral and written domains.

Peer Collaboration

Rogoff (1990) notes that, as adults continuously reassess the child's need for help and attune their level of assistance to the child's understanding of and interest in the activity, so too children actively seek to manage their own learning by requesting help from others when it is necessary for attaining their goals. Recall the "What's that word" example (Chapter 4) in which Amy uses more knowledgeable peers in her reading group as metalinguistic resources for clarifying her understanding about the specific meaning of the assigned activity and the words to be written down. Amy's tactics in recruiting the assistance of others for clarification illustrates the truth of an ancient Chinese proverb (somewhat modified): "I hear and I forget. I see and I remember. I do (with others) and I understand."

Collaborative activity organized through the supportive discourse scaffold serves, then, to facilitate the structure for communication as well as to provide social support in visible ways for the child to reach beyond current levels of competence. As Rogoff (1990) states, "Involvement in the overall process and purpose of the activity, in a manageable and supported form, gives children a chance to see how the steps fit together and to participate in aspects of the activity that reflect the overall goals, gaining both skill and a vision of how and why the activity works" (p. 95).

Transfer of Responsibility

Cazden (1988) cautions that the transformation of the apprentice problem solver into an expert is not a simple mechanical process through which speaking and listening, as overt forms of social interaction, are gradually internalized into covert metacognitive operations. Recall that these metacognitive operations also subsume metalinguistic, metacommunicative, and metacomprehension knowledge as well. When the scaffold can be removed is still unknown. The question of scaffold removal is related to retrospective evaluation and the child's readiness to benefit from involvement with specific kinds of learning activities. Cazden (1988) offers an informal guideline for retrospective decision making on scaffold removal: "If, in fact, the novice takes over more and more responsibility for the task at hand . . . then we can infer, retrospectively, that our help was well timed and well tuned and that the novice was functioning in his or her zone of proximal development, doing at first with help what he or she could very soon do alone" (p. 107).

The Zone of Proximal Development

In order to understand what is meant by the zone of proximal development, also called the *zone of instructional sensitivity* (Brown & Ferrara, 1985), it is necessary to picture a map of a child's readiness to learn. This map includes the boundaries between a child's current level of unaided understanding, which can be construed as the lower end of competence (what N.W. Nelson, 1989, refers to as the communicative strategies and skills a student currently displays), and his or her developmental potential for a higher level of successful comprehension given optimal adult assistance (the communicative strategies and skills that the student may be capable of achieving [N.W. Nelson, 1989]). The distance between these boundaries constitutes the zone of instructional sensitivity, and maximally effective teaching occurs within this zone (Day et al., 1985).

Stated another way, the greater the zone width for a particular learning activity—for example, asking well-formed questions related to the topic being talked about or being able to use the auxiliary *can't* in obligatory linguistic contexts (Fey, 1986)—the greater the flexibility between a child's current developmental level (the lower boundary) and the potential for a higher level of development (the upper boundary). Conversely, the narrower the zone is for any learning activity—for example, as is the case with many children who are mentally retarded—the less likely it is that rapid and efficient learning and transfer of responsibility will occur, even with optimal adult support (Brown & Ferrara, 1985).

Campione and Brown (1987) note the subtlety of intrachild differences in zone widths. For one child engaged in a particular learning activity (e.g., taking more responsibility for sustaining topics in reading activities directed by the teacher or clinician), the zone may be small. A narrow zone of readiness can indicate that the child may not be any more responsive on this type of task with the assistance of scaffolded intervention than prior to intervention. However, for that same child engaged in another learning activity (e.g., shared reading, where peers take more cooperative responsibility for initiating and sustaining topics), the zone may be large. This latter instance suggests a higher degree of readiness to benefit from the well-tuned assistance described by Cazden (1988).

Finally, Day et al. (1985) point out that, if a task is beyond a child's developmental level, consistent failure will be the outcome. On the other hand, if a task is too easy, which means that the child demonstrates completed development, then no new learning will occur. The challenge becomes one of selecting "challenging tasks" (Day et al., 1985, p. 50) that the child cannot solve independently but may be able to solve through the supportive guidance of the teacher or clinician. The degree to which it then becomes necessary to make each step of the task explicit, similar to the Heath (1982) examples cited earlier, is a measure of an individual child's zone of instructional sensitivity (Brown & Ferrara, 1985; Campione & Brown, 1987).

Another Word on Transfer of Responsibility

The problems of transfer and maintenance evidenced by language learning disabled children and adolescents (e.g., in the flexible application of strategies for understanding, remembering, and making themselves understood) are well represented in the concept of transfer of responsibility. Premack's (1989) comments about transfer further put into perspective the seriousness of reduced flexibility in problem solving. Creativity results from the hard work of transfer. Intelligent behavior is often tacitly interpreted as creativity or flexibility; therefore, transfer has a revered status in a literate society, because the allocation of intellectual resources is equated with flexibility in appropriately using those resources (Premack, 1989).

The processes regulating transfer and maintenance of a new skill, what Brown (1982) refers to as the induction underlying independent performance, are not well understood. In fact, significant variations occur in the learning styles of children without language and learning difficulties. These variations are becoming increasingly apparent in how children learn language (K.E. Nelson, 1989) and in their problem-solving approaches.

At the level of formal problem solving, marked differences in learning styles emerge for the speed of strategy learning and in the flexibility of strategy transfer (Brown & Ferrara, 1985). These variations are not fully accounted for by differences in IQ. Transfer is not an all-or-none phenomenon but a dynamic one. Transfer pertains to the flexibility with which a new skill is applied (Brown & Ferrera, 1985; Premack, 1989). Some children learn a strategy quickly and can apply it widely; others learn it slowly but then can apply it widely; still others learn it quickly but can apply it only narrowly. Brown and Ferrara (1985) consider the slow learner as someone whose speed of learning is slow and transfer flexibility is narrow. All of these individual differences in learning styles contribute to problems in accurately differentiating "low achievers" from those with actual disruptions in language and learning. For example, the variability in performance profiles manifested in story recall and story production tasks (Roth & Spekman, 1986, 1989) may reflect differences in learning styles.

Case Study

The description by Palinscar and Brown (1984) of Charles, a seventh-grade student, illustrates the relationships among the zone of instructional sensitivity, the gradual transfer of responsibility from assisted to independent performance, and the criteria of speed in acquisition and flexibility in strategy transfer. Initially, Charles was an apprentice and needed a high level of discourse support from his teacher to formulate relevant questions from his reading of written text. Note that this activity of sentence formulation appears to place a high level of demand on Charles for metacognitive control as well as a high metalinguistic demand for analyzed knowledge about syntactic relations. The excerpt is from a segment about American snakes and shows reciprocal-dynamic modeling in action (*C* stands for Charles and *T* for the teacher; interpretations in brackets are additions):

1. *C:* What is found in the southeastern snakes, also the copperhead, rattlesnakes, vipers—they have—I'm not doing this right. [recognizes there is a problem but uncertain about how to fix it]

2. *T:* All right. Do you want to know about the pit vipers? [explicitly states the main idea]

3. *C:* Yeah.

4. *T:* What would be a good question about pit vipers that starts with the word "why?" [provides an explicit word category cue]

5. *C:* (No response)

6. *T:* How about, "Why are the snakes called pit vipers?" [provides a suggested formulation through modeling, which invites Charles to use this information in building his next attempt]

7. *C:* Why do they want to know that they are called pit vipers? [attempts to build on teacher's model] (Palinscar & Brown, 1984, p. 138)

By day 11, with repeated practice in the context of reciprocal reading activities (teacher and students alternated as "teacher"), Charles demonstrated increasing autonomy by assuming the teacher role in leading a discussion about text content. For example, he was able to generate a topically related and well-formulated question ("What is the most interesting of the insect eating plants, and where do the plants live at?"), indicating that he could participate according to the "rules of the game" (Palinscar & Brown, 1984, p. 141). He also exhibited greater ease in utilizing choice and control. By day 15, the supportive scaffold was removable. Charles was now capable of formulating relevant and cohesive questions by himself within this kind of reciprocal reading activity. In this case, flexibility was reflected in the increasing automaticity with which Charles could participate as a confident communicator and in his feeling more self-assured about his potential as a competent learner.

Benefits of the Supportive Discourse Scaffold

Instructional scaffolding, similar to developmental scaffolding, is dynamic, takes place within routine learning activities, emphasizes collaboration through discourse support, and has as its goal the gradual transfer of responsibility for learning from the teacher to the student. A major benefit of the supportive scaffold is its function as an "interactional safety net." Risk taking is reduced until a level of skill develops that makes the student feel confident enough to test out the skill increasingly on his or her own. Principles of supportive discourse scaffolding, as presented here, also tacitly guide several approaches to language intervention used by speech-language clinicians with language-delayed preschoolers and with school-age children who have language and learning problems. Constable's (1986) scripting approach with preschool children draws on the work of K. Nelson (1986, 1990) and Lahey (1988) (see also Lund & Duchan, 1988, for a variation of scripting). Strategy-oriented, learning-how-to-learn approaches with older children, which emphasize explicit teaching, include Hoskins's (1987, 1990) guided conversation program for adolescents and the approaches of Westby (1989) and Scott (1989b) for facilitating the creation of narrative and expository texts through supporting metacomprehension strategies.

A second benefit is articulated by Campione (1989). If the teacher or clinician does not have a working knowledge of the zone of instructional sensitivity for particular learning activities (see Chapter 12), the probabilities remain high that misclassifications, unnecessary referrals, and even mistaken assumptions about lack of progress will continue to occur for educationally at-risk students, including many students from culturally different backgrounds.

INTEGRATING OBSERVATIONAL TOOLS INTO THE SUPPORTIVE SCAFFOLDING: RECOMMENDATIONS FOR REAL-TIME INTERVENTION

The Intervention Plan

It is helpful to keep in mind that planning for intervention is a metacognitive activity and that an intervention plan is an organizational structure or a model. This model serves as a blueprint for making connections between what needs to be done, how it should be done, and why it needs to be done. Planning involves several steps.

First, the process of planning involves the *prediction* of goals and objectives (subgoals) to be achieved. Predictions are products of previous experience—the clinician's professional knowledge base, personal attitudes, and opinions about the ways communication develops, can be disrupted, and may be nurtured.

Second, planning entails choosing *strategies* that will gradually achieve objectives within the guiding framework of the larger purpose.

Third, planning requires decision making about how strategy effectiveness will be *monitored* on an ongoing and manageable basis and in what situations it will be monitored in order to clarify or revise the original predictions and strategies.

Finally, planning requires *evaluation* of intervention outcomes, that is, whether the outcomes ultimately validate the overarching goals.

The Curriculum and the Intervention Plan

Tools for observing the real-time interaction of the classroom were introduced in Chapters 6–10. Also discussed were the purposes that guided the selection and integration of observational tools. Among these purposes was the development of an intervention plan in which curriculum goals and objectives could be taken into account. The curriculum should be considered, not as a static body of knowledge to be mastered, but as a dynamic whole (Gavelek & Palinscar, 1988). Looked at this way, learning activities, the nature of the content to be learned through learning activities, and the purposes of these activities are the curriculum with which children interact. *How, when,* and *where* children engage with the information processing requirements of the curriculum are functions of their background knowledge, including experiential, analyzed, and strategic knowledge, and their communicative interactions with teachers, clinicians, and peers (Gavelek & Palinscar, 1988).

The recommendations for reaching toward the goal of a communication-centered approach in the classroom incorporate these dynamic concepts of intervention planning and the curriculum. They assume that teaching and learning constitute a collaborative activity between "teachers" and learners. Clearly, these recommendations are not an inflexible set of prescriptions to be followed. Rather, in line with the coparticipation model of collaboration and the observational purposes and procedures discussed in Chapters 5–11, we suggest a set of possibilities generated by the graded lenses of observation. These possibilities can then be considered by clinicians in collaboration with teachers in order to discover what works best for individual children.

Recommendation 1: Design Assessment As Scaffolded Intervention

Aim: To increase the predictive validity of intervention goals and objectives.

The predictive validity of intervention goals and objectives can be enhanced significantly when assessment is included within actual teaching processes in the classroom. In placing assessment within real teaching activities, it becomes possible to "continually change and refine the diagnosis of the individual learner" (Campione & Brown, 1987, p. 88) as the central component of a larger intervention plan. In other words, assessment is not an activity conducted first; rather, assessment is a form of intervention and intervention is a process of continual assessment.

This perspective can broaden one's approach to curriculum-based language assessment and intervention (e.g., Miller, 1989; N.W. Nelson, 1989; Simon, 1987a; Wallach & Miller, 1988). These authors all recommend that the first level of assessment should be directed towards describing matches and incompatibilities between the oral- and written-language-processing requirements of the curriculum and the child. Wallach and Miller (1988) stress the importance of examining the compatibility of the content to be learned with a child's background knowledge as that compatibility is mediated through teaching discourse. They suggest that problems in the curriculum are often due to child-teacher-material interactions (i.e., how particular materials are organized, formatted, or presented), and they recommend a careful task analysis of these interactions. N.W. Nelson's (1989) approach, in contrast, first addresses the task analysis of learning activities easily recognized as language-based, such as comprehension of narrative texts and the expository texts characteristic of science and social studies, as well as activities in academic areas less obviously language-based, such as verbal math problems. Nelson's second phase is the analysis of the metaprocessing strategies that a child uses, misuses, or does not use in comprehending and producing written language. Here the focus is the interaction between the specific learning activity, as reflected in strategy use, and the nature of the content being processed.

It is insufficient for predictive validity merely to have determined what these matches or mismatches may be. Describing a match or mismatch is equivalent to a judgment about a child's current level of competence—or equivalent to an answer to this question: "What kinds of language skills and strategies does the student currently exhibit when attempting to complete academic tasks in the curriculum?"(N.W. Nelson, 1989, p. 174). All of the interpretations derived from the integration of observational lenses and tools presented in Chapter 11— interpretations regarding Billy, Damian, Allison, Jared, Larry, and Cary—can be considered as assessments of what the students are currently doing. While these assessments are rich in detail and are validated through multiple perspectives, they are most likely insufficient in certain individual cases to answer Nelson's second question: "What kinds of language skills and strategies might the student acquire in the future that will lead to greater success in meeting similar curriculum demands?" (1989, p. 174). By curriculum demands, Nelson means both the "official" curriculum and the hidden curriculum of social expectations.

The implication of Nelson's work is to challenge clinicians and their collaborators to determine a child's zone of instructional sensitivity within particular learning activities. This zone is the distance between a child's unassisted level of performance and the child's potential to go beyond current levels given the opportunities to do so through varying the level of discourse support. How might this task be implemented once it has been determined that trouble sources exist for a given child? Four strategies are suggested.

1. Define a learning activity in which potential can be reasonably explored. The regular lens, which was initially aimed at a description of the activity structure or the generation of a running record of a learning activity, can be refocused into a close-up lens in order to define the cognitive and communicative components of a learning activity. For example, in asking children to retell a read-aloud story in class, an important factor is the compatibility of the content with what the child already knows or is presumed to know. This refocusing is a refinement of the traditional definition of task analysis. The analysis should also include the kinds of strategies that the child might be expected to use, such as strategies for facilitating or monitoring comprehension (Brown & Palinscar, 1987). The emphasis is placed on the *might* of strategy use, not the *should*.

The following example of plausible inferencing in oral story comprehension may help one to understand how activities can be used to explore learning potential. A set of pictures depicting lifelike situations is given to a student who is nine years old. The task purpose is to obtain a regular lens picture of how adequately the student can infer "whose fault," which taps into metacommunicative knowledge. The child is asked to "listen carefully in order to answer questions following the story" (Meline & Brackin, 1987, p. 264):

Julie's Record

This story is about Julie and Ben. Ben had borrowed some of Julie's records. At school, Julie asked Ben to come to her house after school and bring back a record (picture displayed: Julie and Ben are talking). Ben says, "yes," and comes to Julie's house with a "Prince" record (picture displayed: Ben is holding a Prince record at the door to Julie's house). Ben gives her the record, and she says, "Thank you" (picture displayed: Ben standing at the record player while Julie thinks about a "Michael Jackson" record; thought portrayed in a cartoonist's "bubble"). That is *not* the record that Julie wanted. She wanted her Michael Jackson record, not the Prince record. (Meline & Brackin, 1987, p. 270)

At the end of the story, the student is asked, "Whose fault is it that Julie did not get the record she wanted?" The student is also asked to justify that decision ("Why?"). Three assumptions are important. One is that the story selection has been based on a careful analysis of the story's organizational structure and cohesiveness. The second assumption is that the story has been considered in terms of its possible demand for analyzed knowledge and control (see Exhibit 12-1). The third assumption is that the content is potentially compatible with the student's background knowledge. The student says that Ben is at fault because he wanted to keep the Michael Jackson record (which is plausible but not necessarily logical based on the information constraints in the story). In fact, using a categorical tool, we could classify the student's responses into five categories (see Meline & Brackin, 1987). The resulting pattern would indicate the student's current level of performance on this kind of activity. Current level means unassisted performance.

The next series of questions to ask concerns how the student might deal with this same problem, or a comparable one, if he or she was supported more explicitly:

- After the pictures are displayed, the student is first given the title and encouraged to predict what may happen in the story.
- Then the student is informed that the story is a problem to be solved together. The problem is to decide whose fault it is that one person (Ben) does not understand another person (Julie). What might happen when

people don't understand one another? What might people do so they can understand each other better?

• As the story is read aloud, the student can be asked to stop the reading if there are places that are unclear.

• When the story is completed, if our student has not determined the most appropriate solution spontaneously, further guidance can include such focusing queries as these:

—Do you want to know whether it was Ben's fault or Julie's?

—What would be a good question to ask that would tell us whose fault it is?

—Do you know now whose fault it is or do you need more help?

The restructuring of the task also restructures the nature of the demands (e.g., demands for independently activating analyzed knowledge and control, including controlled remembering) and makes the purpose of the task clearer from the outset. The critical issue is how *much* assistance the student needs to arrive at the inference, an issue that concerns the speed of learning. It also becomes clearer how the student understands information resources (strategies), such as requesting clarification, when content is purposefully made ambiguous. Suggestions made by Brinton and Fujiki (1989) for the use of clarification strategies can be scaffolded into the degrees of discourse support available for problem solving.

2. Construct challenging teaching situations. A challenging teaching situation is one that is neither too easy nor too hard (Baker & Brown, 1984). For instance, the inference task may be too easy for some children and too difficult for others, as determined by the kinds of procedures just outlined for assisted performance. For an individual student, situations should be orchestrated to determine how responsive the student is to actual strategy instruction (Palinscar & Brown, 1987) when assisted through the supportive discourse scaffold of communication-centered intervention. The notion of multipurpose challenges is also consistent with the goal of facilitating language learning:

On the assumption that multipurpose interactions are processable by the child, then discourse, syntax, and semantic goals, in text, speech, and sign modes, all may be efficiently promoted within the same ongoing conversations. If appropriate challenges are built in, the child rather than the teacher will determine which particular structures are learned and used within a particular stretch of dialogue. (K.E. Nelson, 1989, p. 301)

While Nelson's comments pertain to the young language-delayed child, they are equally applicable to the language and learning problems of school-age children.

The emphasis on constructing multipurpose challenges is an important one. N.W. Nelson (1989) cites a transfer problem with a student who had no difficulty with verbal math problems involving division when the computational form itself was written down. The written numerical format cued an existing strategy for long division. However, the same student encountered serious roadblocks in solving the same math problems when responsible for generating the strategy for the computational format from verbal information alone, for example, "7.2 divided by 3.6" (N.W. Nelson, 1989, p. 180). Whether the second type of problem solving is too hard or potentially challenging needs to be carefully explored. Also, as discussed in Chapter 12, the question of a student's previous classroom experience with solving long division problems in different formats is another variable to take into account when examining situations for the flexibility of transfer.

3. Scaffold the discourse supportively. In a supportive scaffold designed to assess learning potential, assistance is systematically offered through a series of graduated cues as a function of a child's need for assistance (consider, e.g., the case of Charles and also the "whose fault" inference task discussed above). Supportive prompting is a form of dialogic mentoring, or coaching, in which verbal cues or choices are offered as external support for accessing a solution (for discussion of directive prompting in clinical discourse, see Silliman, 1984). As noted earlier, the number of graduated prompts that the child is observed to require in attaining a strategy for mastering a particular type of task can be an index of the speed of strategy learning (Brown & Ferrara, 1985). Other illustrations of supportive prompting are provided below in Recommendation 2. In addition, Pearson (1984) and Westby (1989) outline a similar set of graduated scaffolding procedures for supporting oral narrative comprehension.

According to Butler (1989), by using a graduated series of prompts, from the very general to the very specific, a blueprint is generated for inferring the solution. Notice from the restructured "whose fault" inference task that the supportive dialogic procedure can *explicitly* organize and condense the initial "rule induction" for the child (Connell, 1987) if the task is a challenging one. Note also that a rule and a strategy are not always identical. A strategy regulates how a plan can be implemented, while a rule governs how particular subgoals of the plan may be achieved. Finally, clinicians and teachers should work through possible prompts to be used in a particular learning activity before actually using this procedure. Writing them down initially is a good method for monitoring effectiveness and for deciding where and when modifications may be necessary.

4. Document the zone of instructional sensitivity. The use of systematically graduated prompts also allows the clinician and teacher to determine how much help the child actually needs on a particular kind of learning activity. Documentation of this zone can involve the use of a categorical tool, such as a checklist, to derive quantitative data ("How many prompts are necessary to reach the solution/answer?"), combined with a narrative tool to provide critical qualitative information on how the child reached the solution or answer (Butler, 1989).

Obtaining insight into how the child arrived at the solution, for example, to "7.2 divided by 3.6" (N.W. Nelson, 1989) or "whose fault" (Meline & Brackin, 1987), is essential for two reasons: It helps to establish the predictive validity of the intervention goals and objectives as well as the validity of the teaching strategies selected to realize the aims of communication-centered learning.

Recomendation 2: Scaffold the Strategy Instruction

Aim: To support the gradual internalization of comprehension-enhancing strategies within routine learning activities.

A controversial issue in instruction concerns transfer and maintenance. Should the strategies taught be general or task-specific strategies? Doubt exists about whether any metacomprehension strategy is ever acquired, at least initially, as a general strategy (Brown & Ferrara, 1985; Gavelek & Raphael, 1985; Pressley et al., 1987) or can even be taught as a general metastrategy (Campione & Brown, 1987) particularly to students who have language and learning difficulties (Deshler et al., 1983; Schumaker & Deshler, 1984). However, from a practical perspective, it is important to distinguish between teaching a general strategy and teaching a strategy that naturally transfers to situations that progressively diverge from the original learning situation (Campione & Brown, 1987; Deshler et al., 1983).

We cannot resolve these controversies; however, in light of recent research findings, the strategy instruction focus that we recommend is learning how to learn. The examples chosen are drawn from work on the teaching of specific strategies for enhancing and monitoring oral and reading comprehension, especially the strategy of reciprocal teaching (RT) (Brown & Palinscar, 1987; Palinscar & Brown, 1984). Our choice of RT is motivated by two reasons. First, it exemplifies how a systematic set of dialogic procedures can be sufficiently supportive to lead students at risk because of language and learning differences through transfer within the classroom setting. Second, RT has a rigorous research base and is reported to be easily learned by both teachers and peer tutors. Both of these factors make RT seem potentially useful in collaborative programs involving teachers and speech-language clinicians (see Brown & Palinscar, 1987, for a review of studies; for a critique of RT, see Pressley et al., 1987).

Palinscar (1989) describes the rationale for the RT approach:

> Children can be taught to engage in self-regulated learning when strategy instruction is an integrated part of the curriculum and includes the assessment of current strategy use, explanation regarding the nature and use of strategies, and opportunities to use strategies across the contexts in which they are useful. (p. 37)

RT, as defined by Brown and Palinscar (1987), is an instructional procedure in which a collaborative dialogue (discussion) between the teacher and students is structured by four strategies:

1. summarizing or self-reviewing the essential information in order to determine that the content has been understood (Palinscar, 1989, cites being able to paraphrase as indicative of whether comprehension and retention have occurred; if not, corrective actions may be needed)
2. question generating practiced as an ongoing activity within the larger theme of the lesson and predicated on what a teacher or test might reasonably ask
3. clarifying ambiguous or inconsistent interpretations of oral stories or the written text when gaps in comprehension are detected
4. predicting future content as the means for validating, disconfirming, or modifying how that content fits with previous understanding

These four strategies are task-specific in the sense that they are postulated to be critical for the activity of text (discourse) comprehension in both oral and written domains. Their use is practiced in natural learning situations. The RT procedures were originally validated with expository texts involving science lessons but have also been applied to oral narrative comprehension with Grade 1 "poor listeners" (Brown & Palinscar, 1987). Across curriculum areas, the basic procedures remain similar; however, how the four strategies are taught will differ depending on students' ages and ability to be responsive to the components of the scaffold.

Finally, Butler (1989) remarks that RT parallels approaches to language intervention in which the aim is to foster more active discourse comprehension and production through assisting children to monitor the level and depth of their understanding (e.g., Brinton & Fujiki, 1989; Hoskins, 1990; Norris & Damico, 1990; Scott, 1989b; Wallach & Miller, 1988; Westby, 1989). Elements of the RT approach are also visible in the two communication-centered, collaborative programs described in Chapter 5. We concur with Butler's (1989) assessment; however, an important contribution of RT is the explicitness of its dialogic procedures, including the role of modeling, in guiding children from external regulation to self-regulation of their comprehension.

1. Make the purposes, benefits, and steps of a strategy clear from the beginning. All adherents of strategy instruction, regardless of their theoretical and disciplinary orientations, stress the importance of a shared understanding between the teacher or clinician and the student on why a strategy is valuable, what its steps will consist of, when it will be used, and where it will be used (Pressley et al., 1987). Hoskins (1987), whose guided conversation program for language learning disabled adolescents most closely approximates RT, observes that directive scaffolds often fail to explicitly orient participants regarding what will be done and why it will be done; hence, children and adolescents are often left to infer the reasons, which may never make much sense to them in terms of their daily life inside and outside of school (e.g., see Chapter 4 on conversational routines; see also the "speech therapy dialect" in that chapter).

Purposes, benefits, and steps should also be described in a manner adjusted to the children's level of understanding. For example, Hoskins (1987) advises that, if the purpose of a session is to practice various discourse devices for maintaining a topic, then the purpose can be explained as practicing "keeping a conversation going by asking questions and adding information" (Hoskins, 1987, p. 19). Clarifications should be provided as appropriate.

On the other hand, Wilson (in Weaver, 1988) is a strong advocate of allowing students, with adult guidance, to set their own purposes once they understand that reading, writing, speaking, and listening have many purposes. This relates to the notion of semantic mapping mentioned in Chapter 12, which is intended to connect together why an activity might be important (its purposes) with possible resources for implementing goals (its strategies) and how this information is to be shared (its outcomes). Regardless of whether the choice is to "tell" children the reason why engagement with an activity is important or to lead them in discovering what might be learned, the same outcome is essential—shared understanding of the activity's communicative relevance.

2. Structure interaction so that it is collaborative. The following description of procedures for collaboration is from Brown and Palinscar (1987):

1. The teacher and student take turns leading a dialogue about a segment of text they are jointly listening to and trying to understand.
2. The teacher assigns a segment of the passage to be read and indicates that either it is her turn to be the teacher or the student's turn to teach.
3. After all participants have read the segment silently, the assigned teacher for that unit:
   - summarizes the content
   - asks a question that a teacher or test might reasonably ask
   - clarifies any interpretative difficulties
   - makes a prediction about what the author might say next (pp. 86–87)

During each substep, collaborative rather than evaluative feedback is continuously provided by the teacher and students (Applebee & Langer, 1983). Feedback can consist of acknowledging the relevance of a contribution, requesting explicit clarification when appropriate, adding new information to a previous contribution, or, as was done with Charles, who had difficulties generating questions by himself, providing an explicit model of the question form and function to build on.

3. Sequence the strategy introduction and its practice. Brown and Palinscar (1987) carefully sequence the strategy introduction and its practice. Summarization is taught first, followed by question generating, clarification, and prediction. Once acquired, summarizing and question generating occur after each and every segment read. Moreover, different children may need different levels of scaffolding to learn how to formulate text-relevant questions or summaries. Recall the earlier example of Charles and the high level of discourse support that he needed to generate questions that were both linguistically well formed and textually meaningful.

The clarification and prediction strategies, once understood, are used only when necessary. One justification for the optional use of prediction is that the ability to ask a question that a teacher or test might reasonably ask presumes prediction of what is plausible to ask based on existing background knowledge. However, Brown and Palinscar (1987) make clear from their research that the teaching of all four strategies is more effective than if only summarizing and questioning are taught. Brinton and Fujiki (1989) also underscore the need for teaching clarification strategies, since many children with language learning disabilities not only have comprehension difficulties but "may also fail to realize that they are *supposed* to comprehend" (p. 107). That is, they cannot readily infer that comprehension has a purpose, possibly because of insufficient analyzed knowledge of metacommunication variables. If the need for clarification is not recognized, it will not be requested.

4. Introduce each strategy by verbally demonstrating how it is implemented in both the "teacher" and "student" roles; transfer some responsibility to the child to practice the strategy as "teacher." The teacher or clinician initially demonstrates (models) the desired comprehension activities to make the underlying processes overt, explicit, and concrete (Brown & Palinscar, 1987).

If, for example, a narrative is read aloud, the adult reads the title first and then asks what could be learned from the title, an activity that entails predicting what could happen in the story ("what the problem may be"). This substep also communicates expectations for performance. The first paragraph is then read, followed by modeling the summarization strategy, since it synthesizes what the segment is about. In the next segment, the child is guided by the adult in assuming the teacher "summarizer" role.

An application of the RT approach for summarization is reproduced in Exhibit 13-1, which is an expansion of the Gist Lesson first discussed in Chapter 4.

Exhibit 13-1   Progress in Summarization for Danny (D), Sam (S), and Myron (M) Using Reciprocal Teaching

---

Session 1

Story: Mark Ramsey's "Magic Spaceship," modified from J. Watkins, *Science Fiction Stories* (Indianapolis, IN: Saturday Evening Post, 1975). The passage is the seventh of the modified story and is orally read by the clinician: "Mark walked toward school with his eyes down. Then he saw something weird on the ground. It was a small smooth rock shaped like a clamshell. But it burned like it was on fire."

Myron is the "teacher" and he picks Danny to summarize the main point.

Danny:	It was - um - Mark was looking down and was about to kick (.) a rock/ And . . . it was . . . and it . . . it was . . . and it was glowing and - um - (.) . . . and then -- and so he didn't kick it/
Myron/S:	He didn't kick it/ He didn't kick it/ Did he say he didn't kick?/
Danny:	He did <u>not</u> kick it/
Myron:	Uh - it's okay/ (Evaluation of Danny's summary)
Sam/M:	You can change it if you want to/
Clinician/S:	You can help if you want to/ (Invites assistance)
Myron:	I like it/
Clinician/M:	How could you change Danny's ideas? (General prompt focusing on reformulating)
Myron:	Me?/ Me?/
Clinician/M:	Uh huh you/
Myron:	Um - (.2+) Mark was going to school when he saw a clam on fire/
Danny:	But he was in the -- he was at the - um - school already so how could he be walking to it?/
Myron:	He was walking to school/ He wasn't in there/

The ninth and tenth passages are orally read by the clinician: "Back at the spaceship, sirens went off. The ship shook and the light went dead. The heat shields on the windows slammed shut. The Martians fell off their bunks."

Danny is the teacher.

Danny/S:	You/
Sam:	Okay/
Clinician/D:	What is Sam supposed to do? How would you remind him? (General prompt for purpose and strategy selection)
Danny:	Okay/ Um - um - to try to think of a little -- a sh-short sentence that - um - . . . that - um - summarize what I just read/
Sam:	Okay/ Um - okay the rocket siren went on/
Danny:	Off/
Sam:	Off/ Off whatever/
Danny:	Can you read that? (Showing Sam the word in the passage)
Sam:	(Trying to read) Then - um - um (.) when the sh- um - uh [I don't know]/
Danny:	[If you need help with a word, ask me]

Exhibit 13-1   continued

Session 2

Myron volunteered to summarize the parts of the story covered in the first session.

Myron:	Mark was mad 'cause he couldn't make any friends or (.) and he was late so he was walking to school and he kicked some - um - rocks and - um - ...and - um - kicked some rocks and - um - he kicked the - um - shells/
Danny:	Where is he?
Myron:	And they -- the . . . the people and ran out of - um - . . . ran out of their bunks/ And they -- and he . . . he picked it up and he said I never seen this rock in my . . . in . . . in when his rock co - collection and so he put it in his collection and he put it in his pocket/
Clinician:	That was good!
Sam:	You know when you said - um - he kicked that spaceship, he didn't kick it/ He put it in his po -- [He was gon]
Myron:	[He was gonna kick it]
Sam:	He was gonna kick it but he saw it was glowing/ So he picked it up and put it in his pocket/
Myron:	Pocket right/
Sam:	Yeah and he said emergency emergency/ And then people fell out of their bunks/

Session 3

Story: "Buried Alive" (Merritt & Liles, 1989). Orally read by the clinician: "One day it had been snowing for several hours. The roads were getting bad, and Jim could hardly see where he was going. He wanted to get home safely."

Clinician:	Sam/ What's the main idea?
Sam:	Okay - um/ It was snowing and - uh - and Jim couldn't see/
Danny:	Jim wanted to get home safely/
Clinician/M:	Do you have a main idea or do you like the ones said by Sam and Danny?/
Myron:	I like one of theirs/ I like them put together/
Clinician:	Okay/ How would you put them together?/ (General prompt calling attention to strategy)
Myron:	Jim . . . Jim was in a bad storm and he wanted to go home/
Clinician:	You all did a fantastic job/ (Reads next passage) So, he looked for a wide place at the side of the road, and pulled over his eighteen-wheeler, and fell asleep. He was finally able to relax/ Danny/ What could be the main idea?/ (General prompt inviting an interpretation)
Danny:	Ah - (.2+) he could relax/ He - he pulled over his eighteen-wheeler and fell asleep/
Myron:	Eighteen?/
Clinician:	That was good, Danny/
Danny:	That's a lot of wheels/
Clinician/M:	Do you want to change that idea?/
Sam:	I got one/

Exhibit 13-1   continued

Myron:	Jim pulled over when he found a (.) good spot to relax/
Sam:	I said one/ um - Jim pulled (.) . . . Jim pulled over (.) . . . J - Jim pulled over and fell right asleep/

Source: Based on Brown & Palinscar (1987) and Palinscar & Brown (1984).

The segments are portions of critical incidents identified from the running records of the first three sessions, in which the summarization strategy was introduced, modeled, and practiced. The three boys, Danny (9½ years old), Sam (11½ years old), and Myron (10½ years old), participated in story selection and were developing a cartoon portfolio of the story's events as the various portions were summarized. The first story was a type of "trickster" tale involving deception (Westby et al., 1989). The second story, from Merritt and Liles (1989), concerns a truck driver who becomes trapped in his truck in a snowstorm. Both stories were chosen as challenging tasks. They proved to be the most challenging for Sam, but not too difficult. Each story was divided into mini-episodes for the purpose of reducing the load on intentional remembering in these early sessions.

The transcripts display a variety of things: (1) the presence of multipurpose challenges (K.E. Nelson, 1989), represented by the children's changing interpretation of how the activity could shift focus (e.g., from providing a response to attending to structural variations in the form of the response); (2) the initial "effort" involved in taking on the teacher role; (3) trouble points arising in evaluating another's summary because of misinterpreting key word meanings (e.g., confusion over the multiple meanings of "He didn't kick it" and "off" in Session 1); (4) strategies used to resolve these breakdowns; and (5) an initial willingness to begin taking some metalinguistic risks (e.g., Myron's volunteering to summarize at the start of Session 2 and his choosing to combine "two ideas" in Session 3, and Sam's offering a paraphrased construction that attempts to expand on Myron's summary in Session 3).

Myron and Sam had serious comprehension problems, as reflected in their oral and reading comprehension. Neither could readily obtain the gist of what was read and often misinterpreted classroom language. However, both demonstrated over the course of the three sessions that, with only moderate levels of assistance, they could begin to produce and combine in more deliberate ways sentences that expressed synonymous meaning (Sessions 2 and 3), which is the essence of paraphrase, and monitor the completeness of another's content. Danny, on the other hand, had been designated a "problem learner," but he appeared to be the child with the widest zone of instructional sensitivity in this kind of activity, as measured by the speed with which he could infer the point.

The same kinds of procedures are followed for the introduction of each subsequent strategy: (1) learning to generate questions, (2) requesting clarification, and (3) making predictions. The criteria for acceptable role transfer and strategy use should be flexible. The important point in the initial phases of strategy acquisition is that the child feels safe and successful in participating and that trial and error are expected (Brown & Palinscar, 1987). As skill is acquired in each of the strategies through practice and the child becomes responsive to higher demand levels, the adult gradually shifts to mentoring participation in discussion (Palinscar, 1989), as this second example involving Charles shows:

> *C:* How does the pressure below push the mass of hot rock against the opening? Is that it?
>
> *T:* Not quite. Start your question with, "What happens when?"
>
> *C:* What happens when the pressure from below pushes the mass of hot rocks against the opening?
>
> *T:* Good for you! Good job. (Palinscar & Brown, 1984, p. 139)

These dialogic procedures can also be modified with younger children for oral comprehension of narratives (Palinscar, 1989).

The four metacomprehension strategies supporting the RT dialogue—summarization, question asking, clarification, and prediction—are also found in other collaborative scaffolds (e.g., Harste, Short & Burke, 1988; Hoskins, 1990; Pearson, 1984; Rhodes & Dudley-Marling, 1988; Wilson, in Weaver, 1988; Westby, 1989). The RT approach is distinguished by its sequence of strategy instruction (teaching each strategy separately) and its use of reciprocal-dynamic modeling within the structure of shifting communicative roles. Hence, less inferencing is required initially by the child in learning how to manage the topical continuity of interaction.

An additional difference is that the explicit sequencing of the RT strategy instruction reduces monitoring complexity for the teacher or clinician. For example, Hoskins (1987) uses modeling (verbal demonstration), recapping (summarization), and coaching (prompting) as the dialogic procedures; however, when and where each procedure is to be inserted by the clinician into the ongoing dialogue is dependent on how the situation of the moment is judged, a monitoring task that is not always easy.

5. Plan transfer activities as a routine component of scaffolded intervention. From a practical standpoint, the implementation of the zone of instructional sensitivity by means of the RT scaffolding incorporates transfer within natural learning activities. The zone can be thought of as a continuous spiral in which "students are led to perform at increasingly mature levels" (Brown & Palinscar, 1987, p. 88) within an activity domain. The new level of expertise now becomes the lower edge of apprenticeship as the student is challenged to go beyond once again. Individual differences will appear in the rate of progress; some students may progress only so far and may continue to need high scaffolding support. However, in reaching towards flexibility of transfer in the four comprehension strategies, it is necessary to plan carefully how to achieve this aim. Scott (1989a, 1989b), Wallach and Miller (1988), Westby (1989), and Wilson (in Weaver, 1988) provide guidelines on sequencing the complexity of text processing in both the oral and written realms. In general, flexibility in the use of comprehension strategies for understanding and generating a variety of narrative texts should proceed the introduction of practice with these same strategies in expository texts (e.g., Scott, 1989b). Whether the four comprehension strategies can be taught simultaneously for both narrative and expository texts remains speculative.

Recommendation 3: Systematically Monitor and Evaluate Outcomes through the Use of Observational Tools

Aim: To document progress.

Campione and Brown (1987) suggest that in documenting progress, the teacher or clinician should not be preoccupied with how much overall improvement in performance can be demonstrated. Rather, the documentation of progress should be directed towards determining how much discourse support a child needs from the teacher or clinician to attain a specific level of learning and to apply this learning flexibly to new situations. A further qualification is highlighted by K.E. Nelson (1989). The need for gathering data should not be confused with documenting what is actually learned through an intervention. Increased frequency of a behavior is not sufficient evidence that the behavior has been integrated into the knowledge base. For example, "the frequency with which children . . . will say 'horse' or 'the' or 'on' or 'running' or will point to one half or one third or one quarter of pictures that best illustrates these structures . . . may be gains only for the documentation process and not for the child's language skills" (K.E. Nelson, 1989, p. 285).

The scaffolding of communication-centered intervention readily lends itself to formative evaluation. This form of assessment is ongoing, is directed to the evaluation of behaviors as they are actually developing, is dependent on observational data, and can be tied to immediate modifications in teaching-learning strategies because formative evaluation is a teaching tool. Although formative evaluation systems have not been widely researched and can be time-consuming to use, Howell and Morehead (1987) offer a variety of charting procedures for evaluating changes in learning on a daily, weekly, or monthly basis. However, in using some of these charting procedures, caution should be taken not to reduce the evaluation of progress to frequency counts that are inherent in certain observational tools, such as checklists. In addition, Howell and Morehead (1987) recommend the use of time sampling as the basis for data collection. The advantages and disadvantages of time sampling are reviewed in Chapter 7, and they should be considered before adopting time sampling as the method for charting outcomes.

Formative evaluation procedures can also be utilized without complete dependence on time-sampled frequency counts. Portfolios, which are a kind of narrative tool, can be maintained for each child. For example, dialogue journals, because they are written records, not only allow evaluation of progress in learning the purposes of "dialoguing" but also allow assessment of increasing internalization of spelling rules and changes in sentence structure. Narrative accounts can be compiled from these portfolios and be reverified for interpretation through modifying the multiple perspective procedures described in Chapter 11. Students' self-profiles of progress, also covered in Chapters 5 and 11, can supplement these records.

Other categorical tools, such as rating scales, can be developed for assessing the outcomes of learning activities. For example, Watson and Crowley (in Weaver, 1988) cite a number of areas for inclusion in an integrated assessment of progress: types of assistance sought for problem solving (e.g., child seeks assistance only from teacher, seeks assistance from others, etc.); risk taking (e.g., child contributes own topics, trys to paraphrase what has been read, invents best-fit word for an unfamiliar word; etc.); and attitude toward reading and writing (e.g., child prefers books with predictable structures, enjoys sharing writing, etc.). Many of the metalinguistic, metacommunicative, and metacomprehension behaviors discussed in Chapter 12 and in this chapter can be organized in the format of a rating scale. Functions and quality of use can be assessed. Several of the scales replicated in this volume are also appropriate for an integrated and ongoing review of progress. Chapter 8 is an additional resource for developing rating scales.

A good rule of thumb in selecting the best tool is to consider the purpose of evaluating progress at a particular time. The more detailed the requirement for documenting the status of a particular acquisition, the greater the need for the lenses of observation to be refocused in order to obtain a fine-grained evaluation.

TO THE FUTURE

This book focuses on new collaborative roles and competencies for the speech-language pathologist in the classroom; new tools for observing real-time communication in the classroom; and new intervention goals that center the many and varied functions of communication, functions that serve as the blueprint and motivation for students' advancements in their own learning about language and literacy. In developing themes, it has been emphasized that teaching is collaborative and learning is interactional.

One accomplishment of our efforts may have been to make the familiar obvious. We suspect that much of what is covered is intuitively known by speech-language clinicians and teachers. However, it perhaps has not been fully accessible. Accessibility is related to the power of our observational lenses. Directing these lenses to what children actually do in the classroom can allow recognition of the aspects of language and communication most relevant for individual children, integration of that information with existing knowledge bases, and organization of the discourse scaffolding of intervention in new ways—ways that make use of the strengths of children and their curiosity about language, including what it is and how it works. A singular benefit from this refocusing can accrue to students with language-learning differences—the enhancement of their capacity to participate as full members of a society in which information technologies have revolutionized how we live, work, learn, and communicate.

Recommendations for In-Service Workshops on Classroom Discourse

Elaine R. Silliman, Louise C. Wilkinson, and Amy S. Belkin

DESCRIPTION OF THE FISHER-LANDAU PROGRAM

The Fisher-Landau Program is located in and supported by The Dalton School, New York City. The purpose of the program is to provide support for (1) teacher education, (2) the development of student intervention programs relevant to The Dalton School curriculum, and (3) the creation of diagnostic tools and instructional materials for use in the classroom (e.g., videotapes, publications, and games).

The creation of the Fisher-Landau Program was motivated by the need to serve students with language and learning disabilities in the private-school setting. The Dalton School and the Collegiate School, also located in New York City, were the first independent day schools in the United States to incorporate the Fisher-Landau Program as part of their educational program. In adopting such a program, Dalton acknowledged the presence of gifted students with language learning differences and, at the same time, the school accepted the responsibility for facilitating the linguistic-communicative development of these students.

Currently, the staff of the Fisher-Landau Program includes, among others, a director, a school psychologist, learning disabilities specialists, and a speech-language pathologist. The program is a training site for graduate students and a continuing education site for regular and special education teachers who desire to increase their expertise. Parent volunteers participate in the classroom. Moreover, in-service workshops have been developed for teachers and parents, such as the workshop on classroom discourse. Workshops have also been created exclusively for the Fisher-Landau staff in order to enhance their expertise.

Consistent with the long-term mission of the Fisher-Landau Program, the Dalton staff, in conjunction with Columbia University Teachers College, disseminates the program to other private schools. Workshops and lectures are presented at these schools and at professional conferences.

GUIDELINES FOR ORGANIZING IN-SERVICE WORKSHOPS ON CLASSROOM DISCOURSE

Several areas are discussed below as a guide to the organization of workshops on classroom discourse. These include (1) obtaining key administrative and faculty support, (2) preparing an instructional packet, (3) creating and maintaining a supportive environment, (4) applying descriptive tools and interpreting outcomes, and (5) follow-up.

Obtaining Key Administrative and Faculty Support

The support of the appropriate administrative personnel and teachers is a prerequisite for work in the classroom. One suggestion for obtaining support is to prepare a written proposal for curriculum development and then discuss the proposal with the administrators and teachers who will be involved in the project. This proposal should contain, at a minimum, information on the purposes of the workshop sessions, their procedures, the location (or locations) in which they will take place, their duration, the participants (e.g., teachers), the anticipated outcomes, and any expenditures necessary to hold the workshop initially.

A proposal can emphasize how the workshop content will allow teachers and other team members to become skilled in analyzing their lessons in order to obtain increased insights into and control over the language of teaching. Increased knowledge can also allow teachers the opportunity to acknowledge their strengths or, only if they thought necessary, to modify their instructional style as a tool for facilitating student growth. The overall purpose should not be viewed in judgmental terms. Rather, three aims should be stressed: (1) to offer teachers an overview of the central role of classroom discourse in teaching and learning, (2) to provide teachers with a heightened awareness of why particular children are less able to participate successfully in lesson activity, and (3) to give teachers some practical means for analyzing their own discourse patterns.

Teachers who participate can be encouraged to audiotape or, preferably, to videotape a whole-class or small-group lesson of their own choosing as a way of deciding whether they will participate (see Appendix C for taping procedures). As described in Chapter 7, general guidelines for event sampling can be given. Important points to reaffirm are (1) that making judgments of audiotaped or videotaped activities, whether positive or negative judgments, is not a workshop goal; (2) that teachers' participation is voluntary; and (3) that the information learned will be shared only if the teacher participants choose to do so.

Preparing an Instructional Packet

Once an initial cadre of teachers volunteer, a packet of information can be given to them. The packet should include a schedule, a manual on videotaping and transcribing, and instructional readings.

The *schedule* of sessions should clearly specify the dates by which information is to be learned as well as the dates for the completion of the various aspects of the workshop. In developing goals for each session, it is helpful to segment the information to be acquired in a way that will be manageable given the teachers' available time. It is important not to overwhelm participants with work. In addition, reinforce the point that the focus of sessions will not be determined in advance, but will be determined by the content of the individual videotapes or audiotapes.

The *manual* should explain procedures for (1) transcribing the videotape or audiotape, including a list of coding notations used to depict the transcription graphically (see Appendix B); (2) completing activities related to interpretation of the transcription, such as mapping of the classroom, which describes the physical and social structure of activity (see Chapter 10); and (3) analyzing the transcription using a set of guiding questions (see Appendix B). The manual should also contain a sample transcript that shows how information is to be transcribed, a sample of a completed transcript, and, if desired, a grid designed for tallying the types and distributions of instructional acts.

The manual provided in Appendix B can be used as a reference for developing materials appropriate to the particular setting and circumstances. However, in adapting materials, the clinician should remember that event sampling rather than time sampling is recommended for obtaining samples of teacher-student interaction. This preference for event sampling derives from the importance of preserving contextual aspects of the activity being recorded. As discussed in Chapter 7, event sampling allows preservation of the natural context, while time sampling removes behaviors from their natural context of occurrence. Also, if videotaping is not feasible, other modifications will need to be made in the accompanying materials to accommodate an audiotape analysis.

The *readings* should be related to the workshop purposes and procedures and should help establish a general frame of reference. These can be offered as an enhancement to learning rather than as a requirement. In all likelihood, as the workshop progresses, teachers who choose to participate will want to learn more about a range of language learning issues (e.g., the relationship between language and math or how children's story telling can bridge the gap between oral and more literate uses of language). The clinician should follow up teachers' requests.

Creating and Maintaining a Supportive Environment

To maintain rapport and coparticipation throughout the workshop, participants may need to be reassured that they and their work are valued. The potential for participants to feel embarrassed is present when their communication with students is subjected to rigorous analysis in the workshop.

Several procedures can be employed to create and maintain an atmosphere of trust: (1) The videotapes or audiotapes collected by the participants should not be previewed by the clinician; rather, the participants should maintain personal control of their own tapes. (2) The focus and content of transcription should be decided by the participants; the clinician should act only as a guide in assisting the participants to consider possibilities. (3) The earlier phases of the workshops can be designed so that successful completion of objectives is not dependent on the participants sharing their tapes with the group (i.e., the choice of when to show or hear his or her tape must also remain with each participant). (4) When a participant selects to share a tape, the clinician should not constrain that individual's choice of how to present it. For example, a teacher, in presenting a tape, may believe that he or she must criticize the teaching strategies employed. It's better to indicate that the manner of presentation is the individual's choice, rather than stating that the purpose of the activity is not one of criticism. One person's choice does not obligate others to participate in a similar manner. By creating this "safe" environment, the clinician is encouraging a collective sense of responsibility for how choices are made.

Applying Descriptive Tools and Interpreting Outcomes

The substeps comprising this phase are presented as five separate workshop sessions. However, depending on the overall duration of the sessions, the same substeps can be extended over longer periods of time. While the use of descriptive tools is essential for achieving an in-depth understanding of classroom communication, other observational tools can be used as well.

The First Session

The initial session has two primary purposes: (1) to heighten the participants' sensitivity to the spatial, temporal, and social features of the classroom and (2) to introduce the process and value of transcribing lessons as a means for magnifying awareness of classroom discourse.

The reasons for creating and describing classroom activities are addressed first. The activity structure description, including the classroom map, documents the spatial, temporal, and social orientation of the activity within the school day (see Exhibit 10-1). Depending on the schedule of sessions, the activity description and map may be completed from memory by the participants prior to viewing their own videotapes, then reviewed during this initial session or in the second session. A complete description of the videotaped activity should include the name, the location, the participants, the materials involved, the specific activity structure (e.g., teacher–whole class, teacher–small group, peer groups, etc.), and, if groups are used for the activity, the criteria by which children are grouped.

The second task for this session is to familiarize participants with the vocabulary of transcription, including the mechanics and notations. A blank transcript with four columns is used to achieve this objective (see Exhibit B-1 for organization). Components to be completed in the transcription include (1) identification of the speaker, who the speaker is addressing, and the number of the speaking turn; (2) the actual language used by the teacher and students during the particular speaking turn; and (3) a description of aspects of the context that influence the unfolding of the activity, which helps to substantiate how the teacher or students interpret each other's intentions. The manual includes definitions, descriptions, and examples of these components. Analysis of the fourth component, functions of various types of communicative acts, is reserved for the third and fourth sessions—or it can be extended over other sessions if necessary.

Several issues arise at this point. One pertains to the sufficiency of transcription for basic training purposes. The amount of effort required to capture multiple levels of behavior can be overwhelming for a novice. Experience indicates that a 5- to 7-minute segment is manageable for the beginner; however, the participants will need to agree to transcribe outside of school time. Furthermore, if transcription comes easily to a participant, then the clinician can offer to provide assistance for transcribing a longer segment. In either case, each participant needs to select a segment in which he or she is actively engaged in teaching children (e.g., introducing a new topic unit, clarifying information that was previously unclear, or assisting a student in managing a strategy).

A second issue pertains to the actual process of transcription. While there are many approaches available for the general organization and process of transcription and the coding of units (e.g., Bennett-Kastor, 1988; Cooper, Marquis, & Ayers-Lopez, 1982; DeStefano, Pepinsky, & Sanders, 1982; Dollaghan & Miller, 1986; Dore, 1986; Friel-Patti & Conti-Ramsden, 1984; Ochs, 1979a; Prutting & Kirchner, 1983; Zukow, 1982), ease of use should be one criterion.

Since it is easiest to focus on only one type of behavior at a time, we suggest the following sequence for videotapes:

1. Make an audiotape of the videotape segment to be transcribed and use the audiotape as the source of a draft transcription. This procedure will reduce the information overload that can occur when transcription proceeds directly from a videotape.

2. Transcribe teacher talk first; include everything said including repetitions, filled pauses (*uh, um, ah*), revised utterances, and single words (e.g., *Wait!*). Begin each utterance on a new line using a slash mark (/) rather than a period to mark an utterance boundary.

3. Use the same procedures for transcribing student talk next.

4. Review the audiotape to refine the transcription of both teacher and student talk. Note where a topic seems to start and end by drawing a horizontal broken line (-----) across the page, and name the topic (e.g., "Topic 1: Discussion of Weekend Activity," "Topic 2: Introduction of Digits," etc.).

5. Now use the videotape to verify accuracy.

6. From the videotape, attend to nonverbal-contextual information that occurs simultaneously with talk and may be relevant for the particular transcript, such as gaze behaviors; orientations of head and body; the use of gestures; changes in rate, stress, and volume of speaking; facial expressions; and laughter. Note behaviors on the transcript that appear to be important for maintaining the ongoing flow of interaction; include verbal or nonverbal actions that interrupt the activity flow.

7. Refine the draft further and produce a final copy (refer to Appendix B for specific definitions and examples of this process).

A third issue pertains to what exactly constitutes a topic, much less a shift in topic or a shading of a topic (Brinton & Fujiki, 1989). The decision of when a topic has been changed, either by the teacher or a student, should be left to the teacher's judgment at this time. Heightening participants' sensitivity to topic shifts is an adequate outcome of this first session.

A fourth issue that can emerge concerns participants' feelings of being overwhelmed by the immensity of the subject to be covered. Reassurance is needed that the focus of critical analysis will depend on the particular area of interest and the extent to which the video viewing sessions and the resulting transcript provide relevant information. The transcription thus serves the dual function of defining a focus and limiting it as well. For example, one participant, who taught a kindergarten class, was interested in how she handled topic transitions and presented new information. Her videotape had purposefully included both kinds of discourse behaviors. Because of her dual interest, this teacher made the decision to transcribe the beginnings of two different segments containing these behaviors rather than analyze a more extended segment of one lesson.

A questionnaire can be used as a guide to assist participants in initially interpreting their transcripts. Appendix B contains a sample questionnaire. The rationale underlying the questionnaire derives from the preceding chapters, while its specific content has been compiled from a variety of sources. Nine areas are addressed:

1. the children's knowledge of classroom routines
2. the teacher's expectations for performance in the activity
3. how turns are designated and whether turn-taking is cooperative or competitive
4. teaching choices concerning the introduction, maintenance, and cohesion of topics
5. teaching choices concerning vocabulary selection
6. teaching choices concerning the selection of communicative intents
7. teaching choices concerning the forms and complexity of expression
8. the characterization of speech style
9. possible effects of the classroom listening environment on comprehension

As mentioned previously, the analysis of teaching choices should be reserved for the third and fourth sessions.

The questionnaire is not intended to neglect procedures sensitive to the sociolinguistic diversity that occurs in multicultural and bilingual child populations. Although the particular content of the questionnaire is oriented to classrooms in which majority children predominate, the basic format is sufficiently flexible to incorporate content specific to sociocultural differences. One outcome of increased awareness about sociolinguistic variations in language use is the understanding that these differences are a resource to build upon in achieving the aims of communication-centered learning. The work of Au and Kawakami (1984; Kawakami & Au, 1986) exemplifies this principle. Chapter 4 also contains a number of interdisciplinary references on the richness of variations in language use associated with multicultural and bilingual differences. Other valuable sources for the clinician and interested teachers to review include Cole's (1989) synthesis of demographic variables affecting the direction of clinical service delivery to children and the impact of these variables on possible sources of miscommunication between cultural groups; Cheng's (1989) review of issues and approaches with children having limited English proficiency; and the work by Taylor (1986) and Taylor, Payne, and Anderson (1987) on communication disorders in multiculturally diverse populations.

The Second Session

The purpose of the second session is to increase the sensitivity of participants regarding classroom discourse and to facilitate their realization that teaching choices are being communicated through discourse. Participants need to analyze their own data by the second session. It is beneficial to start by sharing the activity descriptions of the classroom and presenting the classroom maps. Differences between teachers will likely appear with regard to the various aspects of the description. Again, reassurances are needed that these differences are appropriate and that a "standard" description is not expected.

Discussion of the transcriptions is the next step. For clarification purposes only, this discussion is divided into four areas. In actual practice, these topics would naturally be the focus of dialogue about the transcriptions:

1. *Time for transcription.* Discussion should be facilitated on the effort expended to complete the transcription. Our experience indicates that achieving reasonable accuracy on five to seven minutes of transcription, using the procedures just outlined, will take the beginner a minimum of five hours. The amount of effort will also differ depending on how individual participants choose to enhance their transcriptions. For example, a participant may select to color-code each speaker's verbal and nonverbal actions. While this technique may be helpful for enhanced visualization of interactions, it will add considerable time to the transcription task. The clinician will want to learn whether the time allocated for transcription was sufficient or insufficient and whether the experience was a meaningful one in spite of the effort it took. It may be necessary to extend the time between the first two sessions so that participants may be able to fit the five to seven hours of transcription comfortably into their schedules.

2. *Additional notations.* The notations contained in the manual may not be adequate to capture the richness of a particular transcription fully. A tradeoff always exists between less notation, thus risking the loss of valuable detail, and putting in too much notation that is not needed. The problem with extensive notation is that the transcription may not be readable because of its inclusiveness (Ochs, 1979a). Participants should be encouraged to develop useful notations not contained in the manual. The clinician can then decide whether to incorporate these notations into a future revision of the manual.

3. *Transcription.* The process itself should be reviewed relative to its ease and value. Those participants who may have deviated from the recommended procedures (e.g., by transcribing all aspects simultaneously from the videotape) can be asked to share their impressions about the procedures they used.

4. *Learning process.* A key outcome is what the participants learned about the patterns and effects of their discourse from viewing the video sessions and transcriptions. Having placed themselves under scrutiny, the question becomes how adequately they can stand back from themselves to see objectively those hidden aspects of communication to which Mehan (1979) referred.

An example of this objectification process is related to a frequent behavior about which we are often unaware. Many participants become painfully aware of how many times they use *OK*. The essential issue is not its use but the communicative functions served by its frequent use. Some may use *OK* to mark the ending of a topic and immediately follow it with *Now* to convey a topic shift or the beginning of a new activity. Or *OK* may be linked to the E slot of the IRE sequence and serve as a form of an external comprehension check.

The following exchange illustrates these multiple functions in a kindergarten class. The task involved two children taking photographs of classroom activities and then describing what they saw by writing a newspaper. The teacher is assisting Bobby in finding the main idea of Bobby's photographs of a classmate (all names have been changed):

Teacher: So we need to find a picture where we have Donald working/ (Donald is the classmate whose pictures were taken by Bobby)

Can you find a picture of where you can see Donald in the picture?/ (Bobby points to the picture)

Terrific!/

OK/ (External comprehension check)

So we're not gonna use these for our story because we don't have the main idea/

We can't [see all of Donald]/

Bobby: [We can use this one]/ (Bobby overlaps the teacher's turn)

Teacher: Right!/

OK (.) so I'll put these here/ (Puts aside extra pictures and holds up the best one; *OK* again serves as an external comprehension check)

Now (.) can you give me a good sentence about the main idea for this picture?/ (Use of *Now* projects a topic shift)

Other functions of *OK* can include the filling of a gap when a child does not take an expected turn.

Two points warrant emphasis. One is that the general role of teacher is multi-level. It involves teaching academic content, communicating expectations for appropriate conduct in children's roles as students, and acting as a "traffic director" in keeping the conversational flow going. Devices as *OK* serve to maintain this flow of talk. The second point is that the multiple functions of *OK* represent stylistic choices (variations) for moving from one topic to another, for self-clarification, for evaluation, or for keeping talk going. The objective is to facilitate teachers' realization that their language use always reflects choices and that a relationship exists between their teaching choices and what children actually do in response to these choices. The clinician also needs to react positively to the participants' increasing ability to differentiate between discourse choices they believe to be effective and those they would consider modifying. For most participants, the workshop provides the first opportunity they have had to focus on specific aspects of their classroom discourse and the functions communicated by their choice of various discourse devices. The process of bringing automatic linguistic-communicative behaviors to a more conscious level allows teachers to begin exercising more deliberate control over the selection of instructional choices.

The Third and Fourth Sessions

Two major activities are focused on in the next two sessions: (1) helping teachers to better understand their "teaching register," which is characteristic of the instructional mode, by helping them to identify functions of instructional acts, and (2) considering additions and corrections to the manual and questionnaire. Because examination of the instructional mode is somewhat more complex, more time should be allocated to this activity.

Understanding the Teaching Register. This task is essential in order to allow participants to complete their questionnaires and transcripts. Different approaches may be used for realizing this objective. Some may analyze only the small lesson segment that has been the particular focus of the transcript. From a practical standpoint, using a limited text may be adequate given an individual's time constraints. Use of a limited text may also be initially sufficient for the objectives of gaining proficiency in the use of descriptive tools, feeling more secure in analyzing patterns of classroom discourse, and gaining a general sense of the kinds of instructional acts composing the teaching register.

The preferred approach is to use multiple perspectives, however. In this approach, the clinician and the participants jointly view each of the videotapes. As these joint viewing sessions are held, the participants should be encouraged to listen critically for the various kinds of communicative acts that occur. Since this may be the first time that the actual videotapes are shown to the entire group, some teachers may still hesitate to participate. A suggestion for a hesitant teacher is to show only selected sections of a tape that he or she is comfortable sharing.

The example of Laurie Jones, an elementary art teacher who volunteered to present her videotape of an origami lesson with a kindergarten class, illustrates the value of these joint viewing sessions (all teachers' names have been changed). For example, Ms. Jones, in previously viewing her videotape, had recognized that her style of presenting directions was redundant. A directive for children to perform an action was immediately followed by a request that contained much of the same information, as in this example:

> Now I want you to take the top corner/ Can everyone put your hand on the top corner?/ Once you match the corners, I want you to hold the corners with one hand and crease (.) with the other hand/ Make certain your crease is nice and strong/ Does everyone have a nice strong crease?/

Ms. Jones interpreted this pattern as one that offered children additional time to perform the task by providing redundancy of content. On another level, the yes/ no requests afforded her the retrospective verification that children had understood the content. As the viewing progressed, group members also recognized other kinds of communicative acts and patterns and were able to discuss them in relation to similarities and differences in their own teaching discourse, of which they were now increasingly aware. The additional redundancy that Ms. Jones provided through the visual mode was revealed. Simultaneously with her directives, Ms. Jones performed the activities of holding the top corner, matching the top corners, and creasing the fold. Hence, the multiple perspectives of group members in interpreting the meaning of Ms. Jones's verbal and nonverbal actions contributed to strengthening the validity of Ms. Jones's own interpretations while positively acknowledging her teaching choices.

In contrast, let us consider Ms. Smith, a first-grade teacher, who introduced a contrasting focus of interest in her joint viewing session. Ms. Smith wanted a more complete view of her instructional strategies. She began by reviewing the entire videotape several times using the questionnaire and the definitions of communicative acts in the manual. Next, she applied an additional descriptive procedure whereby functions were assigned to each of her utterances and then each token was classified by type. Descriptive systems can also be used to identify preexisting categories that may be found in the data, such as types of communicative acts or types of cohesive devices. Ms. Smith's choice to gather quantitative data again illustrates that qualitative information can readily serve as the base for gathering and interpreting numerical information that has been obtained in the natural context of the classroom.

Feedback on the Utility of the Manual and the Questionnaire. Aspects of either the manual or questionnaire may remain confusing. Completion of the questionnaire and transcript is dependent on the clarity with which concepts and behaviors are explained. Certain definitions can be interpreted as ambiguous or the form in which questions are stated may imply an unintended value judgment. One illustration of a mismatch in intent occurred in an initial version of the questionnaire. The original question regarding teachers' modes of speaking was as follows: "Please characterize your speaking rate: Fast:_____ Slow:_____ Adequate:_____." The teachers' reaction was that predetermined values were implied in the use of "adequate"; that is, the choice implied that fast and slow rates were not adequate. However, in the case of some instructional activities, such as the presentation of new information, a slow, well-modulated speaking rate might be adequate. The end result was the conversion of "adequate" to "average."

The Fifth Session

The primary objective of this final session is to summarize observations emerging from the process of completing the questionnaire. Although, by now, the participants are familiar with their videotaped activities, certain behaviors may not become salient until attention is more narrowly focused through the questionnaire. In other words, the questionnaire can serve to objectify the familiar.

We have found that variations in teachers' language use needs to be made more visible. Some participants become more aware of how many multiply embedded directives and explanations they give, the multiple functions of their utterances, and the complexity of the grammatical structures used in encoding these functions. For example, even a seemingly simple directive can convey permission if it is encoded in a complex construction. An example of the complex encoding of a single-function directive is the multiply embedded structure "You can keep playing while he takes the picture because that's what the picture's about." The issue here is not that complexity confuses all students; rather, the pertinent point is the extent to which the participants have now developed insight into possible sources of comprehension breakdown in individual students and, as a result, have expanded their capacity to generate effective modifications in language use to repair understanding.

Other participants may develop enhanced awareness of how their vocal style of presentation is actually an instructional tool. For example, Ms. Smith became more conscious of how slowly she spoke and how this style contributed to students' interrupting her speaking turns. She became her own agent in identifying and modifying this aspect of her teaching discourse, clearly an effective method for implementing change.

Follow-Up

Follow-up is a critical aspect of the parallel focus consultation model (see Chapter 5). Its purpose is to sustain teacher-clinician dialogue in the monitoring of student progress over time. The duration of follow-up beyond the five basic training sessions is open-ended.

Procedures for follow-up need to be developed in a way that meets the participants' needs. Regardless of the specific procedures that may be devised, two objectives are important: (1) supporting the increasing generalization of newly acquired skills into the routine life of the regular or special education classroom, and (2) maintaining a continuum of coparticipation.

Supporting Generalization

Generalization can be thought of in two different but compatible ways. According to the more familiar notion, generalization is the increasingly independent application of new task analysis and problem-solving skills by the individual teacher. According to the other, less familiar notion, generalization creates a ripple effect. In particular, teachers who are skilled in the principles and practices of coparticipation influence other teachers and administrators and thereby help spread what they have learned.

Independent Application. The fact that a teacher has volunteered for a workshop on classroom discourse indicates at the outset that he or she is motivated and committed to an experience of self-reflection and change. The personal identification gained from analyzing one's own actions from a videotape is more involving and directly applicable to practical problem solving than is observing the videotape of others. Having seen themselves interacting with the very students they teach, teachers will likely engage in more deliberate efforts to utilize the strategies they appreciate and modify those found to be less effective.

Teachers can be supported in their individual efforts to generalize new insights and skills through two direct methods. One method is continual teacher-clinician consultation to promote the goals of coparticipation throughout the school year. The second method, which can be combined with consultation if requested by the teacher, is to videotape subsequent classroom activities for joint viewing. Both of these procedures serve to help a teacher solidify newly acquired skills. Both also permit ongoing self-assessment of interactional styles and strategies relative to their effectiveness for facilitating children's academic and social growth.

Consider the case of Janet Harper, a second-grade teacher. She sought consultation alone as the follow-up means for meeting the curriculum needs of all of her students, including several children who had language learning difficulties.

To enable her to teach differently than she had previously, she requested readings, specific strategies, and relevant tasks that would support her in more effectively communicating the curriculum. She also requested that the clinician sit in on semiweekly reading and language arts lessons to help her problem solve and to assist her in determining the degree of success in achieving goals. During the weekly teacher-clinician meetings, she was always the first to share her perspectives about changes in her students and to analyze the effectiveness of her teaching discourse strategies. Ms. Harper used consultation as an opportunity to assimilate newly developed skills more fully.

In contrast to Ms. Harper, Jeffrey Allen, a preschool teacher, chose to use subsequent videotaping in combination with consultation to identify possible sources of interference that might compromise achieving curriculum objectives. From a follow-up videotaping, Mr. Allen observed several factors that affected his children's ability to attend fully to language arts activities. First, the seating arrangement made it awkward for children to direct their eye gaze to him. Additionally, the routine of setting up snacks during the language arts activity was disruptive: The child snack helpers moved around the room setting the tables while another supervising teacher whispered directions, the school chef's entry into the room with the snacks stopped the language arts activity, and the visibility of the snacks had a strong attentional pull for the children during the remainder of the activity.

Based on his insights from viewing the follow-up videotape, Mr. Allen made specific and immediate modifications that were maintained in subsequent years. The seating arrangement was changed so that, during all lesson activities, children could easily maintain face-to-face interaction with the teacher. Teachers not involved in the activity positioned themselves next to children who needed support to focus on the activity. The hall door was always closed to minimize extraneous ambient noise, and all toys were put aside to facilitate attending to lesson content and to the teacher. Child helpers for snack time were not chosen until after the language arts activity was completed. The school chef did not enter during the activity, and therefore the snacks were no longer visible. Because of his ability to analyze the event in detail and to take practical steps to modify the situation, Mr. Allen remained alert to other management issues that inadvertently affected the ability of individual children to attend.

Creating a Ripple Effect. The second aspect of generalization involves peer teaching. Teachers who had initially volunteered for the workshops subsequently recommended a "buddy" system. With this procedure, teachers participating in previous workshops acted as a support network for teachers currently involved in workshop learning. The clinician continued as the facilitator of the five basic sessions, while the experienced teachers supported the new participants as they worked through each assignment.

The buddy system has two substantial advantages. First, it gives newly involved teachers additional professional and psychological assistance as they move through the stages of change. Since coparticipation is built on a nonjudgmental foundation, peer teaching through a buddy system has the potential for broadening communication and comradery among teachers. The second advantage accrues to experienced teachers. The buddy system offers them an opportunity to reassess and consolidate their own learning, a critical component of independent application.

Another aspect of the ripple effect is the support for coparticipation spread through word of mouth. For example, during meetings of the school faculty, teachers who had participated in workshops were asked to share their experiences. Although each description was unique, a common thread was the personal and professional benefits that teachers received. Thus, word of mouth can serve to increase teacher demand for learning about discourse as the primary tool of teaching.

Finally, the rippling effect can benefit student teachers. Once teachers understand the dynamics of classroom discourse, they will be better able to spontaneously and naturally guide the learning of the less experienced student teachers.

Maintaining a Continuum of Coparticipation

The second objective of follow-up in the parallel focus consultant model is to sustain teachers' feelings of empowerment within their own classrooms. It remains important for teachers to feel comfortable requesting changes in the role of the speech-language clinician as a result of fluctuating needs during the course of a school year. Teacher needs will vary, and it is important that the clinician be attuned to these changing needs. Help may be requested to identify whether a child has language learning difficulties, to develop specific activities or strategies, or to counsel parents. Responding to these and other needs in a flexible manner reinforces the existence of a natural continuum in the clinician's role—from maintenance to an expansion of the traditional role to role release.

Appendix B

Coparticipation Materials

Elaine R. Silliman, Louise C. Wilkinson, and Amy S. Belkin

PROPOSAL DEVELOPMENT

Purpose

Developing a proposal for teacher education on classroom discourse is analogous to developing a proposal for curriculum change. A statement of purpose should emphasize that the goal is to assist teachers to better understand their patterns of classroom communication. The statement should also mention the anticipated long-range benefits from participation in the workshop, as in the following example:

> The specific purpose of this project is to provide teachers with the opportunity to acquire increased insight into the various aspects of their instructional language use in order to achieve two goals: (1) to identify strengths in their teaching style and (2) if warranted, to modify their teaching style as a tool for expanding communicative effectiveness in facilitating children's academic and social growth.

It is necessary to consider whether the aims should also include educating teachers about the dimensions of a language learning disability. Arguments can be presented for exclusion or inclusion. One argument for exclusion is that the scope of building coparticipation is sufficiently broad without incorporating issues relating to a language learning disability. Therefore, it may be efficacious for clinicians to present workshops only from the perspective of classroom discourse. Another argument is that, for the inexperienced teacher, learning about the components of classroom discourse and how to transcribe and analyze a lesson may be sufficiently challenging.

One argument for inclusion is that, during the course of the school year, teachers frequently have students whose communication and learning styles are confusing and who are not benefiting from the standard presentation of the curriculum. These children motivate teachers to search out the speech-language clinician. Typically, teachers are interested in knowing (1) the reasons for a child's language learning difficulties, (2) the kinds of teaching strategies that will assist the child in assimilating the curriculum, and (3) the ways in which the child's language learning difficulties can be described to the parents. Thus, the at-risk child becomes a catalyst for the teacher's engagement with the clinician and a vehicle for that teacher's subsequent professional growth.

In addition, there may be occasions when a teacher appears to make instructional choices that are not in the best educational interests of all of his or her students. By clarifying the educational, social, and affective needs of students with language learning vulnerabilities, it becomes possible to help teachers develop more effective instructional strategies without directly criticizing their style or manner of teaching.

Finally, through the coparticipation process, teachers become highly attuned to their classroom discourse and its impact on children. During the workshop, it can be advantageous to discuss language learning disabled children, because (1) teachers begin to recognize why particular children are less able to participate successfully in lesson activity and (2) problem solving and the generation of alternate choices can be stimulated. The outcome is an expansion of teachers' repertoire of instructional strategies, including strategies better matched to the learning styles of individual children.

Procedures

A description of procedures for the workshops is essential. Another issue important for administrators is the actual scheduling of the workshop.

Determining where the workshop is to be held is not usually a problem. Any room that has an electrical outlet for a videotape monitor and playback is adequate.

Determining when the five sessions are to meet is more complex, because teachers' schedules are usually tightly organized and allow little free time. The sessions can range in duration from 1½ to 2 hours. If a workshop is presented during the school year, scheduling can be especially problematic. One solution is to request that teachers be excused from certain kinds of meetings, such as faculty meetings, for the workshop sessions.

The procedures to be undertaken must also be described specifically, as the following example shows:

Teachers will be asked to join the project on a voluntary basis and to be videotaped in their classroom teaching a whole-class or small-group lesson. Lessons will be approximately 30 minutes in length. During the four initial sessions, the teachers will be taught how to observe the videotapes and transcribe teacher-student discourse and nonverbal interaction. A manual will assist in this endeavor. Additionally, the clinician will be continuously available to assist teachers.

After the transcript is completed, the language and nonverbal interaction between the teacher and students will be analyzed from a variety of perspectives. Both the videotape and transcripts will be used for this purpose. The analysis will be based on the use of a guiding questionnaire, which is enclosed, and will culminate in completing this questionnaire.

Through this process, the effectiveness of various verbal and nonverbal interactions will be highlighted. Possible language behaviors deemed not as effective will be noted and alternate means of presentation explored. Comparison between the responses of various students will be emphasized as a means of analyzing how language can be modified to involve all children.

Expenditures

An account of anticipated expenses should be outlined in detail. For example, depending on the equipment and materials available in a given school or school system, expenditures may be needed for (1) videotapes; (2) audiotapes; (3) rental or purchase of a video camera, a monitor, or audiotape cassettes; (4) reproducing the manual, questionnaire, and supplementary articles; and (5) paper for transcription.

Duration

A coparticipation workshop minimally consists of 1½- to 2-hour sessions. These sessions can be held during the first week of the summer vacation or at various times during the regular school year.

Summer Workshops. When a workshop is held during the first week of summer vacation, the sessions can be presented on four or five consecutive days. A primary benefit is that teachers can immerse themselves in the language of the classroom. Teachers analyze and transcribe videotapes prior to or after each daily session. This concentration is also heightened by the fact that teachers do not have other school obligations. Summer workshops also have some disadvantages. One is that teachers cannot immediately apply their newly learned insights and skills. A second problem involves the retrospective nature of a summer workshop. Teachers are analyzing videotapes of their interactions with students who have now moved up to another grade level. The opportunity to modify teaching choices with these students has been lost. A third possible disadvantage is financial. Depending on a school system's contractual agreements, teacher participation may be contingent upon additional salary.

Workshops during the Regular School Year. One advantage of a workshop scheduled in the school year is that it allows teachers to apply new skills immediately in their classrooms. One disadvantage is the additional commitment of time and effort required for teachers, which can be mitigated to some extent by reducing other nonclassroom obligations. It may be necessary to extend the time between workshop sessions in order to give teachers sufficient time to accomplish tasks associated with the individual sessions.

Participants

The final component of the proposal deals with the participants in the workshop. Since teachers will be volunteers, some problems may arise from having teachers at different grade levels. On the other hand, depending on the circumstances and size of a particular school or school system, it may be feasible to focus on volunteer teachers from within a single grade level. Whether volunteer participation will be sought from across grade levels or from within a particular grade level is an important issue. Additional consideration must be given to the number of participants. Starting with a small group of four or five teachers will permit more opportunity for interaction than would a larger group.

In sum, the components of the proposal should be tailored to a clinician's particular school system; should contain detailed information on the purpose, procedures, anticipated expenditures, duration, and participants; and should have a well-thought-out basis for the presentation of choices.

INSTRUCTIONAL PACKET

The instructional packet is oriented to the classroom teacher; however, its content can be of use to speech-language clinicians who want to develop basic skill with descriptive techniques for the transcription and analysis of their own interactions with children and adolescents.

There are four steps to be taken during the workshop sessions: (1) describing the classroom activity, (2) transcribing the videotape onto paper, (3) analyzing the teaching choices, and (4) completing a questionnaire based on the actual transcription. The questionnaire is designed as an organizing guide for looking at a variety of issues relevant to interaction with students.

Classroom Activity Description

The first step is to describe the general format of classroom activity. The outline for this description is presented on the first pages of the questionnaire. The initial part of the description includes drawing a map of the classroom.

Transcriptional and Notational Procedures

The second step is to analyze a five- to seven-minute segment of the videotape (refer to Appendix A for the seven phases of transcribing from a videotape). Four types of behavior will be examined: (1) teacher talk, (2) child talk, (3) contextual clues that accompany talk, and (4) topic division.

Teacher Talk

First, take some scrap paper and transcribe only the teacher talk during the segment. Transcribe everything said by the teacher during that time, including filled and silent pauses, latchings, self-repairs, and unintelligible utterances as well as overlaps and interruptions of speaking turns (these behaviors are all defined in the next section, "Child Talk"). Each utterance should begin on a separate line irrespective of whether the utterance consists only of a word that stands alone (e.g., "Yes"), a longer phrase (e.g., "on the chair"), or a sentence. Leave multiple spaces between each of your speaking turns so that the children's utterances can later be added in the correct places.

Next, make certain to put a slash instead of a period to mark the end of each utterance. The slash denotes the end of an utterance, which has just been defined as a single word, a phrase, or a sentence. It is more versatile than a period, which is used to indicate the termination of a written "grammatical" utterance (a complete sentence). A question mark continues to denote a question; however, place a slash after the question mark in order to indicate the boundary of the utterance.

Also write down to whom the teacher is talking. The person who has the speaking turn is the addressor; the individuals being talked to are the addressees. An example from a gymnastics class shows how to notate this behavior, as well as how to use the slash and question mark notations (*T* stands for the teacher, while other alphabetic letters denote various children or the entire class):

T/CH:	We start out over here just like you do the Short Bird's Nest/ (Teacher addressing all the children)
T/B:	Bobby, watching?/ (Teacher addressing Bobby only)
T/J,S:	John, Sam, eyes over here, please/ (Teacher addressing John and Sam)
T/CH:	Children, watching?/ (Teacher talking to all the children)

Stress and Volume. Sometimes teachers stress or emphasize important words to make a point clearer to children. Underline these stressed words:

    T/CH: <u>Please</u> do not laugh/

Occasionally teachers need to use a loud voice for class management and other attentional purposes. Draw two arrows pointing up, ↑ ↑, to indicate when the volume was generally loud, as shown here:

    T/CH: This class is nowhere ready to proceed to gym/ ↑ ↑ /

When an utterance is said with less than usual volume, draw two arrows pointing down for example:

    T/CH: Shhhhhh ↓ ↓ /

An accurate transcription requires going through the audio- and videotapes several times in order to record everything that was said.

Child Talk

The next step is to transcribe all of the children's utterances using the basic notational system described. Write these utterances down in the spaces in between the teacher utterances so that interactions between the teacher and the students are apparent. Again, write down who the child was addressing and every word said. Also transcribe any filled pauses, audible silent pauses, latchings, self-repairs, unintelligible utterances, overlaps, or interruptions that may occur. Here's an example from an exchange on the sharing of vacation experiences:

T/A:	Adam?/
A/T:	I went to Disney World/
	And in the hotel the kids have a (.) -- on the first floor = there
	was this game room/
T/A:	Oh, what fun/
	So, you ah - spent a lot of quarters/
A/T:	And I went on my - my first roller coaster!/

Filled Pauses and Silent Pauses. In the above sequence, a filled pause (*ah*) occurs and is notated as ah - . Sometimes filled pauses will be said in multiples, for example, um - um -. Use a single hyphen to mark their boundaries. This same sequence also contains a silent pause within one of Adam's utterances, which is notated as (.). A silent pause in this context means a brief pause that is detectable by the ear (Silliman & Leslie, 1983).

Make certain to note filled and silent pauses in both teacher and child speech. Both types of pauses are commonly found in our construction of talk, are usually located at certain kinds of semantic or syntactic boundaries, and can indicate a searching for words or ideas. Silent pauses may also be used as a teaching device to highlight important information by creating a short space around key words, as in this example:

> *T/CH:*   The spelling word is (.) thunder/

When the duration of a silent pause appears to be more than brief, a different notation should be used. The notation (.2+) means a considerably longer silent pause occurred within parts of an utterance, between utterances in a single speaking turn, or when speaking turns were exchanged. All three situations are illustrated below:

> *T/J:*   John, why did the baby horse feel sad?/
> *J/T:*   Because (.2+) he got lost from his mother/ (located within the utterance boundaries)
>
> --
>
> *T/CH:*   And sit down/ (.2+)
>   Alright, let's try jumping jacks/ (located between utterances in a single speaking turn)
>
> --
>
> *T/L:*   Laura, what month comes after June?/
> *L/T:*   (.2+) um - May?/ (located at the speaking turn exchange)

Latching. The notation = indicates that latching has occurred in the formulation of the utterance, as when Adam said, "on the first floor = there was this game room." Latching means it is difficult to detect audible "spaces" between words. Latching may happen more often when the rate of speaking is rapid. Sometimes latching can also be heard at an apparent utterance boundary, which makes it more difficult to determine where the boundary is, as the following example shows:

> *T/CH:*   Today, we're going to tell what we did over the weekend =
>   then we'll write a story/

Self-repairs. Revising or repairing words, phrases, or sentences as one is actually producing talk indicates that self-monitoring (or self-editing) is taking place. Being able to detect an error in what we are saying, or intend to say, and self-repair it is a relatively sophisticated skill. Self-repairs can also be the result of "reading" listener cues on the clarity of what we are saying, also a sophisticated skill. Self-repairs can be classified into three general types (Brinton & Fujiki, 1989): (1) corrections to the form of the message; (2) adjustments to the content of the message; and (3) covert self-repairs, which can include whole word and phrase repetitions. Covert self-repairs may represent a brief failure in the actual production of talk and not be self-repairs in the strict sense of the term. They may also be mistakenly interpreted as disfluencies (Brinton & Fujiki, 1989; Silliman & Leslie, 1983). Although these kinds of repetitions can affect judgments of fluency, they are not the same as stuttering forms of disfluency. Stuttering disfluencies typically involve repetitions or prolongations of sound units within the word combined with visible or audible muscular effort in production (Silliman & Leslie, 1983).

A double hyphen is the notation for a correction or adjustment to content, while three dots designate repetitions consistent with the covert self-repair category. Examples of how to notate self-repairs follow:

T/CH: We all get -- got colds/ (correction)

C/T: One day we were going for a match (.) car --
    Matchbox car/ (correction)

B/T: My brother said the snow is going -- will change into rain/
    (correction)

A/CH: The roller coaster was scary -- real scary/ (adjustment to content)

B/T: And two of my brother -- my friend's brother took the money/ (adjustment to content)

Yeah, he has a . . . he has a lot of guns/ (covert self-repair)
You don't know what . . . you don't know what's . . . you don't know what that spells/ (covert self-repair)
(From Brinton & Fujiki, 1989, p. 81)

Unintelligible Utterances. Sometimes certain words or utterances may be impossible to understand and may therefore affect the accuracy of transcription. When this happens, use four asterisks for the notation, as indicated below:

T/J: Your **** missing/

Overlaps of Speaking Turns. Sometimes one person's speaking turn can overlap another person's speaking turn. These instances are important to document, since they may reflect a speaker's particular style or the extent to which one can appropriately predict a plausible end to the other speaker's turn. Furthermore, overlap is easy to document. Write the first person's utterance and bracket the section of that utterance during which the overlap occurred. Start the second person's speaking turn at the end of the bracketed section. Also bracket the overlapped section of the second utterance, and then continue the utterance, as in this example:

T/CH: The next word is an easy [one   ]/
J/T: [Me and] (.) me and Danielle are
          going to the country at 2:00 today/

Note that J's overlap occurred at a predictable point, which is a distinguishing feature of an overlap.

Interruption of Speaking Turns. The distinction between an overlap and an interruption is not always easy to make. Most typically, the difference can only be inferred based on the actual behavior of the speaker whose turn is being disrupted at a less predictable point (Silliman & Lamanna, 1986). Examples of these behaviors include (1) ceasing to talk completely (i.e., giving up one's speaking turn); (2) ceasing to talk until the interruption ends, then finishing the speaking turn; and (3) competing for the conversational floor by increasing volume. Despite the problems that may occur in differentiating an overlap from an interruption, try to attune yourself to the distinction.

The method of notation is identical to that for overlaps. What differs is the notation. Use { } to signify an interruption:

T/CH: If you look behind you, those are our letters KAWP/
          And you'll see them in the morning
          {when they say the}
A/T: {KAW is now on the air}
T/CH: announcements/

In this example, the determination that A interrupted the teacher was based on the fact that the teacher stopped talking and then completed her speaking turn following A's turn.

Summary. In this discussion of how to transcribe teacher and student talk onto paper, a number of symbols useful in representing important aspects of talk have been introduced. There are only a few notations to keep in mind:

/   Utterance boundary
?   Question
T/CH   Addressor/addressee
Please   Underline to denote increased stress
↑ ↑   Utterance said with increased volume
↓ ↓   Utterance said with less volume than usual
-        Marks a filled pause (e.g., um - um -)
(.)   Brief silent pause is detectable
(.2+)   Longer than brief silent pause
=   Latching
--   Self-repair of form or content
...   Repetitions of words or phrases
****   Unintelligible words or utterances
[ ]   Overlap of speaking turn
{ }   Interruption of speaking turn

Contextual Clues

The next step is to review the videotape again and describe any accompanying contextual clues that contribute to maintaining the flow of interaction or to its disruption. Contextual clues signaling disruption are on the right-hand side in the following example:

T/CH: Stretch to right/

                                                    B goes to left

T/CH: Stretch to left/

                                                    B goes to right

Frequently, contextual clues or behaviors explain why a particular utterance was spoken, as the following illustrates:

T/J: Bird's Nest and ... and up/

                                        Children laugh as J makes an error

T/CH: Please do not laugh/

Topics

Notice that the teacher's activity is divided into topics. Topics are used to focus attention on particular ideas or subjects, and any activity may consist of multiple topics. For example, children may discuss what they did over the weekend prior to introducing the actual content of the activity. The discussion of weekend experiences is the first topic, while the second topic might start with the teacher's introduction of lesson content. Note when topics start and stop on rough transcript. A simple way to identify topics, as shown below, is to draw horizontal broken lines across the page as boundaries, and then name the topics: "Topic 1: Discussion of Weekend Experiences," "Topic 2: Introduction of Digits," etc.:

Topic 1: Discussion of Weekend Activities

There are times when topics are spontaneously initiated by children. A child might notice a picture on the wall, and a discussion can be created around that topic. Even though the child's contribution may be unrelated to the lesson content or goal, separate the child's topic from the previous one with a broken line and a description. When that topic stops and another begins, draw another broken horizontal line to mark the shift.

The Formal Transcription

Once the teacher talk, child talk, contextual clues, and topic divisions are written down, the formal transcription can be completed. Make certain that the spaces between utterances and behaviors are tightened to show the actual flow of interaction.

The format of the formal transcription consists of four columns to further highlight interactional relationships, as shown in Exhibit B-1.

The first column documents the speaker-listener relations. For example, T/CH means the teacher is addressing all the children. If the teacher addresses all the children for several utterances in a row, then T/CH needs to be written only once. Also, it is important to number speaking turns in order to keep track of the amount of turn-taking occurring between the teacher and the children. Number these turns consecutively beginning with the first turn transcribed:

1   *T/CH:*   First I'll say the sentence/
              And then, Charlie, you repeat it/
              And then you both write it/
              But don't write it until Charlie says it/
              "The dentist has big feet"/

2   *J/T:*   You already said that/

Exhibit B-1   Example of Formal Transcription

Speaker/ Listener	Talk	Contextual Clues	Teaching Choices
1 T/CH:	(Reading a story) Jim heard Danny say "That is some big chicken?"/	Harley raises her hand. Children look at each other questioningly, then laugh.	
2 L/CH:	Chicken?/		
3 T/CH:	"It's a dinosaur," shouted Danny↑ ↑/ Jim came around the corner/ The dinosaur has its <u>arms up over Jim's head</u>/ The dinosaur's teeth were smiling a <u>fierce</u> smile/ Paul said "Look out Jim/ He's going to get you!"/ Is that true? ↑ ↑/	T raises arm. T makes gesture with hand & facial expression.	RI—Choice
4 All CH:	No/	Laughter; all shake head no.	RS—Choice
5 T/CH:	Why?/		RI—Process
6 Y/T:	Because he was dead/ He's dead/		RS—Process
7 T/CH:	Yeah/ There's nothing but what?/	T laughs. T points to picture of dinosaur skeleton.	EVAL—Positive RI—Product
8 All CH:	Bones/		RS—Product
9 T/CH:	Yeah/		EVAL—Positive

A problem can arise in numbering of speaking turns when overlaps and interruptions occur. The simplest solution is to add lowercase letters in designating speaking turns. These examples of interruptions are taken from Silliman and Lamanna (1986, p. 37):

    203   N/T: Sometimes {I   }
    203a   T/N: {How's} your garden N?/
    ----
    26   K/CH: The {back   (.)   } In
    26a   T/CH: {That's a lot of grass}
    26b   K/CH: the back I would have to use the <u>big</u> tractor/

In these two examples, the use of *a* and *b* indicates that the speaker holding the turn is interrupted (or overlapped) by a second speaker (the *a* designation). If N had taken the conversational floor back following the teacher's interruption (e.g., by responding "Fine"), his turn would be numbered 204, because the content of his turn would then be matched to the teacher's question. The second example shows that K chose to continue the message begun in her original turn, as indicated by the *b* notation (26b).

The second column, labeled "Talk," contains what is actually said.

The third column is dedicated to contextual clues. Here is where behaviors can be described that either support or interrupt the continuity of the activity. Place these clues where they occur, as shown below and in Exhibit B-1:

16 *T/CH:*   "Band-it"/

                                        T watching S write word

    T/S: That's beautiful, Sam/

Note that the T/S follow-up is not given a new turn number since S did not take a verbal speaking turn; rather he engaged in a nonverbal action. The teacher's continuation is part of turn 16.

While transcribing the activity into the formal format, remember to mark off the beginning and end of various topics with broken horizontal lines and a brief description of each topic.

The final column is titled "Teaching Choices." This column provides a means of analyzing interaction in relation to language content, form, and use. But this analysis is for another time. For now, concentrate on transcribing the actual talk and nonverbal behaviors in the videotaped activity.

Guiding Questionnaire

The questionnaire is presented as a guide to organizing the analysis of the transcript. It consists of nine interrelated sections that synthesize content and procedures described in Chapters 2–9. Additional sources for the questionnaire are as follows:

- *Section 1:* N.W. Nelson (1985)
- *Section 2:* Gruenewald and Pollak (1990), N.W. Nelson (1985, 1988b)
- *Section 3:* Cazden (1988), Mehan (1979), Silliman (1984), Silliman and Lamanna (1986), Simon (1987b)
- *Section 4:* Brinton and Fujuki (1989), DeStefano and Kantor (1988), Halliday and Hasan (1976), Lahey (1988), N.W. Nelson (1985, 1988b), Simon (1987b)

- *Section 5:* N.W. Nelson (1985, 1988b)
- *Section 6:* Brinton and Fujiki (1989), Cazden (1988), Dore (1986), Gruenewald and Pollak (1990), Mehan (1979), N.W. Nelson (1985), Silliman (1984), Silliman and Leslie (1983)
- *Section 7:* Gruenewald and Pollak (1990), Lahey (1988), N.W. Nelson (1985, 1988b)
- *Section 8:* Gruenewald and Pollak (1990), N.W. Nelson (1985, 1988b)
- *Section 9:* N.W. Nelson (1985, 1988b)

Section 1: Activity Routines

The first section addresses the overall routines of the day and is derived from the activity description and classroom map. Questions refer to each child's ability to follow the daily schedule and to anticipate routines. Although this section really addresses issues beyond the particular activity being analyzed, the ability to follow routines relates to how readily children can anticipate requirements for participating in the activity.

A. Do all the students in the videotaped segment recognize and follow the daily schedule and routine?

Yes: ___ No: ___

Describe behaviors that show they know: _____

_____

_____

Describe behaviors that show they do not know: _____

_____

_____

1. From the daily schedule documented in the description of the activity structure, can your students anticipate the various aspects of the activity?

Yes: ___ No: ___

2. How do you signal that the previous activity is over and a new activity is beginning? _____

_____

a. Do you use a nonverbal means of getting the students' attention, such as raising your hand? _____

b. Or do you primarily highlight this change in activity with language? If so, what do you say? _____

3. How do children respond to your attention getters? _____

_____

4. When you present the activity, do students demonstrate that they distinguish familiar from new information?

Yes: ___ No: ___

Describe behaviors that show how they recognize the difference: _____

_____

_____

5. From your videotape, do all of your students demonstrate that they can attend to essential versus nonessential information?

Yes: ___ No: ___

Describe those behaviors that show how certain students attend only to essential information: _____

_____

Describe those behaviors that show how certain students attend to both essential and nonessential information: _____

_____

Describe those behaviors that show how certain students attend only to nonessential information: _____

_____

_____

Section 2: Teaching Expectations

This section concerns the teacher's expectations regarding children's ability to participate in this particular activity and how these expectations were met.

A. What performance outcomes did you expect from the activity? Briefly describe: _____

_____

Were these outcomes met by all students?

Yes: ___ No: ___

B. How were children primarily expected to respond?

1. Speaking: _____

2. Listening: _____

3. Reading: _____

4. Writing: _____

5. Movement: _____

C. How did you orient children to your expectations for responding during the activity (e.g., "Point to the word that goes with my definition and, when you have found the word, raise your hand."). Briefly describe: _____

_____

_____

_____

D. Did you discuss or question your students about your expectations regarding their performance?
Yes: ___ No: ___
If so, did this serve as a means of clarification?
Specify:_____

_____

E. Did you offer your students time for discussion or questions for the purpose of clarification or did you anticipate that they would demonstrate immediate understanding of the activity's content?
Describe:_____

_____

F. What previous information should students have assimilated in order to successfully participate in the activity? _____

_____

G. Did you expect your students to understand the content of the activity?
Yes: ___ No: ___

H. In fact, was the content understood by your students?
Yes: ___ No: ___

I. Did your students understand the purpose of the activity?
Yes: ___ No: ___
How did you know? _____

_____

_____

J. Did you choose a teacher-directed strategy when presenting this activity or did you stimulate student-directed participation?_____

_____

K. Did all of your students learn from your participation requirements?
Yes: ___ No: ___
Which children did? _____
Which children did not? _____

Section 3: Speaking Turns

Who "has the floor" and how speaking turns are designated are critical parts of any interaction, including instructional interactions. Rules for how and when to take turns teach children about being a member of a learning group and maintaining the topic of talk. This section of the questionnaire concerns the various ways speaking turns were allocated and sustained during the transcribed portion of the activity. The formal transcription in Exhibit B-1 illustrates how to number speaking turns.

A. Did children engage in turn-taking in this activity?

   Yes: ___ No: ___

B. How did you indicate who could have a turn?

   1. Were turns verbally indicated, such as by naming specific children? Describe: _____

   _____

   2. Or were turns cued nonverbally, such as by directing eye gaze to a particular child or pausing to convey that anyone could take a turn? Describe: _____

   _____

C. How did students claim a speaking turn?

   1. Raise hand? _____
   2. Call out? _____
   3. Verbally respond in unison? _____
   4. Other? _____

D. Did particular students appear not to take a turn when it was expected? Describe: _____

   _____

E. When claiming a speaking turn, did students maintain the topic?

   Yes: ___ No: ___

   Describe: _____

   _____

F. Did overlapping of speaking turns occur often?

   Yes: ___ No: ___

   If so, was overlapping more characteristic of students' speaking turns or your speaking turns? Describe: _____

   _____

G. Did interruptions of speaking turns occur often?

   Yes: ___ No: ___

If so, was there a pattern to interruptions? Were they more characteristic of certain students or of your speaking style? Describe: _____

_____

_____

H. Did you have a characteristic way of dealing with interruptions of speaking turns? Explain: _____

_____

_____

The next four sections of the questionnaire deal with instructional acts or the teaching choices through which academic information is communicated.

Section 4: Teaching Choices: Topic (Content)

Topics focus the content of what we say. This section emphasizes how topics were introduced and maintained and how topic shifts related to the original theme of the activity. Three semantic devices that glue a topic together within and across utterance boundaries are also analyzed: pronominal reference, ellipsis, and lexical similarity. Definitions of each follow.

- Pronominal reference. This type of semantic device involves using personal and possessive pronouns (e.g., *he, she, we, they, it, one, my, mine, your, yours, his, her, them, their, theirs*) (Halliday & Hasan, 1976) to refer back to a previously mentioned noun phrase that represents the theme. This kind of referencing consists of the use of identity ties where one lexical choice, such as a third-person pronoun, shares the same meaning with another lexical choice through a rementioning principle (DeStefano & Kantor, 1988; Lahey, 1988). Exhibit B-1 contains examples of pronominal referencing:

> *T/CH:* (reading a story) Jim heard Danny say "That is some big chicken!"/ *"It's* a dinosaur," shouted Danny/ "Look out Jim/ *He's* going to get *you!"*/

The italicized words all mark pronominal reference. *It's* refers back to, or rementions, the noun phrase *some big chicken*. *He's* ties back to *dinosaur*, while *you* depends on *Jim* as its source of meaning. Note that, in this example, *you* occurs as part of quoted speech. In routine conversation, *I, we,* and *you* are not considered as identity ties, because the source of their reference is external to the linguistic context; that is, these first- and second-person pronouns refer to the speaker and addressee, who are defined by the social situation rather than by the linguistic context (Halliday & Hasan,

298 COMMUNICATING FOR LEARNING

1976). The use of identity ties created by third-person and possessive references allows us to recover meaning from the linguistic context itself when the original referent has been clearly stated.

- Ellipsis. A second kind of identity tie is the ellipsis. Here words are deleted, but the deleted information can be recovered from what has been said (Lahey, 1988) in order to maintain the topical flow, as in these examples:

T/CH:	Where was the cat?/
J/T:	In the tree/

T/L:	Did your mother see the report card?/
L/T:	She said so/

Ellipses allow a conversation to continue without the unnecessary repetition of information. In the two examples above, the responding child presumes that the respective referents are *the cat* and *see the report card.*

- Lexical similarity. A third method for binding meaning together is to use similarity ties. In these instances, one lexical choice comes from the same meaning classification as another lexical choice. The equivalence of the semantic class then becomes the device through which similar reference is maintained (DeStefano & Kantor, 1988):

T/CH:	A *dinosaur* is very big/ If you met this *giant lizard,* it might scare you/

M/CH:	My father bought a new *Pontiac.* He likes a big *car.*

A. What was the primary instructional topic of the activity? _____

_____

_____

_____

B. Why has this topic been chosen? Describe: _____

_____

_____

_____

C. In what ways was this topic related to previous or upcoming academic or social experiences? Please choose:

1. Part of an instructional unit: _____

_____

_____

2. Related to objects or events in the classroom: _____

_____

_____

3. Related to past or future events shared by the class: _____

_____

_____

4. Related to "world" knowledge shared by the class (such as an upcoming holiday): _____

_____

_____

5. Other: _____

_____

_____

D. How was the topic of the activity introduced? _____

_____

1. Was your introduction short or lengthy? _____

2. Did your introduction contain all the information students needed to know to meet expectations?
   Yes: ___ No: ___
   If no, briefly explain: _____

_____

_____

3. In your introduction, did you encourage your students to think about personal experience relevant to the topic of the activity?
   Yes: ___ No: ___
   Specify: _____

_____

E. Did all of your students maintain the instructional topic?
   Yes: ___ No: ___

F. In which ways did the students maintain the instructional topic?
   1. Verbal turn-taking (speaking): _____

_____

   2. Writing: _____
   3. Reading: _____

4. Listening (e.g., giving active feedback that they were listening): _____

_____

5. Gestural: _____

6. Other: _____

G. Did all of your students understand that you were referring to the topic when you used third-person or possessive pronouns instead of the topic's name?

Yes: ___ No: ___

If some students became confused, how did they demonstrate this confusion? _____

H. Did all of your students understand that you were referring to the topic when you used similar terms instead of the original topic's name (e.g., *giant lizard* for *dinosaur*)?

Yes: ___ No: ___

If some of the students became confused, how did they demonstrate this confusion? _____

I. In your referring to the topic or in students' understanding questions about the topic, were elliptical utterances used?

Yes: ___ No: ___

If ellipsis was used, was the omitted information easily identified in what had been previously said?

Yes: ___ No: ___

Describe: _____

_____

J. When you used third-person or possessive pronouns, was the original meaning easily retrievable?

Yes: ___ No: ___

From where could the intended meaning be retrieved? Choose:

1. The content of what was previously said: _____

_____

2. Prior lessons (spoken or read): _____

_____

3. Shared "world" or cultural knowledge (such as knowledge about holidays): _____

_____

4. Other: _____

_____

K. During the activity, did your students have an opportunity to share their ideas regarding the topic?

Yes: ___ No: ___

Describe: _____

L. How many total topics were introduced during this activity? Enumerate: ___

_____

_____

M. How did you or your students introduce a new topic within the activity? ____

_____

_____

   1. Did the topic shift(s) change the focus of the topic without changing the subject entirely?

   Yes: ___ No: ___

   Describe: _____

   _____

   2. Did the topic shift(s) involve the presentation of a new theme?

   Yes: ___ No: ___

   Describe: _____

   _____

   3. Did subtopics relate to or interfere with the major theme of the activity?

   Describe: _____

   _____

   4. Did your students recognize that a shift in topic had been made?

   Yes: ___ No: ___ Some: ___

   Describe how they indicated this recognition: _____

   _____

   _____

   Describe how they did not indicate this recognition: _____

   _____

   _____

N. Did your students indicate that they knew when the original topic was reintroduced?

Yes: ___ No: ___

Describe how they indicated this recognition: _____

_____

_____

Describe how they did not indicate this recognition: _____

_____

_____

O. Prior to the activity, how did you anticipate the topic would end? _____

_____

_____

How did you actually end the topic? _____

_____

_____

Section 5: Teaching Choices: Vocabulary (Content)

It is also important that the children know the lexical (vocabulary) terms that are critical for understanding the lesson activity. For example, in a gymnastics lesson, there may be numerous terms that are less familiar, such as *straddle, pike, point toes, scissors, double twist*, etc. In addition, it may be essential for a child's success that he or she has a grasp of spatial terms, in particular, *left* and *right*.

T/CH: Straddle/	
	Children's legs go apart;
	Bobby's legs go together
Stretch to right/	
	Children stretch to right;
	Bobby stretches to left
Now to left/	
	Children stretch to left;
	Bobby stretches to right

Analyzing what vocabulary must be known and how a particular child comprehends or expresses these terms may help clarify a source of difficulty. In Bobby's case, it is clear that he does not know, or has not mastered, some of the gymnastic terms, such as *straddle*, or the spatial terms *right* and *left*.

A. List those vocabulary terms that you considered important for the activity:

_____

_____

1. Enumerate those concepts that serve as the underlying foundations for these vocabulary terms: _____

_____

_____

2. What words did you use to regulate students' behavior throughout the activity? _____

_____

_____

3. Enumerate those concepts that are the underlying foundations for these regulating words: _____

_____

_____

B. Estimate:
   1. How often you used more abstract or less familiar vocabulary terms: _____

   _____

   2. How often you used more familiar or concrete vocabulary terms: _____

   _____

   3. What percentage of vocabulary terms contained multiple meaning: _____

   _____

   4. The approximate percentage of vocabulary terms that were new to the students: _____

C. Did you highlight essential concepts by using specific vocabulary terms or were students expected to identify this information by themselves?
   Yes: ___ No: ___
   Please explain: _____

   _____

   _____

   _____

D. When teaching new vocabulary terms, what supportive materials did you use in order to clarify the meaning of these terms? Please indicate:
   1. 3-dimensional objects: _____
   2. Pictures: _____
   3. Sentences using the word: _____
      a. Orally presented: _____
      b. Presented in written form: _____
      c. Other: _____
   4. No use of supportive material: _____

Section 6: Teaching Choices: Communicative Functions (Use)

Thus far, we have examined choices related to the selection of meaning relationships by which conversational sequences are joined in order to be relevant and clear. However, every utterance also has a purpose or function, because conversational acts (utterances) are goal-directed. A variety of classification systems are available for analyzing the intentions of individual conversational acts. Regardless of the system used, there are several problems associated with the categorization of individual conversational acts.

One problem derives from the fact that every utterance has multiple functions (Dore, 1986). The discussion in Chapter 2 highlighted that each utterance communicates cognitive, social, and affective intents. Another problem, reviewed in Chapter 8, arises from the use of categorical tools that tend to separate the natural flow of talk from its contexts of occurrence. Because discourse is sequentially related, the interpretation of what is intended at any given moment cannot be readily determined without examining what has been said previously, what came after, and the contextual clues that contribute to how conversational partners understand each other. Chapman (1981) describes a third set of problems related to the application of classification systems for coding types of conversational acts. A particular system may be too detailed in terms of the number of subcategories or contain categories that are too broad to be useful. Any of these issues, if not recognized, will significantly affect the reliability and validity of a classification system.

Given these qualifications, it is important that some sensitivity be developed regarding the functional component of teaching choices. The modified system to be applied in analysis is based on Dore (1986) and Mehan (1979). Conversational acts are considered from the perspective of three general categories: requests, statements (explanations and evaluations), and repairs.

1. *Requests.* Requests function to solicit information or action from another. As reviewed in Chapter 4, requests are frequently used by teachers to assess children's knowledge of the information being taught or to regulate children's conduct and are often patterned as IRE conversational sequences. Three subcategories are of interest for analysis: requests for information, requests for action, and requests for clarification.

   • *Requests for information.* Four basic types can be identified; each can vary in its complexity of form or content and in its explicitness.

   —*Choice requests* seek agreement or disagreement or the evaluation of options, most typically through yes/no judgments:

   T/CH: Is that true?/

T/J: Jimmy, do you see how to crease the bunny ears?/

T/CH: Do good things happen or do bad things happen when you're rude?/

—*Product requests* commonly solicit factual pieces of information through wh-forms (what, which, who, when, why, and where) (Dore, 1986, p. 39); replies to product requests are often single words or short phrases (Silliman, 1984):

T/CH: Who was the first president of the United States?/

T/CH: What do the red letters say?

T/CH: When did we visit the chef?/

T/CH: What's another polite word?/

—*Process requests* seek opinions or interpretations (Mehan, 1979) through explanations or extended descriptions; wh-forms also dominate (why, how, what for, what about, and how come) (Dore, 1986, p. 39):

T/CH: Why isn't that true?/

T/CH: How does thunder happen?/ (Silliman, 1984, p. 303)

T/CH: What happens when we are mean and rude to each other?/

—*Metaprocess requests* solicit reflections on the rules, procedures, or mental processes by which informational content is formulated (Mehan, 1979); these reflections are also cued by wh-forms (why, how, etc.) and the use of "meta" vocabulary terms such as *know, think, remember, mean,* and *feel*:

T/B: Ben, why do you think Nancy is in the city?/ How do you know?/

> *T/S:*   Susan, why do you think Nancy was afraid?/ What do you think she will do next?/
>
> --
>
> *T/C:*   And, Carolyn, how did you remember where it was?/ (Mehan, 1979, p. 46)

- *Requests for action.* These types of requests are often referred to as directives, since the speaker expects that the listener will perform or is capable of performing an action; directives can also vary in the complexity of their form and content, in their explicitness, and in their degree of directness. Two types of directives are often found in the instructional setting under the traditional description of directions: procedural requests and indirect requests.

—*Procedural requests* (Mehan, 1979) solicit actions related to regulating conduct in either the physical, attentional, or verbal realms:

> *T/CH:*   Now look up/
>
> --
>
> *T/CH:*   Look over one shoulder as far as you can and then look the other way/
>
> --
>
> *T/CH:*   Everybody open your books to page 71/
>
> --
>
> *T/CH:*   I'm gonna say a sentence and then, Charlie, you repeat it/ And then you both write it/ But don't write it until Charlie says it/

—*Indirect requests* seek action using syntactic forms, such as declaratives or questions, that do not directly obligate the listener; these kinds of directives can be presented as suggestions or even hints. The child needs to infer that a directive is the actual intent.

> *T/CH:*   We're gonna do lower case, alright?/
>
> --
>
> *T/CH:*   Who did something that's so much fun that they want to tell me about it?/
>
> --
>
> *T/S:*   Susan, can you read it?
>
> --
>
> *T/L:*   Linda, why don't you think a minute?/

- *Requests for clarification.* Information is sometimes not understood. When that occurs, the communicative breakdown may be repaired by a request for repetition or specification (Silliman, 1984, p. 304):

C/T:	Um - like yesterday when I was - uh - just about to go jump in the pool with my friend
T/C:	What? ↑ ↑ / (request for repetition)
C/T:	I said when I was just about to jump into my pool with my friend/

C/T:	And then you wind the back and then it goes up the stairs, makes the bed, and everything/
T/C:	<u>What</u> goes up the stairs?/ (request for specification)
C/T:	The person that goes/

2. *Statements.* This category of conversational acts covers assertions, which "report facts, evaluate conditions, or establish roles and rights" (Dore, 1986, p. 39). Two subcategories are the focus of attention: explanations and evaluations.

   - *Explanations.* Explanations express intents related to causal relations, reasons, or predictions (Dore, 1986). In the instructional setting, explanations may often refer to a fact or a skill embedded in a lesson activity, as these examples demonstrate:

T/CH:	Bobby should be next on the beam because he spotted Harry/

T/CH:	No, they're just watching/ That's why they're here/

T/D:	"er"/ Two letters say "er"/ We want two letters saying "er" at the end/

   - *Evaluations.* An evaluation expresses feedback in the form of a personal judgment or attitude (Dore, 1986) about children's performance in the physical, written, spoken, graphic, or attentional domains. Similar to requests, evaluations may have multiple functions and can differ as well in their degree of explicitness and directness.

     —*Positive evaluations* confirm that verbal contributions or other actions meet expectations for accuracy, appropriateness, or originality (informativeness):

T/B: Bobby, open the arms/ (Bobby opens arms) Good/

T/S: "B" for baseball/ That's a good way to do it/

—*Negative evaluations* sanction violations in expectations for accuracy, appropriateness, or originality, for example:

T/S: Bird's nest and . . . and up/ (Sam makes a mistake; children start laughing)

T/C: <u>Please</u> do not laugh / That is not helpful/

T/G: It's "thunder"/ (George misspelling as he writes) But that's not quite "thunder"/

—*Neutral evaluations* express acknowledgement of a contribution; however, depending on the communicative context, a neutral evaluation may also indirectly signal that a contribution is not acceptable or is insufficiently informative:

T/S: Why do you think it rained?/
S/T: 'Cause it was Sunday/
T/S: Hmmm/

—*Extending evaluations* also have multiple functions. They can function as positive feedback for a contribution while simultaneously providing verbal support for the topic to continue:

A/T: And in the hotel -- the kids have a -- on the first floor there was this game room/
T/A: Oh, what fun/ So you spent a lot of quarters/
A/T: And I went on my first roller coaster ride/
T/A: Wow/

—*Comprehension checks* function as a verbal form of external verification for the adult that a child's contribution has been understood. Some or all of the child's response may be restated or the child may be led to provide a response, which is then restated by the adult. Comprehension checks may be combined with other types of evaluation:

T/CH:	What can you do with your mouth?/
S/T:	You can taste things with your mouth/
T/S:	You can taste things with your mouth/ Good/

J/T:	It happened to me on the water slide/ Yesterday/
T/S:	Yesterday?/ Oh really/ What happened?/

3. *Repairs.* Teachers revise what they say in order to repair communicative breakdowns and to help children comprehend information. Your own style determines how and when repairs occur as defined in the section on transcribing child talk. An additional type of repair is *simplification.* In this kind of repair, both the content and the form of what has been said are revised so as to reduce its conceptual complexity. Often, simplifications may function as hints or clues for students to infer the reply that is expected, as illustrated by this example, which was taken from a high school lesson on current events (Blank, 1988, p. 387):

Student:	The war in the Middle East is still going on.
Teacher:	Is it going on in the same way? Frank?
Student:	Egypt asked Syria to intervene. They want a security meeting or quick meeting of the U.N. Security Council.
Teacher:	O.K. for what reason? Do you know? Anyone know why Egypt has called a meeting of the Security Council of the U.N.? What has the Security Council just initiated?
Student:	A cease fire.

Again, repair devices are a teaching tool. The effectiveness of the repairs selected is dependent on the overall purpose of the instructional activity. Enhanced appreciation of how these tools are actually chosen can lead to increased effectiveness in their use.

Before beginning the analysis of communicative functions, refer back to the discussion at the beginning of this section ("Teaching Choices: Communicative Functions (Use)"). The statement was made that the discourse of instruction does not consist of isolated utterances. Rather, teaching discourse has many different functions and is sequenced in a patterned way that we call conversation. We may start with a process request, obtain a process response, then evaluate that response, next clarify the information or repeat a request or statement.

Examining a segment of your teaching discourse will provide a better understanding of your style of teaching; therefore, it would be beneficial to take a section of your teaching discourse and note how the functions that have just been defined are patterned. The following set of notations can be used for this purpose (also see the Teaching Choices column in Exhibit B-1):

- Requests for information (RI)
    RI—Choice
    RI—Product
    RI—Process
    RI—Metaprocess
    RI—Clarification
- Requests for action (RA)
    RA—Procedural (direct)
    RA—Indirect
- Responses (RES)
    RES—Choice
    RES—Product
    RES—Process
    RES—Metaprocess
    RES—Clarification
    RES—Action
    RES—Procedural
    RES—Indirect
- Explanations (EXP)
- Evaluations (EVAL)
    EVAL—Positive
    EVAL—Negative
    EVAL—Neutral
    EVAL—Extend
    EVAL—Compre. check (comprehension check)
- Repairs (RP)
    RP—Correction (to form of message)
    RP—Adjustment (to content of message)
    RP—Repetition (of words or phrases)
    RP—Simplification (of both form and content of message)

Now you should be prepared to begin your analysis of communicative functions.

A. Requests
   1. Estimate from your total number of speaking turns what percentage of your utterances consisted of:
      a. Requests for information: _____
         Give examples: _____
         _____

      b. Direct requests for action (e.g., *Look*; *Let's say it together*, etc.): _____
         _____
         Give examples: _____
         _____

      c. Indirect requests for action (e.g., *Can you give Mary the book? May I have your attention?* etc.): _____
         _____
         Give examples: _____
         _____

   2. Of the total requests for information, give the percentages that were:
      a. Choice requests: _____
         Give examples: _____
         _____

      b. Product requests: _____
         Give examples: _____
         _____

      c. Process requests: _____
         Give examples: _____
         _____

      d. Metaprocess requests: _____
         Give examples: _____
         _____

      e. Clarification requests: _____
         Give examples: _____
         _____

3. How would you characterize the overall informational complexity of your requests for information? Describe: _____

_____

_____

4. How would you characterize the overall informational complexity of your requests for action (both direct and indirect)? Describe: _____

_____

_____

5. Approximate the percentage of requests for action that were presented as:
   a. Direct directions to speak or listen: _____

   _____

   Give examples: _____

   _____

   b. Indirect directions to speak or listen: _____

   _____

   Give examples: _____

   _____

   c. Direct directions relating to conduct or attention: _____
      Give examples: _____

   _____

   d. Indirect directions relating to conduct or attention: _____
      Give examples: _____

   _____

6. During this activity, did your students understand that directions can be presented as indirect requests for action?
   Yes: ___ No: ___
   If yes, give an example: _____

   _____

   If no, give an example: _____

   _____

7. Were your clarification requests effective in clearing up your misunder-standings?
   Yes: ___ No: ___
   If yes, give examples: _____

   _____

   If no, give examples: _____

   _____

B. Explanations
   1. Estimate from your total number of speaking turns what percentage of your utterances consisted of explanations: _____
      Give examples: _____
      _____

   2. Would you characterize the majority of your explanations as notably long, complicated, or unclear?
      Yes: ___ No: ___
      If yes, give examples: _____
      _____

   3. Did some of your students stop participating when the amount of explanation was extensive?
      Yes: ___ No: ___
   4. Did some of your students perform only after they had watched other students' performance?
      Yes: ___ No: ___

C. Evaluations
   1. How did you provide feedback on performance during this activity?
      a. Through verbal evaluations: _____
      b. Through nonverbal evaluations: _____
      c. Through a combination of both verbal and nonverbal evaluation: _____
   2. Estimate what percentage of your evaluations were positive: _____
      Give examples: _____
      _____

   3. Estimate what percentage of your evaluations were negative: _____
      Give examples: _____
      _____

   4. Estimate what percentage of your evaluations provided neutral feedback:
      _____
      Give examples: _____
      _____

   5. Did you use comprehension checks?
      Yes: ___ No: ___
      a. If yes, give examples: _____
      _____

      b. Was your use of comprehension checks specific to certain students?
         Yes: ___ No: ___

    c. Why do you think comprehension checks were used more often with certain students? _____

_____

D. Repairs

  1. During the activity, did you frequently repair the form or content of what you said?

    Yes: ___ No: ___

    If yes, give examples: _____

_____

  2. Estimate how many of your repairs were:

    a. Corrections to the form of what you were saying: _____

    b. Modifications to the content of your message: _____

    c. Repetitions of words or phrases: _____

_____

    d. Simplifications of both the form and content of your message:_____

  3. Did your students indicate that these repairs aided their comprehension?

    Yes: ___ No: ___

    If yes, explain how :_____

_____

Section 7: Teaching Choices: Form

The fourth area of teaching choices concerns the selection of sentence structure. Syntax is the form by which intentions and meanings are expressed. Syntax can be thought of as the surface structure—what is actually said. Some general questions concern the complexity of the syntactic structures you use and whether the level of complexity is appropriate for the developmental and informational needs of your students. Both simple and complex syntactic structures are important for facilitating normal language development at school and home. The goal of analysis in this section is to assist you in becoming more aware of the level of syntactic structures that you use.

A. Approximate how often you expressed information in sentence structures having the expected subject-verb-object word order: _____

B. Approximate how often you expressed information in more complex syntactic structures:

  1. Clauses in which the expected word order is violated (e.g., *Before you turn in your work, make certain to check your answers*): _____

_____

Give examples: _____

_____

2. Clauses containing multiple concepts connected by *that, who*, or *which*:

_____

Give examples: _____

_____

3. Clauses containing multiple concepts connected by *and, then, but, so, or, because, if-then*: _____
   Give examples: _____

_____

C. Did you characteristically present information using the same level of syntactic complexity or did you vary the syntactic complexity? _____

_____

1. Were you aware of the level of syntactic complexity?
   Yes: ___ No: ___
2. Was this level appropriate for meeting your goals in the activity?
   Yes: ___ No: ___
   Briefly describe why this level was or was not appropriate: _____

_____

Section 8: Speech Style

Speech style consists of a number of factors. Among these are the rate of speaking, the volume used, and how important information is stressed. Analyzing your speaking style affords greater control. For example, some children encounter increased difficulty in processing spoken language that is very fast. If you know your rate is habitually fast, then you might be more aware of the need to control it when interacting with such children. Of course, this control only becomes possible with more deliberate awareness of speaking style.

A. Characterize your speaking rate:
   Fast: ___ Slow: ___ Average: ___
B. Did you vary your rate of speaking and your intonational pattern while presenting the activity?
   Yes: ___ No: ___
   Describe: _____

_____

C. Did you slow your rate when presenting new or important information?

Yes: ___ No: ___

Describe: _____

_____

_____

D. When highlighting important points, did you pause prior to and after essential information?

Yes: ___ No: ___

Describe: _____

_____

Section 9: Listening Environment in the Classroom

This final section concerns the noise level of the classroom. A few children may be less able to attend to classroom discourse and to comprehend it effectively because they cannot easily foreground the teacher's voice from ambient (or environmental) noise. Therefore, the noise conditions associated with the implementation of a lesson activity should be assessed.

A. What is the general noise level of your classroom during presentation of lessons and related activities? _____

B. Do you increase or decrease the loudness of your voice when speaking to a large versus a small group of students? _____

C. Can all of your students attend to you while competing noises are heard (e.g., nearby conversations, noise from the hallway or street, etc.)?

Those who can: _____

Those who cannot: _____

Guide to Videotaping in Classrooms

Videotaping can provide contextual, spatial, and temporal information of interest to observers. Visual information that accompanies speech is necessary for interpretation. Body language, including gaze direction, touching, and head orientation, often denotes an intended listener in the absence of any verbal signaling. Additionally, videotapes allow identification of speakers that would, in certain situations, be difficult with the sole use of audiotaping. Videotape recordings preserve the "natural coloring" of an event in ways that prose, anecdotes, and audiotapes cannot.

Videotaping allows an observer to replay an observation, manipulate time and space, make minute examinations of events, and examine actions and behavior by several people after the fact. Taping allows scrutiny of these events in a different setting. While live observations focus on only one aspect of an occurrence of human behavior, videotaped observations can be used to examine a number of these aspects simultaneously. Categorizing and coding data can be done much more reliably, and observers can share actual data samples as well as conclusions. Videotaping can capture occurrences that would have been vastly altered by the presence of a human observer. And even in situations where the presence of an observer would not greatly affect behavior, an observer would not have been physically able to hear, see, and record all that went on simultaneously.

The primary disadvantage in using videotape is the student's heightened awareness of being observed. This problem can be alleviated by placing equipment behind a curtain, one-way mirror, or other facade. Videotaping may be difficult in the home or in school settings. The design of the observation, the children's ages and attitudes, and the videotaper's technique are factors that in-

The material presented here is derived from an unpublished report: L. Wilkinson & M. Brady, *Videotaping in Classrooms: A Guide for Researchers* (Program Report 83-1), University of Wisconsin, Wisconsin Center for Education Research, Madison, WI, 1983.

fluence the effectiveness of videotaping. For example, videotaping cannot capture every syllable uttered by a six-year-old racing around the playground. Other technologies, such as a wireless microphone, might be used, but the more esoteric the application, the less likely the correct hardware will be available. It is important to choose a method of data collection that is compatible with data requirements.

Two general principles guide the approach taken here: (1) the clinician should know the goals in advance of the videotaping, and (2) it is important to do a "dry run" before the actual taping begins.

It is essential to be certain the task is amenable to videotaping. One way to determine whether this is the case is to view your subjects with a frame formed by your thumbs and forefingers, since this indicates what will be seen through the camera lens.

EQUIPMENT CONSIDERATIONS

Having decided that videotaped data is necessary for a particular objective, you must consider issues regarding equipment and materials. Describing the features of the information to be collected is the first step: How many tapes do you want to make and what will be the focus (e.g., whole class, individual child)? Once these requirements have been delineated, the budget (and/or your expectations) should be adjusted accordingly. Renting equipment may be considered; however, rental is costly. Additionally, problems encountered with breakdowns, availability, shoddy maintenance, and lack of backup equipment often make purchase a better choice than rental.

If you decide to purchase equipment, the second step is to select the appropriate hardware, which is largely a matter of anticipating future needs. The current boom in the home video market has produced an array of consumer products for video production as well as for viewing. Over the past 20 years, prices for video equipment have decreased. The features available now—slow motion, remote control, longer recording time, two audio tracks—far surpass those available in the same price range a few years ago. The quality and ease of operation of these new video products have also improved substantially.

The prospective owner of equipment should consider both tape format and equipment maintenance. If the tapes, once recorded, will never leave the school or clinical setting, the format choice may be less important. However, if the tapes will be utilized outside the setting, interchangeability with others' equipment is a must. Helical-scan videotapes may be Beta format (I or II), VHS (video home system), ¾" cassette, or ½" open-reel EIAJ format. Each of these formats requires a different machine for use. There are no great differences in cost or quality, though the length of recording time per cassette or reel varies from 20, 30, or 60 minutes (¾" format) to 6 hours or more (Beta II). The VHS format seems to be most widely distributed. Two other format differences that may be of interest to some are (1) editing capability (there is no way to make clean edits on ½" open-reel tape, but all other formats may be electronically edited) and (2) ease of loading (cassettes are easier to handle in the field and do not require rewinding before unloading, unlike reels). Videotapes can be dubbed to any other format or film (with some loss of visual quality) for showing at in-service workshops, at conferences, in classes, and so on.

The second, and perhaps more important, factor in equipment choice is maintenance. In addition to repairs for breakdowns, periodic maintenance is a must for efficient performance. Although video recorders have solid state circuitry, motors, belts, and video heads do wear out and require replacement. Almost all equipment comes with a 90-day service and a 1-year parts replacement warranty. However, if the vendor is not a factory authorized dealer, it may be necessary to ship the equipment across the country for servicing. For this reason, many universities and some schools employ engineers to maintain electronic equipment. Many dealers will loan equipment while yours is in the shop.

THE PHYSICAL SETUP

Camera Placement

The television picture is two-dimensional but the video camera has the advantage of capturing motion and the ability to zoom from distant to close-up shots, allowing one to focus on aspects of the shot that may be of interest at any given moment. The television frame allows the observer to look at a scene or person from only one angle at a time. For example, suppose the focus of study is two people interacting face to face. Their expressions are of primary importance. Figure C-1 illustrates the choices available for camera placement. First, either one or two cameras can be used. Using two cameras (as illustrated in frames A and B) allows full-face shots. However, it is extremely difficult and expensive to synchronize the two tapes. This approach requires an additional camera and recorder. In frame C, head turning or change of posture by the subjects results in loss of information. When using only one camera, the best choice for camera placement is illustrated by frame D; that is, the subjects are positioned at a 90-degree angle (e.g., at the corner of a table). This provides a three-quarter shot and more visual information.

No one method is better than another. The choice should depend on the important aspects of interaction and the number of video setups. A trial taping is most helpful in determining whether critical features will be captured. If it is necessary to count syllables in slow motion, profile shots will not be very help-

Figure C-1   A, Over-the-shoulder shot—camera A; B, Over-the-shoulder shot—camera B; C, Profile shot—one camera; D, Three-quarter shot—one camera. *Source:* From *Videotaping in Classrooms: A Guide for Researchers* (Program Report 83-1) by L. Wilkinson and M. Brady, an unpublished report by the Wisconsin Center for Education Research, 1983.

ful. If placing students at a table will restrict their natural behavior (because they happen to be four-year olds), it may be necessary to sacrifice full visual information for their comfort and cooperation. And if the design calls for counting the eye blinks of a pair of four-year-olds engaged in interaction, there is something wrong with the design. Pulling the trigger and hoping that the results will turn out the way you want them to guarantees disappointment. Unlike real-time observations, video observations can be replayed, criticized, and analyzed repeatedly. Yet there is no solution for the absence of critical features on the tape.

Mapping the Area

In deciding on the physical setup for recording, it is best to plan the recording setup with a figure or sketch made in a preliminary visit to the research site, so that information about lighting, ambient noise, furniture, and extraneous people is known. An example of this kind of map was presented in an earlier chapter and is given again in Figure C-2. Figure C-3 is a schematic in which the various pieces of video equipment are indicated.

The components that are required for video recording include the following: videotape recorder (VTR/VT), camera with zoom lens (CAM), power adaptor,

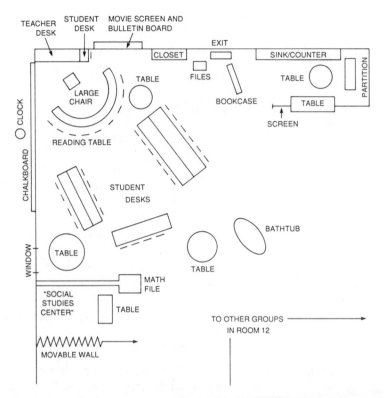

Figure C-2 Classroom Map. *Source:* Drawing by Robert Cavey for Wisconsin Center for Education Research, University of Wisconsin-Madison. From *Communicating in the Classroom* (p. 270) by L. Wilkinson, 1982, New York: Academic Press, Inc. Copyright 1982 by Wisconsin Center for Education Research. Reprinted by permission.

microphone, microphone cable, earphone, 15-foot camera extension cable, electrical adaptor (from three to two prongs), videotape, 15-foot power extension cord, and tripod.

In addition, extra microphones, microphone cords, extension cords, and microphone (table or floor) stands may be needed. Also, a battery may be needed, but use the battery only if it is necessary to be away from an outlet; batteries can be unreliable. Any of these components can break down during recording, so include backup equipment. Every piece of equipment should be tested before taping. Microphone cables and jacks often suffer shorts in the course of normal use. Long cords and cables will allow routing and securing of the wires.

It is necessary to become familiar with the equipment and to simulate the observational setup. Zooming, panning, tilting, and focusing are techniques that

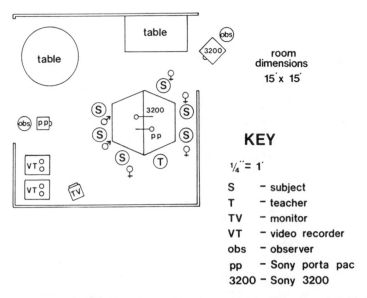

Figure C-3 Videotaping Schematic. *Source:* From *Videotaping in Classrooms: A Guide for Researchers* (Program Report 83-1), by L. Wilkinson and M. Brady, an unpublished report by the Wisconsin Center for Education Research, 1982.

should be mastered. Experimentation with angles, distances, and contrast levels created by different types of lighting is part of this process. The limits and flexibility of the tripod and cables are also important to determine. The observer who is comfortable with the mechanics can more easily concentrate on the salient features of what is being captured on tape. A good technique is to (1) set up the equipment in the actual room; (2) tape assistants playing the roles of subjects; and (3) rewind the tape, play it back, and critique the product. This practice session allows trouble-shooting the design. Realistic assessment at this stage will prevent the production of useless data.

AUDIO RECORDING

Videotaping allows observers to frame visual reality, but this framing, by its very nature, excludes certain information. The audio component of videotape recording gives rise to a separate, yet related issue. Recorded audio is more restricted than live audio. While binaural perception allows one to select and tune in one voice out of the classroom "hubbub," the microphone (mic) treats all sounds as if they come from one source. Thus, upon playback, the listener cannot use directional cues to locate or tune in any one voice. A certain degree of discrimination is lost, which may or may not be important in the particular situation (see Figure C-4).

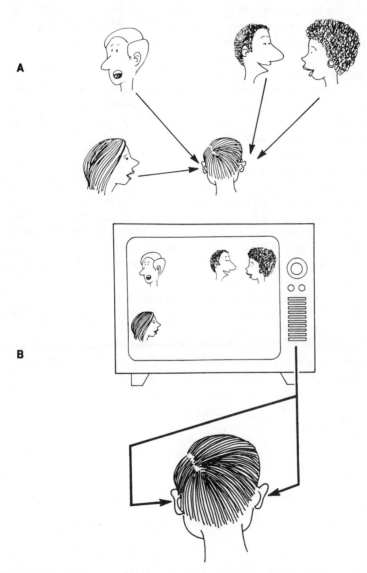

Figure C-4   **A,** Live sound reaches an observer's ears from many directions; **B,** Taped sound reaches an observer's ears from only one direction. *Source:* From *Videotaping in Classrooms: A Guide for Researchers* (Program Report 83-1), by L. Wilkinson and M. Brady, an unpublished report by the Wisconsin Center for Education Research, 1983.

Consider a situation in which you are taping a group of children in order to be able to count the words per minute from one child. It will often be very difficult to distinguish the child's voice from those of his or her peers. You could probably guess by the combination of mouth opening and talking, but unless the child has an extremely distinctive voice, you won't be able to separate out the child's words. Children's voices are all fairly high pitched, with much less variation than adults' voices.

It is possible to approximate the type of audiotaping to be obtained by placing an observer in the position that the microphone will occupy on the set. Discrimination between voices in the live situation will be more accurate than discrimination using the tape. On the other hand, the microphone can be placed where the live observer cannot be placed.

One decision in audiotaping is whether to use omni- or unidirectional microphones. Use unidirectional mics if you are concentrating on only one speaker per microphone. Unidirectional mics pick up sound only from one direction in a roughly cardioid (heart-shaped) pattern, with the speaker facing the mic at the vortex. Most portable video and audio recorders have inputs for only one audio source at a time; without a mixer, only one microphone per recorder can be used. A mixer allows use of several mics per recorder but will necessitate constant audio monitoring. Each mic input has a different volume level, and one subject's heavy breathing may obliterate another's speech unless someone is standing at the controls and correcting for such problems.

Lavalier microphones can be worn about the neck on a string or pinned to the lapel. They are not designed to be placed on a stand or held in the hand. Omnidirectional microphones are designed for use with a stand, placed either on a table or on the floor. They will pick up sound in a half-spherical coverage area, as shown in Figure C-5. While all microphones are somewhat directional, in that

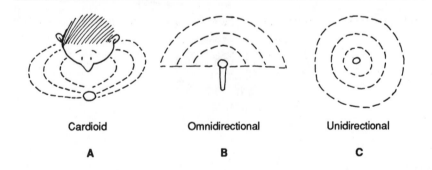

Cardioid   Omnidirectional   Unidirectional

A   B   C

Figure C-5 Patterns of Microphone Recordings. *Source:* From *Videotaping in Classrooms: A Guide for Researchers* (Program Report 83-1), by L. Wilkinson and M. Brady, an unpublished report by the Wisconsin Center for Education Research, 1983.

they will pick up sound better when the source is in front of rather than behind the mic, shotgun mics are the most directional. They require an observer and have a very narrow pickup pattern. They are useful when the target speaker changes frequently, as in a large group discussion. There is also an omnidirectional microphone in the camera itself (internal mic), which may be used as a last resort. This microphone will pick up a lot of extraneous noise, including such things as rings clinking against the tripod and unwanted voices. However, such extraneous noise may be what is desired if the point of interest is, for example, students' abilities to study in a specific environment, such as the cafeteria.

Another consideration when choosing a microphone is the obtrusiveness of the equipment. A subject wearing a lavalier mic cannot be totally mobile. A mic on the table cannot be used to capture the subject's speech when he or she leaves the table to go to the blackboard. The subject might be intimidated by having a shotgun mic pointed directly at his or her face.

An auxiliary recording device, such as a tape recorder, may be helpful, but the tape will not synchronize precisely with the videotape. Such auxiliary devices are sometimes used, although infrequently, to provide additional types of information.

The type of impedance the recorder accepts, as well as the type of connector it receives the signal from, is important to note. More types of connectors are available than are necessary, they are all mutually incompatible, and the terms used to describe each are nonstandard. For audio recording, every "male" plug must be matched by a compatible "female" jack. The inputs on your recorder are female jacks. The outputs on the end of the mic cables are male plugs. Between these two components, adaptors can transfer the signal. Extension cords and mic cables can be wired differently, which also affects audio recording. In general, the fewer adaptors used, the better. Although they do not actually add noise to the signal, they provide one more point along the cord where solder can inopportunely let loose or wires can break. Some videotape recorders have high-impedance mic inputs, and most studio microphones output a low-impedance signal. An inconsistency can cause a "buzz" or "hum" signal. For best results, a low-impedance mic should be matched to a high-impedance video recorder input using an impedance-matching transformer at the tape deck input. This has the advantage of making the signal louder and clearer. Such a transformer is infrequently used, but occasionally it is essential, depending on the criteria of research.

Testing audio equipment is always essential. It is most important to listen to the signal while taping via headphones or earphones. After recording the data, it is also necessary to check the audio recording. The audio signal is susceptible to equipment damage and environmental interference. Audio malfunctioning is typically less obvious than a video problem.

VIDEO RECORDING

Focus

Focusing on buildings and trees is good practice, but focusing on a human face is more difficult. Always focus on the eyes, not the hand or shirt. If the eyes cannot be the object of focus, then focus on the part of the body closest to them, such as the hair or nose. The technique for setting focus is as follows:

1. Zoom in as close as possible to the subject's face.
2. Focus the lens (adjust the focus ring on the lens).
3. Zoom out to frame the subject as desired.

It is not necessary to refocus unless the camera is moved, the subject moves forward or back, or the focus changes to another individual. In other words, zooming in and out is possible without refocusing. It is best to check the focus if it looks a little fuzzy.

Lighting

Placing subjects in front of a brightly lit window results in silhouettes. If subjects already are in such a spot, the camera must be moved so the window is behind it. Ordinary fluorescent lighting in most institutions is fine for videotaping. Incandescent lighting is not quite as even as fluorescent for videotaping, but in high enough wattage it will usually suffice. In homes, it is advisable to bring an auxiliary light source, an extension cord, a tripod, and tape to situate it, since home environments are unpredictably lit.

Camera Placement

The aspects of camera placement most often ignored are camera height and the camera's distance from subjects. If it is not possible to see over someone's head or another obstruction with your lens, the camera must be raised (Figure C-6). The technique of zooming in allows the camera operator to be quite far away (e.g., 20 feet) from the subjects and achieve close-up shots.

TAPE AND EQUIPMENT STORAGE

Tapes should be clearly labeled and boxed in an upright position for storage. Storing them on their sides for long periods can cause an accumulation of magnetic particles that may degrade the image or sound. Cables and cords should be gently coiled, never knotted or wound tightly about the forearm.

Figure C-6   A, View of a speaker can be blocked by other speakers or by obstructions; B, Raising camera often allows a clearer view. *Source:* From *Videotaping in Classrooms: A Guide for Researchers* (Program Report 83-1), by L. Wilkinson and M. Brady, an unpublished report by the Wisconsin Center for Education Research, 1983.

Bibliography

Allington, R.L. (1980). Teacher interruption behavior during primary-grade reading. *Journal of Educational Psychology, 72,* 371–377.

Almy, M., & Genishi, C. (1979). *Ways of studying children.* New York: Teachers College Press.

Anderson, R.C., & Pearson, P.D. (1984). A schema-theoretic view of basic processes in reading comprehension. In P.D. Pearson (Ed.), *Handbook of reading research* (pp. 255–291). New York: Longman.

Applebee, A.N., & Langer, J.A. (1983). Instructional scaffolding: Reading and writing as natural language activities. *Language Arts, 60*(2), 168–175.

Au, K.H., & Kawakami, A.J. (1984). Vygotskian perspectives on discussion processes in small-group reading-lessons. In P.L. Peterson, L.C. Wilkinson, & M. Hallinan (Eds.), *The social context of instruction* (pp. 209–225). New York: Academic Press.

Au, K.H., & Mason, J.M. (1983). Cultural congruence in classroom participation structures: Achieving a balance of rights. *Discourse Processes, 6,* 145–167.

Baker, J.M., & Zigmond, N. (1990). Are regular education classes equipped to accommodate students with learning disabilities? *Exceptional Children, 56,* 515–526.

Baker, L., & Brown, A.L. (1984). Metacognitive skills and reading. In P.D. Pearson (Ed.), *Handbook of reading research* (pp. 353–394). New York: Longman.

Ball, E.W., & Blachman, B.A. (1988). Phoneme segmentation training: Effect on reading readiness. *Annals of Dyslexia, 38,* 205–225.

Bashir, A.S. (1989). Language intervention and the curriculum. *Seminars in Speech and Language, 10,* 181–191.

Bashir, A.S., Kuban, K.C., Kleinman, S.N., & Scavuzzo, A. (1983). Issue in language disorders: Considerations of cause, maintenance, and change. In J. Miller, D.E. Yoder, & R. Schiefelbusch (Eds.), *Contemporary issues in language intervention* (ASHA Reports 12, pp. 92–112). Rockville, MD: American Speech-Language-Hearing Association.

Bates, E. (1976). *Language and context: The acquisition of pragmatics.* New York: Academic Press.

Beattie, G. (1983). *Talk: An analysis of speech and nonverbal behavior in conversation.* Stony Stratford, England: Open University Press.

Becker, L.B., & Silverstein, J.E. (1984). Clinician-child discourse: A replication study. *Journal of Speech and Hearing Disorders, 49,* 104–106.

Bedrosian, J. (1985). An approach to developing conversational competence. In D.N. Ripich & F.M. Spinelli (Eds.), *School discourse problems* (pp. 231–258). San Diego, CA: College-Hill Press.

Bennett-Kastor, T.L. (1986). Cohesion and predication in child narrative. *Journal of Child Language, 13*, 353–370.

Bennett-Kastor, T.L. (1988). *Analyzing children's language.* New York: Basil Blackwell.

Bernstein, D.K. (1989). Assessing children with limited English proficiency: Current perspectives. *Topics in Language Disorders, 9*(3), 15–20.

Bernstein, D.K., & Tiegerman, E. (1989). *Language and communication disorders in children* (2nd ed.). Columbus, OH: Charles E. Merrill.

Bialystok, E. (1986). Factors in the growth of linguistic awareness. *Child Development, 57*, 498–510.

Bialystok, E., & Ryan, E.B. (1985). A metacognitive framework for the development of first and second language skills. In D.L. Forrest-Pressley, G.E. MacKinnon, & T.G. Waller (Eds.), *Metacognition, cognition, and human performance* (Vol. 1, pp. 207–252). New York: Academic Press.

Biber, D. (1988). *Variation across speech and writing.* New York: Cambridge University Press.

Birdsong, D. (1989). *Metalinguistic performance and interlinguistic competence.* New York: Springer-Verlag.

Blachman, B.A. (1989). Phonological awareness and word recognition: Assessment and intervention. In A.G. Kamhi & H.W. Catts (Eds.), *Reading disabilities: A developmental language perspective* (pp. 133–158). Boston: College-Hill Press.

Blank, M. (1988). Classroom text: The next stages of intervention. In R.L. Schiefelbusch & L.L. Lloyd (Eds.), *Language perspectives: Acquisition, retardation, and intervention* (pp. 367–392). Austin, TX: Pro-Ed.

Bloom, L. (1970). *One word at a time.* New York: Teachers College Press.

Bloom, L. (1988). What is language? In M. Lahey (Ed.), *Language disorders and language development* (pp. 1–19). New York: Macmillan.

Bloome, D. (1987). Reading as a social process in a middle school classroom. In D. Bloome (Ed.), *Literacy and schooling* (pp. 123–149). Norwood, NJ: Ablex.

Bloome, D., & Knott, G. (1985). Teacher-student discourse. In D.N. Ripich & F.M. Spinelli (Eds.), *School discourse problems* (pp. 53–76). San Diego, CA: College-Hill Press.

Bloome, D., & Theodorou, E. (1988). Analyzing teacher-student and student-student discourse. In J.L. Green & J.O. Harker (Eds.), *Multiple perspective analyses of classroom discourse* (pp. 217–248). Norwood, NJ: Ablex.

Bobkoff, K., & Panagos, J.M. (1986). The "point" of language interaction. *Child Language Teaching and Therapy, 2*, 50–62.

Boehm, A.E., & Weinberg, R.A. (1977). *The classroom observer: A guide for developing observation skills.* New York: Teachers College Press.

Boggs, S. (1972). The meaning of questions and narratives to Hawaiian children. In C.B. Cazden, V.P. John, & D. Hymes (Eds.), *Functions of language in the classroom* (pp. 299–330). New York: Teachers College Press.

Bossert, S.T., Barnett, B.G., & Filby, N.N. (1984). Grouping and instructional organization. In P.L. Peterson, L.C. Wilkinson, & M. Hallinan (Eds.), *The social context of instruction* (pp. 39–51). New York: Academic Press.

Boyce, N.L., & Larson, V.L. (1983). *Adolescents' communication: Development and disorders.* Eau Claire, WI: Thinking Ink Publications.

Brennan, A.D., Bridge, C.A., & Winograd, P.N. (1986). The effects of structural variation on children's recall of basal reader stories. *Reading Research Quarterly, 21*, 91–104.

Brinton, B., & Fujiki, M. (1989). *Conversational management with language impaired children.* Gaithersburg, MD: Aspen Publishers, Inc.

Brown, A.L. (1982). Learning and development: The problems of compatibility, access, and induction. *Human Development, 25*, 89–115.

Brown, A.L., Campione, J.C., & Day, J.D. (1984). Learning to learn: On training students to learn from texts. In A.L. Harris & E.R. Sipay (Eds.), *Readings on reading instruction* (3rd ed.) (pp. 317–326). New York: Longman.

Brown, A.L., & DeLoache, J.S. (1983). Metacognitive skills. In M. Donaldson, R. Grieve, & C. Pratt (Eds.), *Early childhood development and education* (pp. 280–289). New York: Guilford Press.

Brown, A.L., & Ferrara, R.A. (1985). Diagnosing zones of proximal development. In J.V. Wertsch (Ed.), *Culture, communication, and cognition* (pp. 275–305). New York: Cambridge University Press.

Brown, A.L., & Palinscar, A.S. (1987). Reciprocal teaching of comprehension strategies. In J.D. Day & J.G. Borkowski (Eds.), *Intelligence and exceptionality: New directions for theory, assessment, and instructional practice* (pp. 81–132). Norwood, NJ: Ablex.

Bruner, J. (1985). Vygotsky: A historical and conceptual perspective. In J.V. Wertsch (Ed.), *Culture, communication, and cognition: Vygotskian perspectives* (pp. 21–34). New York: Cambridge University Press.

Bryan, T.H. (1986). A review of studies on learning disabled children's communicative competence. In R.L. Schiefelbusch (Ed.), *Language competence: Assessment and intervention* (pp. 227–259). San Diego, CA: College-Hill Press.

Bryan, T., Bay, M., & Donahue, M. (1988). Implications of the learning disabilities definition for the regular education initiative. *Journal of Learning Disabilities, 21*, 23–28.

Bryan, T., Donahue, M. & Pearl, R. (1981). Learning disabled children's peer interactions during a small group problem solving task. *Learning Disability Quarterly, 4*, 13–22.

Butler, K.G. (1984). The language of the schools. *Asha, 26*(5), 31–35.

Butler, K.G. (1989). Classroom strategies and reciprocal teaching. Paper presented at the Institute on Language Learning Disabilities, Emerson College, Boston.

Buttrill, J., Niizawa, J., Biemer, J., Takahashi, C., and Hearn, S. (1989). Serving the language learning disabled adolescent. *Language, Speech, and Hearing Services in Schools, 20*, 185–204.

Calfee, R., & Sutter, S. (1982). Oral language assessment through formal discussion. *Topics in Language Disorders, 2*(4), 45–55.

Campione, J.C. (1989). Assisted assessment: A taxonomy of approaches and an outline of strengths and weaknesses. *Journal of Learning Disabilities, 22*, 151–165.

Campione, J.C., and Brown, A.L. (1987). Linking dynamic assessment with school achievement. In C.S. Lidz (Ed.), *Dynamic assessment: An interactional approach to evaluating learning potential* (pp. 82–115). New York: Guilford Press.

Catts, H.W. (1989a). Phonological processing deficits and reading disabilities. In A.G. Kamhi & H.W. Catts (Eds.), *Reading disabilities: A developmental language perspective* (pp. 101–132). Boston: College-Hill Press.

Catts, H.W. (1989b). Speech production deficits in developmental dyslexia. *Journal of Speech and Hearing Disorders, 54*, 422–428.

Catts, H.W., & Kamhi, A.G. (1987). Relationship between reading and language disorders: Implications for the speech-language pathologist. *Topics in Language Disorders, 8*, 377–392.

Cazden, C.B. (1988). *Classroom discourse: The language of teaching and learning.* Portsmouth, NH: Heinemann.

Cazden, C.B., John, V.P., & Hymes, D. (1972). *Functions of language in the classroom.* New York: Teachers College Press.

Cazden, C.B., Michaels, S., & Tabors, P. (1985). Spontaneous repairs in sharing time narratives: The intersection of metalinguistic awareness, speech event, and narrative style. In S.W. Freedman (Ed.), *The acquisition of written language* (51–64). Norwood, NJ: Ablex.

Cerussi, F., & Stern-Levine, L. (1988). *Working with individual needs: Classroom strategies to help students succeed.* Tucson, AZ: Communication Skill Builders.

Chapman, R.A. (1981). Exploring children's communicative intents. In J. Miller (Ed.), *Assessing language production in children* (pp. 111–136). Baltimore: University Park Press.

Cheng, L.L. (1987). *Assessing Asian language performance: Guidelines for evaluating limited English-proficient students* (pp. 195–196). Gaithersburg, MD: Aspen Publishers, Inc.

Cheng, L.L. (1989). Intervention strategies: A multicultural approach. *Topics in Language Disorders, 9*(3), 84–91.

Cherry, L. (1978). Teacher-student interaction and teachers' expectations of students' communicative competence. In R. Shuy & M. Griffin (Eds.), *The study of children's functional language and education in the early years.* (Final report to the Carnegie Corporation, New York.) Arlington, VA: Center for Applied Linguistics.

Cherry, L. (1979). A sociocognitive approach to language development and its implications for education. In O. Garnica & M. King (Eds.), *Language, children, and society* (pp. 115–134). New York: Pergamon.

Christensen, S.S., & Luckett, C.H. (1990). Getting into the classroom and making it work. *Language, Speech, and Hearing Services in Schools, 21,* 110–113.

Cochrane, O., Cochrane, D., Scalena, S., & Buchanan, E. (1984). *Reading, writing and caring.* Winnipeg: Whole Language Consultants.

Cohen, E. (1984). Talking and working together: Status, interaction and learning. In P. Peterson, L. Wilkinson, & M. Hallinan (Eds.), *The social context of instruction* (pp. 171–189). Orlando, FL: Academic Press.

Cole, K.N., & Dale, P.S. (1986). Direct language instruction and interactive language instruction with language delayed preschool children: A comparison study. *Journal of Speech and Hearing Research, 29,* 206–217.

Cole, L. (1989). E pluribus unum pluribus: Multicultural imperatives for the 1990's and beyond. *Asha, 31*(9), 65–70.

Comkowycz, S.M., Ehren, B.J., & Hayes, N.M. (1987). Meeting classroom needs of language disordered students in middle and junior high schools: A program model. *Journal of Childhood Communication Disorders, 11,* 199–208.

Connell, P.J. (1987). Teaching language rules as solutions to language problems: A baseball analogy. *Language, Speech, and Hearing Services in Schools, 18,* 194–205.

Constable, C.M. (1986). The application of scripts in the organization of language intervention contexts. In K. Nelson (Ed.), *Event knowledge* (pp. 205–230). Hillsdale, NJ: Lawrence Erlbaum.

Conti-Ramsden, G. (1990). Maternal recasts and other contingent replies to language-impaired children. *Journal of Speech and Hearing Disorders, 55,* 262–274.

Cook-Gumperz, J., & Gumperz, J. (1982). Communicative competence in educational perspective. In L.C. Wilkinson (Ed.), *Communicating in the classroom* (pp. 13–26). New York: Academic Press.

Cooper, C., Marquis, A., & Ayers-Lopez, S. (1982). Peer learning in the classroom: Tracing developmental patterns and consequences of children's spontaneous interactions. In L.C. Wilkinson (Ed.), *Communicating in the classroom* (pp. 69–84). New York: Academic Press.

Corson, D. (1988). *Oral language across the curriculum*. Clevedon, England: Multilingual Matters.

Craig, H.K., & Evans, J.L. (1989). Turn exchange characteristics of SLI children's simultaneous and nonsimultaneous speech. *Journal of Speech and Hearing Disorders, 54*, 334–347.

Craig, H.K., & Gallagher, T.M. (1983). Adult-child discourse: The conversational relevance of pauses. *Journal of Pragmatics, 7*, 347–360.

Cronbach, L. J. (1970). *Essentials of psychological testing* (3rd ed.). New York: Harper & Row.

Crystal, D. (1985). *A dictionary of linguistics and phonetics* (2nd ed.). New York: Basil Blackwell.

Damico, J.S. (1987). Addressing language concerns in the schools: The SLP as consultant. *Journal of Childhood Communication Disorders, 11*, 17–40.

Day, J., French, L.A., & Hall, L.F. (1985). Social influences on cognitive development. In D.L. Forrest-Pressley, G.E. MacKinnon, & T.G. Waller (Eds.), *Metacognition, cognition, and human performance* (Vol. 1, pp. 33–56). Orlando, FL: Academic Press.

Deshler, D.D., Warner, M.M., Schumaker, J.B., & Alley, G.R. (1983). Learning strategies intervention model: Key components and current status. In J.D. McKinney & L. Feagans (Eds.), *Current topics in learning disabilities* (pp. 245–283). Norwood, NJ: Ablex.

Despain, A.D., & Simon, C.S. (1987). Alternative to failure: A junior high school language development-based curriculum. *Journal of Childhood Communication Disorders, 11*, 139–179.

DeStefano, J.S. (1984). Learning to communicate in the classroom. In A. Pellegrini & T. Yawkey (Eds.), *The development of oral and written language in social contexts* (pp. 155–165). Norwood, NJ: Ablex.

DeStefano, J.S., & Kantor, R. (1988). Cohesion in spoken and written dialogue: An investigation of cultural and textual constraints. *Linguistics and Education, 1*, 105–124.

DeStefano, J.S., Pepinsky, H.B., & Sanders, T.S. (1982). Discourse rules for literacy learning in a classroom. In L.C. Wilkinson (Ed.), *Communicating in the classroom* (pp. 101–129). New York: Academic Press.

Dollaghan, C.A. (1987). Comprehension monitoring in normal and language-impaired children. *Topics in Language Disorders, 7*(2), 45–60.

Dollaghan, C., & Miller, J. (1986). Observational methods in the study of communicative competence. In R.L. Schiefelbush (Ed.), *Language competence: Assessment and intervention* (pp. 99–129). San Diego, CA: College-Hill Press.

Donahue, M. (1985). Communicative style in learning disabled children: Some implications for classroom discourse. In D.N. Ripich & F.M. Spinelli (Eds.), *School discourse problems* (pp. 97–124). San Diego, CA: College-Hill Press.

Dore, J. (1986). The development of conversational competence. In R.L. Schiefelbusch (Ed.), *Language competence: Assessment and intervention* (pp. 3–60). San Diego, CA: College-Hill Press.

Dreeben, R. (1984). First-grade reading groups: Their formation and change. In P.L. Peterson, L.C. Wilkinson, & M. Hallinan (Eds.), *The social context of instruction* (pp. 69–84). New York: Academic Press.

Duchan, J.F. (1984). Language assessment: The pragmatics revolution. In R.C. Naremore (Ed.), *Language science* (pp. 147–180). San Diego, CA: College-Hill Press.

Duchan, J.F. (1988). Assessment principles and procedures. In N.J. Lass, L.V. Reynolds, J.L. Northern, & D.E. Yoder (Eds.), *Handbook of speech-language pathology and audiology* (pp. 356–376). Canada: B.C. Decker.

Dudley-Marling, C. (1987). The role of SLPs in literacy learning. *Journal of Childhood Communication Disorders, 11*, 81–90.

Duncan, S., & Fiske, D. (1977). *Face to face interaction: Research, methods, and theory.* Hillsdale, NJ: Lawrence Erlbaum.

Durkin, D. (1978–1979). What classroom observations reveal about reading comprehension instruction. *Reading Research Quarterly, 14*, 481–533.

Eder, D. (1982). Differences in communicative styles across ability groups. In L.C. Wilkinson (Ed.), *Communicating in the classroom.* (pp. 245–264). New York: Academic Press.

Ehri, L.C. (1989a). Movement into word reading and spelling: How spelling contributes to reading. In J.M. Mason (Ed.), *Reading and writing connections* (pp. 65–81). Boston: Allyn & Bacon.

Ehri, L.C. (1989b). The development of spelling knowledge and its role in reading acquisition and reading disability. *Journal of Learning Disabilities, 6*, 356–365.

Eller, R.G. (1989). Ways of meaning: Exploring cultural differences in students' written compositions. *Linguistics and Education, 1*, 341–358.

Erickson, F. (1981). Timing and context in everyday discourse: Implications for the study of referential and social meaning. In W.P. Dickson (Ed.), *Children's oral communication skills* (pp. 241–269). New York: Academic Press.

Erickson, F. (1982). Classroom discourse as improvisation: Relationship between academic task structure and social participation structure in lessons. In L.C. Wilkinson (Ed.), *Communicating in the classroom* (pp. 153–181). New York: Academic Press.

Erickson, F., & Mohatt, G. (1982). Cultural organization of participation structures in two classrooms of Indian students. In G. Spindler (Ed.), *Doing the ethnography of schooling: Educational anthropology in action* (pp. 132–174). New York: CBS College Publishing.

Erickson, F., & Shultz, J. (1982). *The counselor as gatekeeper: Social interaction in interviews.* New York: Academic Press.

Ervin-Tripp, S. (1977). Wait for me roller-skate. In S. Ervin-Tripp & C. Mitchell-Kernan (Eds.), *Child discourse.* New York: Academic Press.

Ervin-Tripp, S. (1982). Structures of control. In L.C. Wilkinson (Ed.), *Communicating in the classroom* (pp. 27–48). New York: Academic Press.

Evertson, C., & Green, J. (1986). Observation as inquiry and method. In M. Wittrock (Ed.), *Handbook of research on teaching* (3rd ed.) (pp. 119–213). Washington, DC: American Educational Research Association.

Fey, M.E. (1986). *Language intervention with young children.* Boston: College-Hill Press.

Fitzgerald, J., & Spiegel, D.L. (1983). Enhancing children's reading comprehension through instruction in narrative structure. *Journal of Reading Behavior, 15*(2), 1–17.

Fivush, R. (1983). Negotiating classroom interaction. *Quarterly Newsletter of the Laboratory of Comparative Human Cognition, 5*(4), 83–86.

Flanders, N. (1970). *Analyzing teaching behavior.* Reading, MA: Addison-Wesley.

Fletcher, J.M., Espy, K.A., Francis, D.J., Davidson, K.C., Rourke, B.P., & Shaywitz, S.E. (1989). Comparison of cutoff and regression-based definitions of reading disabilities. *Journal of Learning Disabilities, 22*, 334–338.

Florida Department of Education. (1987, May). *English skills IV: Parallel alternative strategies for students,* Tallahassee, FL: Author.

Florida Department of Education. (1989). *Inservice training for SLD and EH secondary teachers: Implementing the strategies intervention model* (Research Report 9). Tallahassee, FL: Division of Public Schools, Bureau of Education for Exceptional Students.

Florio, S., & Shultz, J. (1979). Social competence at home and at school. *Theory into Practice, 18*(4), 234–243.

Frankel, R.M. (1982). Autism for all practical purposes: A micro-interactional view. *Topics in Language Disorders, 3*(1), 33–42.

Friel-Patti, S., & Conti-Ramsden, G. (1984). Discourse development in atypical language learners. In S.A. Kuczaj, II (Ed.), *Discourse development* (pp. 167–194). New York: Springer-Verlag.

French, P., & MacLure, M. (1981). Teachers' questions, pupils' answers: An investigation of questions and answers in the infant classroom. *First Language, 2*, 31–45.

Fressola, D.R., & Hoerchler, S.C. (1989). The speech and language evaluation scale (SLES). Columbia, MO: Hawthorne Educational Services.

Galaburda, A.M. (1989). Ordinary and extraordinary brain development: Anatomical variation in developmental dyslexia. *Annals of Dyslexia, 39*, 67–80.

Gallagher, T. (1983). Pre-assessment: A procedure for accommodating language use variability. In T. M. Gallagher & C.A. Prutting (Eds.), *Pragmatic assessment and intervention issues in language* (pp. 1–28). San Diego, CA: College-Hill Press.

Garton, A., & Pratt, C. (1989). *Learning to be literate.* New York: Basil Blackwell.

Gavelek, J.R., & Raphael, T.E. (1985). Metacognition, instruction, and the role of questioning activities. In D.L. Forrest-Pressley, G.E. MacKinnon, & T.G. Waller (Eds.), *Metacognition, cognition, and human performance* (Vol. 2, pp. 103–136). New York: Academic Press.

Gavelek, J.R., & Palinscar, A.S. (1988). Contextualism as an alternative worldview of learning disabilities: A response to Swanson's "Toward a metatheory of learning disabilities." *Journal of Learning Disabilities, 21*(5), 278–298.

Gee, J.P. (1985). The narrativization of experience in the oral style. *Journal of Education, 167*, 9–35.

Genishi, C. (1983). Studying classroom verbal interaction; unpublished paper as cited in C. Evertson & J. Green, Observation as inquiry and method. In M. Wittrock (Ed.), *Handbook of research as teaching.* New York: Macmillan.

Genishi, C., & Dyson A. (1984). *Language assessment in the early years.* Norwood, NJ: Ablex.

German, D.J. (1987). Spontaneous language profiles of children with word finding problems. *Language, Speech, and Hearing Services in Schools, 18*, 217–230.

German, D.J., & Simon, E. (in press). Analysis of children's word finding skills in discourse. *Journal of Speech and Hearing Disorders.*

Geschwin, N. (1985). Biological foundations of reading. In F.H. Duffy & N. Geschwin (Eds.), *Dyslexia: A neuroscientific approach to clinical evaluation* (pp. 197–211). Boston: Little, Brown & Co.

Gillam, R.B., & Johnston, J.R. (1985). Development of print awareness in language-disordered preschoolers. *Journal of Speech and Hearing Research, 28*, 521–526.

Goldfield, B.A., & Snow, C.E. (1985). Individual differences in language acquisition. In J.B. Gleason (Ed.), *The development of language* (pp. 307–330). Columbus, OH: Charles E. Merrill.

Goodman, K. (1986). *What's whole in whole language.* Portsmouth, NH: Heinemann.

Gordon, C.J., & Braun, C. (1985). Metacognitive processes: Reading and writing narrative discourse. In D.L. Forrest-Pressley, G.E. MacKinnon, & T.G. Waller (Eds.), *Metacognition, cognition, and human performance* (Vol. 2, pp. 1–75). New York: Academic Press.

Green, J.L., & Harker, J.O. (1982). Gaining access to learning: Conversational, social and cognitive demands of group participation. In L.C. Wilkinson (Ed.), *Communicating in the classroom* (pp. 183–221). New York: Academic Press.

Green, J., & Weade, V. (1987). In search of meaning: A sociolinguistic perspective on lesson construction and reading. In D. Bloome (Ed.), *Literacy and schooling* (pp. 3–34). Norwood, NJ: Ablex.

Green, J.L., Weade, R., & Graham, K. (1988). Lesson construction and student participation: A sociolinguistic analysis. In J.L. Green & J.O. Harker (Eds.), *Multiple perspective analyses of classroom discourse* (pp. 11–47). Norwood, NJ: Ablex.

Griffin, P., & Shuy, R. (Eds.). (1978). *The study of children's functional language and education in the early years* (Final report to the Carnegie Corporation). Arlington, VA: Center for Applied Linguistics.

Grimes, J.E. (1982). Topics within topics. In D. Tannen (Ed.), *Analyzing discourse: Text and talk* (pp. 164–176). Washington, DC: Georgetown University Press.

Gruenewald, L.J., & Pollak, S.A. (1990). *Language interaction in curriculum and instruction* (2nd ed.). Austin, TX: Pro-Ed.

Gumperz, J. (1970). Verbal strategies in multilingual communication. In J. Alatis (Ed.), *Roundtable in language and linguistics* (pp. 88–103). Washington, DC: Georgetown University Press.

Hall, W.S., & Cole, M. (1978). On participants' shaping of discourse through their understanding of the task. In K. Nelson (Ed.), *Children's language*, (Vol. 1, pp. 445–465). New York: Gardner Press.

Halliday, M.A.K. (1975). *Learning how to mean: Explorations in the development of language.* New York: Elsevier.

Halliday, M.A.K., & Hasan, H. (1976). *Cohesion in English.* London: Longman.

Hammill, D.D. (1990). On defining learning disabilities: An emerging consensus. *Journal of Learning Disabilities, 23,* 74–84.

Harste, J.C., Short, K.G., & Burke, C. (1988). *Creating classrooms for authors.* Portsmouth, NH: Heinemann.

Heald-Taylor, G. (1987). Predictable literature selections and activities for language arts instructions. *The Reading Teacher, 41*(1), 6–12.

Heap, J.L. (1988). On task in classroom discourse. *Linguistics and Education, 1,* 177–198.

Heath, S.B. (1982). Questioning at home and at school: A comparative study. In G. Spindler (Ed.), *Doing the ethnography of schooling: Educational anthropology in action* (pp. 102–131). New York: CBS College Publishing.

Heath, S.B. (1983). *Ways with words.* New York: Cambridge University Press.

Heath, S.B. (1989). The learner as cultural member. In M.L. Rice & R.L. Schiefelbusch (Eds.), *The teachability of language* (pp. 333–350). Baltimore: Paul H. Brookes.

Hoffman, L.P. (1990). The development of literacy in a school-based program. *Topics in Language Disorders, 10*(2), 81–92.

Hoskins, B. (1987). Conversations: Language intervention for adolescents. Allen, TX: DLM Teaching Resources.

Hoskins, B. (1990). Language and literacy: Participating in the conversation. *Topics in Language Disorders, 10*(2), 46–62.

Howell, K.W., & Morehead, M.K. (1987). *Curriculum-based evaluation for special and remedial education.* Columbus, OH: Charles E. Merrill.

Hubbell, R.D. (1988). *A handbook of English grammar and language sampling.* Englewood Cliffs, NJ: Prentice-Hall.

Idol, L., Paolucci-Whitcomb, P., & Nevin, A. (1987). *Collaboration consultation.* Austin, TX: Pro-Ed.

Iglesias, A. (1985). Cultural conflict in the classroom: The communicatively different child. In D.N. Ripich & F.M. Spinelli (Eds.), *School discourse problems* (pp. 79–96). San Diego, CA: College-Hill Press.

Irwin, D., & Bushnell, D. (1980). *Observational strategies for child study.* New York: Holt, Rinehart & Winston, Inc.

Johnston, J.R. (1983). What is language intervention?: The role of theory. In J. Miller, D.E. Yoder, & R. Schiefelbusch (Eds.), *Contemporary issues in language intervention* (ASHA Reports No.12, pp. 52–57). Rockville, MD: American Speech-Language-Hearing Association.

Johnston, J., Blatchley, M., & Olness, G.S. (1990). Miniature language system acquisition by children with different language learning proficiencies. *Journal of Speech and Hearing Research, 33,* 335–342.

Kagan, S.L. (1989). Assessing young children: Reconciling conflicting needs and strategies. *Partnerships in education: Toward a literate America* (ASHA Reports No. 17, pp. 13–17). Rockville, MD: American Speech-Language-Hearing Association.

Kail, R., & Leonard, L.B. (1986). *Word-finding abilities of language-impaired children* (ASHA Monographs No. 25). Rockville, MD: American Speech-Language-Hearing Association.

Kaiser, A.P., & Warren, S.F. (1988). Pragmatics and generalization. In R.L. Schiefelbusch & L.L Lloyd (Eds.), *Language perspectives: Acquisition, retardation, and invention* (2nd ed., pp. 393–442). Austin, TX: Pro-Ed.

Kamhi, A.G. (1989). Language disorders in children. In M.M. Leahy (Ed.), *Disorders of intervention: The science of intervention* (pp. 69–102). New York: Taylor & Francis.

Kamhi, A.G., & Catts, H.W. (1986). Toward an understanding of developmental language and reading disorders. *Journal of Speech and Hearing Disorders, 51,* 337–347.

Kamhi, A.G., & Catts, H.W. (1989a). Language and reading: Convergences, divergences, and development. In A.G. Kamhi & H.W. Catts (Eds.), *Reading disabilities: A developmental language perspective* (pp. 1–34). Boston: College-Hill Press.

Kamhi, A.G., & Catts, H.W. (1989b). Reading disabilities: Terminology, definitions, and subtyping issues. In A.G. Kamhi & H.W. Catts (Eds.), *Reading disabilities: A developmental language perspective* (pp. 35–66). Boston: College-Hill Press.

Kamhi, A.G., Gentry, B., Mauer, D., & Gholson, B. (1990). Analogical learning and transfer in language impaired children. *Journal of Speech and Hearing Disorders, 55,* 140–148.

Kamhi, A.G., & Lee, R.F. (1988). Cognition. In M.A. Nippold (Ed.), *Later language development.* Boston: Little, Brown & Co.

Kavale, K., & Forness, S. (1985). *The science of learning disabilities.* San Diego, CA: College-Hill Press.

Kawakami, A., & Au, K. (1986). Encouraging reading and language development in cultural minority children. *Topics in Language Disorders, 6*(2), 71–80.

Kerlinger, F. (1973). *Foundations of behavioral research.* New York: Holt, Rinehart & Winston, Inc.

King, D.F., & Goodman K.S. (1990). Whole language: Cherishing learners and their language. *Language, Speech, and Hearing Services in Schools, 21,* 221–227.

Kronick, D. (1988). *New approaches to learning disabilities: Cognitive, metacognitive, and holistic.* New York: Grune & Stratton.

Lahey, M. (1988). *Language disorders and language development.* New York: Macmillan.

Lease, B.V., & Hoffman, L.P. (1990). *Communication development program manual* (Available from L.P. Hoffman, SMA, 800 Governors Highway, Flossmor, IL 60422).

Leonard, L.B. (1981). Facilitating linguistic skills in children with specific language impairment. *Applied Psycholinguistics, 2,* 89–119.

Leonard, L.B. (1988). Lexical development and processing in specific language impairment. In R.L. Schiefelbusch & L.L. Lloyd (Eds.), *Language perspectives: Acquisition, retardation, and intervention* (pp. 69–87). Austin, TX: Pro-Ed.

Leong, C.K. (1989). Productive knowledge of derivational rules in poor readers. *Annals of Dyslexia, 39*, 94–115.

Letts, C. (1985). Linguistic interaction in the clinic—How do therapists do therapy? *Child Language Teaching and Therapy, 8*(1), 321–331.

Liles, B.Z. (1985). Cohesion in the narratives of normal and language-disordered children. *Journal of Speech and Hearing Research, 28*, 123–133.

Liles, B.Z. (1987). Episode organization and cohesive conjunctions in narratives of children with and without language disorder. *Journal of Speech and Hearing Research, 30*, 185–196.

Lund, N.J., & Duchan, J.F. (1988). *Assessing children's language in naturalistic contexts.* Englewood Cliffs, NJ: Prentice-Hall.

Marvin, C.A. (1987). Consultation services: Changing roles for SLPs. *Journal of Childhood Communication Disorders, 11*, 1–15.

Masling, J., & Stern, G. (1969). The effect of the observer in the classroom. *Journal of Educational Psychology, 60*, 351–354.

McKinley, N.L., & Lord-Larson, V. (1985). Neglected language-disordered adolescent: A delivery model. *Language, Speech, and Hearing Services in Schools, 16*, 2–15.

McTear, M. (1985). *Children's conversation.* New York: Basil Blackwell.

Mehan, H. (1979). *Learning lessons.* Cambridge, MA: Harvard University Press.

Mehan, H. (1983). The role of language and the language of role in institutional decision making. *Language in Society, 13*, 187–211.

Mehan, H. (1987). Language and power in organizational processes. *Discourse Processes, 10*, 291–301.

Mehan, H., Hertweck, A., Combs, S.E., & Flynn, P.J. (1982). Teachers' interpretations of students' behavior. In L.C. Wilkinson (Ed.), *Communicating in the classroom* (pp. 297–322). New York: Academic Press.

Mehan, H., Hertweck, A., & Meihls, J.L. (1986). *Handicapping the handicapped: Decision making in students' educational careers.* Stanford, CA: Stanford University Press.

Meline, T.J., & Brackin, S.R. (1987). Language-impaired children's awareness of inadequate messages. *Journal of Speech and Hearing Disorders, 52*, 263–270.

Menyuk, P. (1983). Language development and reading. In T.M. Gallagher & C.A. Prutting (Eds.), *Pragmatic assessment and intervention issues in language* (pp. 151–170). San Diego, CA: College-Hill Press.

Merritt, D.D., & Liles, B.Z. (1987). Story grammar ability in children with and without language disorders: Story generation, story retelling, and story comprehension. *Journal of Speech and Hearing Research, 30*, 539–552.

Merritt, D.D., & Liles, B.Z. (1989) Narrative analysis: Clinical application of story generation and story retelling. *Journal of Speech and Hearing Disorders, 54*, 438–447.

Merritt, M. (1982a). Repeats and reformulations in primary classrooms as windows on the nature of talk engagement. *Discourse Processes, 5*, 127–145.

Merritt, M. (1982b). Distributing and directing attention in primary classrooms. In L.C. Wilkinson (Ed.), *Communicating in the classroom* (pp. 223–245). New York: Academic Press.

Michaels, S. (1981). "Sharing Time": Children's narrative styles and differential access to literacy. *Language in Society, 10*, 423–442.

Michaels, S. (1986). Narrative presentations: An oral preparation for literacy with first grade. In J. Cook-Gumperz (Ed.), *The social construction of literacy* (pp. 94–116). New York: Cambridge University Press.

Michaels, S., & Cazden, C.B. (1986). Teacher/child collaboration as oral preparation for literacy. In B.B. Schieffelin & P. Gilmore (Eds.), *The acquisition of literacy: Ethnographic perspectives* (pp. 132–154). Norwood, NJ: Ablex.

Miller, L. (1989). Classroom-based language intervention. *Language, Speech, and Hearing Services in Schools, 20*, 153–169.

Miller, L. (1990). The roles of language and learning in the development of literacy. *Topics in Language Disorders, 10*(2), 1–24.

Montague, M., Maddux, C.D., & Dereshiwsky, M.I. (1990). Story grammar and comprehension and production of narrative prose by students with learning disabilities. *Journal of Learning Disabilities, 23*, 190–197.

Morine-Dershimer, G. (1985). *Talking, listening, and learning in elementary classrooms*. New York: Longman.

Muma, J.R. (1986). *Language acquisition: A functionalist perspective*. Austin, TX: Pro-Ed.

Naremore, R.C., & Hopper, R. (1990). *Children learning language* (2nd ed.). New York: Harper & Row.

National Association of Teachers of English (NATE). (n.d.). *The first 21 years 1963–84*. Sheffield, England: NATE.

Nelson, K. (1986). Event knowledge and cognitive development. In K. Nelson (Ed.), *Event knowledge*. Hillsdale, NJ: Lawrence Erlbaum.

Nelson, K. (1990). Language development in context. *Annals of the New York Academy of Sciences, 583*, 93–108.

Nelson, K.E. (1989). Strategies for first language teaching. In M.L. Rice & R.L. Schiefelbusch (Eds.), *The teachability of language* (pp. 263–310). Baltimore: Paul H. Brookes.

Nelson, N.W. (1984). Beyond information processing: The language of teachers and textbooks. In G.P. Wallach & K.G. Butler (Eds.), *Language learning disabilities in school-age children* (pp. 154–178). Baltimore: Williams & Wilkins.

Nelson, N.W. (1985). Teacher talk and child listening—Fostering a better match. In C. Simon (Ed.), *Communication skills and classroom success: Assessment of language learning disabled students* (pp. 65–102). San Diego, CA: College-Hill Press.

Nelson, N.W. (1988a). The nature of literacy. In M.A. Nippold (Ed.), *Later language development* (pp. 11–23). Boston: College-Hill Press.

Nelson, N.W. (1988b). *Planning individualized speech and language intervention programs*. Tucson, AZ: Communication Skill Builders.

Nelson, N.W. (1989). Curriculum-based language assessement and intervention. *Language, Speech, and Hearing Services in Schools, 20*, 170–184.

Nippold, M.A. (1988a). Verbal reasoning. In M.A. Nippold (Ed.), *Later language development* (pp. 159–177). Boston: College-Hill Press.

Nippold, M.A. (1988b). Figurative language. In M.A. Nippold (Ed.), *Later language development* (pp. 179–210). Boston: College-Hill Press.

Nippold, M.A., Erskine, B.J., & Freed, D.B. (1988). Proportional and functional analogical reasoning in normal and language impaired children. *Journal of Speech and Hearing Disorders, 53*, 440–448.

Nippold, M.A., Martin, S.A., & Erskine, B.J. (1988). Proverb comprehension in context: A developmental study with children and adolescents. *Journal of Speech and Hearing Research, 31*, 19–28.

Nippold, M.A., & Sullivan, M.P. (1987). Verbal and perceptual analogical reasoning and proportional metaphor comprehension in young children. *Journal of Speech and Hearing Research, 30*, 367–376.

Norris, J.A. (1989). Providing language remediation in the classroom: An integrated language-to-reading intervention method. *Language, Speech, and Hearing Services in Schools, 20*, 205–218.

Norris, J.A., & Damico, J.S. (1990). Whole language in theory and practice: Implications for language intervention. *Language, Speech, and Hearing Services in Schools, 21*, 212–220.

Norris, J.A., & Hoffman, P.R. (1990). Language intervention within naturalistic environments. *Language, Speech, and Hearing Services in Schools, 21*, 72–84.

Nye, C., Foster, S.H., & Seaman, D. (1987). Effectiveness of language intervention with the language/learning disabled. *Journal of Speech and Hearing Disorders, 52*, 348–357.

Ochs, E. (1979a). Transcription as theory. In E. Ochs & B.B. Schieffelin (Eds.), *Developmental pragmatics* (pp. 43–72). New York: Academic Press.

Ochs, E. (1979b). Planned and unplanned discourse. In T. Givon (Ed.), *Syntax and semantics, Vol. 12: Discourse and syntax* (pp. 51–80). New York: Academic Press.

Palinscar, A.S. (1989). Roles of the speech-language pathologist in disadvantaged children's pursuit of literacy. *Partnerships in education: Toward a literate America* (ASHA Reports No. 17, pp. 34–40). Rockville, MD: American Speech-Language-Hearing Association.

Palinscar, A.S., & Brown, A.L. (1984). Reciprocal teaching of comprehension fostering and comprehension monitoring activities. *Cognition and Instruction, 1*, 117–175.

Palinscar, A.S., & Brown, D.A. (1987). Enhancing instructional time through attention to metacognition. *Journal of Learning Disabilities, 20*, 66–75.

Panagos, J.M., Bobkoff, K., & Scott, C.M. (1986). Discourse analysis of language intervention. *Child Language Teaching and Therapy, 2*, 211–229.

Panagos, J.M., & Griffiths, P.L. (1981). Okay, what *do* educators know about language intervention? *Topics in Learning and Learning Disabilities, 1*(2), 69–82.

Parnell, M.M., Amerman, J.D., & Harting, R.D. (1986). Responses of language-disordered children to wh-questions. *Language, Speech, and Hearing Services in Schools, 17*, 95–114.

Parnell, M.M., Patterson, S.S., & Harding, M.A. (1984). Answers to wh-questions: A developmental study. *Journal of Speech and Hearing Research, 27*, 297–305.

Pearl, R., Donahue, M., & Bryan, T. (1986). Social relationships of learning-disabled children. In J.K. Torgesen & B.Y.L. Wong (Eds.), *Psychological and educational perspectives on learning disabilities* (pp. 194–224). New York: Academic Press.

Pearson, P.D. (1984). Asking questions about stories. In A.J. Harris & E.R. Sipay (Eds.), *Readings on reading instruction* (3rd ed.) (pp. 274–283). New York: Longman.

Pearson, P.D., & Gallagher, M.C. (1983). The instruction of reading comprehension. *Contemporary Educational Psychology, 8*, 317–344.

Pennington, B.F. (1989). Using genetics to understand dyslexia. *Annals of Dyslexia, 39*, 81–93.

Peterson, C., & McCabe, A. (1983). *Developmental psycholinguistics: Three ways of looking at a child's narrative.* New York: Plenum Press.

Philips, S. (1972). Participation structures and communicative competence: Warm Springs children in community and classroom. In C.B. Cazden, V.P. John, & D. Hymes (Eds.), *Functions of language in the classroom* (pp. 370–394). New York: Teachers College Press.

Porter, R., & Conti-Ramsden, G. (1987). Clarification requests and the language impaired child. *Child Language Teaching and Therapy, 3*, 133–150.

Premack, D. (1989). Some thoughts about transfer. In M.L. Rice & R.L. Schiefelbusch (Eds.), *The teachability of language* (pp. 239–262). Baltimore: Paul H. Brookes.

Pressley, M. (1983). Making meaningful materials easier to learn: Lessons from cognitive strategy research. In M. Pressley & J.R. Levin (Eds.), *Cognitive strategy research; Educational applications* (pp. 239–266). New York: Springer–Verlag.

Pressley, M., Borkowski, J.G., & O'Sullivan, J. (1985). Children's metamemory and the teaching of memory strategies. In D.L. Forrest-Pressley, G.E. MacKinnon, & T.G. Waller (Eds.), *Metacognition, cognition, and human performance* (Vol. 1, pp. 111–153). New York: Academic Press.

Pressley, M., Forrest-Pressley, D.L., Elliot-Faust, D., & Miller, G. (1985). Children's use of cognitive strategies, and what to do if they can't be taught. In M. Pressley & C.J. Brainerd (Eds.), *Cognitive learning and memory in children*, (pp. 1–47). New York: Springer-Verlag.

Pressley, M., Johnson, C.J., & Symons, S. (1987). Elaborating to learn and learning to elaborate. *Journal of Learning Disabilities, 20* (2), 76–91.

Prutting, C.A. (1982). Pragmatics as social competence. *Journal of Speech and Hearing Disorders, 47*, 123–134.

Prutting, C.A., Bagshaw, N., Goldstein, H., Juskowitz, S., & Umen, I. (1978). Clinician-child discourse: Some preliminary questions. *Journal of Speech and Hearing Disorders, 43*, 123–139.

Prutting, C.A., & Kirchner, D.M. (1983). Applied pragmatics. In T.M. Gallagher & C.A. Prutting (Eds.), *Pragmatic assessment and intervention in language* (pp. 29–64). San Diego, CA: College-Hill Press.

Prutting, C.A., & Kirchner, D.M. (1987). A clinical appraisal of pragmatic aspects of language. *Journal of Speech and Hearing Disorders, 52*, 105–119.

Pugach, M. (1987). Teacher education's empty set: The paradox of preparing teachers of learning disabilities. In B.M. Franklin (Ed.), *Learning disabilities: Dissenting essays* (pp. 163–177). Philadelphia: Falmer Press.

Ramirez, A. (1988). Analyzing speech acts. In J.L. Green & J.O. Harker (Eds.), *Multiple perspective analyses of classroom discourse* (pp. 135–163). Norwood, NJ: Ablex.

Rees, N.S. (1979). Breaking out of the centrifuge. *Asha, 21*(1), 992–997.

Rhodes, L.K., & Dudley-Marling, L.K. (1988). *Readers and writers with a difference: A holistic approach to teaching learning disabled and remedial students.* Portsmouth, NH: Heinemann.

Richardson, S. (1990, March). Evolution of approaches to beginning reading and the need for diversification in education. Paper presented at the Orton Dyslexia Society Conference on Whole Language and Phonics, Bloomington, MN.

Ripich, D.N. (1989). Building classroom communication competence: A case for a multiperspective approach. *Seminars in Speech and Language, 10*, 231–240.

Ripich, D.N., & Griffith, P.L. (1988). Narrative abilities of children with learning disabilities and nondisabled children: Story structure, cohesion, and propositions. *Journal of Learning Disabilities, 21*, 165–173.

Ripich, D.N., Hambrecht, G., Panagos, J.M., & Prelock, P. (1984). An analysis of articulation and language discourse patterns. *Journal of Childhood Communication Disorders, 7*, 17–26.

Ripich, D.N., & Panagos, J.M. (1985). Accessing children's knowledge of sociolinguistic rules for speech therapy lessons. *Journal of Speech and Hearing Disorders, 50*, 335–346.

Ripich, D.N., & Spinelli, F.M. (1985). An ethnographic approach to assessment and intervention. In D.N. Ripich & F.M. Spinelli (Eds.), *School discourse problems* (pp. 199–217). San Diego, CA: College-Hill Press.

Rogoff, B. (1990). *Apprenticeship in thinking.* New York: Oxford University Press.

Romaine, S. (1984). *The language of children and adolescents.* New York: Basil Blackwell.

Roth, F.P., & Spekman, N.J. (1986). Narrative discourse: Spontaneously generated stories of learning disabled and normally achieving children. *Journal of Speech and Hearing Disorders, 51,* 8–23.

Roth, F.P., & Spekman, N.J. (1989). The oral syntactic proficiency of learning disabled students: Spontaneous story sampling analysis. *Journal of Speech and Hearing Research, 32,* 67–77.

Ryan, E.B., & Ledger, G.W. (1984). Learning to attend to sentence structure: Links between metalinguistic development and reading. In J. Downing & R. Valtin (Eds.), *Language awareness and learning to read* (pp. 149–171). New York: Springer-Verlag.

Sacks, H., Schegloff, E., & Jefferson, G. (1974). A simplest systematics for the organization of turn-taking in conversation. *Language, 50,* 696–735.

Schegloff, E.A. (1986). Sequencing in conversational openings. In J.J. Gumperz & D. Hymes (Eds.), *Directions in sociolinguistics: The ethnography of communication* (pp. 346–380). New York: Basil Blackwell.

Schegloff, E.A., Jefferson, G., & Sacks, H. (1977). The preference for self-correction in the organization of repair in conversation. *Language, 53,* 361–382.

Schery, T.K., & Lipsey, M.W. (1983). Program evaluation for speech and hearing services. In J. Miller, D.E. Yoder, & R. Schiefelbusch (Eds.), *Contemporary isues in language intevention* (ASHA Reports No. 12, pp. 261–274). Rockville, MD: American Speech-Language-Hearing Association.

Schumaker, J.B., & Deshler, D.D. (1984). Setting demand variables: A major factor in program planning for the LD adolescent. *Topics in Language Disorders, 4*(2), 22–40.

Schumaker, J.B., Deshler, D.D. & Ellis, E.S. (1986). Intervention issues related to the education of LD adolescents. In J.K. Torgesen & B.Y.L. Wong (Eds.), *Psychological and educational perspectives on learning disabilities* (pp. 329–365). New York: Academic Press.

Schunk, D.H. (1989). Social cognitive theory and self-regulated learning. In B.J. Zimmerman & D.H. Schunk (Eds.), *Self-regulated learning and academic achievement* (pp. 83–110). New York: Springer-Verlag.

Scott, C.M. (1988). Spoken and written syntax. In M.A. Nippold (Ed.), *Later language development* (pp. 49–95). Boston: College-Hill Press.

Scott, C.M. (1989a). Learning to write: Context, form and process. In A.G. Kamhi & H.W. Catts (Eds.), *Reading disabilities: A developmental language perspective* (pp. 261–302). Boston: College-Hill Press.

Scott, C.M. (1989b). Problem writers: Nature, assessment, and intervention. In A.G. Kamhi & H.W. Catts (Eds.), *Reading disabilities: A developmental language perspective* (pp. 303–344). Boston: College-Hill Press.

Searle, J.R. (1975). Speech acts and recent linguistics. In D. Aronson & R.W. Rieber (Eds.), *Developmental psycholinguistics and communication disorders* (Vol. 263, pp. 27–38). New York: New York Academy of Sciences.

Senf, G.M. (1986). LD research in sociological and scientific perspective. In J.K. Torgesen & B.Y.L. Wong (Eds.), *Psychological and educational perspectives on learning disabilities* (pp. 27–53). New York: Academic Press.

Shatz, M. (1978). Children's comprehension of question directives. *Journal of Child Language, 5*, 39–46.

Shriberg, L., & Kent, R. (1982). *Clinical practice*. New York: John Wiley & Sons.

Shuy, R. (1988a). Identifying dimensions of classroom language. In J.L. Green & J.O. Harker (Eds.), *Multiple perspective analyses of classroom discourse* (Vol. 28, pp. 115–134). Norwood, NJ: Ablex.

Shuy, R. (1988b). The oral language basis for dialogue journals. In J. Staton, R.W. Shuy, J.K. Peyton, & L. Reed (Eds.), *Dialogue journal communication* (pp. 73–87). Norwood, NJ: Ablex.

Sidner, C.L. (1983). Focusing and discourse. *Discourse Processes, 6*, 107–130.

Silliman, E.R. (1984). Interactional competencies in the instructional context: The role of teaching discourse in learning. In G.P. Wallach & K.G. Butler (Eds.), *Language learning disabilities in school-age children* (pp. 288–317). Baltimore: Williams & Wilkins.

Silliman, E.R. (1987). Individual differences in the classroom performance of language-impaired children. *Seminars in Speech and Language, 8*, 357–373.

Silliman, E.R. (Ed.). (1988). Interdisciplinary perspectives on classroom discourse. *Topics in Language Disorders, 6*(2).

Silliman, E.R. (1989). Narratives: A window on the oral substrate of written language disabilities. *Annals of Dyslexia, 39*, 125–139.

Silliman, E.R., Campbell, N., & Mitchell, R.S. (1989). Genetic influences in autism and assessment of metalinguistic performance in siblings of autistic children. In G. Dawson (Ed.), *Autism* (pp. 225–259). New York: Guilford Press.

Silliman, E.R., & Lamanna, M.L. (1986). Interactional dynamics of turn disruption: Group and individual effects. *Topics in Language Disorders, 6*(2), 28–42.

Silliman, E.R., & Leslie, S.P. (1983). Social and cognitive aspects of fluency in the instructional setting. *Topics in Language Disorders, 4*(1), 61–74.

Silliman, E.R., & Paris, V.S. (1984). A study of self-repairs in two special education classrooms. Paper presented at the Northeastern Educational Research Association, Ellenville, NY.

Simon, C.S. (1987a). Out of the broom closet and into the classroom: The emerging SLP. *Journal of Childhood Communication Disorders, 11*, 41–66.

Simon, C.S. (1987b). Classroom communication screening procedure for early adolescents. Tempe, AZ: Communi-Cog Publications.

Sleeter, C. (1987). Literacy, definitions of learning disabilities and social control. In B.M. Franklin (Ed.), *Learning disabilities: Dissenting essays*. Philadelphia: Falmer Press.

Smitherman, G. (1977). *Talkin' and testifyin': The language of Black America*. Boston: Houghton Mifflin.

Snow, C. (1977). Mothers speech research. In C. Snow & C. Ferguson (Eds.), *Talking to children* (pp. 11–23). New York: Cambridge University Press.

Snow, C., Midkiff-Borunda, S., Small, A., & Proctor, A. (1984). Therapy as social interaction: Analyzing the contexts for language remediation. *Topics in Language Disorders, 4*(4), 72–85.

Snyder, L.S. (1984). Cognition and language development. In R.C. Naremore (Ed.), *Language science* (pp. 107–145). San Diego, CA: College-Hill Press.

Snyder, L.S., & Silverstein, J. (1988). Pragmatics and child language disorders. In R.L. Schiefelbusch & L.L. Lloyd (Eds.), *Language perspectives: Acquisition, retardation, and intervention* (pp. 189–222). Austin, TX: Pro-Ed.

Spinelli, F.M., & Ripich, D.N. (1985). A comparison of classroom and clinical discourse. In D.N. Ripich & J.M. Spinelli (Eds.), *School discourse problems* (pp. 179–196). San Diego, CA: College-Hill Press.

Stahl, S.A., & Miller, P.D. (1989). Whole language and language experience approaches for beginning reading: A quantitative research synthesis. *Review of Educational Research, 59*(1), 87–116.

Stallings, J. (1977). *Learning to look.* Belmont, CA: Wadsworth.

Stanovich, K.E. (1986). Matthew effects in reading: Some consequences of individual differences in the acquisition of literacy. *Reading Research Quarterly, 21,* 360–407.

Stanovich, K.E. (1988). Explaining the differences between the dyslexic and the garden-variety poor reader: The phonological-core-variable-difference model. *Journal of Learning Disabilities, 21,* 590–604, 612.

Stanovich, K.E. (1989). Learning disabilities in broader context. *Journal of Learning Disabilities, 22,* 287–291, 297.

Staton, J., Shuy, R.W., Peyton, J.K., & Reed, L. (Eds.). (1988). *Dialogue journal communication.* Norwood, NJ: Ablex.

Stein, N.L. (1982). What's in a story: Interpreting the interpretations of story grammars. *Discourse Processes, 5,* 319–335.

Stein, N.L. (1983). On the goals, functions, and knowledge of reading and writing. *Contemporary Educational Psychology, 8,* 261–292.

Stein, N.L., & Glenn, C.G. (1979). An analysis of story comprehension in school children. In R.O. Freedle (Ed.), *New directions in discourse processing* (pp. 53–120). Norwood, NJ: Ablex.

Sternberg, R.J. (1987a). A unified theory of intellectual exceptionality. In J.D. Day & J.G. Barkowski (Eds.), *Intelligence and exceptionality: New directions for theory, assessment and instructional practices* (pp. 135–172). Norwood, NJ: Ablex.

Sternberg, R.J. (1987b). A unified theoretical perspective on autism. In D.J. Cohen & A.M. Donnelan (Eds.), *Handbook of autism and pervasive developmental disorders* (pp. 690–696). Silver Spring, MD: V.H. Winston.

Stewart, R.S. (1987). Language: Creating a literate environment for reading and writing development. *Journal of Childhood Communcation Disorders, 11,* 91–106.

Stiggins, R.J. (1990). Relevant assessment training for educators. *Newsletter for Educational Psychologists of the American Psychological Association, 13*(2), 3–4.

Stodolsky, S.S. (1984). Frameworks for studying instructional processes in peer work-groups. In P.L. Peterson, L.C. Wilkinson, & M. Hallinan (Eds.), *The social context of instruction: Group organization and group processes* (pp. 107–124). New York: Academic Press.

Stone, C.A., & Wertsch, J.V. (1984). A social interactional analysis of learning disabilities remediation. *Journal of Learning Disabilities, 17,* 194–199.

Tattershall, S., & Creaghead, N. (1985). A comparison of communication at home and school. In D.N. Ripich & F.M. Spinelli (Eds.), *School discourse problems* (pp. 29–51). San Diego, CA: College-Hill Press.

Taylor, O.L. (Ed.). (1986). *Treatment of communication disorders in culturally and linguistically diverse populations* (pp. 29–51). San Diego, CA: College-Hill Press.

Taylor, O.L., Payne, K.T., & Anderson, N.B. (1987). Distinguishing between communication disorders and communication differences. *Seminars in Speech and Language, 8,* 415–427.

Tharp, R.G. (1982). The effective instruction of comprehension: Results and description of the Kamehameha early education program. *Reading Research Quarterly, 17*(4), 503–527.

Tindal, G. (1985). Investigating the effectiveness of special education: An analysis of methodology. *Journal of Learning Disabilities, 18,* 101–112.

Tindal, G., & Marston, D. (1986). Approaches to assessment. In J.K. Torgesen & B.Y.L. Wong (Eds.), *Psychological and educational perspectives on learning disabilities* (pp. 55–84). New York: Academic Press.

Torgesen, J.K. (1989). Cognitive and behavioral characteristics of children with learning disabilities: Concluding comments. *Journal of Learning Disabilities, 22*, 166–168, 175.

Tunmer, W.E., & Grieve, R. (1984). Syntactic awareness in children. In W.E. Tunmer, C. Pratt, & M.L. Herriman (Eds.), *Metalinguistic awareness in children* (pp. 92–104). New York: Springer-Verlag.

van Kleeck, A. (1984a). Metalinguistic skills: Cutting across spoken and written language and problem-solving abilities. In G.P. Wallach & K.G. Butler (Eds.), *Language learning disabilities in school-age children* (pp. 128–153). Baltimore: Williams & Wilkins.

van Kleeck, A. (1984b). Assessment and intervention: Does "meta" matter? In G.P. Wallach & K.G. Butler (Eds.), *Language learning disabilities in school-age children* (pp. 179–198). Baltimore: Williams & Wilkins.

van Kleeck, A. (1985). Issues in adult-child interaction: Six philosophical orientations. *Topics in Language Disorders, 5*(2), 1–15.

van Kleeck, A. (1990). Emergent literacy: Learning about print before learning to read. *Topics in Language Disorders, 10*(2), 63–80.

van Kleeck, A., & Richardson, A. (1988). Language delay in children. In N. Lass, L. McReynolds, J. Northern, & D. Yoder (Eds.), *Handbook of speech-language pathology and audiology* (pp. 655–684). Canada: B.C. Decker.

van Kleeck, A., & Richardson, A. (in press). Assessment of speech and language development. In J. Johnson & J. Goldman (Eds.), *Developmental assessment in clinical child psychology*. Elmsford, NY: Pergamon.

van Kleeck, A., & Schuele, C.M. (1987). Precursors to literacy: Normal development. *Topics in Language Disorders, 7*(2), 13–31.

Vygotsky, L.S. (1962). *Thought and language.* Cambridge, MA: MIT Press.

Vygotsky, L.S. (1983). School instruction and mental development. In M. Donaldson, R. Grieve, & C. Pratt (Eds.), *Early childhood development and education* (pp. 263–269). New York: Guilford Press.

Wallach, G.P. (1990). Magic buries Celtics: Looking for broader interpretations of language learning and literacy. *Topics in Language Disorders, 10*(2), 63–80.

Wallach, G.P., & Miller, L.M. (1988). *Language intervention and academic success.* Boston: College-Hill Press.

Watlawick, J., Beavin, J., & Jackson, D. (1967). *The pragmatics of communication.* New York: W.W. Norton.

Watson, D., & Crowley, P. (1988). How can we implement a whole-language approach? In C. Weaver (Ed.), *Reading process and practice* (pp. 232–279). Portsmouth, NH: Heinemann.

Weaver, C. (1988). *Reading process and practice.* Portsmouth, NH: Heinemann.

Weiner, C.A., & Creighton, J.M. (1987). Documenting and facilitating "school readiness language" in the kindergarten classroom. *Journal of Childhood Communication Disorders, 11*, 125–131.

Wertsch, J.V. (1985). *Vygotsky and the social formation of the mind.* Cambridge, MA: Harvard University Press.

Wertsch, J.V., & Stone, C.A. (1985). The concept of internalization in Vygotsky's account of higher mental functions. In J.V. Wertsch (Ed.), *Culture, communication, and cognition: Vygotskian perspectives* (pp. 162–179). New York: Cambridge University Press.

West, J.F., & Brown, P.A. (1987). State departments of education policies on consultation in special education: The state of the states. *RASE*, 8 (3), 45–51.

West, J.F., & Cannon, G.S. (1988). Essential collaboration consultation competencies for regular and special educators. *Journal of Learning Disabilities, 21*, 56–63, 28.

West, J.F., Idol, L., & Cannon, G. (1989). *Collaboration in the schools*. Austin, TX: Pro-Ed.

Westby, C.E. (1984). Development of narrative language abilities. In G.P. Wallach & K.G. Butler (Eds.), *Language learning disabilities in school-age children* (pp. 103–127). Baltimore: Williams & Wilkins.

Westby, C.E. (1985). Learning to talk—talking to learn: Oral-literate language differences. In C. Simon (Ed.), *Communication skills and classroom success: Therapy methodologies for language-learning disabled students* (pp. 181–213). San Diego, CA: College-Hill Press.

Westby, C.E. (1989). Assessing and remediating text comprehension problems. In A.G. Kamhi & H.W. Catts (Eds.), *Reading disabilities: A developmental language perspective* (pp. 199–259). Boston: College-Hill Press.

Westby, C.E. (1990). The role of the speech-language pathologist in whole language. *Language, Speech, and Hearing Services in Schools, 21*, 228–337.

Westby, C.E., & Costlow, L. (in press). Whole language in special education. *Topics in Language Disorders*.

Westby, C.E., & Rouse, G.R. (1985). Culture in education and the instruction of language learning–disabled students. *Topics in Language Disorders, 5*(4), 15–28.

Westby, C.E., Van Dongen, R., & Maggart, Z. (1989). Assessing narrative competence. *Seminars in Speech and Language, 10*, 63–76.

Wiig, E.H. (1989). *Steps to language competence: Developing metalinguistic strategies*. San Antonio, TX: Psychological Corporation.

Wiig, E.H., & Semel, E. (1984). *Language assessment and intervention for the learning disabled* (2nd ed.). Columbus, OH: Charles E. Merrill.

Wilcox, K. (1982). Differential socialization in the classroom: Implications for equal opportunity. In G. Spindler (Ed.), *Doing the ethnography of schooling: Educational anthropology in action* (pp. 268–309). New York: CBS College Publishing.

Wilkinson, L., Wilkinson, A., Spinelli, F., & Chiang, C. (1984). Metalinguistic knowledge of pragmatic rules of school age children. *Child Development, 55*, 2130–2140.

Wilkinson, L.C. (Ed.). (1982). *Communicating in the classroom*. New York: Academic Press.

Wilkinson, L.C., & Calculator, S. (1982). Effective speakers: Students' use of language to request and obtain information and action in the classroom. In L. C. Wilkinson (Ed.), *Communicating in the classroom* (pp. 85–100). New York: Academic Press.

Wilkinson, L.C., Calculator, S., & Dollaghan, C. (1982). Ya wanna trade—just for awhile: Children's requests and responses to peers. *Discourse Processes, 5*, 161–176.

Wilkinson, L.C., Milosky, L.M. & Genishi, C. (1986). Second language learners' use of requests and responses in elementary classrooms. *Topics in Language Disorders, 6*(2), 57–70.

Wilkinson, L.C., & Silliman, E.R. (in press). Sociolinguistic analysis: Non-formal assessment of children's language and literacy skills. *Linguistics and Education*.

Wilkinson, L.C., & Spinelli, F. (1982). Applications for education. In L.C. Wilkinson (Ed.), *Communicating in the classroom* (pp. 323–328). New York: Academic Press.

Williams, J.P. (1986). The role of phonemic analysis in reading. In J.K. Torgesen & B.Y.L. Wong (Eds.), *Psychological and educational perspectives on learning disabilities* (pp.399–416). Orlando, FL: Academic Press.

Wilson, M. (1988). How can we teach reading in the content areas? In C. Weaver (Ed.), *Reading process and practice* (pp. 280–320). Portsmouth, NH: Heinemann.

Wong, B.Y.L. (1985). Metacognition and learning disabilities. In D. L. Forrest-Pressley, G.E. MacKinnon, & T. G. Waller (Eds.), *Metacognition, cognition, and human performance* (Vol 2, pp. 137–180). New York: Academic Press.

Wong, B.Y.L. (1986). Problems and issues in the definition of learning disabilities. In J.K. Torgesen & B.Y.L. Wong (Eds.), *Psychological and educational perspectives on learning disabilities* (pp. 1–26). New York: Academic Press.

Wong-Fillmore, L., Ammon, P., Ammon, M.S., Delucchi, K., Jensen, J., McLaughlin, B., & Strong, M. (1983). *Learning English through bilingual instruction: Second year report* (Contract 400–80–0030). Washington, DC: National Institute of Education.

Wright, H. (1960). Observational child study. In P. Mussen (Ed.), *Handbook of research methods in child development* (pp. 71–139). New York: John Wiley & Sons.

Zukow, P. (1982). Transcription systems for videotaped interactions: Some advantages and limitations of manual and computer rendering techniques. *Applied Psycholinguistics, 3,* 61–79.

Index

About the Authors

ELAINE R. SILLIMAN is a professor of communication sciences and disorders at the University of South Florida and is a former chair of the Department of Communication Sciences and Disorders. Her other appointments include professor and director of the Program in Communication Sciences at Hunter College of the City University of New York (CUNY), membership on the Ph.D. faculty in speech and hearing sciences of the CUNY Graduate School and University Center, and a visiting professor at Tel Aviv University. Dr. Silliman is a Fellow of the American Speech-Language-Hearing Association. She also holds the Honors of the New York State Speech-Language-Hearing Association, and is a recipient of the Distinguished Alumni Achievement Award from the CUNY Graduate School and University Center. She has presented numerous seminars and lectures regionally, nationally, and internationally on language learning disabilities in school-age children. Her publications include a variety of chapters and articles on classroom and clinical discourse and metalinguistic awareness, as well as an issue editorship of *Topics in Language Disorders* on interdisciplinary perspectives on classroom discourse. Dr. Silliman received her B.S. from Syracuse University in speech pathology and her Ph.D. from CUNY in speech and hearing sciences.

LOUISE CHERRY WILKINSON is Dean of the Rutgers Graduate School of Education and a professor of educational psychology and psychology at Rutgers. She is the former executive officer of the Ph.D. program in educational psychology at the Graduate School of the City University of New York and a former chair of the Department of Educational Psychology at the University of Wisconsin-Madison. Dr. Wilkinson was elected Fellow of the American Psychological Association and Fellow of the American Psychological Society. Since 1977, she has served as a member of various review panels for the U.S. Department of Education and is vice president for the Division of Learning and Instruction,

American Educational Research Association, for 1990 to 1992. She is the author of more than 70 chapters and articles on classroom communication and the development of pragmatic knowledge. She is also the editor or coeditor of three volumes on classrooms published by Academic Press, *Communicating in the Classroom*, *The Social Context of Learning*, and *Gender Influences in the Classroom*, and since 1989 she has been the series editor of *The Rutgers Symposia on Education*, published by Prentice-Hall. Dr. Wilkinson received her B.A. in psychology from Oberlin College and her Ed.M. and Ed.D. in human development from Harvard University.